The Cambridge Companion to Periyar

E. V. Ramasamy (1879–1973), popularly called Periyar, was a rationalist and radical social reformer. A household name in Tamil Nadu and the central figure of the Dravidian movement, he is best known for his polemics against religion, fervent propagation of atheism, support for proportional representation for backward and scheduled castes, and the demand for political autonomy for south Indian states. His opposition to the caste system and the oppression of women and his engagement with questions of identity, culture, religion, nationalism, and economy are exemplified in his writings and speeches spanning more than five decades.

The Cambridge Companion to Periyar presents a comprehensive account of his interventions on these topics and his complex politics, and brings conversations from the Tamil world to a global audience.

The chapters are contributions from established and emerging academics in different fields and look at Periyar from diverse disciplinary perspectives. Crucial events from Periyar's life are discussed, as are critical aspects of Periyar's thought. New published material is engaged with and old scholarship is revisited, reflecting the core concerns of Periyar and placing them in broader intellectual and historical contexts.

The volume aims to draw attention to a non-canonical thinker whose important intellectual and political contributions transcend the limits of his context. Drawing upon new sources, challenging myths, and crossing disciplinary boundaries, it presents a Periyar for the times.

A. R. Venkatachalapathy is Professor at the Madras Institute of Development Studies, Chennai. He is a prolific author and has published widely in both Tamil and English. His contribution to Tamil has been recognized by two lifetime achievement awards.

Karthick Ram Manoharan is Assistant Professor of Social Sciences at the National Law School of India University, Bengaluru. He is the author of *Periyar: A Study in Political Atheism* (2022) and *Frantz Fanon: Identity and Resistance* (2019) and the co-editor of *Rethinking Social Justice* (2020).

Cambridge Companions to History

Cambridge Companions to History provide accessible and thought-provoking introductions to key topics, eras, places and figures, invaluable to both the student and scholar. Edited by leading academics, each volume contains specially-commissioned essays by a team of expert contributors from around the world, presenting cutting-edge research and suggesting new paths of inquiry for the reader. Companions are designed not only to offer a comprehensive overview of their chosen topic, but also to provoke debate and discussion. Like the highly successful Cambridge Companions to Literature and Cambridge Companions to Philosophy series, these volumes are ideal for use by students, and will be of interest also to the curious general reader.

A full list of recent titles in the series can be found at the following address: www.cambridge.org/gb/universitypress/subjects/history/series/cambridge-companions-history

The Cambridge Companion to Periyar

Edited by
A. R. Venkatachalapathy
Karthick Ram Manoharan

Shaftesbury Road, Cambridge CB2 8EA, United Kingdom

One Liberty Plaza, 20th Floor, New York, NY 10006, USA

477 Williamstown Road, Port Melbourne, VIC 3207, Australia

314–321, 3rd Floor, Plot 3, Splendor Forum, Jasola District Centre, New Delhi – 110025, India

103 Penang Road, #05–06/07, Visioncrest Commercial, Singapore 238467

Cambridge University Press is part of Cambridge University Press & Assessment, a department of the University of Cambridge.

We share the University's mission to contribute to society through the pursuit of education, learning and research at the highest international levels of excellence.

www.cambridge.org
Information on this title: www.cambridge.org/9781009605366

© Cambridge University Press & Assessment 2025

This publication is in copyright. Subject to statutory exception and to the provisions of relevant collective licensing agreements, no reproduction of any part may take place without the written permission of Cambridge University Press & Assessment.

First published 2025

Printed in India

Cover image: Photograph of Periyar. Image courtesy: Dravidar Kazhagam, Chennai.

A catalogue record for this publication is available from the British Library

ISBN 978-1-009-60536-6 Hardback
ISBN 978-1-009-60535-9 Paperback

Cambridge University Press & Assessment has no responsibility for the persistence or accuracy of URLs for external or third-party internet websites referred to in this publication, and does not guarantee that any content on such websites is, or will remain, accurate or appropriate.

For EU product safety concerns, contact us at Calle de José Abascal, 56, 1°, 28003 Madrid, Spain, or email eugpsr@cambridge.org.

In memory of
Bernard Bate (1960–2016),
scholar, *mensch*

Contents

Preface and Acknowledgements — ix

Introducing an Iconoclast — 1
A. R. Venkatachalapathy and Karthick Ram Manoharan

Part I Events That Made Periyar

1. Periyar and the Vaikom Satyagraha — 17
   Pazha. Athiyaman

2. Periyar, Ambedkar, and the Poona Pact — 35
   A. Thiruneelakandan

Part II The Politics of Periyar

3. EVR's Non-Brahmin Cosmopolitanism, Periyar's Dravidian Nationalism, and the Appearance of Humankind — 57
   Matthew H. Baxter

4. Periyar and the Forging of a Horizontal Dravidian–Tamil Solidarity — 78
   Vignesh Karthik K. R.

5. The Double-Barrelled Gun: Periyar and Anna after the Split in the Dravidar Kazhagam — 93
   A. R. Venkatachalapathy

Part III Religion, Caste, and Identity

6. The Rationale for Reason: Periyar on Religion — 113
   Sundar Kaali

7. Periyar's Anti-Aryanism: A Genealogy, a Synopsis, and a Critique — 129
   Karthick Ram Manoharan

8. Periyar in Singapore: Transnationalism and Decolonization — 147
   Darinee Alagirisamy

Part IV Women and Culture

9. Periyar, the Women's Question, and Maniammai — 167
   Karthick Ram Manoharan and Vilasini Ramani

10. Periyar's Engagement with Literature — 182
    Antony Arul Valan

11. Periyar, Art, and Cinema — 198
    Swarnavel Eswaran

Part V Labour and Dignity

12. The Social Subsumes the Economic: Periyar's Reading of Economic Power in Caste Society — 217
    M. Vijayabaskar

13. Liberation Notes, Dignity, and Periyar: A Radical Cultural Psychology Perspective — 234
    Ramaswami Mahalingam

For Further Reading — 249
About the Contributors — 252
Index — 256

Preface and Acknowledgements

The Cambridge Companion to Periyar has been jointly edited by two researchers belonging to two different generations. When the first editor began his writing career in the mid-1980s, Periyar's was not a name that could be taken in genteel, academic circles. By the time the second editor began his doctoral work at a British university in 2011, the topic was a study in political theory, comparing Periyar with a major international thinker (Frantz Fanon). In the intervening generation, much had changed in the fortunes of academic writing on Periyar. After decades of being ignored or consigned to the margins by Indian sociologists and historians, we can say that Periyar has arrived in global scholarship. This volume exemplifies this turn.

Paralleling Periyar's rising influence during these intervening decades, there has been vigorous academic interest in studying the Dravidian movement. Newer and newer editions of Periyar's writings—covering the spectrum from multivolume sets to popular paperbacks—are being published every year. Any visitor to the annual Chennai Book Fair would be amazed by the piles of books by and on Periyar. The transformation of the Periyar Library and Research Centre housed in the Chennai headquarters of the Dravidar Kazhagam (DK) from a sweltering hall roofed by an asbestos sheet in 1981, when the first editor first consulted it, to a comfortable air-conditioned hall with expanded print resources indexes the growing academic interest in Periyar. Social media is also abuzz with young readers discussing animatedly the ideas of Periyar. If the dominant political organizations in Tamil Nadu still swear by Periyar, the right-wing backlash underlines his importance even more. Reservations for backward castes, Dalit assertion, conversations on social justice, the rise of Hindu communalism, developments in Indian feminism(s), and debates on federalism—all highlight the continuing relevance of Periyar's ideas.

Would Periyar have been happy with this situation? Perhaps not. Periyar hoped for a utopian progressive future when he would be seen as an outdated thinker rather than as a radical. On the other hand, we would like to believe it would please Periyar to note that quite a few scholars from the social classes that his movement empowered have broken into formerly gatekept academic cloisters. If he might be more than a tad disappointed that this volume includes only two women contributors, we plead guilty. Edited volumes are strange creatures subject to circumstances beyond the editors' control.

Periyar often ended his long speeches by calling upon his audiences not to accept him in toto but to reflect critically and make up their own minds. It is our hope that in studying his life and thought, we have measured up to this litmus test.

* * *

The Cambridge University Press team showed remarkable patience over the long time this volume took to develop and were prompt to help. We are thankful to Qudsiya Ahmed for first approaching us with this book idea and to Anwesha Rana for firmly pushing us to the finishing line in the face of a raging pandemic on the one side and health issues and job moves on the side of the editors. We are also grateful to Priyanka Das and to the Press's copyediting team for their meticulous work.

Karthick Ram Manoharan's research for this volume received funding from the European Union's Horizon 2020 research and innovation programme under the Marie Sklodowska-Curie grant agreement no. 895514. He is thankful to Meena Dhanda for supervising this project at the University of Wolverhampton. He also benefitted greatly from his time as Bliss Carnochan International Visitor at the Stanford Humanities Center, and he is thankful to Anna Bigelow and Lalita du Perron for nominating him for the position. National Law School of India University, Bengaluru, provided him an excellent atmosphere to complete his work. He would like to thank M. Gautaman and R. Thirunavukkarasu, who introduced the joys of intellectual life to him when he was an undergrad student.

A. R. Venkatachalapathy pays homage to 'Mugam' Mamani (1931–2022), who first introduced him to Periyar when he was a student of class ten. A school dropout who went on to become a noted cultural figure, Mamani typifies the numerous people whom Periyar transformed through his life, thought, and work. In thanking him, Venkatachalapathy acknowledges the many scholars and institutions who have shaped him, with a special mention of the Madras Institute of Development Studies, Chennai.

Chennai/Bengaluru
17 September 2024

A. R. Venkatachalapathy
Karthick Ram Manoharan

Introducing an Iconoclast

*A. R. Venkatachalapathy and Karthick Ram Manoharan**

One of the most honoured figures in the state of Tamil Nadu, arguably home to the highest number of temples in India, is an atheist who profaned the gods. E. V. Ramasamy (1879–1973), popularly called 'Periyar' (the Great One), was a rationalist and radical social reformer. A household name in the region and the central figure of the Dravidian movement, he is best known for his polemics against religion, fervent propagation of atheism, support for proportional representation for backward and scheduled castes, and demand for political autonomy for south Indian states. His opposition to the caste system and the oppression of women are exemplified in his writings and speeches spanning over five decades. One of the first things that Dravida Munnetra Kazhagam (DMK) leader M. K. Stalin did on assuming office as chief minister of Tamil Nadu in 2021 was to declare Periyar's birth anniversary (17 September) as 'Social Justice Day'—underscoring his reputation as a crusader for social justice.

In 2018, statues of Periyar were vandalized across Tamil Nadu, reportedly by Hindu right-wing activists. His statues outside temples, bearing the inscription 'There is no god, there is no god, there is no god at all. He who invented god is a fool. He who propagates god is a scoundrel. He who worships god is a barbarian' have been an eyesore for the Hindu right, and its leaders have been promising to have them removed.

Many other accusations have been heaped on Periyar: anti-national, anti-Hindu, anti-Brahmin, anti-Tamil, secessionist, pro-dominant non-Brahmin castes, neglectful of Dalit interests, supporter of promiscuity, and enemy of family and nation. Fifty years after his death, Periyar continues to be a controversial figure in Tamil politics, but also an unavoidable one.

Social Milieu

The late nineteenth century was a time of considerable social churning in south India. Following the Poligar wars (1799–1805) and the 1857 revolt, India was taken over by the British Crown and the imperial power began taking an active interest in the society that came under its governance.

---

* The authors would like to thank Rinku Lamba for her feedback.

Religion, culture, language, and, yes, caste became objects of academic and administrative scrutiny. The censuses conducted in the late nineteenth and early twentieth centuries, aided by colonial philologists and anthropologists, were unprecedented exercises in counting and categorizing social groups in India. Diverse *jati*s, now read as 'castes', were enumerated. But the colonial apparatus did not stop with a mere empirical data-gathering exercise; it was an ideological project as well. The making of the census was greatly informed by the *varna* system, which colonial scholars became acquainted with owing to interaction with the Indian elite castes, mostly the Brahmins. Not only were the castes counted, they were also located in the *varna* hierarchy, or out of it, as was the case of the 'untouchable' communities. Policies were designed favouring recruitment of some castes, granting additional rights to some, criminalizing some, and so on. As holders of property *and* knowledge, Brahmins and other upward landowning and mercantile castes held a decisive advantage in the new state that was forming. Across India, several castes contested the positions they were assigned to. Regional histories across the country record several pre-colonial religious and spiritual movements that contested social hierarchies. In modern times, anti-caste movements became more focused on the secular terrains of education, employment, and political power. Maharashtra and Tamil Nadu in particular gave rise to strong non-Brahmin movements led by powerful anti-caste thinkers whose influence continues to animate our times.

In the Madras Presidency (a straggling province that included most of what is now Tamil Nadu, Andhra Pradesh, northern Kerala, and parts of Karnataka), the colonial government assumed a tripartite division of society into Brahmins, Sudras, and Untouchables. The 'Sudra' categorization was nebulous, as the diverse castes that were lumped together under this nomenclature shared few common interests or histories. Powerful landowning castes and economically weak artisanal castes were dubbed as Sudras on the criterion that they were not Brahmin and not untouchable. Many among these castes contested this label and some of the more active ones petitioned the colonial authorities against it. Further, the disproportionately greater representation of Brahmins in positions of power and educational institutions was seen as posing hurdles for the empowerment of emergent groups.

In the late nineteenth century, non-Brahmin elites of the Madras Presidency played a key role in galvanizing relatively egalitarian opinions through social and religious reforms, literary and cultural interventions, and, inevitably, political activism. Writers, poets, novelists, spiritual thinkers, and political leaders challenged Brahmin domination and the caste system. A significant number were from the Vellalar community, though there were many others from subaltern castes. In the decade that Periyar was born in, an eclectic group called the Madras Secular Society was active, which opposed caste and called for reform in all spheres of society. This was a time when secularist, Saivite, and Buddhist thinkers were proposing new ways of imagining an egalitarian society. A consciousness of being Tamil, with pride in the distinctiveness of Tamil culture and history, was the *zeitgeist*. This eventually took the form of Dravidian politics.

E. V. Ramasamy, before He Became 'Periyar'

Periyar was born to Erode Venkatappa Naicker and Chinnathayammal in the town of Erode in western Tamil Nadu. The family belonged to the Balija Naidu caste, a Kannada-speaking, upwardly mobile community involved in trade in this region. Rising from humble origins, Venkatappa Naicker was a successful businessman and a devout Vaishnavite. He named his two male children after avatars of Vishnu. The older was Krishnasamy, a lifelong backer of his famous brother. The younger, Ramasamy, a rebel from an early age, would later gain considerable notoriety in his lifetime and after for his criticisms of the deity he was named after. The quintessential *enfant terrible*, Periyar even in his initial school days defied caste boundaries and ritual prohibitions, causing much consternation at home. He would also bedevil the sadhus and sanyasis who thronged his home, invited for the religious sermons (and free dinners) that his father hosted, with irreverent questions about caste and religion. Quitting school at the age of eleven, he was soon involved in the family business.

Periyar married Nagammai at the relatively older age of nineteen. Contrary to his family's hopes, the marriage did little to tame him. Along with caste and religion, marriage would also be an institution that Periyar relentlessly attacked in his public life, criticizing it for the enslavement of women and distracting individuals from pursuing the common good. Nagammai, Periyar's wife for thirty-five years, was initially socially conservative but eventually joined her husband, actively participating in both political and social reform movements. A child was born to the couple, which passed away in five months. Following this and some troubles with his father, Periyar ran away from home and set off to Varanasi as a mendicant. In his autobiographical recollections made at various times, he stated that it was this holy place that exposed to him the vices that religion conceals. Returning to take over his father's business, Periyar soon developed an interest in local municipal politics and later in the Indian National Congress.

As a local notable, Periyar held important positions in the Erode Devasthanam (Religious Endowment) Board, the Erode municipality, and the taluk board. He began observing the Congress from 1907 and started attending its meetings soon after—he even took shares in the Swadeshi Steam Navigation Company of V. O. Chidambaram Pillai (an early nationalist of the Tilak faction in the Congress). The grand old party of India also took note of him, given his popularity in that district. When he was nearing forty, Periyar became acquainted with an eminent Congress leader from the nearby town of Salem, C. Rajagopalachari (later the chief minister of the Madras Presidency/State and the last governor-general of India). The Periyar–Rajaji friendship would span over five decades, despite them being harsh critics of each other's political and religious views.

In the years after the First World War, Periyar joined the Non-Cooperation Movement and resigned from all positions of office. Following M. K. Gandhi's call, Periyar actively campaigned for the promotion of khadi. His agitations for prohibition led to his arrest in 1922. In 1924, he became president of the Tamil Nadu Congress Committee (TNCC). Even as a Congress activist, he demanded proportional representation in various political offices for various communities and wanted the party to take a stronger line against caste. In that same year, he cut his teeth as an activist and organizer by taking a leadership role in the Vaikom Satyagraha for the rights of lower castes to use public roads around the Sri Mahadeva Temple in the then princely state of Travancore. This was the first major political protest in Periyar's life where he confronted caste-based injustices. Nagammai as well as his younger sister Kannammal were also actively involved in the agitations.

Coevally, he confronted his fellow Congressmen over the Cheranmadevi Gurukulam controversy. At a traditional school founded by Congressman V. V. S. Aiyar, there was preferential treatment to Brahmin students and discrimination against the rest, though the funds came overwhelmingly from the Congress party and from non-Brahmin patrons. Periyar raised this issue repeatedly within the party and in public forums. The Cheranmadevi experience greatly coloured his views about the hypocrisy of the Congress and its Brahmin leaders towards caste. He continued making a strong case for proportional representation in the emerging political bodies. Criticizing the party's lackadaisical approach to these demands, Periyar quit the Congress in late 1925 and started the Self-Respect Movement (SRM) soon after.

Key Goals and Ideas

The SRM had three major goals—*samathuvam* (equality), *jaathi ozhippu* (annihilation of caste), and *penn viduthalai* (liberation of women). Periyar elucidated these goals through his newly started weekly, *Kudi Arasu*. Piqued by the lack of reportage of non-Brahmin political leaders and interests in the predominantly Brahmin press, Periyar had planned this paper earlier and had it registered in 1923. However, *Kudi Arasu* was formally launched on 3 May 1925 in Erode. Incidentally, a reformist Saivite saint, Sivacharya Swamigal (popularly known as Gnaniyar Swamigal), inaugurated the launch. Periyar editorialized and commented in its pages regularly. *Kudi Arasu* carried reports, commentaries, satires, and notes by Periyar and his fellow Self-Respecters. It also gave space to critics to place their views. This was the forum where Periyar's students and later leaders of the DMK such as C. N. Annadurai and M. Karunanidhi learnt the ropes as writers and journalists.

Kudi Arasu closed down in 1949. Started in 1936, the daily *Viduthalai*—still in circulation as of 2025—became the official organ of his party. The other papers published by Periyar and his movement were *Revolt* (English weekly, 1928–1930), *Puratchi* (Tamil weekly, 1933–1934), *Pagutharivu* (Tamil daily, 1934; weekly, 1934–1935; monthly, 1935–1939), *Unmai* (Tamil monthly, established 1970, still in publication), and the *Modern Rationalist* (English monthly, established 1971, still in publication). Though Periyar wrote extensively, he was more of a speaker than a writer; his speeches were reported and reproduced in these publications.

Periyar was a propagandist all his life, trying to convince and convert people to his views by argumentation and exposition. Towards this end, he also published numerous booklets. Printed on cheap paper, they were priced very low and sold at party meetings. Often, even his wife, Maniammai (whom he married in 1949), would herself spread out the books on the ground and hawk the publications. Though most of these booklets remain in print and in wide circulation and there are rival and competing multi-volume compilations, a critical and comprehensive edition of his collected works remains a desideratum. In the last years of Periyar's life, some of his selected works were systematically compiled—thematically and with reference to original sources—by V. Anaimuthu. This three-volume collection that began with Periyar's authorization has become the mainstay for much of Periyar scholarship since then. An expanded edition—in twenty volumes—published in 2011 however left much to be desired. The *Kudi Arasu Kalanjiyam* published by the Periyar Self-Respect Propaganda Institution, running into forty-three volumes, only covers the *Kudi Arasu*. A separate thematically organized series from the same publisher, titled *Periyar Kalanjiyam*, runs into thirty-eight volumes and covers Periyar's writings from 1925 to 1973, a comprehensive but not yet complete collection. In 2023, the first volume of *Viduthalai*, covering 1936, appeared under the same imprint; two subsequent volumes have appeared since. The Dravidar Viduthalai Kazhagam has published thirty-eight volumes of writings from *Kudi Arasu* running up to 1938. (This was the subject of litigation with the Madras High Court ruling in favour of its publication.

As of September 2024, the matter is under appeal in the Supreme Court of India.) In a major initiative, the Thanthai Periyar Dravidar Kazhagam has announced the publication of the facsimile edition of the full run of *Kudi Arasu*. There are other multi-volume editions which are useful. Despite the spate of compilations and editions of his writings and thought, the lack of critical editing apparatus such as dating and variant readings have rendered the task of contextualizing his ideas challenging.

The SRM aimed to be a social reform movement that eschewed direct involvement in politics. Periyar saw religion and 'tradition' as the cornerstone of the oppression of the lower castes and women. The goals of social equality, annihilation of caste, and the liberation of women could not be achieved without dismantling these. To that extent, Periyar launched unsparing attacks on Brahminical Hinduism. He was of course not the first modern reformer to confront caste. Vallalar Ramalinga Adigal (1823–1874), a reformist Saivite saint, promoted an egalitarian spirituality and influenced other Tamil thinkers and religious and secular reformers. Saivite thinkers such as 'Manonmaniam' Sundaram Pillai, Maraimalai Adigal, M. S. Purnalingam Pillai, and Somasundara Nayagar and Buddhist revivalists such as Iyothee Thass, P. Lakshmi Narasu, and M. Singaravelar reimagined religion and challenged Brahminical orthodoxy and what they saw as Aryan supremacy. Concurrently, Christian missionaries also influenced intellectual opinions on caste. The contributions of these thinkers, many of whom were Periyar's predecessors in time, to the formation of Dravidian political thought cannot be understated.

However, the intellectual legacy to place Periyar in would be that of the Madras Secular Society and its affiliated thinkers led by Athipakkam Venkatachala Nayakkar (1799[?]–1897). These were a group of non-Brahmin intellectuals active in the late nineteenth century who argued for atheism and subjected religion to critical scrutiny. Greatly influenced by the freethinkers of the National Secular Society in England, they contributed to the creation of an intellectual atmosphere where rationalism and opposition to casteism were seen as interlinked. In his personal life, Periyar was influenced by Kaivalya Swamiyar (1877–1953), a *sanyasi* who was sharply critical of *sanatana dharma* and supportive of rationalism.

How did Periyar achieve a reach and popularity that eluded his predecessors and contemporaries? From the start the SRM was conceived not as an intellectual project but as a mass movement targeting the common people. Periyar's speeches and writings were in direct and colloquial Tamil. A performer, his long and rambling speeches were laced with humour, satire, and, often, profanity. Periyar was aiming neither at a sophisticated critique of religion nor to construct a rigorous philosophical defence of any system of thought. An eclectic reader, mostly in Tamil, he was not however systematic in espousing his thought. Through popular rhetoric, he was able to consistently link multiple forms of oppression to Brahminism and appeal to diverse audiences. He did not see Brahminism as being confined to Brahmins alone, but as an all-pervasive ideology that coloured social, religious, and political institutions in India and contributed to the oppression of women and subaltern castes.

Another aspect that made Periyar unique was that he did not assume an egalitarian Tamil culture or past to counterpose against the Aryan-Brahminical—in contrast to the perspective of the Saiva reform movement, which was later appropriated and championed by the DMK. If he was critical of the Sanskrit texts of the *Ramayana* and the *Manusmriti* for what he argued were casteist aspects, he was also critical of canonical Tamil texts such as *Thirukkural* and *Silappathikaram* for what he claimed were their patriarchal aspects. Women's liberation and annihilation of caste could not be achieved by invoking religion or tradition. Rather, self-respect, rationalism, and socialism were the way forward.

The SRM was rooted in three key Periyarist ideas—*suyamariyadhai* (self-respect), *samadharmam* (socialism), and *pagutharivu* (rationalism). Periyar founded the SRM along with S. Ramanathan, an erudite socialist and lifelong rationalist. Periyar was also in conversation with other prominent socialist leaders like M. Singaravelar and later with M. N. Roy and Ram Manohar Lohia. But he believed that in India, socialism had to prioritize self-respect and a sense of dignity and worth which had been denied to the lower castes and also foreground a criticism of religion since it contributed to both ideological and material impoverishment of the subaltern populations. Indian communists were however loathe to give primacy to the caste question and even less enthusiastic to campaign for atheism.

Periyar expressed his opposition to Hinduism as early as in 1924 when he supported the proposal of the Government of Madras to take control of the admittedly corrupt temple administration. By 1927 he had gone much further as evidenced by his meeting with Gandhi in Bangalore. While Gandhi insisted that it was possible to use religion positively and to reform Hinduism, Periyar was resolute that Hinduism would have to be destroyed for any social progress to be achieved. Throughout his life, he held this belief and campaigned for atheism. While he did occasionally say positive things about Islam and Christianity, he also offered harsh criticisms of these religions in different contexts. The one religion he was most sympathetic to was Buddhism, that too because he saw it as a non-religion and as an atheist philosophy. Religion, Periyar believed, made brutes of humans.

Going Left

The editorials of *Kudi Arasu* began taking a leftist turn in the early 1930s. Periyar admired the pro-atheist aspect of socialism. In 1931, he wrote a strong editorial supporting Bhagat Singh and his ideas and condemned his execution. A few years later, *Kudi Arasu* published a serialized translation of Bhagat Singh's *Why I Am an Atheist*. The early 1930s were also a time when Periyar set out on foreign travels. In late 1929 to early 1930, Periyar met Tamils in Malaya and spoke to them about the principles of the SRM. In December 1931, he set out on an eleven-month tour of countries in the West along with Ramanathan. The United Kingdom, France, Germany, Spain, Greece, and Turkey were some of the countries he visited. His longest stay was in the Union of Soviet Socialist Republics (USSR), where he was hosted by an atheist league from February to May 1932. He met and had a pleasant exchange with Mikhail Kalinin, the head of state of the USSR. Periyar also interacted with atheist groups like the League of the Militant Godless and the staff of the anti-religious newspaper *Bezbozhnik*. He met with socialist groups, anti-imperial activists, freethinkers, and nudist campaigners in Berlin and Madrid. During his visit to London, he connected with the communist leader Shapurji Saklatvala, joining him in working-class protest meetings. A highlight of his London visit was his participation in a meeting in support of the Scottsboro Boys.

On his return to India, *Kudi Arasu* began publishing translated works on socialism and atheism. If the partial translation of *The Communist Manifesto* predated his European tour, Bertrand Russell's *Why I Am Not a Christian* and works of Lenin, Ingersoll, Bhagat Singh, and others followed soon.

By this time, Nagammai had become an integral part of the movement. In Periyar's absence, she took charge of *Kudi Arasu*. When she passed away in 1933, Periyar and his fellows mourned the loss of a comrade.

In 1933, Periyar launched the short-lived weekly *Puratchi* (Revolution). This paper promoted socialist ideas aggressively and declared its support to the Soviet Union. In collaboration with M. Singaravelu, the SRM and the communists devised a programme popularly known as the 'Erode Plan' which included an agenda for land distribution, opposition to colonial and capitalist rule, and radical social reform. For his militant advocacy of socialism, Periyar was arrested in December 1933 and the activities of the SRM were repressed by the colonial state. Fearing that the social reform activities of the SRM would suffer a severe setback if he pursued this line of action, Periyar openly distanced himself from the communists. This was also consistent with his principles—Periyar felt that annihilation of caste and birth of common rights, such as equal access to education and employment and proportional representation, should take precedence over the fight for communism. Thus, though sympathetic till the end of his life to the USSR and socialism, he was highly critical of the Indian communists for their lack of will to tackle the caste question head-on.

For Justice

This was also the period when Periyar moved close to the Justice Party. Founded in 1917 as the South Indian Liberal Federation (but popularly known after its English journal, *Justice*) following the publication of *The Non-Brahmin Manifesto*, the Justice Party was active as the face of non-Brahmin constitutional politics. Though they brought about important institutional reforms while in power such as an executive order for reservations for the backward and scheduled castes in universities and a rudimentary midday meal scheme in schools, it was perceived to be a party of non-Brahmin elites. After a run of electoral successes in the 1920s, the party was routed by the Congress in the first provincial elections under the Government of India Act in 1937. Recognizing the absence of popular leaders in their ranks, Periyar was approached in 1938 to take over its reins. Little did they anticipate that he would wreck the party from within.

Periyar was sympathetic to the political non-Brahminism of the Justice Party. Proportional representation for non-Brahmins in education and positions of power was important. But this alone was not enough to solve the problem of caste. Dismantling caste, Periyar believed, required upending the political, religious, cultural, and social systems that legitimized it. While the Justice Party's methods had ushered in limited progress, they would hardly bring about a social revolution. There were many occasions when Periyar lashed out at the elite non-Brahmins for seeking political positions for themselves and not aspiring for the uplift of the subaltern masses. However, Periyar did not devise a long-term agenda for this social revolution but was more involved in agitations for immediate causes.

Periyar was elected *in absentia* as leader of the Justice Party as he was jailed in 1938 for participating in anti-Hindi agitations. In the Madras Presidency and later in Tamil Nadu, the imposition of Hindi in schools was seen as an infringement on the cultural and linguistic rights of the Tamils. A contentious issue since the 1930s, a massive series of anti-Hindi agitations in the mid-1960s led to the DMK coming to power in Tamil Nadu in 1967, heralding a 'Dravidian era' with only Dravidian parties having been in power in the state ever since. In 1938, Periyar raised the slogan of

'Tamil Nadu for Tamils' in response to the pro-Hindi policies of the ruling Congress party. Periyar viewed the imposition of Hindi as establishment of north Indian cultural and political domination. He also upped his anti-Aryan rhetoric.

The idea that Aryans and Dravidians were separate racial–cultural groups, with Aryans as invaders from the north and Dravidians as indigenous peoples of the south, was in circulation much before Periyar arrived on the scene. Some of the Tamil Saivite and Buddhist thinkers mentioned in the preceding paragraphs also opposed Aryan domination, often relying on missionary scholar Robert Caldwell's 1856 work, *A Comparative Grammar of the Dravidian or South Indian Family of Languages*, to bolster their claims. However, it would be reductive to view the opposition to Aryanism as solely influenced by the colonial–missionary discourse. Influential Indian Hindu thinkers from Bal Gangadhar Tilak to Sarvepalli Radhakrishnan viewed the Aryans as a noble conquering race who brought civilization to India, if not to the world at large. On the other hand, anti-caste thinkers such as Mahatma Jyotirao Phule saw the Aryans as oppressors who, by force and fraud, enslaved the natives of India and suppressed egalitarian forms of living. Periyar used 'Aryan' interchangeably to connote an oppressor race and an oppressive religious–cultural ideology.

The late 1930s were an eventful period for Periyar. It was in 1938 that E. V. Ramasamy was formally conferred the title of 'Periyar' at the Tamil Nadu Women's Conference, organized by Neelambigai Ammaiyar, the daughter of Maraimalai Adigal, in Chennai. Though Ramasamy was referred to as Periyar even by the late 1920s, it was after this that the honorific stuck to him. And it was apt, given Periyar's concern for women's liberation. Periyar viewed women as the first oppressed caste in history, and there were many occasions when he said that fighting the oppression of women was his first priority. That he advocated for greater education for women and their economic independence, and called on them to actively participate in political life, is well known. In addition, his calls for the abolition of marriage, advocacy of contraception, urging women to give up child-bearing, and support for their sexual freedom were unprecedented in India. Many of these themes are covered in *Penn Aen Adimaiyaanal?* (Why Was the Woman Enslaved?), a series of articles beginning from the late 1920s and put together as a book in 1934. Periyar remained an advocate of women's liberation throughout his life. His radical position on this issue upset many, not excepting many of his comrades and fellow travellers.

While Periyar opposed Hindi imposition, he did not support Tamil nationalism. Likewise, though sharply critical of Aryan culture, he did not spare Tamil culture either. Periyar found many things in Tamil tradition, the ancient Tamil texts, and the works of Bhakti literature which reinforced the oppression of women and/or the subordination of the lower castes. His criticisms of these earned him the ire of Tamil nationalists, who continue to revile him much like the Hindu nationalists. What Periyar saw as 'Dravidian' was an alternative to a culturalist or nationalist imagination. While he occasionally used racial terminology to describe the Dravidians as an oppressed indigenous race of the south, he also viewed 'Dravidian' as a flexible category that could include all non-Brahmins in India—even foreigners if they subscribed to anti-caste ideals. In Periyar's imagination, identity and ideology overlapped to constitute the 'Dravidian', while leaving space for change in the future.

A crucial event in the early 1930s that throws light on Periyar's approach to caste, especially his support for the Dalits, is the Poona Pact (1932). Periyar had earlier advocated reservation for the Depressed Classes and opined that they needed it even more than other non-Brahmin castes. In the run-up to the Poona Pact, he strongly supported the idea of separate electorates for the Depressed

Classes proposed by B. R. Ambedkar. From 1932 to 1944, *Kudi Arasu* published at least forty articles in support of Ambedkar's opinions. It was in this period that Periyar drifted further from Gandhi's position, sharply criticizing his opposition to separate electorates, and stood firmly by Ambedkar. At a time when Ambedkar was marginalized by all dominant political formations, Periyar was one of the earliest leaders to recognize him as *the* representative of the Dalits and played no small role in popularizing him in Tamil Nadu. The first ever (and immediate) translation of Ambedkar's *Annihilation of Caste* in any Indian language was in Tamil—commissioned by Periyar and published in serial form in *Kudi Arasu* and soon as a booklet as well. Periyar met Ambedkar for the first time in 1940 in Mumbai, where M. A. Jinnah was also present. In a meeting that Ambedkar and Periyar addressed jointly, both criticized Brahminism. Periyar also spoke about the possibility of a separate 'Dravida Nadu'. Periyar's engagement with Ambedkar continued over the years until the latter's death.

Dravidar Kazhagam

'Dravida Nadu' was imagined as a confederation of south Indian states. Later, it became a stand-in for a separate Tamil Nadu. In the 1940s, Periyar wrote many articles arguing for the secession of Dravida Nadu from India. In 1944, the Justice Party he headed was dismantled and reconfigured as the Dravidar Kazhagam (DK). An influx of activists from subaltern backgrounds and a radical political agenda in the DK led to the flight of the old elite. The DK claimed to focus on social reform as well as the separation of Dravida Nadu. However, unlike the Muslim League, they conducted no major agitations for separation. Periyar spoke of Dravida Nadu to counter Hindi imposition and what he dubbed as the Brahmin–Baniya rule of New Delhi. He had no action plan for separation. Further, his criticism of Tamil cultural nationalism and linguistic pride and his advocacy of a future stateless society in texts such as *Inivarum Ulagam* (The World to Come, 1944) undermined the potential for separatism to be put into practice. Even though he continues to be reviled as a secessionist, it is evident that Periyar's rhetoric was intended only as shock treatment to hasten social reform, to assert linguistic rights, and to demand autonomy for the south Indian states within India. Similarly, much is made out of Periyar's observance of 15 August 1947 as a day of sorrow. Yet, at three crucial moments in post-Independence India—the Sino-India war of 1962 and the Indo-Pakistan wars of 1965 and 1971—Periyar supported the Indian war effort.

Periyar's negative comments on Independence Day were also not taken well by some within the ranks of the DK. Further, while the DK wanted to eschew politics and instead function as a pressure group, trying to influence those in power to bring about egalitarian policies, younger leaders groomed by the party wanted to contest elections in a new democratic India. Periyar's marriage with the thirty-two-year-old Maniammai in 1949 became the trigger for the exodus of this group. Maniammai, the daughter of a Justice Party volunteer, was an activist in the DK. Contributing to *Kudi Arasu*, she also assisted Periyar and managed party affairs. An aging Periyar saw in her a comrade and a worthy successor to his party and its assets. Dissidents in the DK accused Periyar of betraying principles and broke away from the organization. Led by the astute and charismatic C. N. Annadurai, they formed the DMK in 1949 as a political party that would contest elections to fight for political and cultural autonomy for Tamil Nadu and to improve the socio-economic conditions of the Dravidians. Periyar saw them as backstabbers. Until 1967, when the DMK came to power, Periyar was merciless in his criticisms of the newly formed party. Soon, he started supporting the Congress again.

But before that, he came into confrontation with an old friend. In 1953, with Rajaji as chief minister of Madras, the Modified Scheme of Elementary Education was introduced. Under this scheme, children would take classes in one session and learn their father's occupation in the afternoon. Dubbed by Rajaji's opponents as the 'Kula Kalvi Thittam' (Caste Education Scheme), it was criticized as being casteist and meant to propagate Brahmin dominance. Periyar, who was already sparring with Rajaji over the *Ramayana*, spearheaded the campaign against the scheme which led to Rajaji's ouster from power. Rajaji's successor K. Kamaraj promptly scrapped the scheme.

In Kamaraj, Periyar saw a *pachai Tamilan*—a true Tamil. Kamaraj, who hailed from the Nadar community (a caste which had earlier faced much social discrimination), is recognized in Tamil Nadu for his contribution to expanding literacy in the state. He is particularly known for the effective implementation of the noon meals scheme, introduced earlier in a rudimentary form by the Justice Party. Periyar saw Kamaraj's regime as a boon for the subaltern castes and threw his full weight behind him. The DMK, which was steadily growing, had to now confront two very popular leaders, one of them their ideological parent.

Periyar travelled with Maniammai to Burma in 1954 to attend the World Buddhist Conference. He met Ambedkar there for the last time. Periyar subsequently endorsed Ambedkar's conversion to Buddhism and, on the latter's demise, wrote a glowing tribute hailing him as one of the greatest thinkers of the time. In the following years, Ambedkar's birth and death anniversaries were routinely commemorated by Periyar and his party with huge public meetings and Buddhist conferences were also organized.

In the 1950s and early 1960s, Periyar continued his propaganda against caste and religion, combining this with criticisms of Indian nationalism and the constitution. Periyar claimed that the constitution was protecting religion and caste and further alleged that it strengthened the centre at the cost of the states. The 1950s were also a time when Periyar created considerable controversy by iconoclastic acts directed at Hindu gods and by making some aggressive speeches against the Brahmins. However, apart from a few sporadic incidents involving the cutting of the sacred threads of some Brahmins, no violence attended Periyar's anti-Brahmin speeches. Periyar's politics was rooted in non-violence. While provocative sloganeering was used by him, as by many others the world over in the fight for social justice, it was meant to shake public commonsense thinking and not to incite violence. Whenever he felt that the masses were agitated, he took caution to defuse the possibility of aggression.

Many of Periyar's comments on religion were offensive. But equally, if not more, were his remarks on leaders of the DMK. Periyar felt that the DMK was needlessly glorifying an imagined pristine and hoary Tamil past and was compromising on immediate questions of caste and gender. The DMK's politics of Tamil pride, in his view, was incompatible with his politics of self-respect, which had to take a critical rationalist approach to all traditions and religions without exception. In 1963, Kamaraj abdicated and passed the chief minister's chair to M. Bhaktavatsalam, a party man with no popular appeal. Yet Periyar continued to back the Congress party owing to Kamaraj's presence. The DMK intensified their anti-Hindi agitations, and Bhaktavatsalam responded in a ham-fisted manner. There was extensive repression and brutal use of police force. Periyar, who was in principle opposed to Hindi imposition, condemned not the police but the DMK for resorting to aggressive means of protest and for destroying public property. This was of a piece with his disavowal of popular violence.

But the DMK's popularity had grown exponentially. Anna (elder brother), as Annadurai was popularly known, was aided by an able group of lieutenants who were gifted writers and orators and who could take the DMK's politics to wider audiences. The DMK also made extensive use of popular cinema to convey their message. M. Karunanidhi as writer and M. G. Ramachandran (MGR) as film star were widely known in Tamil homes. In Periyar's considered view, cinema was a corruptive medium that spread irrationalism. Politically, the DMK had more clarity and precision on means and ends. Periyar had the burden of supporting a Congress party that was getting unpopular with the Tamil masses. Thus, a political revolution with Anna at the helm preceded the social revolution that Periyar desired. The DMK came to power in 1967 with Anna as chief minister.

Final Years

In the initial months, Periyar was suspicious of the DMK in power. Anna broke the two-decade-long bitterness by magnanimously meeting Periyar and dedicating the new government to him. With the DMK legalizing 'self-respect marriages' (marriages conducted without an officiating priest or traditional rituals) and initiating efforts to legalize *archaka*s (temple priests) from all castes, Periyar mended fences with them. He recognized the merits of the DMK. But this support was not uncritical and he chided them for policies on culture that he felt were irrational. Periyar wanted Dravidian politics to cultivate a scientific rationalist temper. When Anna passed away, he supported Karunanidhi's candidature as his successor. When a rift occurred between Karunanidhi and MGR, he tried to resolve it. When MGR was determined to float his own party, Periyar opposed it. Even in his nineties, in failing health and catheterized for a urinary disorder, Periyar was very much an active force in Tamil Nadu's politics and did not fail to attract controversy. The superstition eradication conference organized by the DK in 1971 in Salem, where the image of the Hindu deity Rama was reportedly disrespected, is one such incident.

One of Periyar's early biographers, Anita Diehl, notes that in the last year of his life, Periyar had no less than 176 public engagements. He passed away on 24 December 1973 at the age of 94. His body was laid for public viewing at Rajaji hall, as if to honour his best friend, and the procession passed by the tomb of Anna, his most accomplished understudy. He was buried, with full state honours, at Periyar Thidal, which now hosts the DK headquarters, a publishing house, a bookstore, a venue for 'self-respect marriages', and a hub for conversations on Periyar.

In his long public career, Periyar's political affiliations and activities varied over time, sometimes even being diametrically opposed. Starting off as a Congress leader, he subsequently called it an evil to be eradicated but campaigned wholeheartedly for it again in the latter part of his life; while he supported Gandhi's movement for prohibition, he later called for a prohibition of Gandhism itself, but also wanted India to be named 'Gandhi Naadu' following Gandhi's assassination; he engaged with socialism and adopted it as a core idea, but was critical of Indian communists for not taking caste seriously, and yet, when they faced repression such as the 1950 Salem prison massacre, DK was one of the few organizations to stand by them; he advocated atheism while campaigning for the rights of all castes to access temples; he mercilessly lampooned the DMK and went to the extent of calling for a ban on the party, but later saw it as the only party capable of providing social justice measures; he opposed the imposition of Hindi as the national language of India while simultaneously satirizing the views of his Tamil nationalist contemporaries. Finding coherence or consistency in

Periyar's politics or thought is no easy task, but there are some pointers from his works. In the last year of his life, Periyar reiterated his commitment to the goals of *samathuvam*, *jaathi ozhippu*, and *penn viduthalai* and reaffirmed the importance of the ideas of *suyamariyadhai*, *samadharmam*, and *pagutharivu*. These were consistent concerns for him in his long and distinguished political life.

Periyar's Vision: A Postscript

Periyar envisaged a sociocultural revolution, and this was intimately linked to his political and economic ideas and the driving force for his life-long activism. Imagining the DK primarily as a social organization, he sought to bring about a change from below. He aimed to take the message of rationalism to the masses. For him, atheism was not an exercise in intellectual dialogue but a public engagement where he sought to confront religious beliefs, notions of scriptural authority, and superstitions, often using direct, blunt arguments, addressing mostly non-elite masses. His speeches on religion were provocative, but so were his opinions on caste, patriarchy, and nationalism. For instance, when Periyar was invited to speak at caste conferences, he had no reservations using that platform to challenge such castes, in places where they were dominant, to give up claims to superiority and work for a common cause. Likewise, he also used wedding events where he was asked to preside to advocate for the abolition of marriage.

The reception of Periyar's vision is varied. The DK continues to promote Periyar's works and thoughts in several forums. Other Periyarist outfits, such as the DK's offshoots, the Dravidar Viduthalai Kazhagam and the Thanthai Periyar Dravidar Kazhagam, function as radical activist groups. These are groups that do not contest elections but instead seek to effect social change following Periyar's ideas. The centering of Periyar as an important figure in Tamil Nadu owes much to the repeated electoral success of the Dravidian political parties, especially the DMK, though the All-India Anna Dravida Munnetra Kazhagam (AIADMK) has not lagged behind in commemorating Periyar. Periyar's birth centenary was celebrated with gusto by MGR's AIADMK government which, among other things, adopted Periyar's Tamil script reform and established a memorial in Vaikom. Leaders of Dalit parties like Thol. Thirumavalavan of the Viduthalai Chiruthaigal Katchi (VCK) uphold Periyarist thoughts and highlight his contributions to the struggles of the marginalized. Feminists, anti-caste activists, leftists, and rationalists have had much to take from Periyar. Though the impact of his ideas has largely been among Tamil audiences, a small number of Lohiaties in Bihar and Uttar Pradesh have engaged with Periyar's thoughts with much sincerity. Lalai Singh of Uttar Pradesh, who was involved with the rationalist anti-caste organization Arjak Sangh, translated a controversial booklet of Periyar on the *Ramayana* to Hindi. There has been a greater interest in Periyar among secular and anti-caste circles in India since 2010, largely owing to the decisive electoral victories of the Dravidian parties—the J. Jayalalithaa-led AIADMK in the 2014 national election and 2016 state election and the M. K. Stalin-led DMK in the 2021 state election and the 2019 and 2024 national elections—over the Hindu nationalist Bharatiya Janata Party (BJP).

However, electoral parties that uphold Periyar as an icon have also had to moderate several of his iconoclastic views. Specifically, his profanation of religion, sharp criticism of all nationalisms, and promotion of a radical libertarian approach to the women's question are difficult positions to take for any politician expecting to succeed in popular elections. As is the case of great thinkers with radically utopian ideas, Periyar is received and applied in parts: the manageable image of Periyar is as a leader of social justice. While pragmatic politics requires such compromises, theory and history cannot shy away from contending with the radical, controversial, and erratic elements of Periyar's thoughts.

Periyar was uncompromising on the goal of annihilation of caste and was keen to explore all means available. An agitator, he was willing to negotiate with the state to secure representation for underprivileged castes. At certain points in his life, he advocated conversion to other religions to fight caste. But generally, he felt that not only was religion unnecessary, it was also an impediment to the creation of an egalitarian society. Texts such as *Inivarum Ulagam* (1944) provide an account of his utopian vision of a casteless, classless, religion-less, and gender-just society. His understanding of and opposition to caste, commitment to Dalit emancipation, and support for women's liberation are topics that merit books by themselves. His writings on literature, culture, cinema, identity, economy, religion, and nationalism deserve new and critical attention. This volume offers a panoramic view of Periyar's interventions on these topics, providing a ready handbook on Periyar and Periyarist thought.

The chapters of this volume seek to provide a reasonably coherent account of Periyar's complex politics and his thought. We invited contributors from different fields, established and emerging academics, to look at Periyar from diverse disciplinary perspectives. Crucial events from Periyar's life are discussed, as are critical aspects of his thought. New published material is engaged with, while old scholarship is revisited. There have been remarkable works on the lives and thoughts of leaders such as Tagore, Gandhi, Nehru, Ambedkar, Bose, and others who have a pan-Indian presence. While Periyar's political reach has mostly been within Tamil Nadu, we, the editors, believe that his goals and ideas have much wider significance. To that extent, our chapters reflect the core concerns of Periyar and place them in broader intellectual and historical contexts.

In the past decade, there have been a handful of significant publications on Dravidian politics, some of which engage with Periyar in detail. It is indeed a matter of regret that more attention was not paid to this significant thinker earlier, but we are glad that there has been a rebirth of intellectual interest in his thought in Tamil Nadu and beyond. To do justice to a thinker like Periyar, the multiple dimensions of his thought, his politics, and his contexts have to be considered. We hope that this volume measures up to one such effort. Many of the topics discussed here by our contributors, the materials used, arguments advanced, and conclusions drawn took us by surprise, despite our own longstanding engagement with Periyar. It was a pleasure to work on this volume and what we have learnt in the process is immeasurable. *The Cambridge Companion to Periyar* aspires to serve as a useful entry point for future research and intellectual conversations on this iconoclast. We are also confident that general readers will have much to take away from this volume and will discover a Periyar who is relevant to the times they are in.

Part I

Events That Made Periyar

1

Periyar and the Vaikom Satyagraha

Pazha. Athiyaman

Edited and translated from Tamil by A. R. Venkatachalapathy

The years leading up to Periyar's break from the Indian National Congress and the founding of the Self-Respect Movement (SRM) were marked by two significant events. The first was the controversy over discrimination in the Cheranmadevi Gurukulam, a nationalist school, of which the centenary history of *The Hindu* says: 'The controversy was one of the contributing factors for E. V. Ramaswami Naicker drifting away from Congress and later forming an organisation of his own whose avowed objective was to eliminate Brahmins and Brahmin influence in Tamil Nad which it wanted to secede from India' (Parthasarathy, 1978, p. 337).

The bitterness caused by the Cheranmadevi Gurukulam controversy was accentuated by the Vaikom Satyagraha, which Periyar for the most part led during 1924–1925. If the nationalist *gurukulam* in Cheranmadevi provided separate seating for Brahmins and non-Brahmins in the dining hall, in the temple town of Vaikom in Kerala, Ezhavas and other Depressed Classes were not even permitted entry into the streets surrounding the Mahadeva (Siva) Temple, not to speak of entry into the temple precincts. The Vaikom experience gave Periyar a fuller understanding of nationalist politics and left an indelible imprint on his future career. Periyar returned to these experiences in his speeches and writings all through his life.

These two struggles and the campaign for communal representation (equitable share of seats for non-Brahmins in representative political bodies and in employment and education) were what led Periyar to leave the Congress, of which he had been a part from around the time of the First World War. It was the Vaikom Satyagraha that earned Periyar his first moniker, 'Vaikom Veerar', that is, 'the hero of Vaikom'.[1] At least a decade before he came to be venerated as Periyar, he had won this distinction.

There are many studies—both full-length monographs and articles—on the Vaikom Satyagraha. Of varying quality, a common feature of this scholarship is the inadequate space and importance given to Periyar.[2] Based on extensive research into hitherto unexplored archives, this chapter seeks to map Periyar's central role in the Vaikom Satyagraha.[3]

***

In colonial India, Travancore was one of the six big princely states under British paramountcy—the largest in south India. (Travancore; Cochin, another princely state; and the Malabar district of the Madras Presidency were brought together in 1956 to form what is present-day Kerala.) At the beginning of the Vaikom Satyagraha, Travancore was ruled by Sri Moolam Thirunal Rama Varma (4 August 1885–7 August 1924). At the height of the movement, he died and was succeeded by a minor king, Chithira Thirunal Balarama Varma, with the real power vested in Sethu Lakshmi Bayi as maharani regent. The Congress followed a policy of non-interference in the affairs of native states even though many of them were loyalist and anti-people.

If Travancore had won praise as 'a Hindu Kingdom', it had also gained notoriety, in the angry words of Swami Vivekananda, as 'a lunatic asylum' for its brazen and inhuman forms of caste discrimination.

The caste structure of Travancore may be broadly divided as follows: Brahmins, Nairs, Ezhavas, and Pulayas. Constituting a small minority, Brahmins included Nambudris, Tamil Brahmins, and some Gaud Saraswats. Warriers, Nambissans, Poduvals, Marars, and some others were a separate group of castes related to the temple and its administration (Ambalavasi castes) and were considered superior to the Nairs. Though regarded as Sudras, Nairs were a powerful caste below them. The numerous Ezhavas—referred to as Shanars (Chanars) and Tiyyas in other parts of the Malayalam-speaking region—were treated as untouchables and experienced unspeakable social disabilities, including limited access to education and no rights to Vedic or Brahminical temples. While 'untouchability' also marked the caste system in other parts of India, in Travancore it was compounded by the even worse forms of 'unseeability' and 'unapproachability'. Not only the touch, in Travancore, proximity to and even the very sight of certain castes was deemed to be polluting to upper castes.

In the Kottayam district of the state was situated the Mahadeva temple. In the streets around the temple, untouchables and Ezhavas, a caste just above the former in the caste hierarchy, were not permitted entry. Vaikom was the locus of the first Gandhian *social* experiment in *satyagraha* in that it was employed to rectify a social problem unlike his earlier use of it to protest against British political rule. The *satyagraha*, started under the aegis of the Congress, achieved partial success after nearly twenty months on a rollercoaster path: three of the approach roads were thrown open in November 1925. More than a decade later, in November 1936, the historic Travancore Temple Entry Proclamation was issued removing caste restrictions on entry into temples.

The *Satyagraha*

Before we reconstruct and analyse Periyar's central role in the Vaikom Satyagraha, let us first sketch its course and end result.

Though the Vaikom Satyagraha is generally designated as a temple entry movement, it was in fact only a protest against the bar on entry into the temple streets. Nevertheless, it was a momentous struggle. It came at the zenith of a long process of protest for liberty, equality, and dignity by the Ezhavas. Dr P. Palpu's Ezhava Mahajana Sabha, founded in 1896, marked the beginnings of organized efforts among the community for their upliftment. Sree Narayana Guru (1856–1928), their pre-eminent social and spiritual leader, and his Sree Narayana Dharma Paripalana Yogam (SNDP, established 1903) were central to the social movement among the Ezhavas.

T. K. Madhavan (1885–1930), active in the SNDP from a young age, was the editor of *Desabhimani*, a weekly published from Kollam. A Congressman and an Ezhava leader, he was the first to raise the demand for entry into the Vaikom temple streets. Elected to Travancore's Sree Moolam Praja Sabha in 1918, he consistently voiced this demand, asking for the removal of the demeaning signboards (*theendal palaka*) that barred Ezhavas. Long agitated by this injustice, he met M. K. Gandhi in Tirunelveli in September 1921, seeking the Mahatma's approval for a *satyagraha*. When Gandhi asked if this was a priority when there were more pressing issues such as education, Madhavan explained the Travancore situation and won his approval. The support of all-India leaders such as C. R. Das and Motilal Nehru followed at the Kakinada session of the Congress in December 1923. The Congress resolved to form an all-India committee to eradicate untouchability while provincial committees were to carry out the task in their respective regions. Subsequently, in January 1924, the Kerala Congress Anti-Untouchability Committee was constituted by the Kerala Provincial Congress Committee. This was a radical break from the Congress's policy of non-interference in native states (Ouwerkerk, 1994, p. 4). As a consequence of this policy, its organization had been rather weak in Travancore, leading to difficulties in coordinating the Vaikom Satyagraha.

The *satyagraha* began on 30 March 1924. Gandhi's statement on unqualified non-violence was first read out. Heralded by T. K. Madhavan, K. P. Kesava Menon, A. K. Pillai, Velayudha Menon, and T. R. Krishnaswami Iyer, three *satyagraha* volunteers stepped into the prohibited streets. All three were immediately arrested by the Travancore police. Kesava Menon was arrested on 7 April followed by George Joseph on 11 April.

A *satyagraha* ashram was set up to house the volunteers and organize the struggle. Volunteers came from all castes including the *savarna*s (upper castes). Regular public meetings were held, usually at the foreshore, to explain the rationale for the struggle. Printed notices were distributed. The *satyagraha* was offered at the entrance to the approach roads. Every day, two or three batches of volunteers courted arrest. Volunteers took out *charka*s and spun on them at the *satyagraha* site apart from making house-to-house collections for funding the *satyagraha*. Regular *bhajanai* parties were held.[4]

The Travancore State took a strong stance against what it saw as open defiance of its authority. But after initial arrests, it gave up imprisoning leaders and volunteers, instead barricading the approach streets. The policy of non-arrest necessitated the continuous presence of police pickets. Following Gandhi's orders not to fast as it would amount to coercion rather than persuasion, the *satyagraha*'s leaders were at a loss as to measures to counter this. Gandhi's instructions not to seek outside help further hampered the *satyagraha*. Paid goons of the obdurate upper castes harassed and beat up the non-violent volunteers, worsening matters. The weather too played truant. In late July there were heavy rains causing floods, cutting off Vaikom from the outside world, but the volunteers remained undeterred.[5]

On Gandhi's advice, two *jatha*s (long marches) to Thiruvananthapuram, the seat of the royal family, were organized in November. Consisting purely of upper castes, one *jatha* started from Vaikom and another from Kottar in the extreme corner of south Travancore. A twelve-member deputation from the two *jatha*s met the maharani regent and presented a memorial urging the removal of the disabilities imposed on the untouchables in public places and institutions. The deputation was disappointed as the maharani regent favoured the status quo. But the *jatha*s nevertheless succeeded in sensitizing and shaping public opinion in favour of their demand.

The deputation having failed, the *satyagraha* was at an impasse. Gandhi sought to effect a compromise and arrived in March 1925 in Vaikom. Apart from negotiating with the upper castes, he also met the maharani regent. Though no headway was made in relation to the demands of the *satyagraha*, the government removed some restrictions on the volunteers and permitted peaceful protests. But the *satyagraha* continued—more as a symbolic struggle—for the better part of 1925.

However, on 23 November 1925, the government granted major concessions. All the roads around the temple with the exception of two short lanes leading to the eastern approach road—one from the south and one from the north—were opened to everyone. A new road was planned to join the eastern approach road to the northern road. With the granting of unrestricted access to three streets surrounding the temple, victory was proclaimed. Police Commissioner W. H. Pitt observed that the use of the roads by all people had 'long been accepted by the general public as fair and are now accepted by the Satyagrahis themselves who have at last found a suitable occasion for withdrawing'.[6] A typical Gandhian passive victory had been achieved.

On 17 November 1925, a celebratory event was organized under the aegis of the Kerala Congress Anti-Untouchability Committee in Vaikom. When the news that the public roads would be thrown open 'to all classes of people without distinction' was received, the committee resolved that 'the object of the Satyagraha [had] been achieved' 'under the advice from Mahatmaji'. The meeting was also of the view that the public opinion in Travancore had 'clearly expressed itself in favour of temple entry for all Hindus' and therefore the task was to strengthen that opinion, 'conciliate and enlist the sympathy of the orthodoxy'.[7]

The victory meeting, attended by over 4,000 people, was presided over by Periyar. Why?

Enter Periyar

As the *satyagraha* was launched, practically all the leaders and volunteers were arrested within the first two weeks. With the *satyagraha* being headless, there was a desperate search for leaders. It was in this context that urgent messages were sent to Periyar.

Why Periyar? Given the challenge posed by the Justice Party (founded in 1917) to the Brahmin-dominated Congress, Periyar had moved swiftly in the Congress party hierarchy by demonstrating his organizational skills during the Rowlatt Satyagraha and the Non-Cooperation Movement. In 1924, he became president of the Tamil Nadu Congress Committee (TNCC). As he explained later, 'I was good at exposing the barbarity of untouchability and had also gained fame as an excellent agitator.' On hearing from the *satyagraha*'s organizers, he handed over charge of the party organization to the senior leader of Madras, C. Rajagopalachari, and set off stating that 'this was an excellent opportunity to serve an excellent cause' (Anaimuthu, vol. 1, 1974, pp. 110–111).

Though Periyar was enthusiastic about going to Vaikom, he wanted to be sure that his presence was indispensable. Periyar was wary of jumping the gun considering the official Congress policy of non-interference. Further, not only was Gandhi against turning the *satyagraha* into an all-India affair, he had also forbidden the involvement of outsiders. C. Rajagopalachari too took a similar line: he had even asked George Joseph what purpose would be served by him or Periyar being jailed for a year. Not only was untouchability not going to be eradicated anytime soon, nationalist work too would be hampered.[8] This explains Periyar's detailed statement at the time of his departure to Vaikom wherein he set out the timetable of his correspondence regarding the invitation from the leaders of the *satyagraha*.

The first cable was from Kurur Neelakandan Namboodiripad, one of the *satyagraha* leaders, on 4 April 1924, asking Periyar to hasten to Vaikom. To this Periyar had replied with a wire, followed by a detailed letter, asking if he had to come immediately given that he was scheduled to attend a Congress district conference in Kulitalai. When on 6 April, George Joseph too wrote to Periyar, he responded in similar terms. On 12 April, Kurur Neelakandan Namboodiripad wrote again reiterating the importance of Periyar's presence: 'Vykom situation grave. All leaders arrested. Eighteen Satyagrahis on hunger strike. Myself just leaving for Vykom. My immediate arrest probable. Lead movement. Wire advise, etc.' Initially, Periyar was hesitant considering the ongoing *khadi* work in Tamil Nadu but found 'the command from the neighbouring province of Kerala is irresistible. A grave situation has arisen. Repression is rampant.' The removal of untouchability being 'the cornerstone of our Mahatma's programme', this factor 'outweighed' all other considerations in his mind and he set out immediately though 'I may also be arrested but it is nothing.'[9]

Ironically, when Periyar arrived, he was officially welcomed by Travancore state officials. He was informed that the maharaja had instructed them to make the necessary board and lodging arrangements. Sometime earlier, Periyar had made excellent arrangements for the maharaja who had stopped in Erode on his way to Delhi and the maharaja was reciprocating his generosity. However, Periyar refused to accept the hospitality as the purpose of his visit was to agitate against the government. Periyar recalled later that the royal welcome extended to him served the purpose of introducing him to the public and greatly enhanced his prestige (Anaimuthu, vol. 1, 1974, pp. 110–111). The royal welcome has passed into oral lore and no discussion in Tamil circles of Periyar's role in the *satyagraha* is complete without mentioning it.

Periyar's arrival gave a fillip to the movement. As T. K. Ravindran, the first historian to write in detail about the *satyagraha*, remarks, Periyar's 'lead gave a new life to the movement' (1980, p. 89). With local leaders behind bars, Periyar had to shoulder the entire responsibility. As soon as he arrived on 14 April, he led from the front, joining two batches of *satyagrahi*s.

As its leader, organizing the *satyagraha* on a day-to-day basis fell upon Periyar. Choosing volunteers, arranging for their board and lodging, raising funds and accounting for them, and generally managing the *satyagraha* ashram were his tasks. In addition, he gave daily public talks—his Tamil speeches translated into Malayalam—in Vaikom and in adjoining districts to raise funds as well sensitize the public about the inhumanity of untouchability. As police records and newspaper reports attest, barely a day passed without him giving a well-attended talk.

Periyar toured the state, including Cherthala and Kottayam in central Travancore and Thiruvananthapuram and Nagercoil in south Travancore. He was often accompanied by C. A. Ayyamuthu, his friend and Congressman from Coimbatore. His associate S. Ramanathan too joined him for some time. *The Hindu* described Periyar's speeches in the Malayalam country as 'inspiring'.[10] According to Ravindran, his 'speeches were especially impressive and their savage force cut through the prestige of the Travancore government' (1980, p. 90). However, despite his commitment to non-violence, Periyar's speeches were described as 'violent' by the district magistrate.[11] We should read them as being strident and assertive.

The report presented at the annual session of the Tamil Nadu Congress in Tiruvannamalai (15–16 November 1924) sums up Periyar's role in the *satyagraha* in the following terms: Periyar 'travelled across Travancore state and through his propaganda speeches explained the necessity of the satyagraha, clarified doubts regarding it and mobilized support among the public, and in the process suffered imprisonment twice'.[12]

The people of Travancore, as subjects, held the maharaja in the highest esteem, little short of worship. Periyar's criticism of him therefore was quite novel to them and caused considerable surprise and wonder. One reason adduced by the government for not throwing open the streets was that they were the property of the temple over which it had no control. If that was the case, Periyar asked, had the maharaja not dedicated the entire kingdom to Lord Padmanabha and ruled it only as his *dasa* (servant)? 'By virtue of this,' he argued, 'everything in Travancore has become the property of the Devaswam', and therefore was not the entire state the property of the temple? Why should the temple streets alone enjoy such a privilege? He went so far as to identify the government and the raja '[as the] real opponent[s]'.[13] Speaking in Nedunkana on 4 September, he said that 'the British Govt. which was the suzerain power did not observe any distinction between different castes. Therefore, it passed his understanding why subordinate states like Travancore & Cochin also should observe such a practice.'[14] It speaks for Periyar's daring that he indulged in relentless criticism of the king despite it not going down well with the Ezhavas who held strong loyalist sympathies.

Given the difficult circumstances of organizing the *satyagraha*, Periyar called for volunteers from Tamil Nadu to join, apart from contributing funds. This was a radical move, considering that Gandhi was not in favour of outsiders joining the *satyagraha*. In response to Periyar's appeal, *The Hindu* observed, volunteers were coming from Tamil Nadu 'in large numbers'.[15] Periyar also deputed C. A. Ayyamuthu to go to Tamil Nadu to collect funds and for propaganda work. Ayyamuthu was specially tasked with attending the Kongu Vellalar Conference taking place in Rasipuram to mobilize support.[16]

Periyar's wife Nagammai and sister S. R. Kannammal too arrived in Vaikom soon after Periyar. Probably they were the first women volunteers to take part in the *satyagraha*. *Swadesamitran* reported that a troop of women volunteers was being formed and that the wives of Periyar, Govindan Chanar, and T. K. Madhavan were to lead it.[17]

In the company of four other women, Nagammai offered *satyagraha*.[18] In one instance, Nagammai even pushed her way through an opening in the barricade but was stopped by the police when she insisted on taking the wife of A. K. Govindan Chanar, an *avarna* (lower caste) with her. As it started raining, the policemen offered umbrellas but Nagammai refused, preferring to get drenched in the downpour.[19] Similarly, the wives of Emperumal Naidu, Sankara Iyer, and Dhanumalaya Perumal—all from Tamil Nadu—too joined the *satyagraha*.

Following the entry of Nagammai and other women, the police had to face the novel situation of dealing with women *satyagrahi*s. On 22–23 May, when Nagammai, Kannammal, Thirumalai Ammal, Bhakkiyam Ammal, and others offered *satyagraha*, a police officer, Pichai Aiyangar, is said have instructed Inspector Sarma not to extend any special privileges to them but treat them like other (male) *satyagrahi*s.[20]

Nagammai and Kannammal also joined Periyar on his propaganda tours. According to a police report, Nagammai accompanied Swami Satyavrath, K. Velayudha Menon, and K. Krishna Namboodripad on a tour of Alleppey to collect funds.[21] She was also present at a meeting in Chingoli on 16-1-1100 (Malayalam calendar; Gregorian calendar equivalent: 31 August 1924) before proceeding to Kollam.[22]

With Periyar giving the lead, the struggle intensified, garnering all-India attention. Leaders from outside Travancore were forced to take note. Rajagopalachari, who had refused to depute anyone from Tamil Nadu to join the *satyagraha*, himself visited Vaikom. Another leading Congress figure, S. Srinivasa Iyengar, visited Vaikom to confer with all the parties and surveyed the streets that were the bone of contention.[23] Congress leader C. V. Venkataramana Aiyangar came towards the end of April 1924 and was involved in peace talks with the various parties. Apart from C. A. Ayyamuthu and S. Ramanathan mentioned earlier, Dr Emperumal Naidu of Nagercoil, Sankara Iyer of Kallidaikurichi, Chakravarthi Iyengar of Kumbakonam, and Thirumeninathan of Aruppukkottai too became part of the *satyagraha*. Some of them joined the *jatha*s, campaigned for the cause, and even courted arrest. At least fifty-three volunteers from Tamil Nadu participated, apart from the many who contributed funds and lent a helping hand in other ways (Athiyaman, 2020, pp. 636–640).

The Resident of Travancore C. W. E. Cotton's observation that '[i]n fact, the movement would have collapsed long ago but for the support it has received from outside Travancore though the question of opening this road is a domestic problem' attests to the success of Periyar's leadership and his call for mobilization.[24]

Proceedings against Periyar

As the struggle gathered intensity and Periyar's campaign gained traction, the Travancore government had to take note of him. From grudgingly acknowledging that 'One Ramaswami Naicker is now leading the movement',[25] soon it had to take steps to restrict him, prohibiting him from speaking in public. The order imposing a ban for fifteen days was served on 29 April 1924 as his speeches were likely 'to create hostility among classes'.[26] Another order followed after the first one lapsed, with the district magistrate prohibiting him from addressing the public in Kollam district.[27]

With the prohibition orders doing little to stop him, the state next moved to externing him from Vaikom. In response, Periyar declared from Vaikom on 17 May that he would violate this order.[28]

Following his defiance, Periyar was prosecuted along with 'Sahodaran' K. Ayyappan and Emperumal Naidu. An offence was made of speeches delivered on 20 April in Vaikom and 25 April in Thiruvananthapuram, and he was charged under sections 117, 145A, and 508 of the Travancore Penal Code.[29]

Meanwhile, on 19 May 1924, Periyar was served with an externment order prohibiting him from entering Kottayam district—which, according to the special branch of the Madras police, 'he has acknowledged but intends to disobey'.[30] His reply to the district magistrate was expressed in the following terms:

> The primary condition for the success of Satyagraha is non-violence, peace and goodwill. It is therefore just to prevent violence and affray that I came, stayed and worked in Vaikom. I am convinced that this is clear to you from my speeches and activities. I am also convinced that your order is intended to prevent me from my peaceful activities and somehow cause riot or affray and then to kill the movement in a calculated manner. So, I feel bound to disobey the order.[31]

Soon, speaking at the *satyagraha* camp, Periyar said, amidst 'loud and prolonged cheers', that he had replied to the district magistrate saying 'I cannot obey this lying order. It is the Government that wants to cause riot or affray and not the Satyagrahis.' Referring to the earlier two orders prohibiting him from speaking in public, he said they 'left me room to do something towards [the] Vaikom Satyagraha though the orders themselves were illegal'. But the externment order left him with no option 'except to become the Rajah's guest', meaning a state prisoner. The arrest, rather than affecting the struggle, he said, would only help it, adding tongue in cheek, 'I go to jail therefore gladly and for much deserved leisure'.[32]

The government complied with his wish. Stating that he did not expect the court to be fair in dispensing justice, Periyar refused to cooperate with it. The purpose of his coming to Vaikom was to ensure that everyone had access to the temple streets and he was prepared to accept any punishment.[33] On 22 May, the court sentenced Periyar to simple imprisonment for one month.[34]

Periyar served time in the lock-up at the Arookutty police station. When he was behind bars, Rajagopalachari visited Vaikom at the urgent call of the Anti-Untouchability Committee and met Periyar.[35] P. Varadarajulu Naidu too paid him a visit. The cell he was confined to, Naidu described, was 'very small, dark and insanitary' and the medical arrangements far from satisfactory.[36]

On being released on 21 June, rather than returning to Erode, Periyar set out to Vaikom again where he was given an enthusiastic welcome. 'Mr E. V. Ramaswami has arrived today. He was received and taken to the camp from the boat-jetty in a grand procession of the volunteers,' said a police report.[37]

At Vaikom, Periyar was perturbed to see the *satyagrahi*s being assaulted by hired goons, with the police turning a blind eye.[38] On occasion, they even smeared lime on the volunteers' eyes. Addressing a large gathering on the foreshore, Periyar condemned 'police terrorism'; however, he also exhorted volunteers to remain non-violent. Even as he was speaking, stones were thrown at him which missed him but injured a boy.[39]

The district magistrate of Kottayam was furious that Periyar had entered the district again and pulled up the police for letting him in.[40] On 26 June, another prohibition order was served on him under section 127 of the Code of Criminal Procedure (CrPC) 'to prevent a probable riot'.[41]

Periyar was free for barely a month before he was put behind bars again. He had planned a tour of Travancore to campaign against untouchability but cancelled it on account of barbarities unleashed by upper castes and their hired goons.[42] Even as the externment order remained in force, he refused to leave the district, preferring to wait for the summons for his disobedience. The summons came the next day.[43]

In between, Periyar made a quick visit to Erode for some urgent personal work.[44] Returning to Vaikom on Sunday, 6 July 1924, he met leading merchants in the place and collected rice worth over 300 rupees for feeding the volunteers. Meanwhile, Kumara Pillai, the district superintendent of police, met him in the *satyagraha* ashram and informed him that the police would no more confiscate the *charka*s as long as the spinners worked them without obstructing passage. Periyar promised that they would not.[45] But he soon clarified that his undertaking did not mean that they were indeed causing obstruction earlier.[46]

Meanwhile, prohibition orders were extended by the district magistrate of Kollam.[47] The fresh orders forced Periyar to take a stance on courting imprisonment. In a public statement, he said that C. Rajagopalachari had expressly told him both 'personally and in writing' to not disobey orders and avoid getting arrested at any cost given that every leader was in prison and the *satyagraha* needed a leader. He had decided to ignore the externment order because he was 'anxious to remain here as long as I possibly could so that I might satisfy myself that the Satyagrahis remained perfectly non-violent, and willingly and cheerfully bore all the indignities and affronts hurled on them by their opponents'. On finding that 'lawlessness and terrorism' had been let loose on the *satyagrahis* and they had been 'assaulted, fisted and brutally handled' and that the authorities were 'conniving at this sort of hooliganism', Periyar said he had decided to disobey the order.[48]

Given that he had violated the prohibition order a second time, the Kottayam magistrate summoned Periyar demanding an explanation. Periyar appeared in the court on 8 July, but the enquiry was adjourned to a week later.[49] In convicting him, on 16 July, the magistrate stated that the 'reports and enquiries made of the speeches and other activities [revealed] … that [his] entry and stay would lead to riot and affray'.[50]

The convicting judge noted that '[a] spirit of defiance and revolt to law and order is evidenced by his conduct'. '[H]aving a second time disobeyed the prohibition order' indicated that a 'punishment of reformatory character has already been proved to be ineffective'. The magistrate not only sentenced Periyar to four months of rigorous imprisonment but also stated that 'I do not consider that he must be given any special treatment'.[51]

Following his conviction, there was a delay in transporting Periyar to Thiruvananthapuram due to the floods that had cut off Vaikom from the outside word.[52] On this occasion, he was lodged in Thiruvananthapuram Central Jail along with K. P. Kesava Menon and George Joseph who had earlier been sentenced in the Vaikom Satyagraha. However, while all others were treated as political prisoners, Periyar was treated as an ordinary criminal. K. P. Kesava Menon, the president of the Kerala Pradesh Congress Committee, wrote to the government demanding that Periyar be treated like a political prisoner. He referred to Periyar as his counterpart in the TNCC and said that as a noble patriot and a former chairman of the Erode Municipal Council, he deserved better treatment (Menon, 1963, p. 66).

Expressing his consternation in similar terms, Rajagopalachari stated that he was 'reliably informed' that Periyar was being treated 'as an ordinary convict in the matter of diet and accommodation'. He was dressed in 'jail clothes and ankle iron[s], and [was] confined in a solitary cell far away from the other Satyagraha prisoners'. Describing him as someone who had 'deliberately spurned the pleasures of wealth and position and chosen the hard and rugged path, not in form only like many of us but in all reality', Rajagopalachari paid encomiums to his 'indomitable soul'. Openly criticizing the government for treating him harshly, he demanded 'civilized treatment [as] is due to prisoners of conscience'.[53]

Though he was sentenced to imprisonment for four months, Periyar was released in a little over a month, on 30 August, along with eighteen other *satyagrahis* due to an unexpected change in the polity. On 7 August, Maharaja Moolam Thirunal passed away. Following this, a twelve-year-old Chithira Thirunal Balarama Varma ascended the throne—as it turned out, he was the last maharaja of Travancore—and Rani Sethu Lakshmi Bayi became maharani regent. If the *satyagraha* was suspended for three days as a mark of respect,[54] following their ascension, the government reciprocated by granting remission to the prisoners.

On their release, a statement signed by Periyar and Kesava Menon, among others, expressed the hope that their release was a sign that everyone could walk on the public streets. If it was not so, they expressed their determination to continue with the *satyagraha*.[55]

Despite the rough treatment he had received at the hands of jail authorities, Periyar made light of it. Tongue in cheek, he said at a public meeting that he was 'leading a quiet life in jail without anxiety'. Rather, 'the release had given him anxiety. If the Government [did] not lay open the roads and paths [a]round Vaikom temple to all persons without distinction of caste or creed, he [would have] to work again and prepare himself to go to jail.'[56]

Challenges to the *Satyagraha*

In the absence of local leaders, Periyar had to face various challenges: both organizational and political. As the Congress's 'branch in Travancore … existed merely in name' (Ouwerkerk, 1994, p. 4) —a situation accentuated by the arrest of local leaders—Periyar faced innumerable organizational challenges, both in terms of people and money.

The first was the stance of Gandhi. Gandhi's various restrictions on the conduct of the *satyagraha* effectively meant fighting with one's arms tied to one's back. Refusing to see this as a civil matter but a religious one, Gandhi forbade George Joseph, a Syrian Christian, from leading the agitation. (George Joseph disagreed but complied; in any case, he was arrested and removed from the scene.)

Next, Gandhi expressly forbade outside help underlining the exclusive efforts of the local people. The Akali Sikhs who had established a free kitchen for the *satyagrahi*s had to consequently wind it up, and from 16 July, the SNDP started a free kitchen.[57] The support of the Arya Samaj under Swami Shraddhananda of Delhi was also disavowed.

Gandhi further prohibited the use of fasting as a weapon against the *savarna*s as it would amount to coercion and not persuasion. To the *savarna*s themselves, he proposed what he called 'three sportive offers': of arbitration, a referendum, and an examination by selected pandits of scriptures. His appeals to reason, humanity, and Hinduism failed to make the impression he hoped on the oppositionists. To the *satyagrahi*s themselves he advised 'tremendous patience'. As public opinion in and outside Vaikom, and even across the world, was growing strongly in their favour, he asked them to play their game nobly and silently.[58]

Gandhi's impositions were such that there were reports of the *satyagrahi*s getting impatient 'at the gentle and slow methods'.[59] Even though Periyar did not see eye to eye with Gandhi on these issues, as a committed follower of Gandhi, he obeyed the commands in both letter and spirit. Periyar's reservations were expressed only many years later, after he had moved far from the Gandhian creed.

The second, major challenge was the participation of the Ezhavas. For a struggle that primarily sought to win the *sanjara* (free movement) right of Ezhavas to the temple streets, the involvement of Ezhava leaders, at least initially, was limited (see Chandramohan 2016, pp. 184–191). P. Palpu was actively against the protest and few Ezhava leaders other than T. K. Madhavan and Govindan Chanar participated. Kesava Menon, Kelappan, and Munnoth Padmanabhan were all Nairs. Ayyankali, the great Pulaya leader, seems to have largely ignored the *satyagraha*.

Most interestingly, the peerless spiritual and community leader of the Ezhavas, Sree Narayana Guru, seemed to have reservations on the methods adopted to win the right. As a contemporary newspaper observed somewhat disingenuously, 'As a saint, he has very little to do with these movements and is practically outside the range of Politics.'[60] But the *satyagraha* ashram itself was located on SNDP land.[61] Even if it did not have Narayana Guru's express permission, his silent consent was assumed. When his reservations became public, Gandhi wrote about them in

Young India.⁶² It was after this intervention that Narayana Guru stopped indicating his reservations. Only in September 1924, almost six months after the *satyagraha* had commenced, did he bless the movement launched by his prime disciple, T. K. Madhavan. He also donated a sum of 1,000 rupees on learning that the movement was strapped for funds. Ultimately, it was after Gandhi's visit to Vaikom in March 1925 that Ezhavas participated in large numbers.

Periyar was clear that a movement for the rights of Ezhavas could not succeed without their own participation. And even if the campaign did succeed without them, it could not be consolidated without their involvement. Just before his first prison sentence, within a month of his arrival at Vaikom, he addressed Ezhavas in the following terms:

> My Ezhava brothers and sisters! If the Satyagraha campaign that in now going on at Vaikom does not bring about the desired result, it will mean a great loss and everlasting discredit on the whole of India. Besides it will give an irreparable setback to the Ezhava community who will, if the movement fails, never again be able to regain their lost position and prestige. It therefore behoves every Ezhava male or female in Travancore, Cochin and British India to do his or her duty in continuing the campaign to a successful close. Let not this appeal be unheeded by them and let it not be said of them, when the test came, they were found wanting and that they proved traitors to their country and their community. This is my humble prayer to them.⁶³

In urging the Ezhavas to join the struggle, he also emphasized the participation of women.

Again, in early July, Periyar reiterated his appeal. Asking if 'they were justified in not taking up the conduct of the campaign in their own hands', he called on Ezhava leaders to take charge of all the executive functions of the movement and carry out the Mahatma's command. They were dutybound to falsify the argument that local Ezhavas were unconcerned about the situation and that the struggle was being instigated by outsiders. 'Brethren, you have now all India behind you in your campaign; you have the blessings of the greatest patriots and reformers of the country, and you have the guidance of Mahatma Gandhi.'⁶⁴

Periyar also spoke at a public meeting to mark the second anniversary of the Karapuram Ezhava Yuvajana Seva Sangam on 16 April 1924. In this meeting, where the welcome address was given by 'Sahodaran' Ayyappan, Periyar 'delivered a lengthy speech in Tamil' which was translated into Malayalam. Funds were collected and volunteers raised. Underlining the non-violent message of Gandhi, he emphatically stated that 'Independence, Equality and Brotherhood could be established only after putting an end to unapproachability and untouchability, that all human beings are equal and that there is only one religion and one caste.' On hearing his appeal to women to join the struggle, the wife of the secretary of the youth volunteer association not only immediately came forward to donate 100 rupees to the campaign fund but gave a list of 100 volunteers as well. Periyar also drew parallels with the hardships experienced by Indians in Kenya and South Africa.⁶⁵

Periyar: Vaikom in Hindsight

Periyar had led the struggle for social justice in Vaikom as the president of the Tamil Nadu Congress. By the time the movement had succeeded to an extent, his political path had changed dramatically. From being a provincial president, he left the party in November 1925 coinciding with the victory celebrations in Vaikom. From an ardent foot soldier of Gandhi, Periyar turned into his vehement critic in the following years. Though he completely distanced himself from the picketing of toddy shops and *khadi* propaganda after he left the Congress, he never reneged on the importance of the Vaikom Satyagraha. In his writings and speeches, he returned to the *satyagraha* over and over again innumerable times over the next fifty years of his life. Ironically, the Congress which led the Vaikom Satyagraha did not claim credit for it. Consequently, Periyar reaped the full credit for the *satyagraha*'s success.

Speaking at the celebratory event on 17 November 1925, Periyar extolled the strength of *satyagraha*. He, however, emphasized that the goal was nothing less than the eradication of untouchability from the temple itself.

> It is through patiently putting up with the hardships of *satyagraha* that we have reached this point. If we had indulged in violence or expressed our anger in violent terms, we would never have overcome the forces against us. Our objective is not simply to walk on the streets that even dogs and swine walk on. The idea is to demonstrate that there should be no difference among men in public life. Our struggle does not stop with the right to walk on the streets. It is the duty of all humans to demonstrate that freedom inside as well. When the Maharani and the Mahatma conferred, the Maharani asked, on granting the right to walk on the streets, would you not then [also] attempt entry into the temple? The Mahatma replied that though this was the ultimate objective, he would not venture into that unless he was convinced that the people were prepared to show adequate patience and calm and were ready to make the required sacrifices to be able to enter the temple. Until then he would prepare for that.[66]

So even at the time of the *satyagraha*, Periyar's goals were at variance with those of Gandhi. While Gandhi clearly did not advocate temple entry, much less inter-caste dining or marriage, Periyar was already disagreeing with him.

While Periyar had expressed qualified jubilation on 29 November 1925 when the three temple streets were thrown open, when the Temple Entry Proclamation was made after eleven years, he was far from happy. Writing on the occasion, he said:

> Many believe, speak and write that the Vaikom Satyagraha is the cause for the Temple Entry Proclamation. I too have received many letters to this effect. Whether this proclamation is good or bad for the human community is a big question. As far as I am concerned, it is my opinion that it may in one way cause harm to human society at large and Indian society and the Depressed Classes in particular.

> What Adi Dravidars have gained by the temple entry is that all efforts for their progress have now been blocked. Rather than realize the cause for their economic ills, it may impel them to blame God and fate and slip into slumber.[67]

Periyar's views seem to be in tune with Ambedkar's on this matter. It may be recalled that Ambedkar did not welcome the temple entry bill of 1933.

Even when he was in the Congress, Periyar was stridently critical of the party's position that social reform could be pursued after political freedom was achieved.

> How many had to go to jail to be able to walk on the streets of the Vaikom temple? Who was behind the imposition of section 144? Who approached the government for its imposition? Where then were the virtuous men who harped on resolving differences between and betwixt ourselves? Where were the noble men who called for resolving our own differences when it was argued that only Brahmins should be educated in a public-funded *veda patashala*?[68]

This view only got strengthened.

> If a person in a human body has no right to obtain *darshan* of his deity, how can he be said to have any self-respect? What is the need for swaraj for such a society? What does it matter what raj they live in? If a demonic community which subjugates another community in this manner were to gain *swaraj*, will it result in any benefit to the latter? If it is claimed that *swaraj* is meant for the subjugated community as well, is the reason for the latter being prevented from seeing and obtaining *darshan* of their gods and being unable to walk on the streets and staying out of sight only because there is no *swaraj*?[69]

Periyar was often ambivalent about the victory in Vaikom. He wondered if it would benefit the entire nation. Following Vaikom, there were *satyagraha*s on similar grounds in Suchindram (1926) in south Travancore and Kalpathi (1926) in Palakkad of the Malabar district. Even after this, Periyar observed:

> The success of the Bardoli satyagraha may be a victory for Bardoli. But of what use is it for its neighbouring region? For instance, at Vaikom, we have had the occasion to say that we achieved victory in terms of being able to walk on the streets. As a result, we could even say, some achieved name and fame. But this yielded no benefit to even adjacent places such as Alappuzha and Ambalapuzha where old injustices (*kodumai*) continue here and there. (Anaimuthu, 1974, vol. 3, p. 2633)

After Vaikom

One important outcome of Periyar's leadership of the Vaikom Satyagraha was his continued association with the Depressed Classes of Kerala, especially the Ezhavas. The relationship forged with Ezhava leaders grew stronger over the years.

Worthy of note was his deep friendship extending over the decades with 'Sahodaran' Ayyappan. When Periyar's wife Nagammai passed away in 1933, Ayyappan was invited to the unveiling of her portrait.[70] 'Sahodaran' Ayyappan presided over the Coimbatore District Self-Respect Conference in Erode on 25–26 November 1933.[71] Again, in October 1935, he was scheduled to speak at the Trichy District Self-Respect Conference but could not make it at the last moment.[72] *Kudi Arasu* was jubilant when 'Sahodaran' Ayyappan was elected uncontested to the Cochin legislature.[73] A biographer of Ayyappan states that 'the speeches of E. V. Ramaswamy Naicker figured prominently in several issues of the *Sahodaran*' (Sahadevan, 1993, pp. 73–74). More such instances could be cited.

Similarly, Periyar was invited to many Ezhava conferences in subsequent years and decades. On 21 February 1929, the leaders of the SNDP met under the chairmanship of T. K. Madhavan and decided to organize three conferences—the SNDP's 26th annual conference, the Kerala Temple Entry Conference, and the Travancore State Self-Respect Conference—in Kottayam in April.

The last of these conferences was to be presided over by Periyar (the other two presidents being P. Palpu and Pandit Madan Mohan Malaviya).[74]

In May 1936, Periyar was scheduled to participate in an Ezhava conference in Kottayam.[75] Speaking at the conference, he said: 'After the Vaikom Satyagraha and the radical reform activities of their inimitable leader Narayana Guruswamy, Ezhavas have sworn not to live even for a moment as an untouchable caste or a Panchama caste and are launching a big struggle.'[76]

At an Ezhava conference in September 1933, Periyar continued in the same vein:

> From the time of the Vaikom Satyagraha, 25 lakh Ezhava comrades have made much effort to break every bond that shackles them. And having also succeeded largely in these efforts, all of them, that is, 25 lakhs of them have unanimously come together as an organization and decided that they do not need any religion.[77]

Many more instances of Periyar being invited to Ezhava conferences and reciprocation by his organization can be cited from subsequent years.

Conclusion

'Every incident at Vaikom is so fully reported in the papers that I do not propose to deal with each day's happenings at any length,' wrote C. W. E. Cotton, Governor-General's Agent, Madras State, reporting the *satyagraha* to the Government of Madras.[78] Ironically, it was only towards the end of the Vaikom Satyagraha that Periyar came to have an independent mouthpiece—in the form of the weekly *Kudi Arasu*—to express his views. His reactions to and criticisms of every step in the *satyagraha* are thus not documented. But in later days, when he repeatedly recalled his involvement in the *satyagraha*, Periyar expressed many differing views. He went to the extent of disavowing the method of *satyagraha*, often referring to it derisively as plain obstinacy and stubbornness.

Even at the victory conference in November 1925, he had hinted at some disagreements. Periyar began his speech with the caveat that it was too soon to talk about the victory or failure of the *satyagraha*. During the time of the *satyagraha* too, he had had some reservations. Probably not wanting to weaken the movement, he had maintained a strategic silence. In later years, he expressed the view that he had led the movement to victory despite the efforts of Gandhi and Rajagopalachari to hamper it.

The evidence is patchy but based on newly discovered material, we can see that Periyar made at least seven visits to Vaikom in the course of the year-and-a-half-long *satyagraha*. During these visits, he spent seventy-four days in prison and sixty-seven days in the struggle, devoting a total of 141 days. No one else from outside Travancore had spent this long in the *satyagraha*.

Periyar came into his own as a leader during the Vaikom Satyagraha. The *satyagraha* gave him his first experience of independently leading a movement. That he achieved this against the heaviest odds in a region that was not his own redounds to his credit. This experience was to stand him in good stead as he led movement after movement over the next fifty years of his life. Not for nothing was Periyar celebrated as 'Vaikom Veerar'.

Notes

1. The conferrer of the moniker was the respected journalist, public speaker, labour leader, and nationalist personality Thiru. Vi. Kalyanasundara Mudaliar (1883–1953).
2. T. K. Ravindran's *Eight Furlongs of Freedom* (1980), originally published as *Vaikkam Satyagraha and Gandhi* (1975), is a pioneering work. A more recent and extended work is Mary Elizabeth King's *Gandhian Nonviolent Struggle and Untouchability in South India* (2015). Important articles include Panikkar (2016) and Kusuman (2000). Chandramohan (2016) has a perceptive section (pp. 175–195) on the *satyagraha*. Studies with scattered references to the *satyagraha* include Ouwerkerk (1994) and Kawashima (1994).
3. This chapter draws extensively from Athiyaman (2020).
4. Vaikom Satyagraha Bundle (VSB), no. 4. The Travancore government proceedings regarding the Vaikom Satyagraha are lodged in the Kerala State Archives (KSA), Thiruvananthapuram, in ten bundles. In a badly damaged condition, the papers are not in any discernible sequence nor do they have clear running page numbers. Some page numbers are stamped with a numbering machine while some page numbers are in pencil.
5. *The Hindu*, 2 August 1924.
6. Commissioner Pitt to Chief Secretary, 2 December 1925, VSB, no. 10.
7. Report by Inspector of Police, Vaikom, to Commissioner of Police, 19 November 1925, of the proceedings and resolutions passed at the meeting, VSB, no. 10. The resolutions were also forwarded to the Dewan of Travancore by K. Kelappan, secretary of the Anti-Untouchability Committee, on 17 November itself.
8. *The Hindu*, 17 April 1924.
9. Periyar's statement to *The Hindu*, 15 April 1924. For the Tamil version, see *Swadesamitran*, 13 April 1924.
10. *The Hindu*, 19 April 1924.
11. District Magistrate to Chief Secretary, 3 April 1925, VSB, no. 9.
12. Annual Report of TNCC, 1924; *Swadesamitran*, 22 November 1924.
13. *The Hindu*, 21 May 1924.
14. Report to the Commissioner of Police, 4 September 1924, VSB, no. 4, file pp. 1260–1263, handwritten pp. 157–159.
15. *The Hindu*, 24 May 1924.
16. *The Hindu*, 15 July 1924.
17. *Swadesamitran*, 22 April 1924.
18. *The Hindu*, 21 May 1924.
19. *The Hindu*, 23 May 1924.
20. *Viduthalai: Periyar Nootrandu Malar* [Viduthalai: Periyar Centenary Number, Chennai, 1978], p. 133. As Nagammai had passed along the barricade where Ezhavas stood, she was even prevented from worshipping in the temple on the ground that she had been polluted! *The Hindu*, 16 June 1924.
21. K. Rama Varier, report of Inspector of Police, Vaikom, 15-1-1100 (Malayalam calendar) (Gregorian calendar equivalent: 30 August 1924), VSB, no. 1, file p. 1233, handwritten p. 136.
22. Report of Inspector of Police, Haripad, 17-1-1100 (Malayalam calendar) (Gregorian calendar equivalent: 1 September 1924), VSB, no. 4, file pp. 1239–1240, handwritten pp. 168–169.

23. Srinivasa Iyengar's statement during this visit is marked by sharp legal acumen and a rationale that greatly strengthened the *satyagraha*.
24. C. W. E. Cotton, Agent to Governor-General, Madras States to the Chief Secretary, Government of Madras, quoted in Ravindran (1980, p. 287).
25. The Satyagraha Movement, Vaikom [an official narrative], VSB, no. 3.
26. Madras Police Abstracts of Intelligence (MPAI), Tamil Nadu Archives, Chennai, 1924, para 263; also *The Hindu*, 30 April 1924.
27. Also *Malayala Manorama*, 13 May 1924.
28. *The Hindu*, 21 May 1924.
29. Chief Secretary, Travancore to W. H. Pitt, Commissioner of Police, Travancore, May 1924, VSB, no. 1.
30. MPAI, 1924, para. 274. Also see *Swadesamitran*, 19 May 1924, carrying Periyar's statement confirming his intention to defy the order.
31. *The Hindu*, 19 May 1924.
32. *The Hindu*, 21 May 1924.
33. *Swadesamitran*, 22 May 1924.
34. MPAI, 1924, para. 286. Also see *The Hindu*, 23 May 1924.
35. *The Hindu*, 19 May 1924; 27 May 1924.
36. *The Hindu*, 7 June 1924.
37. Report of K. Rama Variar, Inspector of Police to the Commissioner of Police, Trivandrum, 9-11-99 (23 or 24 June 1924). Also see Subramanyam, District Magistrate, Kottayam to the Chief Secretary, Trivandrum, 24 June 1924, VSB, no. 3, file p. 2413, handwritten p. 697.
38. *The Hindu*, 7 July 1924.
39. *The Hindu*, 24 June 1924.
40. Subramanyam, District Magistrate, Kottayam to the Chief Secretary, Trivandrum, 24 June 1924, VSB, no. 3, file p. 2413, handwritten p. 697.
41. District Magistrate, Quilon (Kollam) to the Chief Secretary, Trivandrum, 26 June 1924, VSB, no. 3, file p. 356/g, handwritten p. 723.
42. *The Hindu*, 28 June 1924; *The Hindu*, 2 July 1924.
43. *The Hindu*, 3 July 1924.
44. *The Hindu*, 5 July 1924.
45. *The Hindu*, 9 July 1924.
46. *The Hindu*, 15 July 1924.
47. MPAI, 1924, para. 387, quoting *Trivandrum Daily News*, 16 July 1924.
48. *The Hindu*, 7 July 1924.
49. *The Hindu*, 9 July 1924.
50. Judgment, Stationary Second-Class Magistrate, Vaikom, VSB, no. 3, file p. 356/g, handwritten p. 724.
51. District Magistrate, Kottayam to the Chief Secretary, Trivandrum, 2 August 1924. For a newspaper report, see *The Hindu*, 21 July 1924, VSB, no. 1, file p. 2788, handwritten p. 57.
52. *The Hindu*, 2 August 1924.
53. *The Hindu*, 27 August 1924.
54. *The Hindu*, 16 August 1924.

55. *Swadesamitran*, 3 September 1924.
56. Report of Inspector of Police, Kottar, 23-1-1100 (Gregorian calendar equivalent: 7 September 1924), VSB, no. 4, Roc no. 460/24.
57. *The Hindu*, 21 July 1924.
58. MPAI, 1925, para. 198.
59. CID inspector's report,10 March 1925, VSB, no. 9.
60. 'Sri Narayana Guru', *Western Star*, 29 July 1924.
61. 'Sri Narayana Guru', *Western Star*, 29 July 1924.
62. *Young India*, 19 June 1924, cited in Gandhi (1967, pp. 259–260).
63. *The Hindu*, 24 May 1924; for the Tamil version, see *Swadesamitran*, 24 May 1924.
64. *The Hindu*, 7 July 1924.
65. B. Ananta Shenai, Inspector of Police, Shertalai (Cherthala) to the District Superintendent of Police, Kottayam (camp: Vaikom), 5-9-1099 (Gregorian calendar equivalent: 17 April 1924), VSB, no. 5, file p. 563/g, handwritten p. 97.
66. *Kudi Arasu*, 6 December 1925.
67. *Kudi Arasu*, 6 December 1936.
68. *Kudi Arasu*, 22 November 1925.
69. *Kudi Arasu*, 24 January 1926.
70. *Puratchi*, 3 December 1933.
71. MPAI, 1933, para no. 1673.
72. *Kudi Arasu*, 13 October 1935 and 27 October 1935.
73. *Kudi Arasu*, 12 May 1935.
74. *Kudi Arasu*, 3 March 1929.
75. *Kudi Arasu*, 10 May 1936.
76. *Kudi Arasu*, 10 May 1936.
77. *Kudi Arasu*, 24 September 1933.
78. C.W.E. Cotton, Agent to Governor-General, Madras States to the Chief Secretary, Government of Madras; Ravindran (1980, p. 288).

References

Anaimuthu, V. (ed.). 1974. *Periyar E. V. R. Chintanaigal*, 3 vols. Trichy: Thinkers' Forum.
Athiyaman, Pazha. 2020. *Vaikom Porattam*. Nagercoil: Kalachuvadu Pathippagam.
Chandramohan, P. 2016. *Developmental Modernity in Kerala: Narayana Guru, SNDP Yogam and Social Reform*. New Delhi: Tulika Books.
Gandhi, M. K. 1967. *The Collected Works of Mahatma Gandhi*, vol. 24. New Delhi: Publications Division, Government of India.
Kawashima, Koji. 1994. 'Missionaries, the Hindu State and British Paramountcy in Travancore and Cochin, 1858–1936'. Unpublished PhD thesis, School of Oriental and African Studies, University of London.
King, Mary Elizabeth. 2015. *Gandhian Nonviolent Struggle and Untouchability in South India: The 1924–25 Vykom Satyagraha and the Mechanisms of Change*. New Delhi: Oxford University Press.
Kusuman, K. K. 2000. 'Vaikom Satyagraha: The Lead of T. K. Madhavan'. In *Aspects of South Indian History: A Felicitation Volume in Honour of Professor K. Rajayyan*. Nagercoil: Rajesh Publications.

Menon, K. P. Kesava. 1963. *Bandhanathil Ninnu*. Kozhikode: Mathrubhumi Printing and Publishing Limited.

Ouwerkerk, Louise. 1994. *No Elephants for the Maharaja: Social and Political Change in Travancore*. New Delhi: Manohar.

Panikkar, K. N. 2016. 'Vaikom Satyagraha: Struggle against Untouchability'. In *Essays in the History and Society of Kerala*. Thiruvananthapuram: Kerala Council for Historical Research.

Parthasarathy, Rangaswami. 1978. *A Hundred Years of The Hindu: The Epic Story of Indian Nationalism*. Madras: Kasturi & Sons.

Ravindran, T. K. 1975. *Vaikkam Satyagraha and Gandhi*. Trichur: Sri Narayana Institute of Social and Cultural Development.

———. 1980. *Eight Furlongs of Freedom*. New Delhi: Light Life Publishers.

Sahadevan, M. 1993. *Towards Social Justice and Nation Making: A Study of Sahodaran Ayyappan*. Palakkad: Sophia, D.G.

2

Periyar, Ambedkar, and the Poona Pact

A. Thiruneelakandan

Edited and translated from Tamil by A. R. Venkatachalapathy

The Poona Pact, 1932, was a watershed moment in the history of Dalit politics. Nearly a century later, it remains the subject of debate and discussion. A definite setback to the independent mobilization of the Depressed Classes, the Poona Pact deprived them of the historic right to a separate electorate with a double vote granted by the British government. This chapter seeks to describe and analyse the stance taken by Periyar and his Self-Respect Movement (SRM) towards what B. R. Ambedkar described as 'a mean deal' (Ambedkar, 2014 [1994], p. 40).[1]

The pact was signed at a time when the Indian National Congress was in the ascendant and had demonstrated its all-India character and strength through a series of mass agitations. In response to its rise, in south India, the non-Brahmin castes had mobilized under the Justice Party and Periyar's SRM. At the all-India level, the Depressed Classes had become a force to be reckoned with under the leadership of Ambedkar. Both Periyar and Ambedkar viewed the Congress primarily as a formation that represented the Brahmins and Hindu upper castes.

To understand the position taken by Periyar on the Depressed Classes' question, we need to trace the emergence of Depressed Class consciousness and the formation of political organizations representing the interests of Depressed Classes in south India—a group that Eleanor Zelliot describes as 'the other [apart from that of western India] politically vocal group of Untouchables', the largest in terms of numbers in any region of India then (2013, p. 115). Even though the political demands of the Depressed Classes coalesced only at the time of the Simon Commission (1928), their roots can be traced back much further. Writing in 1909, Iyothee Thass Pandithar stated: 'Lord Morley, under the mistaken impression that India comprises of only two classes [Hindus and Muslims], has promised representation to them in the legislative councils. He seems completely ignorant of the existence of six million Dravidians who are called Paraiyars and are oppressed by the Hindus.'[2] Expressing a similar view, the Justice Party's Tamil daily *Dravidan* noted:

> Whenever racial discrimination is practiced in legislative councils, there is a howl from Brahmins. But when the issue of caste discrimination is raised, they keep mum as though they don't exist. The Panchamas are denied even the right a dog has. If only a Panchama is made a member of

the legislative council, would he not argue forcefully about the hardships experienced by his people? Would he not impress upon the ruling British that Panchamas too should enjoy the same benefits of British rule as Brahmins?[3]

Following such demands, in 1919, as recommended by the Southborough Committee on Franchise, appointed by the British government as part of the Montagu–Chelmsford Reforms to consider representation of Indians in government, two members from the Depressed Classes were nominated to the Madras Legislative Council—in other presidencies, legislative councils had only one such member. M. C. Rajah— who will figure prominently in this chapter—was the first to be so nominated in Madras. However, in later days when complaints arose that only non-Adi Dravidars were nominated, *Dravidan* demanded that it should not be so.[4] Following this, the Raja of Panagal, the Justice Party leader, argued for and formulated a rule that only Adi Dravidars could represent Adi Dravidars in legislative councils and local self-government institutions.

The question of separate political representation for Depressed Classes had come to the forefront in the 1920s, and the Indian Statutory (Simon) Commission arrived in the country at this moment. The arrival of the commission, the representations made to it, and its final report—all these together made the demand for representation central to official political discourse. As *Revolt*, an SRM weekly edited by Periyar with his friend S. Ramanathan, observed, 'The Simon enquiry has brought to the fore a sharp conflict of opinion on the question of joint versus separate electorates'[5] and the 'discussions as to [their] relative merits … are growing in intensity.'[6]

Contemporary writings indicate that the maturing of this question was rooted in the dialogue between the Depressed Classes and the Dravidian movement. The substance of this demand was that the Depressed Classes were a distinct social and political entity, different from Hindus, and therefore required separate representation; moreover, only members of the Depressed Classes could and should represent them. A further refinement of the demand—referred to as 'separate electorates'—was that such members be elected only by the Depressed Classes.

Separate Electorates

The political idea of 'separate electorates' had its origins in the introduction of local self-government bodies, limited enfranchisement (as opposed to universal adult franchise), and such other rudimentary democratic institutions under colonialism. The idea emerged in the context of conflict between democratic principles and a hierarchical caste society. Given the infirmities flowing from an unequal, hierarchical society, Depressed Classes demanded representation that was both quantitatively and qualitatively different from representation for other communities. The model was the separate electorates granted to Muslims by the India Councils Act, 1909, as part of the Morley–Minto reforms. As the Communal Award of 1932 stated, the logic of separate electorates was that based on a vote in general constituencies alone, it would be unlikely 'for a considerable period' of time for the Depressed Classes to acquire adequate representation.

By the late 1920s, such a demand was fully articulated in Dravidian movement journals.[7] This demand conceived of a separate electorate that would exist alongside a joint electorate in the same electoral constituency. Thus, a voter from the Depressed Classes would exercise two votes: one as a voter in the joint electorate where they would vote for candidates belonging to any community along with other voters and another for electing a representative from among candidates from the Depressed Classes by casting a vote along with members of their community. The corollary of such a scheme was that a Depressed Classes representative did not require the vote of other communities. As a result, the representative would be able to articulate the political demands of the Depressed Classes without any compromise. If Ambedkar called this double vote 'a priceless privilege' and argued that 'its value as a political weapon was beyond reckoning' (2014 [1994], p. 90), Periyar called it 'the very life breath of the Depressed Classes'.[8]

The importance of the demand for separate electorates was two-pronged. On the one hand, it sought to shape the Depressed Classes as a separate political group. On the other, it precluded the absorption of the Depressed Classes within a monolithic Hindu identity being forged by Brahmins and upper castes.

The Simon Commission and Separate Electorates

As stated earlier, the Simon Commission, whose terms of reference included recommendations for political reforms, was the immediate context for the powerful articulation of the separate electorate demand. The commission spent nearly eight months in India, in two spells between February 1928 and April 1929, as part of its exercise to elicit responses from the political classes. During these two visits, it met with political representatives in the Madras Presidency on 26 February 1928 and 18 August 1929. When the commission came to Madras, it was assisted by the Indian Central Committee consisting of members of the Central Legislative Assembly (including M. C. Rajah, the pioneering leader of the Depressed Classes from Madras and Ambedkar's rival, and C. Sankaran Nair, the legal luminary, former Congress president, and champion of social reform) and the Madras Provincial Committee (including N. Sivaraj, a prominent leader of the Depressed Classes from Madras, and A. P. Patro, a Justice Party leader) (Indian Statutory Commission, 1930).

The Congress, rejecting the commission on the ground that it did not have a single Indian member, organized a nationwide agitation with the catchy slogan 'Simon, go back!' On the other hand, Periyar, Ambedkar, and other subaltern leaders welcomed the commission. In countering the Congress's argument that the commission did not have any Indian representation, *Kudi Arasu* stated that 'given that Indian representation would only mean the inclusion of a member of the Brahmin caste with its monopoly over power, we should consider ourselves lucky that no Indian has been nominated'.[9] The boycott, it further argued, would only result in stonewalling efforts to communicate the aspirations of the people to the commission.[10] This dovetailed with Ambedkar's view that he felt 'relieved of great anxiety by the decision of the Parliament not to appoint an Indian' and that 'this exclusion … was no small mercy to the Depressed Classes. For their non-appointment, the Depressed Classes are … saved the prejudice that would have otherwise been caused to their case …' (Ambedkar, 2019a, p. 430).

Addressing a meeting of the Depressed Classes at Napier Park in Madras City, Periyar said:

When the Simon Commission arrived, 'patriots' shouted that it should be boycotted and that it should 'Go Back'. It is our party that welcomed it … As a result, some of your representatives voiced your views to the commission. It was thus that the commission, and the larger world, had the opportunity to understand your grievances.[11]

The SRM further assured the Depressed Classes that '[t]he commission will inquire into your grievances.... You should represent your grievances in written form and as oral witnesses.'[12] It also warned: 'If Adi Dravidars miss this opportunity, they will have no chance of salvation for a very long time to come.'[13] It further stated:

> Even if A. Ramaswamy Mudaliar [a Justice Party leader] could not achieve anything by attending the all-party meeting, it is significant that he emphasized the need for communal representation.... The sole objective of Brahmins is to abolish communal representation. That is the logic behind the boycott of the commission.[14]

Thus, in the view of Periyar and his movement, historical necessity made it imperative for the Depressed Classes to approach the Simon Commission and underline the importance of both communal representation and separate electorates.

Periyar and Ambedkar's argument for separate representation rested on the foundation that the Depressed Classes formed 'a separate political class'. But on the question of what shape the demand for a separate electorate should take, the SRM took a different view from Ambedkar's early formulation. To grasp this difference, we need to look at the evidence presented by Ambedkar to the Simon Commission and the SRM's response to it.

When the Simon Commission arrived in Madras, two delegations of the Depressed Classes met its members and presented evidence. The first deputation to present evidence was a committee constituted at a conference of the Depressed Classes of the Madras Presidency on 29 January 1928. Its members were Rettamalai Srinivasan (its spokesperson), V. G. Vassudevan, R. Veeraiyan, V. I. Munuswamy Pillai, V. Dharmalingam Pillay, M. V. Gangadhara Siva, Swami Sahajanantham, H. M. Jaganath, S. Subramania Mupanar, S. Venkiah, A. Murugesam, and P. V. Rajagopal Pillai. The other was, in fact, comprised of two organizations, the Registered All-India Adi Dravida Mahajana Sabha and the Madras Arundhathi Mahajana Sabha, which presented a written memorandum and appeared before the commission jointly. The deputation of these two organizations consisted of R. T. Kesavalu, L. C. Guruswami, P. V. Subramaniam Pillai, M. C. Madurai Pillai, J. Sivashanmugam Pillai, M. Devendrudu, Kusuma Venkataramiah, Chokalingam, T. Ponniah, R. Thangavelu, and Venkatapathi. The latter deputation consisted of both Adi Dravidars and Arundhathiars (from the Tamil as well as Telugu districts of the Madras Presidency). Apparently, the second most numerous Depressed Class, the Devendrakula Vellalars, went unrepresented.

That the Depressed Classes were represented by two deputations was not innocent. There were divisions which clearly emerged during the oral evidence presented, and M. C. Rajah was at pains to lay these bare. In his conversation with R. Srinivasan, who was the spokesperson of the Depressed Classes of the Madras Presidency (the Madras Provincial Depressed Classes Federation), Rajah asked if he was not aware that 'now and then mushroom Associations crop [up]'. To this barb, he got this sharp response: 'You have experience as I have.' To a pointed question, Srinivasan replied that the federation was formed before the commission came to Madras and not after. When Rajah stated 'I did not hear of it', the response was 'We did not advertise.' The situation was so charged that Srinivasan confronted Rajah bluntly. Claiming that he represented 'about seven important sections amongst the Depressed Classes', Srinivasan added

… this Federation is not the same as the Association which Rao Bahadur M. C. Rajah has been running for the last ten years. He had an Association called the Adi-Dravida Mahajana Sabha. All that was merely a one-man show, and he kept all the intelligent men out of it. We tried several times to reach him, but he kept us out. (Indian Statutory Commission, 1930, p. 282)

The Registered All-India Adi Dravida Mahajana Sabha, which appeared before the commission jointly with the Madras Arundhathi Mahajana Sabha, was also subjected to a series of questions by M. C. Rajah. This led to information revealing that the Madras Adi Dravida Central Sabha was also combined with it, that the association was active from 1917, and that it had waited on deputation serially to Edwin Montagu, the Franchise and Functions (Southborough) Committee, the Lee Commission, Lord Chelmsford, and Lord Reading—that is, Rajah was trying to show that the federation was an upstart and therefore not representative (Indian Statutory Commission, 1930, p. 286).

What was the position of these two bodies regarding separate electorates? R. Srinivasan, whose stellar work in the cause of the Depressed Classes began in the late nineteenth century, acting as the spokesperson, clearly stated that the nomination of members from the Depressed Classes to political bodies would be adequate: 'Our people are not yet advanced to have separate electorates' (Indian Statutory Commission, 1930, p. 281). The other association was also content with nomination. If elections were to be held, it would have to be under adult franchise, but they vehemently disagreed with reserved seats in a general electorate (Indian Statutory Commission, 1930, pp. 286–287). M. C. Rajah demanded a separate electorate from the beginning. (However, as we shall see, Rajah later reneged.)

Across India, of the twenty Depressed Classes associations that appeared before the commission, sixteen demanded separate electorates (Zelliot, 2013, p. 125). Some leaders feared that such a demand would alienate them from the larger Hindu community.[15]

Curiously, Ambedkar himself did not make a demand for separate electorates. In the words of Eleanor Zelliot, not only was his evidence marked by moderation, it also expressed a deep-seated faith in democracy (2013, p. 127). In a written statement on behalf of the Bahishkrita Hitakarini Sabha on 17 May 1928, he stated:

Although I am for securing special representation for certain classes, I am against their representation through separate electorates. Territorial electorates and separate electorates are the two extremes which must be avoided in any scheme of representation that may be devised for the introduction of a democratic form of Government in this undemocratic country. The golden mean is the system of joining electorates with reserved seats. Less than that would be insufficient, more than that would defeat the ends of good Government. (Keer, 2016 [1954], p. 123)

Two weeks later, in his oral evidence, Ambedkar outlined the shape elections in the country should take: 'Free election in general constituencies is … out of the question as far as the Depressed Classes are concerned.' However, he '[did] not wish to ask for Communal electorates…. it would be sufficient if the Depressed Classes are provided with reserved seats in the general constituencies' (Ambedkar, 2019a, p. 431).

From this it would appear that Ambedkar, in the early days, was content with a joint electorate with reserved seats for the Depressed Classes and not in favour of separate electorates.

Although the SRM was at one with Ambedkar vis-à-vis the Simon Commission, from the very outset it opposed a joint electorate. This was forcefully argued in two editorials published in *Revolt*: 'The Fallacy of Joint Electorates' and 'Separate Electorate.'[16] In declaiming the fallacy of joint electorates, it went to the extent of disagreeing with Ambedkar: 'Even Dr Ambedkar, who put forward a strong case for keeping the Depressed Classes as a distinct electoral unit, appeared to be very willing to accept the method of reservation of seats in joint constituencies as an alternative….'[17]

The Round Table Conference

Following the submission of the Simon Commission's report—which accepted the principle of separate representations but in a joint electorate—to assuage the opposition, the British government invited representative Indians for a Round Table Conference at London.

Ambedkar and R. Srinivasan were the two representatives of the Depressed Classes. If Ambedkar called it 'a landmark in [the] history [of the Depressed Classes]'—for the first time they represented themselves as an exclusive community outside the Hindu fold (Ambedkar, 2014 [1994] p. 40)—the SRM was far from happy with the quantum of representation: 'if only two or three delegates were to represent the Depressed Classes who number five crores, it only demonstrates that not only the Hindus but also the [British] government is trying to hoodwink them'.[18]

Ambedkar's position on the representation of the Depressed Classes underwent a shift during the First Round Table Conference (November 1930–January 1931) largely in response to the vociferous demands of minorities for separate electorates. In the beginning he stated: '… if you give us adult universal suffrage, the Depressed Classes, barring a short transitional period which they want for their organisation, will be prepared to accept joint electorates and reserved seats; but if you do not give us adult suffrage, then we must claim representation through separate electorates' (Ambedkar, 2019a, p. 533). Striking a strident note, he went further:

> … the Depressed Classes demand a complete partition between ourselves and the Hindus…. We have been called Hindus for political purposes, but we have never been acknowledged socially by the Hindus as their brethren. They have taken to themselves all the political advantage with our numbers, with our voting strength, have given to them, but in return we have received nothing. All that we have received is a treatment which is worse than the treatment that they themselves have accorded to other communities whom they do not call Hindus. (Ambedkar, 2019a, p. 533)

Ambedkar was clearly veering away from a position of reserved seats in a joint electorate by making it conditional on universal adult franchise. In the absence of universal adult suffrage, separate electorates were inescapable.

Ambedkar's contention was that to bring the Depressed Classes and the upper castes, who had no social intercourse with each other, under one umbrella of 'the Hindus' was nothing but a ploy for electoral gain. In other words, the political identity of 'the Hindu' denied that the Depressed Classes constituted a separate class and thus amounted to nothing less than their exploitation.

Thus, the representational strategy of a separate electorate was the path to ensure their political emancipation.

Even earlier, in his statement to the Simon Commission, Ambedkar had argued that the Depressed Classes and the Hindus were differentiated in terms of 'community' and 'religion' given that the former were not even admitted into Hindu temples (Ambedkar, 2019a, p. 431). By the time of the First Round Table Conference, his differentiation had expanded to include 'political representation' and 'law'.

As noted in the preceding paragraphs, Ambedkar had made universal adult franchise a precondition for joint electorates. However, when this question was debated, at one point, he demanded separate electorates for a period of ten years irrespective of universal adult franchise (2019a, p. 540). Therefore, by mid-January 1931, his demands on the nature of representation had solidified into the need for a separate electorate.

Kudi Arasu welcomed this change wholeheartedly and reported Ambedkar's speech under the title 'Either of the Two: Ambedkar's *Aaptha Mozhigal* [Axiomatic Statements] in the Round Table Conference'.[19] We can discern that by now Ambedkar's standing had risen further in the estimation of the SRM. In May 1931, Ambedkar was elected the president for the Third Self-Respect Conference to be held in Virudhunagar. Periyar wired M. R. Jayakar to 'kindly make him consent'.[20]

With Ambedkar committing to a separate electorate, it became central to the political discourse of the times. Arguments both for and against were articulated across the political spectrum. As noted, the SRM, from the outset, was for separate electorates.

Gandhi's Opposition

But Gandhi had other ideas.[21] The Congress had boycotted the First Round Table Conference. But following the Gandhi–Irwin Pact, it now nominated Gandhi as its sole representative in the Second Round Table Conference. From the outset the Congress—Gandhi in particular—and the Hindu Mahasabha were opposed to separate electorates. For Gandhi, a separate electorate would erect a wall in the Hindu fold that could never be broken down.

On 17 September 1931, at the Second Round Table Conference, Gandhi stated that the Congress was 'reconciled … to special treatment of the Hindu–Muslim–Sikh tangle. There are sound historical reasons for it but the Congress will not extend that doctrine in any shape or form' (quoted in Ambedkar, 2014 [1994], p. 57). Speaking two weeks later, he argued that 'there are ways and ways of guaranteeing protection to every single interest' (quoted in Ambedkar, 2014 [1994], p. 62). Soon he was even contesting Ambedkar's credentials to represent the Depressed Classes. Even before the Round Table Conference, the Congress, with the help of the nationalist press, portrayed Ambedkar as one who had no right to speak for the Depressed Classes, a pattern that was repeated after the conference as well, according to Ambedkar's most recent biographer, Ashok Gopal (2023, p. 407). The *Bombay Chronicle*, for instance, dubbed him 'a self-styled leader of the Depressed Castes' (Gopal, 2023, p. 408). Non-Mahar leaders such as P. N. Rajbhoj, Palwankar Baloo, and Balkrishna Devrukhbar (all of the Chambhar community) and K. K. Sakat (a Mang leader) declared their faith in the Congress and Gandhi, stating that Ambedkar had little authority to speak on their behalf (Gopal, 2023, p. 419). From declaring that 'the Congress will share the honour with

Dr Ambedkar of representing the interests of the Untouchables', by 13 November Gandhi challenged Ambedkar's standing; he now claimed to be the sole representative of the Depressed Classes. In words bordering on hubris, he stated: 'I claim myself in my own person to represent the vast mass of the Untouchables. Here I speak not merely on behalf of the Congress, but I speak on my own behalf, and I claim that I would get, if there was a referendum of the Untouchables their vote, and that I would top the poll' (quoted in Ambedkar, 2014 [1994], p. 68). While he had no objection to the Depressed Classes converting to Christianity or Islam, he would not countenance the division of the Hindu community as a result of separate electorates, declaring emphatically that 'if I was the only person to resist this thing, I would resist it with my life' (quoted in Ambedkar, 2014 [1994], p. 69).

Ambedkar mocked Gandhi's claim: 'I can only say that it is one of the many false claims which irresponsible people keep on making, although the persons concerned with regard to those claims have been invariably denying them' (2019b, p. 65). But opposition was being stoked from within. In this context, M. C. Rajah was also claiming to be the foremost representative of the Depressed Classes (Gopal, 2023, p. 432). The Hindu Mahasabha had succeeded in driving a wedge among the Depressed Classes.

The SRM fully backed Ambedkar. Though Periyar was on a nearly year-long European tour at the time (see Venkatachalapathy 2018), his movement continued its strident support of Ambedkar. A *Kudi Arasu* editorial stated:

> Ambedkar declared in the plainest terms that there was little in common between the Congress and the Depressed Castes and that there were no Depressed Castes in the Congress. Yet, Gandhi keeps parroting that he and the Congress are their representatives. If those who make such claims have even an iota of shame or self-respect, they should first give a convincing reply to Ambedkar.[22]

Further, the SRM laid bare the contradictions in Gandhi's position and the exalted status he claimed for himself. An article titled 'The Secret Behind Mr Gandhi's Rejection of Separate Electorates', referring to his acceptance of separate representation for certain historical reasons, said:

> Gandhi's attitude is laid bare here. His assumption seems to be that since Muslims and Sikhs were a glorious ruling class once upon a time, they have the right to political privileges while the Untouchables do not deserve the protection of a separate electorate because, traditionally, they lived in thrall with no freedom.[23]

In the SRM's view, the purpose of Gandhi's participation in the Round Table Conference was to safeguard *varnashrama dharma* and act 'as an agent of Brahmins' to establish a Ram Rajya.[24]

Even before his statement in the Round Table Conference, Gandhi, speaking at a meeting of Indian students in London, had stated that he would lay down his life to thwart the attempt to divide the Depressed Classes from Hindu society. A *Justice* editorial (of 14 October 1931)—a translation of which appeared in *Kudi Arasu*—condemned Gandhi's resort to every tactic to deprive the Depressed Classes of their political rights.[25] Elsewhere, *Kudi Arasu* argued that '[i]f Muslims, Christians, and the Depressed Classes were to gain separate electorates',

... their true representatives would number more or less equally in legislative bodies. Muslims and the Depressed Classes are not enemies of emancipatory measures. Consequently, it is likely that socially just bills and socialist legislation may be passed. This would result in the destruction of orthodox Hindu religion. This is why Mr Gandhi refuses to budge on the question of separate electorates.[26]

This dovetails with the SRM's call for the backward castes to follow the Depressed Classes in leaving the Hindu fold and its attempt to forge an alliance with the Depressed Classes and Muslims.

One Rathinasabapathy, writing in *Kudi Arasu*, countered Gandhi's argument that a separate electorate for the Depressed Classes would create a divide between them and the Hindus, wondering how separate electorates for Muslims would foster Hindu–Muslim unity that was so dear to the Mahatma's heart.[27]

Gandhi not only opposed Ambedkar's demand for separate electorates but was also involved in closed-door talks with Muslim representatives to thwart it—an overture that they did not encourage (Ambedkar, 2014 [1994], pp. 72–74). Ambedkar and R. Srinivasan's statement in the *Times of India* (12 October 1931) pointing this out was translated into Tamil by a Self-Respect journal, *Sandamarutham*, and reproduced in *Kudi Arasu*.[28] Ambedkar also spoke about this on his return to Bombay in a public meeting on 5 February 1932—a meeting once again reported in both *Sandamarutham* and *Kudi Arasu* under the title 'Gandhi's Tactic or Conspiracy in London: Ambedkar's Explanation'.[29]

Following the antagonistic stance taken by Gandhi and the Congress, the Depressed Classes, Muslims, Christians, Anglo-Indians, and Europeans came together, leading to a 'Minorites Pact' on 12 November 1931. Safeguarding minority political rights and separate electorates formed the crux of this pact.

Kudi Arasu welcomed the Minorities Pact. Emphasizing the political unity of the Depressed Classes and Muslims, it drew attention to the British prime minister's assurance that in coming to a decision on the communal question, the government would take into serious consideration the Minorities Pact.[30]

As the debate on separate electorates raged in London and in India, a negative shift was seen in the stance of M. C. Rajah. Rajah, who at the time of the Simon Commission had argued for separate electorates, was now beginning to champion joint electorates. Early signs of this began to be visible at the time of the Second Round Table Conference with Ambedkar emerging into prominence. It was first articulated in a resolution passed in the All-India Depressed Classes Conference that he organized in Gurgaon (then in the Punjab) on 18 October 1931.

It was this disposition that pushed M. C. Rajah close to the Hindu Mahasabha president, B. S. Moonje, leading to an agreement (1 March 1932) between them. The meeting between the two was facilitated by the Mahar leader, G. A. Gawai. In what Ashok Gopal describes as 'somersaults', Moonje, who had earlier conceded to Ambedkar separate electorates for five years, now offered joint electorates to Rajah. In turn, Rajah who had all along been arguing for separate electorates assented to Moonje's offer (Gopal, 2023, p. 431–432). In a dramatic about-turn, he now applauded the Hindu Mahasabha for inviting the All-India Depressed Classes Association to work together with it to eliminate untouchability—a call he described as 'an earnest attempt on the part of Caste Hindus' (Gopal, 2023, p. 432). The subtext, according to Gopal, was that Rajah was claiming to be the pre-eminent representative of the Depressed Classes (2023, p. 432). Thus, the Hindu Mahasabha had driven a wedge among the Depressed Classes and they were 'quite literally split into two camps' (Kumar, 1985, p. 96).

Ambedkar roundly condemned the Moonje–Rajah agreement and *Kudi Arasu* published a full translation of his refutation under the rubric, 'Dr Ambedkar Explains'.[31] Just when the time was ripe for winning a separate electorate, this agreement had been hatched to sow discord among the Depressed Classes. As he further pointed out, the All-India Depressed Classes Association, a signatory to the agreement, was an organization only in name and had no branches or following in Assam, Bengal, Madras, Bombay, Bihar, Orissa, the Punjab, and many other regions. And thus it was least representative of the Depressed Classes of India. Describing the agreement as 'a fraud', he attributed this volte-face to Rajah's desire for a ministerial position.[32]

The SRM took upon itself the task of defending Ambedkar's stance and criticized the backsliding of Rajah. One of the specious arguments put forward by Rajah in defence of joint electorates was that Depressed Class candidates would have to tour various districts in order to canvass for votes—an impossibility considering their poverty. *Kudi Arasu* editorialized in the following terms: 'In a separate electorate, there would be no need at all for candidates to tour around the constituency as the Depressed Class voters would be able to identify the leaders who are aware of their true interests.' Further, it stated emphatically: 'It was because Ambedkar and Srinivasan fought sincerely at the Round Table Conference in defence of separate electorates that even though neither of them travelled around the country to meet the people on this question, Depressed Classes have passed resolutions advocating separate electorates.'[33]

A *Dravidan* editorial titled 'Jai to Ambedkar' too condemned the Rajah–Moonje agreement stating that Rajah did not represent the Depressed Classes, and nor did he reflect their real sentiments.[34]

Another *Kudi Arasu* editorial, describing the joint electorates as 'a vile net' of the caste Hindus, declared that Rajah's thoughts against separate electorates were his own personal views and in line with the interests of caste Hindus and not those of the Depressed Classes.[35] The editorial also drew attention to a public meeting in support of separate electorates in Kampti near Nagpur from 5–8 May 1932, presided over by V. I. Munuswamy Pillai and attended by Ambedkar, which drew a crowd of over 2,000 people (Gopal, 2023, p. 432). P. N. Rajbhoj, a supporter of Rajah, suffered injuries when he tried to voice his protest (Gopal, 2023, pp. 432–433). A rival meeting in Bombay on 10 July 1932 organized by M. C. Rajah for joint electorates saw less than 200 persons in attendance. An equal number of Ambedkar's supporters broke into the conference and a scuffle ensued leading to injuries and the intervention of the police (Gopal, 2023, pp. 435–436).

Here it would be pertinent to record the activities of the SRM in the public sphere in support of separate electorates. A survey of SRM journals indicates that between September 1931 and November 1932, more than forty meetings were organized by the SRM in collaboration with Depressed Class organizations.[36] The weight of the resolutions passed in these meetings and the drift of the deliberations in them may be summarized as follows: a distrust in the bona fides of Gandhi and the Congress, especially in relation to the Depressed Class question; criticism of the changed stance of M. C. Rajah and his agreement with Moonje; demand for separate electorates for the Depressed Classes; affirmation of faith in Ambedkar and Srinivasan; and demand for the government to grant separate electorates.

Of these meetings, one deserves special mention. Organized by the Madras Mahajana Sabha, a nationalist organization dating to the 1880s and presided over by one Das Panthulu, it saw members of the SRM and the Depressed Classes defeat a motion in support of joint electorates and succeed in passing a resolution in favour of separate electorates.[37]

The Fast and the Pact

No consensus on the question of separate or joint electorates was arrived at in the Second Round Table Conference, and it concluded with the agreement that the British prime minister would take a decision on the matter. Gandhi returned to India in the first week of January 1932 with the strong feeling that the government was disposed to granting separate electorates. Soon he announced a *satyagraha* in protest. Declaring that the Gandhi–Irwin Pact had been broken, the government arrested Gandhi and lodged him in the Yervada prison in Pune. By March, Gandhi warned that he would undertake a fast unto death if separate electorates were granted.

On 17 August 1932, the government announced the Communal Award granting the demand of the Depressed Classes for a double vote with a separate electorate. Clause 9 read as follows:

Members of the 'depressed classes' qualified to vote will vote in a general constituency.... [In addition] a number of seats will be assigned to them.... These seats will be filled by election from special constituencies in which only members of the 'depressed classes' electorally qualified will be entitled to vote. Any person voting in such a special constituency will ... also be entitled to vote in a general constituency. (Ambedkar 2014 [1994], p. 81)

On 9 September 1932, Gandhi wrote to the British Prime Minister Ramsay MacDonald that separate electorates amounted to 'the injection of poison that is calculated to destroy Hinduism and do no good to the Depressed Castes' (Pyarelal, 1932, p. 111). Gandhi declared that he would commence a fast unto death if the Communal Award was not rescinded (Pyarelal, 1932, p. 111). Ambedkar sensed the threat of violence in Gandhi's statement—'the Mahatma's act will result in nothing but terrorism by his followers against the Depressed Classes all over the country'—and expressed the vain hope that 'the Mahatma will not drive me to the necessity of making a choice between his life and the rights of my people' (Ambedkar, 2014 [1994], p. 316; Gopal, 2023, p. 439).

The SRM for its part welcomed the Communal Award wholeheartedly, and *Kudi Arasu* ran an editorial titled 'Is there any reason to complain?'[38] The announcement of Gandhi's fast only added fuel to the SRM's criticisms. Special mention needs to be made of Kuthoosi S. Guruswamy's article in *Kudi Arasu*. Guruswamy asked if Gandhi was any different from an obdurate *kallulimangan*, a roadside conjuror indulging in self-flagellation in front of shops and refusing to budge until the shopkeeper spared a few coins. Urging the government to charge Gandhi under the relevant clause of the Indian Penal Code (IPC) for attempted suicide, he warned Depressed Class comrades not to spare a single coin for the *kallulimangan*.[39]

A *Dravidan* editorial reassured Ambedkar with the title 'Fear Not, Ambedkar!' Underlining that separate electorates were the very life breath of the Depressed Classes, it emphasized that it was entirely in Ambedkar's hands to safeguard them. Asking him not to fall into a trap, it posed some blunt, even brutal questions. If Ambedkar was to give in, would it not amount to a betrayal of the trust of the 7.5 crore people who were his loyal adherents? Somewhat insensitively it further asked: 'If a Gandhi was willing to lay down his life for safeguarding Hinduism, why does Ambedkar not do the same in pursuit of his people's rights?'[40] Another *Dravidan* editorial titled 'Gandhi's Final Testimony' argued that the rights of crores of people of the Depressed Classes were more valuable than Gandhi's life.[41]

But Ambedkar was caught in a ring of fire. The pressure of Gandhi's fast was crushing. In this dire situation, on 19 September, the editor of *Dravidan*, T. V. Subramaniam, wired to Ambedkar in Bombay on behalf of the Madras Central SRM.[42] Advising him not to be disheartened by Gandhi's threat to fast unto death, the telegram urged him to remain steadfast.

> Comrade, in south India alone, the Self-Respect Movement has three and a half lakh members. It has the overwhelming support of the Depressed Classes. The movement has steadfastly supported the separate electorate demanded by you. Please therefore do not accede to the general electorate demand. There is no need to fear Mr Gandhi's devious political ruse to starve to death. … If he was really committed to their cause, why not warn all those who follow Brahminism and Hinduism that by a certain date if all temples and pilgrim rest houses are not thrown open, he would starve to death? If you give up on the separate electorate demand, you will certainly be seen as a betrayer. Be brave. Do not give in. Please do not let down the poor people.

On the same day, a similar telegram was sent—by Indrani Balasubramaniam, chair of the Provincial Women's Self-Respect Conference—on behalf of the women's wing of the SRM.[43]

P. Sivapichai, the president of the Trichy Adi-Dravidar Mahajana Sabha and an adherent of the SRM, too wired Ambedkar. Praising the latter for his struggle to achieve separate electorates, he hoped that he would not succumb to the tantrums of Gandhi and Rajah. 'If you were to give in, you would be doing great harm to the Depressed Classes,' he warned.[44]

Among the many telegrams sent to Ambedkar during the crisis of the Communal Award, that sent by Periyar is worthy of special mention. It was sent when the latter was on his nearly year-long European tour (from 13 December 1931 to 1 November 1932). Speaking at a conference of Pallars, a Depressed Class, in Mohanur in the then Salem district on 2 February 1935—more than two years after the Poona Pact—Periyar referred to this telegram sent from Paris.[45] Posing the question whether Adi Dravidars should support the Congress, he stated: 'When I was touring Europe, I sent a telegram to Comrade Ambedkar stating that the lives of 6 or 7 crores of Depressed Class people are not inferior to the life of Gandhi and therefore, without fearing this savage bogeyman-ship, I asked him not to murder this community.' However, he charged that Ambedkar, charmed by Gandhi's toothless smile and fooled by the blessings of the Brihaspatis, Madan Mohan Malaviya and C. Rajagopalachari, had signed the pact and ruined the liberation of the Depressed Classes. Clearly, the SRM saw Gandhi as the external enemy and M. C. Rajah as the internal enemy of the Depressed Classes.

Gandhi's fast, the backsliding of many Depressed Class leaders, the death threats made by Pune's upper-caste Hindus to Ambedkar (Ambedkar 2019b [1979], pp. 162–163), and the continued propaganda by some Congressmen and Hindu Mahasabha leaders that the Depressed Classes would not be permitted access to public places[46]—all these put Ambedkar in a difficult situation and exerted tremendous emotional pressure on him. On 19 September, the day before Gandhi's fast was to begin, a meeting of Hindu leaders to save Gandhi's life was held in Bombay in the Hall of the Indian Merchants' Chamber. Between then and the actual signing of the Poona Pact, the national bourgeoise and the Indian mercantile class led by G. D. Birla played a significant role behind the scenes. The Hindu communal leader Madan Mohan Malaviya headed this group. P. G. Solanki, M. C. Rajah, B. S. Moonje, V. D. Savarkar, Chamanlal Harilal Setalvad, Walchand Hirachand, K. Natarajan, Palwankar Baloo, and others participated in the meeting (Keer, 2016 [1954], p. 208; Gopal 2023, p. 442). Speaking there, an unflinching Ambedkar stated: 'It has fallen to my lot to be the villain of the piece. But … I shall not deter from my pious duty and betray the just and legitimate interests of my people even if you hang me on the nearest lamppost in the street' (Keer, 2016, p. 209). Instead, he demanded that the Hindu leaders ask Gandhi to postpone his fast by a week and seek a resolution to the problem. Following this, the meeting was adjourned for two days. However, Gandhi started his fast as planned. But, at the behest of upper-caste Hindu leaders, Ambedkar and Gandhi met on 22 and 23 September.

As Gandhi's fast went ahead, many important leaders of the Depressed Classes began to waver. As noted, M. C. Rajah had changed his position on separate electorates. Further, not only N. Sivaraj and V. Dharmalingam Pillai but even R. Srinivasan, who had stood shoulder to shoulder with Ambedkar at the Round Table Conference, changed their stance. R. Srinvasan, it is said, was swayed by the arguments of C. Rajagopalachari and T. Prakasam (Irschick, 1986, p. 160). Irschick argues that the Congress succeeded in converting the Depressed Class leaders of south India by coopting them (1986, p. 160).[47]

All these pressures, in the words of *Kudi Arasu*, shook even 'the intrepid and resolute' Ambedkar. In the deliberations with the leaders of both sides on 24 and 25 September, Ambedkar's hands were forced: he signed the pact. B. R. Ambedkar, M. C. Rajah, R. Srinivasan, Palwankar Baloo, P. G. Solanki, P. N. Rajbhoj, Biswas, and G. A. Gawai signed on behalf of the Depressed Classes. For the caste Hindus, the signatories included Madan Mohan Malaviya, C. Rajagopalachari, M. R. Jayakar, Tej Bahadur Sapru, Rajendra Prasad, A. V. Thakkar, Devadas Gandhi, and Shankerlal Banker. Apart from them, some big business magnates such as G. D. Birla, Lallubhai Samaldas, and Walchand Hirachand too appended their signatures (Pyarelal, 1932, pp. 155–156).

In a statement to the press on 26 September, Gandhi, while acknowledging that 'the settlement … [was] a generous gesture on all sides', reserved his 'Hindu gratitude' for 'Dr Ambedkar, Rao Bahadur Srinivasan and their party on one hand and Rao Bahadur M. C. Raja on the other' (Gandhi, 1972, p. 144; Pyarelal, 1932, p. 143).[48] Clearly, Gandhi was speaking as a representative of the Hindus, especially of the *savarna* castes. This is of a piece with *Kudi Arasu*'s characterization of Gandhi's fast as a measure to save Hinduism and not to safeguard the political rights or interests of the Depressed Classes.

The Poona Pact, consisting of nine clauses, rejected both separate electorates and double electorates for the Depressed Classes. In their stead, it recommended joint electorates with reserved seats for them. However, rather than the 71 seats granted by the Communal Award, the Poona Pact conceded 148 seats—more than double. Moreover, it also proposed a preliminary election ('electoral college') where both the candidates and voters would be exclusively from the Depressed Classes; the four persons with the highest number of votes would be candidates for the general electorate.[49]

In *Kudi Arasu*'s view, 'Mr Gandhi's starving has ruined three-quarters of the good resulting through the Depressed Classes' representation in the legislatures.'[50] It further claimed that Gandhi who had originally rejected reserved seats in any form for the Depressed Classes had conceded separate representation only after the propaganda and agitation of the SRM.[51] The SRM continued to voice its anger at Gandhi's tactics in ambushing the political benefits resulting from the Communal Award. It was not beyond using harsh, if not callous, words in condemning Gandhi. Stating that Gandhi's life was saved by begging at Ambedkar's feet,[52] it went so far as to say: 'If someone argues that it was only because of the mercy and sacrifice of the Depressed Classes that Gandhi's wife was spared widowhood, not even an ungrateful person can deny that argument.'[53]

A letter penned by eight members of the Depressed Classes from Siluvathur village of Vadamadurai firka in Dindigul taluk of Madurai district is noteworthy in this context.[54]

> Sir—We the Adi Dravidar public write as follows through the editor of *Kudi Arasu*. We have realized the great harm done to our interests by Comrade Gandhi. He has closed the doors to our demand for separate electorates and done great harm to us by depriving us of our rights to common resources. By calling us Harijans, he has humiliated us. He is deceiving the common people by writing in a devious manner. We do not support his motions on untouchability and temple entry. He deceived our representative Dr Ambedkar into signing the Poona Pact. Only heeding the plea to save Gandhi's life did our representative affix his signature. But his cunning will not win any more. Rather than cooperating with Gandhi, if our representative Dr Ambedkar were to join hands with Comrade E. V. Ramasamy, we shall soon be enlightened and make progress.[55]

An analysis of this letter throws light on how the Depressed Classes responded to the ideological campaign of the SRM and its impact on them. It could be said that much of what *Kudi Arasu* chronicled and argued in its pages reflected and articulated their political aspirations, views, and desires. In the absence of other forums, not excepting autonomous Depressed Classes' journals at the time, it functioned as their primary mouthpiece.

The SRM expressed its righteous indignation about Ambedkar succumbing to the pressure of Gandhi and his allies. Leading up to the Poona Pact, D. V. Subramanian speaking at Napier Park, Madras, on 24 September stated that

> … whatever comes, we are sure that Ambedkar will not give up separate electorates.… Even if he were to give in, we know how to deal with it. Not one Ambedkar, even if a thousand Ambedkars come, they cannot stall our efforts.… As far as the Madras Presidency is concerned, we will campaign with the Prime Minister and the Secretary of State for India and win separate electorates.[56]

Another commentator said in somewhat uncharitable terms that 'Despite Comrade E. V. Ramasamy sending a long telegram from Europe explaining the facts of the matter and warning him not to be fooled, Ambedkar ignored everything and lured by the fact that he was invited by some, he vainly signed the pact and lost your rights.'[57]

The SRM, as indicated earlier, organized many meetings across the presidency, especially in the Tamil districts. The substance of the resolutions passed in these meetings was annulling the Poona Pact, demanding separate electorates at least in the Madras Presidency, reiterating that separate and double electorates were more meaningful than the increased seats offered by the Poona Pact, condemning the new nomenclature of 'Harijan' with its reactionary and religious overtones employed by the Congress and the Hindu Mahasabha to refer to the Depressed Classes, and declaring that temple entry was an epiphenomenon used to distract from the real issue of adequate and meaningful political representation.

While taking an uncompromising stand regarding the definite setback to the political rights of the Depressed Classes, the SRM viewed two aspects of the Poona Pact in a positive light: the possibility of at least some representatives being elected who could genuinely articulate Depressed Class interests and Gandhi's acknowledgment of Ambedkar as the undisputed leader of the Depressed Classes from his earlier dismissal of the latter's rightful claim to that status.[58]

On 25 September, two days after the Poona Pact was signed, Ambedkar addressed a meeting in Bombay. Speaking on the resolution welcoming the pact, he reiterated his own view that separate electorates were the only solution to the question of the political rights of the Depressed Classes.[59] However, he expressed certain positive views on the Hindu religion that were at variance with what he had said some time earlier and what he continued to hold until his death.

This passage points to a fleeting new faith in Gandhi and in Hinduism. The vacillation was likely due to the enormous stress caused by the wranglings leading up to the Poona Pact. The context of the meeting, the presence of the nationalist and orthodox Hindu personalities who were signatories to the pact, and the overwhelming crowds gathered in support of his acquiescence to the compromise may have also swayed Ambedkar. But this was entirely political and not ideological. That he was soon disabused of upper-caste good intentions is made clear in his speech on 13 October 1935 at a conference in Yeola. Stating that 'degenerated Hinduism was rightly called Brahminism because it benefited only the Brahmin hierarchy as a class', he recounted the deplorable situation of the Depressed Classes and referred, for instance, to the inhuman treatment meted out to the volunteers of the Kalaram Temple entry movement. He declared forcefully that while he could not help having been born a Hindu Untouchable, 'he [would] not die a Hindu' (Keer, 2016 [1954], pp. 252–253; Gopal, 2023, p. 510).

Conclusion

In a combative paper, Karthick Ram Manoharan has drawn attention to the 'not uncommon' instances of some 'critics in Tamil Nadu accusing Periyar … of side-stepping the Dalit question or of being irrelevant to it' (Manoharan, 2020, p. 136). Strengthening this assertion, a recent essay on the Poona Pact, while excoriating mainstream Indian historians for neglecting Ambedkar's role in the making of modern India, makes no mention of Periyar and the Dravidian movement's championing of Ambedkar (Karuppusamy, 2021).

This chapter demonstrates that, at a crucial point in the tortuous history of the Dalit struggle for political representation—the watershed moment of the Poona Pact—Periyar and the SRM strongly stood by Ambedkar. Rather than seeking to represent itself as the voice of the Depressed Classes, the SRM recognized that Ambedkar was their sole spokesperson and as such espoused and elaborated on his views. When even the Mahars' 'first knowledge of Ambedkar' (Zelliot, 2013, p. 128) came at the time of his nomination to the Round Table Conference, the rising importance of Ambedkar as a distinct and autonomous voice was noticed by Periyar much earlier and efforts were made to establish contact with him. This was especially noteworthy at a time when the dominant political forces, especially the Congress and Gandhi, questioned Ambedkar's credentials to speak for his people.[60] When other leaders from the Depressed Classes laid claim to that status and joined hands with reactionary forces, the SRM stood solidly behind him.

Despite its strong articulation of the Poona Pact disappointment, it was through the pages of *Kudi Arasu* that the understanding that Ambedkar was the real leader of the Depressed Classes was firmly established. There was also an expectation among the SRM that Ambedkar should recognize the strength of allying with them and Periyar in this regard. Unfortunately, we are unable to trace any evidence of this in the extant documents of Ambedkar. This is probably because much of the articulation was in Tamil with the exception of two weeklies in English: *Revolt* and *Justice*. Though important Depressed Class leaders from Madras such as R. Srinivasan, N. Sivaraj, and V. I. Munuswamy Pillai were in close touch with Ambedkar, it is not clear how much of Periyar and the SRM's support was communicated to him.

Nevertheless, the SRM remained unwavering in its support of Ambedkar. *Kudi Arasu* was the first to translate 'The Annihilation of Caste' and serialize the book in its pages. Shortly thereafter, it was also published as *Jatiyai Olikka Vali* (1936), a book that has continued to be in print for almost nine decades. Periyar and Ambedkar met on many occasions—in 1940, in 1944, in 1947, and finally at the World Buddhist Conference in Rangoon, two years before the latter's death in December 1956.

This chapter has drawn our attention to the strong ties between Periyar's movement and Ambedkar's politics in the early stages of the latter's career. Their interaction in the subsequent decades demands further study.

Notes

1. Since Ambedkar's writings came into the public domain in 2016, numerous editions of his *Writings and Speeches* have appeared. I have relied on the Dr. Ambedkar Foundation edition.
2. *Tamilan*, 3 March 1909.
3. *Dravidan*, 3 October 1917.
4. *Dravidan*, 15 December 1920; also see *Kudi Arasu*, 27 November 1932.
5. 'The Fallacy of Joint Electorates', *Revolt*, 14 November 1928.
6. 'Separate Electorates', *Revolt*, 28 November 1928
7. See for instance, *Revolt*, 14 November 1928; 28 November 1928.
8. *Kudi Arasu*, 10 February 1935.
9. *Kudi Arasu*, 27 November 1927.
10. *Kudi Arasu*, 8 January 1928.
11. *Kudi Arasu*, 27 November 1932.
12. *Kudi Arasu*, 29 January 1928.
13. *Kudi Arasu*, 12 February 1928.
14. *Kudi Arasu*, 26 February 1928.
15. 'The Fallacy of Joint Electorates', *Revolt*, 14 November 1928.

16. *Revolt*, 14 November 1928; 28 November 1928.
17. *Revolt*, 14 November 1928.
18. *Kudi Arasu*, 28 June 1931. Periyar often took a harsh view of British rule in India. 'Even though 150 years have passed since British rule, it is a great shame on the Empire that untouchability still remains to be abolished. This alone is enough to show that the British are unfit to rule' (*Kudi Arasu*, 4 December 1932).
19. *Kudi Arasu*, 11 January 1931.
20. *Kudi Arasu*, 8 February 1931; 8 March 1931; Periyar to M. R. Jayakar, telegram, Erode, 2 May 1931. M. R. Jayakar Papers, F. No. 36, National Archives of India. Jayakar replied to Periyar congratulating him on the 'excellent choice' and indicated that he had written to Ambedkar asking him to accept. In his letter to Ambedkar, Jayakar expressed the hope that the latter would accept the invitation and commended the SRM with the words, 'It is an excellent movement, and I am sure you will find that it suits your ideas. They are anxious that you should accept their invitation and have requested me to put in a word.' There is no further paper trail of this correspondence but for whatever reason Ambedkar did not make it to the conference.
21. Gandhi's position regarding political representation for the Depressed Classes, especially in the context of the Poona Pact, was contemporaneously documented by Pyarelal (1932). The earliest scholarly assessment was Ravinder Kumar's pioneering article 'Gandhi, Ambedkar and the Poona Pact, 1932' (1985). A more recent summation is Guha (2018, esp. pp. 411–422), where, despite being Gandhi's biographer, Guha shows more sympathy towards Ambedkar than to his hero.
22. *Kudi Arasu*, 8 November 1931.
23. *Kudi Arasu*, 22 November 1931.
24. *Kudi Arasu*, 30 August 1931; 27 September 1931.
25. *Kudi Arasu*, 18 October 1931.
26. *Kudi Arasu*, 22 November 1931.
27. *Kudi Arasu*, 15 May 1932.
28. *Kudi Arasu*, 8 November 1931.
29. *Kudi Arasu*, 7 February 1932.
30. *Kudi Arasu*, 19 June 1932.
31. *Kudi Arasu*, 10 April 1932.
32. *Kudi Arasu*, 17 July 1932.
33. *Kudi Arasu*, 28 February 1932.
34. *Dravidan*, 1 March 1932.
35. *Kudi Arasu*, 17 July 1932.
36. For a full list of these meetings, see Thiruneelakandan (2014).
37. *Dravidan*, 20 September 1932.
38. *Kudi Arasu*, 28 August 1932.
39. *Kudi Arasu*, 18 September 1932.
40. *Dravidan*, 19 September 1932.
41. Reproduced in *Kudi Arasu*, 18 September 1932.
42. *Dravidan*, 19 September 1932.
43. *Dravidan*, 20 September 1932.

44. *Dravidan*, 22 September 1932.
45. *Kudi Arasu*, 10 February 1935. Also see Periyar's speech on 8 December 1957, reported in *Viduthalai*, 12 December 1957.
46. *Kudi Arasu*, 20 November 1932.
47. By 1937, V. I. Munuswamy Pillai even joined the Congress and became a minister in the first cabinet of the Madras Province.
48. It was in this statement that he referred to 'my Harijan friends, as I would like henceforth to name them' (Gandhi, 1972, p. 125).
49. For the full text of the Poona Pact, see Pyarelal (1932, pp. 153–155) and Ambedkar (2014 [1994], pp. 88–89).
50. *Kudi Arasu*, 20 October 1932.
51. *Kudi Arasu*, 2 October 1932.
52. *Kudi Arasu*, 23 October 1932.
53. *Kudi Arasu*, 27 January 1935.
54. The signatories were Ku. Lakshmanan, Ra. Azhagan, Tha. Rangan, R. Azhagarsami, M. Ahagan, Poo. Si. Andi, Pallikoodathan, and Sandaikavakkaran.
55. *Kudi Arasu*, 19 March 1933.
56. *Dravidan*, 28 September 1932.
57. *Kudi Arasu*, 9 May 1937.
58. *Kudi Arasu*, 2 October 1932.
59. *Kudi Arasu*, 2 October 1932.
60. For instance, *The Hindu* achieved the curious feat of writing an editorial on the Poona Pact without so much as mentioning Ambedkar. See 'The Poona Pact', editorial of 26 September 1932 reproduced in *The Hindu Speaks* (1978).

References

Ambedkar, B. R. 2014 (1994). 'What Congress and Gandhi Have Done to Untouchables (1945)'. In *Dr Babasaheb Ambedkar: Writings and Speeches*, vol. 9, pp. 1–387. New Delhi: Dr Ambedkar Foundation.

———. 2019a. *Dr Babasaheb Ambedkar: Writings and Speeches*, vol. 2. New Delhi: Dr Ambedkar Foundation.

———. 2019b (1979). *Dr Babasaheb Ambedkar: Writings and Speeches*, vol. 17, pt 1. New Delhi: Dr Ambedkar Foundation.

Gandhi, M. K. 1972. *Collected Works of Mahatma Gandhi*, vol. 51. New Delhi: Publications Division, Government of India.

Gopal, Ashok. 2023. *A Part Apart: The Life and Thought of B. R. Ambedkar*. New Delhi: Navayana.

Guha, Ramachandra. 2018. 'Arguments with Ambedkar'. In *Gandhi: The Years That Changed the World, 1914–1948*, pp. 405–430. New York: Alfred Knopf.

Indian Statutory Commission, 1930. *Indian Statutory Commission*, vol. 17, pt 2. London: His Majesty's Stationery Office.

Irschick, Eugene F. 1986. *Tamil Revivalism in the 1930s*. Madras: Cre-A.

Karuppusamy, Karthik Raja. 2021. 'Foregrounding Justice in Indian Historiography: Interrogating the Poona Pact'. In *B. R. Ambedkar: The Quest for Justice*, vol. 2: *Social Justice*, edited by Aakash Singh Rathore, pp. 252–279. New Delhi: Oxford University Press.

Keer, Dhananjay. 2016 (1954). *Dr Ambedkar: Life and Mission*. Mumbai: Popular Prakashan.

Kumar, Ravinder. 1985. 'Gandhi, Ambedkar and the Poona Pact, 1932'. *South Asia: Journal of South Asian Studies* 8(1–2): 87–101.

Manoharan, Karthick Ram. 2020 'In the Path of Ambedkar: Periyar and the Dalit Question'. *South Asian History and Culture* 11(2): 136–149.

Pyarelal. 1932. *The Epic Fast*. Ahmedabad: Mohanlal Maganlal Bhatt.

The Hindu Speaks. 1978. Bombay: Interpress.

Thiruneelakandan, A. 2014. 'Dravidar Iyakkamum Thazhthapattorum'. Unpublished PhD thesis, Department of History, Manonmaniam Sundaranar University, Tirunelveli.

Venkatachalapathy, A. R. 2018. 'From Erode to Volga: Periyar EVR's Soviet and European Tour, 1932'. In *India and the World in the First Half of the Twentieth Century*, edited by Madhavan K. Palat, pp. 102–133. London and New York: Routledge.

Zelliot, Eleanor. 2013. *Ambedkar's World: The Making of Babasaheb and the Dalit Movement*. New Delhi: Navayana.

Part II

The Politics of Periyar

3

EVR's Non-Brahmin Cosmopolitanism, Periyar's Dravidian Nationalism, and the Appearance of Humankind

Matthew H. Baxter

The popular focus on Periyar and Dravidian—as a person leading his loyal people—may invite placing nationalism's assertion, rather than critique, at the heart of political thought in twentieth-century Tamil-speaking South India. 'Nationalism' names the intuition that 'France [is] for the French, England for the English ... and so forth' (Shaw, 2013) or, more generally, 'nationalism is a theory of political legitimacy ... requir[ing] that ethnic boundaries should not cut across political ones', insisting on 'congruence of state and nation', and refusing 'ethnic divergence between rulers and ruled' (Gellner, 1983, pp. 1, 134). Much turns on 'ethnic'. Considerations include whether 'ethnic' is 'racial' or 'historically constituted' (Lenin and Stalin, 1970, pp. 66–68) and nationalism's 'inherent contradictoriness', both because its 'rational and progressive' promises of modernity are often premised on 'traditional and conservative' gestures to the past and because its anti-colonial articulation usually adopts the very imperial 'representational structure ... nationalist thought seeks to repudiate' (Chatterjee, 1986, pp. 22, 38). So, when the August 1944 creation of the Dravidar Kazhagam (DK) was heralded with 'Long live Periyar, Dravida Nadu for the Dravidian, let the Dravidar Kazhagam flourish'[1]—entrenching an 'ethnic' idiom for Tamil-speaking South India's politics—an invitation for 'a chapter on Periyar and nationalism' encourages the interrogation of a twinned presumption of coherence: not simply of 'Dravidian' as a people loyal, but of 'Periyar' as a person leading.

In what follows, I argue that 'Periyar' and 'Dravidian' are the failures—not fulfilments—of someone named E. V. Ramasamy Naicker (EVR) and a project called 'Non-Brahmin'. While their shared concerns were importantly 'not confine[d] ... to caste but included the overarching question of power ... traced to the figure of the Brahmin', we should cautiously regard claims about their 'overlaps ... engaging simultaneously with several identities' and the extent to which these terms were mutually 'substitutable' or could serve as a 'part standing for the whole' (Pandian, 2007, p. 188; Chatterjee, 2020, p. 95). EVR's Non-Brahmin focused on the equality of humankind by prioritizing 'Self-Respect' (*suyamariyadhai*) over 'Self-Rule' (*suyarajyam* or 'swaraj'); as EVR claimed 'humbl[y] but decisive[ly]' in 1926: 'Self-Respect is more essential than Self-Rule, regardless of the society and nation.'[2] This prioritization understood nationalism as always already a Brahminical ideology of elite benefit and mass cost. In contrast, Periyar's Dravidian focused on the independence of a kind of human through the demand 'Dravida Nadu for the Dravidian'. This demand embraced, rather than refused, nationalist logics and thus risked adopting, rather than critiquing, 'Brahminism'.

This argument has two sections; their viability relies on a conceit. Non-Brahmin artefacts consist of edited periodicals, rushed to meet production deadlines, publishing hastily transcribed improvised speeches alongside innumerable essays—all from hundreds of varied figures. EVR's own authorship—a man with an elementary education—is sometimes speculation. Their study—unlike more canonical academic work—may therefore not be about articulation's delicate *consistency* but concern's raw *persistence*. We might call this persistent project 'Non-Brahmin political theory',[3] whose political puzzle and theoretical premise wrestled with Self-Respect's achievement through Self-Rule's deferral or, more generally, with whether humankind's equality could be produced through the postponement of independence premised on human kinds. Crudely, its *early period* involves EVR's Non-Brahmin, from the weekly *Kudi Arasu*'s May 1925 publication[4] to the February 1937 electoral victory of Gandhi's Congress saturating the political horizon with 'Self-Rule'.[5] Its *late period* centres on Periyar's Dravidian, from March 1937's recalibrations after Brahminical 'Self-Rule's' electoral victory[6] to the August 1944 creation of the organization 'Dravidar Kazhagam'.[7] These periods are the focus of this chapter despite EVR speaking and publishing through India's independence until his death. Though EVR's Non-Brahmin and Periyar's Dravidian were used differently at different moments, this chapter maintains that the former's persistent core revolved around the equality of humankind by prioritizing Self-Respect over Self-Rule while the latter's revolved around the independence of human kinds in demanding Dravida Nadu for the Dravidian.

The first section outlines the reversals from EVR to Periyar and from Non-Brahmin to Dravidian. I suggest that Non-Brahmin is a *phenomenal* project, emphasizing the inclusivity of appearance's address through changing roles, while Dravidian is a *noumenal* identity, emphasizing the exclusivity of biological reality through enduring race. EVR is a character critiquing authority, while Periyar a figure assuming it.

The second section focuses on EVR's Non-Brahmin negotiation of 'cosmopolitanism' to imagine international Self-Respect over nationalist Self-Rule. Non-Brahmin cosmopolitanism is not cross-cultural literacy, appreciating different human kinds, but identity's iconoclastic refusal asserting humankind's equality; EVR's 'cosmopolitan' subsequently prioritized human law over different peoples. While dismissing local attachments, Non-Brahmin cosmopolitanism reframed, rather than resisted, politics through an unresolved tension between *actualizing appearances* defining humankind and the *mere appearance* of human kinds.

By way of conclusion, I gesture to the world-historical moment where nationalism's assertive demand of the 1940s eclipsed nationalism's critical deferral of the 1920s in South India: when the Non-Brahmin project's political and theoretical tensions were faced with the simultaneous 1930s rise of the 'Aryan' on continent and subcontinent and, subsequently, of a world hospitable—rather than hostile—to a familiar figure of tremendous Tamil worry.[8]

EVR's Non-Brahmin to Periyar's Dravidian: Phenomenal Role, Noumenal Race

Whether in announcements that 'Periyar founded "The Self-Respect Movement" [SRM]. The Non-Brahmin … had to learn to assert his worth before he could look his oppressor in the face

Non-Brahmin Cosmopolitanism, Dravidian Nationalism, and Humankind 59

and say "No"' (*Economic and Political Weekly*, 1974) following his December 1973 death or in claiming 'Known as "The Father of the Dravidian Movement", Periyar fought for gender and caste equality in Tamil Nadu' (*Indian Express*, 2022) in response to his statues' January 2022 desecration, 'Periyar' seems a regional hero of unquestionable influence. Since 1938, Dravidian publications have ensured 'Periyar's' common sense:

There is no other Buddha after Buddha. There is no further Gandhi after Gandhi. There cannot be another Periyar after Periyar.

Periyar is a movement (institution), not an individual person. Like 'Marxism,' 'Periyarism' is a philosophy, a principle, an objective.[9]

The problem, however, is that EVR often opposed being associated with *periyar*s (distinguished-figures) prior to 1937. As he declared in 1931, commenting on the abuse 'written about me and my wife' on nearby walls:

[T]here is more profit for me in saying that I am a scoundrel, a thief, a fool, [and] self-interested … than in considering me … a mahatma …[or] a buddha … [I]f my words and positions should … get the correct value they actually have, those who campaign so that I should be considered a scoundrel … are in fact doing me a service. Do not burden me with any characteristic that exceeds the quality of the human … Were I happy to see 'The distinguished-figure Ramasamy [Ramasamy *periyar*] should live a long and blessed life' written, I would have been saddened by the claim 'that ass Ramasamy should die and go to hell'. Similarly, only were I to feel joy in seeing written that 'Ramasamy's wife is a chaste-woman' … would I have been aggrieved by the claim 'Ramasamy's wife Nagammal is a whore'.[10]

Here, in 1931, EVR refused praise as a *periyar* associated with mahatmas or buddhas lest 'I myself should … do me injury'. Being a *periyar* 'exceeds … the quality of the human', crippling the assessment of 'words and positions'. 'Correct value' is possible through suspicion of scoundrels or whores, not adulation of mahatmas or buddhas. Rather than 'Periyar found[ing] "The Self-Respect Movement"', Self-Respect's premise was the rejection of *periyar*s.

Moreover, 'Periyar' did not found the SRM as much as the SRM founded 'Periyar'. As is widely cited, this occurred at a November 1938 women's conference in Chennai where

a resolution was passed that hereafter Comrade E. V. Ramasamy Naicker shall be called 'Periyar.' The meaning of 'periyar' is 'great human' [*periya manitar*].

But EVR is not only a great human; he is the periyar among all of India's periyars …

His aim is that the people should first be free from those who deceive them in the name of God and that labourers should be free from the power of capitalists …

… [H]is Self-Respect Movement is the true movement of reason …

Therefore, it is he who is the true leader. There shall never be another … leader such as EVR.[11]

Undoubtedly, EVR frequently spoke highly of *periyars*—among whom he counted radicals 'slandered as atheists' such as Socrates, Jesus Christ, Buddha, and the Prophet Muhammad.[12] But EVR imagined their actualization of Self-Respect through the suspicious refusal they encouraged, not the devotional adulation they commanded.

EVR's preference for 'scoundrel' over 'periyar' has implications for nationalism. Not only does it challenge presumptions of a person leading, but EVR's 1931 speech quoted previously continues to challenge the idea of a loyal people:

> It is said that I often make changes in my principles.... [I]s it all that righteous ... if a human remains ... a thief from birth until today? Why do you desire that any ... should remain in the same condition? What is it to you? Is change progressive or regressive ... good or evil...? The duty of those with understanding is the need to be concerned with things like these.... I may change many times, somersault a lot ... or be a chameleon. What harm will come to you? When seeing a play in a playhouse, just think whether or not ... you see acting involving a human changing costume [*vesham*] over and over ... and go about praising the actor. Have you been deceived...? Think of us just like that and listen to what we say.[13]

EVR's invitation to think of 'us'—Non-Brahmin Self-Respecters—in terms of acrobatic somersault, camouflaged chameleon, or theatrical costume as opportunity to be heard, not misleading deception, suggests that the Non-Brahmin cannot rely on some enduring deeper reality to constitute identity, as one might presume of a loyal national people existing 'from birth until today'. Instead, Non-Brahmin actualization is a matter of theatrical performance and change in appearance.

The relationship between appearance and reality has a long philosophical history on both continent and subcontinent. Crudely, I refer to EVR's Non-Brahmin investments as 'phenomenal' and those of Periyar's Dravidian as 'noumenal', taking initial direction from Kant's distinction between 'mere appearances' and 'things in themselves' (Kant, 2004 [1783]), p. 66; Merleau-Ponty, 2005 [1945]). Efforts to locate power's productivity not in some pre-political noumena behind the human but instead in the political phenomena displayed by the human (Nietzsche, 2006) have emphasized the 'performative' in articulating identities like gender (Butler, 1990). Such phenomenal emphasis has also found traction in theorizing 'publics'. A public exists 'by virtue of being addressed', bound 'by its own discourse rather than by external frameworks', and is identified 'primarily through ... participation' unknowable 'in advance' (Warner, 2002, pp. 56, 82). The suggestion here: EVR's Non-Brahmin, grammatically configured through absence (Non-/-*allatu*), was subsequently available to such phenomenal 'stranger-sociability' ('Put on a show, and see who shows up') rather than requiring noumenal 'positive content' ('nations, religions, races, guilds'). Such actualizing phenomenal appearance, available to performative roles defining a public, contrasted with Periyar's Dravidian as one of underlying noumenal reality, insisting on biological race defining a nation.

In 1925, EVR noted the performative inclusivity of address in constituting a 'whole-heartedly united' Non-Brahmin through 'a common aim' that overcomes 'meaningless' and 'paltry community differences' in 'politics', 'religion', and 'livelihood' in order to 'live as humans with Self-Respect and get away from Brahmin manipulation and strategy': 'the name "Non-Brahmin" has been customary for the common masses ... Non-Hindus such as Christians, Mohammedans, and Anglo-Indians are Non-Brahmins ... [T]he many Hindus distinct from the Brahmin and ... the large group ... pushed aside and called "Untouchable" ... are also Non-Brahmins.'[14] One need not be of a particular Indian community, or even have clear Indian origins, to be 'Non-Brahmin'. Rather, 'Non-Brahmin' was a public available to humankind constituted by those responding to an address: to 'live as humans with Self-Respect' against 'Brahmin manipulation'.

This *Non*-Brahmin was not *Anti*-Brahmin; phenomenal address was constituted through *absence* not *elimination*. EVR makes this clear, refusing the slanderous 'fiction' that 'abolishing Brahminism is the abolition of Brahmins'.[15] Non-Brahmin neither opposed nor addressed human kinds, rather it targeted the more general 'superstition', 'arrogance', and 'deceitful philosophy' of hierarchical structures demarcating 'superior' from 'inferior' based on 'some bogus about birth', preventing humankind's actualization in 'human dharma' and 'Self-Respect'. 'Non-Brahmin' was an inclusive category of humankind's egalitarian possibility. As EVR implied in December 1928, anticipating the Simon Commission's promise of 'communal representation', Non-Brahmin named the

> need to pay attention primarily to abolishing superiority–inferiority at birth ... to establishing equality, and to ... liv[ing] with Self-Respect.... Some societies and some individual people in our country are in an unliveable situation as a result of the lack of equality and feeling of Self-Respect brought about among the people.... [T]hroughout history ... in any given country at any given time, there has always been this sort of group devastating the people's interest out of their self-interest.[16]

Non-Brahmin and Brahmin are world-historical categories of address. Non-Brahmin addresses those who demand humankind's equality, Brahmin those who benefit from the inequality possible from arrangements distinguishing kinds of human. Such categories are based on relational phenomenal performances of participatory address, as roles among humankind, rather than underlying noumenal realities with positive content, as races distinguishing kinds of humans.

Though the Non-Brahmin addressed humankind, as world-historical, the term was riven by temptations to name a kind of human, as regionally specific. Ironically, perhaps the earliest such dramatic instance occurred in late 1926 as EVR argued for a distinct 'Self-Respect Movement':

> [W]e have seen that every nation, every religion, every society, and every class in the world has been trying to secure power and progress, directly or indirectly, by creating movements ... to remove their own ills and achieve their own progress....With regard to our country, we have seen ... institutions established ... in common among Non-Brahmins (Dravidian, Tamilian) ... to escape from the atrocities that have been inflicted upon them ... and to repudiate ... obstacles to their Self-Respect and equality.[17]

EVR used the parenthetical '(Dravidian, Tamilian)' to qualify 'Non-Brahmin' as a kind of human in arguments for creating a 'Self-Respect Movement' to challenge the 'hostility' posed by '[t]he enemies of our Self-Respect (Brahmins and their coolies)'. This tension between Non-Brahmin to name humankind's role, as the phenomenal performance happening in 'any given country at any given time', and Non-Brahmin to name an ethno-linguistic kind of human, such as with the noumenal reality suggested by this parenthetical, was a persistent challenge in Non-Brahmin political theory.

For example, in his anticipation of the Simon Commission quoted in the preceding paragraphs, EVR enumerates 'the common masses—specifically the Mohammedans, Christians, Non-Brahmins, the Depressed, the oppressed, and those dismissed as Untouchables'.[18] Non-Brahmin here was a kind of human, not the 'common masses' of humankind. Yet the Non-Brahmin's phenomenal availability to humankind persisted despite noumenal assertions as kinds of humans.

In contrast to EVR's earlier Non-Brahmin availability to the phenomenal possibilities of participatory address, Periyar's 1940s Dravidian largely relied on the noumenal reality of positive content. Bracketing important debates over subcontinental terms for grouping, such as *vakuppu* for 'community', Tamil *inam* as 'race' became Dravidian identity's noumenal ground.[19] As EVR claimed at Chennai's 1943 celebration of Untouchability Eradication Day:

> We (Dravidians or Tamilians) may make a nation of our existing border.… For those who have Tamil as a mother language, their mother country can exist as Tamil country so far as they do not mix with other blood. Therefore, the Tamilian, in making Tamil country into mother country, needs to exist separately with unity hereafter as one nation, as one race, and push away the political, the social, the religious, the economic, and the educational in so far as they are related to the foreigner. However, today this is possible only through Islam. This is not at all possible through the Hindu religion …[20]

EVR carried forward previous commitments to Islamic conversion as effective egalitarian articulation (Baxter, 2019, pp. 264–281), but conversion now worked because an underlying Tamil- or Dravidian-ness remained unchanged. Though the speech elsewhere wrestles with *vesham*'s guise (further discussed in the following paragraphs), it is language, land, and blood—classic noumenal markers of nationalism—that bind native Dravidians against the 'foreigner'. The absence of 'Non-Brahmin' from the parenthetical defining 'we' as 'Dravidian or Tamilians' is telling, suggesting 'Dravidian' noumenally binds while 'Non-Brahmin' phenomenally did. Likewise, for example, a resolution passed at the June 1940 Kanchipuram 'Separation Conference', exploring the viability of Dravida Nadu to thwart 'Self-Rule', 'requests the Dravidian people to remain united without the difference of Muslim, Christian, and Tamilian' in opposition to 'Comrade Savarkar' whose Hindutva forces threatened South India.[21] Rather than gathering 'Muslim, Christian, and Tamilian' as Non-Brahmins through their shared role played on humankind's stage, they are gathered as Dravidian through their shared race—a kind of human—in the world.

The Dravidian subsequently sometimes racialized the 'foreigner' in a manner colonized by 'color-line' articulations (Du Bois, 2007 [1903]). As EVR wrote in one of many discussions of the Sanskrit epic the *Ramayana* as a narrative of South India's subjugation to north India: 'In Vedic literature, the black humans (Dravidians) are called inhuman-infidels, murderers, and, often, those capable of becoming demons by Indo-Europeans (that is, Aryans).'[22] This 'black' Dravidian against presumably white Aryans would have excluded the 'Anglo-Indian' Non-Brahmin referred to previously. Moreover, EVR had earlier *attacked* these very epidermal optics for erasing caste and legitimating Brahmin-led anti-colonial nationalist conflicts against Whites over Non-Brahmin-led anti-caste internationalist struggles against Brahmins. As early as 1925, EVR was furious that Brahmins expressed outrage over *Indians* being unable to 'walk on the street' in South Africa or needing 'to give a "salam" even to Whites of no integrity because they are the conquering caste' with high salaries while 'no matter how much integrity we [Indians] have, we will remain coolies', but who turned around and dismissed as mere 'envy' or 'bigotry' those Indians who expressed outrage over *Non-Brahmins* needing to give a 'salam' to high-salaried *Brahmins* of no integrity while Non-Brahmins of integrity remained coolies unable to walk on South India's streets.[23] EVR's Non-Brahmin subsequently interrogated Brahminism's epidermal emphasis: 'in what way are the Whites worse? … One might even say that White rule is better than living under this Brahmin rule and system of oppression.'[24]

The messy shift from a politics of Non-Brahmin phenomena (performative appearance) to one of Dravidian noumena (racialized reality) paralleled shifts from EVR, as a figure demanding authority's critique, to Periyar, as a figure disposed to authority's assumption. At the moment of the DK's formation, 'Periyar' reportedly claimed:

> I do not think that dictatorship is something flawed. As responsibility rises, power will certainly rise. If there is more responsibility, and if I happen to assume all responsibility and more power, I would need to become a dictator.… [M]y nature is to consider that I am the one responsible and that [a movement's] full weight is on my shoulders.[25]

To be fair, *sarvatikaram* is more textured than 'dictatorship': it names projects from Hitler and Mussolini,[26] renders Marxism's 'dictatorship of the proletariat',[27] and features in discussions of Rousseau's 'General Will'.[28] That said, Periyar confidently assuming the responsibility of authority amidst claims of 'Dravida Nadu for the Dravidian' seems quite different from EVR refusing adulation as a scoundrel amidst claims that 'Self-Respect is necessary before Self-Rule'.

In sum, the relationship between 'Non-Brahmin' and 'Dravidian' is not one of interchangeable substitution: EVR's Non-Brahmin, a phenomenal project of performance premised on the equality of humankind ('Self-Respect') and authority's constant critique, was overtaken by Periyar's Dravidian, a noumenal project of racialization premised on the freedom of human kinds ('Self-Rule') and authority's naturalized assumption. However, such reductive clarity misses the constant challenge Non-Brahmin political theory faced when prioritizing equality's Self-Respect over Self-Rule's independence. Understanding 'Periyar and nationalism' invites an appreciation of EVR at his most Non-Brahmin, such as when embracing interwar cosmopolitanism.

EVR's Non-Brahmin Cosmopolitanism

Crudely put, the study of political thought in colonial South Asia has had three phases: top–down hagiographies (1950s–1970s), bottom–up subaltern studies (1980s–1990s), and round-and-round global histories (2000s–2020s). The recent phase, focused on the world-wide circulations of people and ideas, has accordingly engaged cosmopolitanism, exploring how South Asian anticolonial projects operated 'within global horizons' and defied the 'semantics of cosmopolitanism in the West'—which rigidly opposed particularity and universalism while caught in structural East–West differences—through the pragmatic 'socially situated need to solve problems' with 'highly different others' (Bose and Manjapra, 2010). Yet such semantics gloss over the origins of *kosmopolites* with the eccentric ancient Greek Diogenes, whose dramatic and violent opposition to conventions suggests that being a 'citizen of the world' is 'not the well-travelled man's interest in alien cultures … but rather a reaction against every kind of coercion imposed by the community on the individual' (Dudley, 1998 [1937], pp. 34–37).[29] Studies of South Asian anti-colonial cosmopolitanism, insofar as they focus on itinerant intellectuals and educated activists articulating 'different universalisms', risk following cosmopolitanism's well-worn *literate* semantic registers of pluralism—favouring 'respectable', 'low-key and academic methods of scrutinizing customs' like 'literature and history', 'cross-cultural study', and the 'cognitive moral development' of reason to battle 'divisive passions'—rather than cosmopolitanism's originary eccentric semantic register of iconoclasm—whose 'confrontational tactics' to 'unsettle and awaken' are dismissed as mere 'street theater', 'strikingly apolitical and defiant' with 'little in the way of developed … political thought' (Nussbaum, 1997) and where Diogenes's politics is regarded as 'doubtless a contradiction' (Dudley, 1998 [1937]). Literate cosmopolitanism's appreciation of different attachments can get so far from cosmopolitanism's origins in iconoclastic refusals of all attachments that the world may appear impossible without the word:

> since one cannot see … the world … or humanity, the cosmopolitan optic is not one of perceptual experience but of the imagination … Literature creates the world and cosmopolitan bonds … because it enables … imagin[ing] a world through its powers of figuration … [and] desir[ing] to share … through universal communication. (Cheah, 2008, pp. 26–27)[30]

Yet when modern politics remains caught in what Hannah Arendt calls 'the secret conflict between state and nation'—where 'the same nation [is] at once declared to be subject to laws … flow[ing] from the Rights of Man [that is, humankind], and sovereign, that is, bound by no universal law and acknowledging nothing superior to itself [that is, kinds of human]'—one may wonder whether democratic fulfilment is best achieved through diverse attachment's literate appreciation or its iconoclastic refusal (Arendt, 1973 [1958]), pp. 229–231). EVR emphasized the latter as 'cosmopolitan'.

EVR explicitly discussed cosmopolitanism on two important occasions during the early period of Non-Brahmin political theory—in July 1930 as a transliterated *kasmapalittan* and in December 1933 as a translation of 'Citizen of the World'. Against iconoclastic cosmopolitanism's dismissal as 'apolitical' and without 'political thought', EVR articulated an iconoclastic cosmopolitanism to refigure political attachments without literary 'powers of figuration'. Iconoclasm's insistence on humankind's equality, rather than literate appreciations of differences among kinds of human, generated Non-Brahmin politics.

We can read Non-Brahmin cosmopolitanism as challenging the political frame presumed across literate cosmopolitanism *and* cosmopolitanism's critics: Self–Other. Whether with a fuzzy multicultural concern that 'a denial of difference contributes to social group oppression … argu[ing] for a politics that recognizes rather than represses difference' in pursuit of 'unassimilated otherness' (Young, 1990, pp. 10, 227) or a frigid Schmittian understanding of 'the political' as 'the distinction … between friend and enemy … as … the other, the stranger … existentially something different' (Schmitt, 2007, pp. 26–27; Mouffe, 2005), Self–Other binaries seem foundational for 'developed … political thought'. But EVR's Non-Brahmin prioritization of 'Self-Respect' above 'all else … as the birth-right … possessed by … every human being' framed the Self-Indian/Other-British presumption behind Self-Rule as always already Brahminical, generating degradation rather than preserving non-assimilation:

> The great Tilak says 'Self-Rule is a birth-right' because he is a Varnashrama Dharma Brahmin and so thinks it is a birth-right to consider others as degraded with respect to the Brahmin. He thus ... use[s] the word 'Self-Rule', which, in our experience, is related to a politics that is meaningless and greatly deceptive.... We are not those who need to subsist by deceiving someone, but rather are those who need to know true humanity.[31]

Self–Other politics subsidized anti-colonial nationalism's plausibility with degrading deception.

In contrast, Non-Brahmin politics targeted the ternary gradations of high/middle/low perpetuating hierarchy. As humans, 'we rejoice in the thought that it is enough if someone is lower than us' and thus the political challenge is that 'no single person can get rid of every kind of untouchability':

> Though someone claims that the one beneath him is an Untouchable ... to those who are above him, that very person is likewise an Untouchable.... This is not a mere custom, since we see that all of these fellows are joined together as Untouchables ... marked by still more inferiority under the Europeans who are the caste that rules us. Consequently ... the eradication of untouchability will not be brought about only by Panchama progress ... nor by preventing only the atrocities committed against them but, rather, ... requires the removal of the atrocity and degradation held within every one of us.[32]

EVR therefore frequently dismissed 'the political', with its Self–Other difference, to emphasize the high/middle/low hierarchy (what EVR often calls 'the social'). For example, in reference to his Non-Brahmin project, EVR suggests we

> call this matter neither politics [*araciyal*] nor theology [*mata iyal*] but instead human-ology [*manita iyal*], that is, let's call it Self-Respect-ology [*suyamariyatai iyal*], which means humanism.... Otherwise ... we'll be kept down as suckers ... Politics is hucksiering.... Don't think that what I am saying is something that looks [only] at the present political condition.... [W]hat is usually called politics in the world is not concerned in the slightest with who assists the common people ... but rather ... is only about ... who experiences the benefit of rule if exercised and who gets power if power is passed along.

Accordingly, the Non-Brahmin targeted Self–Other political frames, declaring cross-cultural difference as always already a matter of Brahmin assertions of superiority, able to claim any challenge to their 'power' or 'profit' as 'acts of national betrayal ... pos[ing] a danger to their religion, their language, and their arts'.[33]

Therefore, for EVR's Non-Brahmin, any 'developed ... political thought' was not about different kinds of human (Self–Other) but, instead, about humankind's opposition to difference's hierarchical availability (high/middle/low).[34] A politics premised on *anything other than* iconoclastic cosmopolitanism was therefore 'doubtless a contradiction'. EVR subsequently articulated a politics defined by the cosmopolitanism of Non-Brahmin Self-Respect rather than the nationalism of

Brahmin Self-Rule: 'nationalism is different, politics is different … Politics is not the issue of "who rules us". "What kind of political system should our people have"—that is our political issue.'[35] But this (cosmo)political question of 'how to rule' over humankind, displacing nationalism's question of 'who should rule' over human kinds, wrestled with the political sustainability of iconoclastic cosmopolitanism's adamant detachment against literate cosmopolitanism's self-reflective attachments.

The July 1930 headline 'Kodaikanal *Kasmapalittan* Reading Room: Opening Festivity'[36] seemingly betrays the wager so far: if Non-Brahmin cosmopolitanism was iconoclastic rather than literate, why a reading room? EVR's speech interrogated what literacy means with regard to cosmopolitanism—particularly important under conditions where Self-Respect's Non-Brahmin masses, unlike Self-Rule's Brahmin elites, were overwhelmingly unlettered.

Literate cosmopolitanism suggests education could cultivate moral reason grounded in the appreciation of difference. But for EVR, a reading room does not lead to reason; rather, reason leads to a reading room:

> In this country, there are two reasons for people not understanding the significance of a reading room. For one, people do not have the education sufficient for [a reading room] to be necessary. For another, people do not have reason. These two turn the people away from founding a reading room to the work of … building a temple … [T]he feeling of reason that has arisen in you has inspired you to take this precious action …

If reason leads to valuing reading, rather than the reverse, whence comes reason? Literate cosmopolitanism presumes domestically available schooling through which one appreciates foreign as native, redistributing value's origin *in* Self *to* Other. For the Non-Brahmin, however, value is premised on foreign/Other *opposition to* the domestic/Self. Though the British 'arrived 150 years ago' saying 'everyone may study',

> White rule … ha[s] been acting according to the wishes of Brahmins, whose principle is that everyone should not study.… Our Brahmins and their Non-Brahmin buffoons stand on stage and say that it is because the White government did not let Indians study that 93 percent of persons were kept illiterate.… [J]udge for yourselves whether White rule is the reason that others in India, apart from Brahmins, are not educated, or whether it is Brahmin religious rule …

Brahminism's force cripples indigeneity's democratic value. Iconoclastic cosmopolitanism refusing indigeneity's attachment is necessary under conditions where global citizenship does not start *inside* but *outside*. That is, valuing foreign as oneself is meaningless without first valuing oneself. Iconoclastic cosmopolitanism's value originates *elsewhere*. Blasphemy, rather than fidelity, is therefore central:

> The people do not have self-understanding and they have been prevented from listening to the understanding of others. When making an effort to get rid of these obstacles, God, religion, and religious-priests come and interfere via the Brahmin … [I]t is necessary to throw them far away. But then we are called religious traitors, God opposers, and blasphemers of religious-priests by the self-interested.

Furthermore, unlike literate cosmopolitanism's preference for 'academic methods' as understanding's premise, EVR names *arivu*'s 'understanding'—the grammatical root of *pakuttarivu*'s 'reason'—as canonical study's antithesis:

> remember that study is different from understanding. You can mention ... many examples ... of studied fools ... [whose] study ... is useless for worldly life and the basis for the survival of scoundrels.... That is, apart from ... the Vedas ... they nominally gather grammar and literature, memorize them, and take the exam.... The north-language [Sanskrit] sources translated into Tamil are illustrious under many guises [*vesham*], but not in a way that'll create understanding and the feeling of Self-Respect for the people.

Study is *mere appearance*—*vesham's* 'guise'—rather than *actualizing appearance* if it does not create humankind's understanding and Self-Respect, whose cultivation is distinct from literate study and indigeneity's valuing oneself as native. Instead of literate sophistication, understanding is achieved through fearless iconoclasm, critically refusing cross-cultural indigeneity's association with customs, religion, nationalism, and so on. Thus making 'people of understanding' and a 'country ... [of] liberty ... can only be done through work that is afraid of neither slander nor contempt'.

Literate cosmopolitanism fails to cultivate *arivu*'s understanding, crippling *pakuttarivu*'s reason, by presuming the value of the self's nativity when, in Non-Brahmin political theory, such value is Brahminism—a demand for the independence of human kinds (that is, nationalism) rather than eradication of humankind's inequality (that is, untouchability). EVR's world-historically progressive investments in cosmopolitanism are distinct from, if not opposed to, academic appreciations of difference—an iconoclastic investment in Self-Respect's fearless refusal of humankind's history of divisive hierarchy:

> The Self-Respect Movement was established so as to bring about the equality, fraternity, and liberty of our Tamil Country's people.... [I]ts primary principle is ... totally abolish[ing] the difference of high caste and low caste at people's birth, the claim that man is high and woman low, and the difference in superiority–inferiority that has existed in claims of rich or poor, king or subjects, guru or disciple, God or devotee. The feeling of difference in superiority or inferiority has enslaved the people. Instead of this feeling of difference, the feeling of equality and the feeling of liberty have been spreading in all countries.

Rather than literate cosmopolitanism's global sociability enabled by textual figuration, presuming a world inaccessible without the word, EVR's iconoclastic cosmopolitanism located world-making and humanity-belonging in particularity's furious refusal—lower-caste rage over inequality, not upper-caste pleasures of difference.

Moreover, bringing about humankind's Self-Respect and understanding through targeting 'difference in superiority–inferiority' generates local possibilities of sociability facilitated, not activated, by reading rooms: 'the development of understanding' requires 'opportunities ... to understand the nature of the world. Reading rooms provide a facility for reading materials that are sources for that and for joining and becoming familiar with many people and speaking with them.' EVR's iconoclastic cosmopolitanism does not refuse literacy, for reading certainly provides world-understanding opportunities, but rooms for reading are not simply about literacy but interaction, not printed words imaginatively figuring worlds but chances to gather with people whose Self-Respect investments require world-making projects 'afraid of neither slander nor contempt'. In short, the *kasmapalittan* excavates possibilities of humankind's membership not through 'universal communication' achieved by sophisticated literacy, as Brahmins bestowing self-value onto others, but through fearless egalitarian assertion refusing particular exploitation, as Non-Brahmins reallocating value from others to themselves. Reading rooms are not responsible for cultivating reason through academic appreciation of differences among human kinds. Instead, a furious insistence on humankind's equality cultivates the reason responsible for building reading rooms.

At a December 1933 conference held in EVR's hometown of Erode under the theme 'Today's Civilization Seen in India', EVR delivered a speech titled 'What Does Civilization Mean?'[37] He asked the question begged by the conference: before discussing 'Indian civilization', what do we mean by 'civilization' at all? The speech featured a translation of cosmopolitanism, with the English parenthetical '(Citizen of the World)' following the Tamil phrase 'compassion for human life, world fraternity, people's own-honour',[38] and furthered the iconoclastic investments EVR earlier explored through a transliterated *kasmapalittan*, getting beyond kinds of humans marked by hierarchy towards the egalitarian actualization of humankind. Whereas July 1930 revolved around literacy and understanding, December 1933 revolved around change and progress. Yet EVR's cosmopolitanism throughout insisted that being *here* is to be a part of the world in the same way as being *there*, and therefore *kasmapalittan* understanding, as a '(Citizen of the World)', requires not educated literacy of foreign difference as much as iconoclastic refusal of indigenous hierarchy.

Cosmopolitanism's appeal in December 1933 remained its challenge to nationalism's fraudulence. Whereas the transliterated *kasmapalittan* emphasized the *agency* of fraudulence, that is, 'Brahmin' as naming the interests generating nationalism, the translated '(Citizen of the World)' partly named the Non-Brahmin's unfortunate *availability* to such fraudulence, that is, the context of interminable world-historical change ripe for co-optation. 'The meaning of the word "civilization" is not a thing easily grasped … [E]veryone has given a distinct meaning for "civilization"'—'compassion' to some, 'slavery' for others, different relations between 'husband' and 'wife', and so on—'significantly chang[ing] according to the people's society, behaviour, food, and all sorts of attitudes.… Somehow everything goes on changing.'

Yet EVR believes this constant flux of civilizational difference has culminated in the present possibility of cosmopolitanism: overcoming particular attachments to appreciate humanity itself.

Discussing history's ceaseless civilizational reversals, whereby something like 'the spinning wheel … in the political matters of today' cycled through 'trash' and 'worth' over the past 'thousand years', EVR demands the elimination of 'fighting over pride' through difference's civilizational assertion of a 'separate and distinct philosophy' to become 'the highest caste'. Instead, cosmopolitan promise is to be realized by 'the common human, who is without any kind of attachment (nation, religion, caste)':

> At one time we considered nation, nationalism or national-attachment as civilization. But today we have come forward to firmly push away all … these … and consider that … compassion for human life, world fraternity, people's own-honour (*Citizen of the World*) is civilization.

> Today we have been making fun of what was considered as civilization at one time... forcefully refuting all these, claiming them to be the ruin of sense and contradictory.... [T]oday we have begun to well realize that support for one caste means crime to another, and welfare for one nation means injury to another.

The train of terms from 'compassion' to 'own-honour' renders 'Citizen of the World'. Any 'philosophy' bound by particular attachments, whether caste or nation, is dismissed. Differences of human kinds perpetuate interminable zero-sum games.

EVR's world-historical culmination—from a long past of hierarchical differences, to a near future of global equality—is grounded in Marxist terms of universal exploitation 'attend[ing] deeply to all humans' where the lived experience of injustice *here* provides 'understanding' of experiences *there*:

> Comrades ... it is said we have been progressing through the research of understanding and maturity of experience.... For example, we see that merchants join into a faction to attain profit and spoil the well-being of people's society, that moneylenders corrupt human society, that the class [*varkkam*] holding religious power are the enemies of human society.... One's own-honour of caste, own-honour of relation, own-honour of language, and own-honour of nation should all disappear.

EVR's cosmopolitan investments trace an iconoclastic fearlessness targeting local factions of profit and exploitation. The 'maturity' of EVR's near future moment marks history's culmination, when the 'honour' attached to one's own kind of human—caste, relation, language, nation—is overcome through the 'Respect' attached to the 'Self' as humankind's member. Like Diogenes, the performative aspect of personal attachment's refusal *here*, not 'low-key ... academic methods' of difference's appreciation *there*, makes one *kasmapalittan*.

One might subsequently wonder, in folk psychological terms: did such Non-Brahmin cosmopolitanism create an abhorrent vacuum of attachment inevitably later filled by Dravidian separatist-nationalism? There are at least two reasons to resist this conclusion. Both return us to Non-Brahmin actualization through performative address—but highlight *vesham*'s inconsistent ability to index phenomenal appearance's priority over noumenal reality despite EVR's provocative metaphor of a playhouse actor repeatedly 'changing costume' as a model for 'listen[ing] to what we say'.

The first has to do with the actor's costume.

We would expect EVR's Non-Brahmin cosmopolitanism to reject attachments that claim an underlying noumenal reality distinguishing human kinds (nation/caste/race) in favour of the constant change in phenomenal appearance actualizing humankind (*vesham*/costume). Yet in December 1933, *vesham* seemed implied when EVR named local attachments as *mere* appearance— 'style', 'clothing', 'food', 'attitude', 'moustache', 'hairstyle'—which are obstructive 'customs of the national affairs of the age', 'unsuitable for sense and understanding' given progressive global 'struggles whose basis is reason' generating 'the freedom of the people'. 'There will never be any obstruction to the flow ... of the age ... bringing about revolution' evident in progress from *mere appearance* to what *actually appears*: 'nowadays ... we value more that which is made clear through explanation of what is directly-seen-before-us [*pratyaksa*] and the experts who have learned from books' based in 'science'.

And we would expect Periyar's Dravidian nationalism to dismiss mere phenomenal appearance as distracting from an underlying noumenal reality grounding identity. Instead, Periyar is far more ambivalent. Take the December 1943 speech quoted earlier, which continued EVR's insistence on conversion from Hinduism to Islam, based on this-worldly 'Self-Respect' rather than other-worldly 'sacred texts', 'as the best religion for … creating unity and social Self-Respect for yourselves—not a spiritual act'.[39] On the one hand, *vesham* is associated with religious difference as superficial cover for underlying shared identity, as we might expect.

> Many Muslims have put on a costume [*vesham*] like Hindus … [and] like Europeans…. If you go and look at Nagore, you'll know whether there is any sort of difference between Hindus and Muslims apart from costume…. [At its] temple and festival … [t]here is Hindu–Muslim in costume only. Moreover, there is not the slightest difference in religious principles … between a Hindu of Self-Respect and a Muslim of Self-Respect …

With an underlying Self-Respect as members of humankind, 'Muslim' and 'Hindu' are mere *vesham*. Yet, on the other hand, *vesham* seems to be the definitive feature of Islamic conversion:

> By Islam, do not think that I am speaking about the God, Prophet, or Quran of Islam. I am speaking about the topi and lungi of Islam.
>
> Put on the Turkish topi and wear the red lungi. Look at what'll happen. No matter how afflicted with asthmatic disease, if someone puts on a military uniform, it is as if a stiffness comes to him…. If someone wears the topi and lungi himself—no matter how much he may be a coward, dishonourable, or self-interested without the feeling of honour—he'll get bravery, honour, and the courage to lay down his life for society. It'll give an appearance that will cause hesitation, from the Government to the Brahmin, and put a bit of fire in their mind.

Vesham—topi and lungi—is not *mere* appearance but *actualizing* appearance. The noumenal—as some deeper biological (asthmatic disease) or psychological (cowardly self-interest) reality—is overcome through *vesham*'s realization of humankind's Self-Respect. Self-Respect is distinct from *mere* costume. Yet *actualizing* costume creates Self-Respect.

In short, the phenomenon of *vesham*'s appearance in Non-Brahmin Self-Respect persists despite the rise of the noumenon of *inam*'s race with Dravidian Self-Rule. The unresolved role of the actor's costume in Non-Brahmin political theory—where *vesham* is *mere appearance*, irrelevant for humankind, or *actualizing appearance*, performatively constituting humankind—troubles any folk psychology suggestion that the detachments of EVR's Non-Brahmin *kasmapalittan*, as humankind, were necessarily remedied by the attachments of Periyar's Dravidian *neshan*, as a kind of human. Instead, the shift from EVR's Non-Brahmin to Periyar's Dravidian did not resolve *vesham*'s tensions but revealed the importance of their persistence.[40]

The second reason has to do with a confused stage.

Rather than Dravidian nationalist attachments filling some vacuum left by Non-Brahmin cosmopolitan detachments, the Non-Brahmin suddenly found itself by 1937 sharing a hostile global stage with Aryanism's transcontinental rise across Hitler's Nazi Europe and Gandhi's Congress India:

> ... Aryan division and caste either destroy or take non-Aryans as slaves ... The principle of Hitler and the Nazi establishment is that the non-Aryan should be destroyed. The principle of our country's Congress and the principle of Gandhi used as an Aryan coolie is just like that.... [S]aying that 'India should be revived according to the Congress, Manu Dharma, and the path of the Varnashrama' proves our claim. Furthermore, regardless of which bases one may provide for the Aryan, the non-Aryan country is a *mleccha* country, the non-Aryan language is a *mleccha* language, [and] non-Aryans are *mleccha*, demon, and devil—one can see such rationalizing even today.[41]

With a world no longer humankind's egalitarian refuge, as EVR suggested in the 1920s, freedom for human kinds gained appeal for Periyar by the 1940s. Though space does not permit further elaboration, suffice it to say here that the historical conjuncture where Brahminical Aryanism at home was understood to saturate the world abroad preceding the 1944 collapse of the Non-Brahmin SRM into the DK troubles any claim that cosmopolitanism's detachment left a vacuum inevitably filled by nationalism's attachment. Dravidian nationalism may not have been filling the void of Non-Brahmin cosmopolitanism as much as the world stage was no longer an egalitarian scene of cosmopolitan remedy to local hierarchies but instead a brutally hierarchical proscenium demanding egalitarian home remedies. On this account, the Dravidian may have simply been an effort to give Non-Brahmin phenomenal hope a noumenal chance—consequently complicating performative actualizations through *vesham*'s appearance.

Conclusion

The conjunction 'and' in a 'chapter on Periyar and nationalism' is no accidental feature of political thought in twentieth-century Tamil-speaking South India. 'Periyar' is the name of a leader for a people called 'Dravidian', and both were taking shape after 1937 alongside the growing nationalist demand 'Dravida Nadu for the Dravidian'. However, the separatist nationalism behind Periyar's Dravidian was not the fulfilment but the failure of the humanist internationalism behind EVR's Non-Brahmin. Rather than a person leading his loyal people, EVR was critical of leadership's authority while 'Non-Brahmin' addressed humankind refusing loyalties to kinds of human. More specifically, I have argued that EVR's Non-Brahmin, revolving around *vesham*'s costume, emphasized the equality of humankind through the phenomena of transformational performative roles and inclusive address prioritizing 'Self-Respect'. In contrast, Periyar's Dravidian, revolving around *inam*'s biology, emphasized the independence of kinds of humans through the noumena of an underlying racial reality and exclusive identity prioritizing 'Self-Rule'. Read as addressing democratic tensions between state and nation, EVR's Non-Brahmin cosmopolitanism was the iconoclastic refusal of attachments to create 'Self-Respect' rather than the literate appreciation of attachments animating anti-colonial 'Self-Rule', thereby suggesting humankind's law stood above any peoples as kinds of humans.

One might claim that Periyar's Dravidian race was simply one of EVR's Non-Brahmin roles. If so, this resolution of *inam* into *vesham* must account for the unresolved tension between Periyar's Dravidian and EVR's Non-Brahmin. Consider two pieces published in December 1944, shortly after the creation of the DK: an editorial titled 'Hitlerism and Aryanism', representing late period investments, and a speech titled 'The Evils Coming from Aryanism Produce Danger for the World' by S. Ramanathan, a formative figure of the early period. Both frame Tamil-speaking South India as world-historical vanguard: Aryanism's recent brutality abroad had been experienced at home for millennia.

The editorial suggests that continental efforts provide a model for subcontinental ones in a national frame. Noting that 'the *ariyanicam* (Aryanism) called *hitlaricam* (Hitlerism)', originating 'from the subcontinent called India', now experienced world-wide 'in the very same distinct manner', had inspired difference-based 'fighting to get back lost independence and rights ... protect[ing]' each nation's 'arts, language, civilization, and customs', the editorial concludes:

> If such tremendous effort is made to eradicate Hitlerism, which has taken root [in Europe] for only a few years, just consider how much greater effort must be made ... to chop down the poisonous tree of the Aryan [in India], grown as tall as a skyscraper, whose taproot ... has taken hold for many thousands of years.[42]

Ramanathan's speech suggests, instead, that subcontinent provides a model for continent. Naming 'Hitlerism ... not Hitler' as today's 'most important problem', Ramanathan notes how a 'nationalist' Congress fosters 'Gandhism like the Hitlerism' posing 'such great danger for the world' through hierarchical brutality:

> Hitlerism was born from the Aryan womb; the Varnashrama, the Hindu religion ... and Gandhism were born from the Aryan womb just like that. Why, when it is said that Hitlerism should be destroyed, shouldn't these be destroyed? ... In South India, it was the Non-Brahmin party that had the might to understand and oppose Gandhism's danger ... [I]t is we that have been opposing Aryanism for the longest time. Therefore it is Dravida Nadu that should ... destroy Aryanism–Gandhism ... to shine as a guide to the world.[43]

Furthermore, the editorial's Dravidian underscores *inam*'s race and Periyar's authority:

> the people living in South India are all the same race ... [A]mong us there is no difference—none superior, none inferior ... [The]...only...way before us today ... is to be disciplined with the feeling of the Dravidian race, to swell and rise as one race, and to stand under the leadership of the indefatigable Periyar and fight ... [T]he Dravidar Kazhagam ... has been formed ... so as to swell as one ... to eradicate Aryanism and ... to free this country's people from Aryan slavery ...

Ramanathan, in contrast, repeatedly identifies with the Non-Brahmin project, sidelining Periyar while worried about the Dravidian's focus on race:

> In this country, the Muslim League, the Scheduled Class, and the Non-Brahmin should join together and fight ... the real danger of Gandhism ... I believe that the Dravidian Movement will act in a manner that will illustrate to the world the equality of all, without the difference of caste–religion [or] ... mahatma and ordinary people. [But] claiming that there is a Dravidian

'race' is not clear to me. If some of the doubts I have were resolved, I could join this Dravidian Movement ...

Ramanathan delivered this speech in Erode at a DK celebration chaired by 'General Comrade C. N. Annadurai'. Annadurai's meteoric rise during the late period of the SRM would propel him to lead the Dravidian into postcolonial electoral politics with his 1949 'Dravida Munnetra Kazhagam' (DMK) becoming the first regional party to win Indian state-level elections in 1967. The summary of events after Ramanathan's conclusion displays remarkable brevity: 'after ... the Chair spoke clearly with evidence about "race"'. Whatever such clarity entailed, Ramanathan's speech illustrates the persistence of EVR's Non-Brahmin Self-Respect, where an equality premised on the phenomenal performance of roles actualized a cosmopolitan humankind, despite the rise of Periyar's Dravidian Self-Rule, where an independence premised on the noumenal reality of race established the nationalism of kinds of human. Given temptations towards authoritarianism, essentialisms, and Great-Men histories, perhaps our political challenge remains how being available to a suspect's address allows us to go undeceived: 'When seeing a play in a playhouse ... you see acting involving a human changing costume over and over ... Think of us just like that and listen to what we say.'[44]

Notes

1. 'S. I. L. F. (Justice) Province Conference: A Conference Unseen [before in] Salem: A Procession of 30,000 Individuals ... Long Live Periyar, Dravida Nadu for the Dravidian, Let the Dravidar Kazhagam Flourish...' and Editorial, 'Salem Conference', *Kudi Arasu* 2 September 1944, p. 1.
2. E. V. Ramasamy, 'Shriman E.V. Ramasamy Naicker in Tiruvarur: The Essence of His Speech: 28-3-26', *Kudi Arasu*, 18 April 1926, pp. 2, 4.
3. This phrase draws inspiration from Geetha and Rajadurai (1998).
4. *Kudi Arasu*, 2 May 1925.
5. For more on the immediate Non-Brahmin reaction to the outcome of the 1936–1937 provincial elections mandated by the Government of India Act, 1935, see 'Loss to Congress in Every Province', *Kudi Arasu*, 14 February 1937.
6. Justice, 'Congress and the Non-Brahmin', *Kudi Arasu*, 14 March 1937, pp. 9, 16. For Non-Brahmin opposition to the Congress's mandatory Hindi, see related articles from Putuvai Cuvami Cuttananta Paratiyaravarkal, 'Does the Tamilian Want Hindi? We Want the Mother Language and English', *Kudi Arasu*, 31 October 1937, pp. 9, 13, to 'Mandatory Hindi's Annihilation: The Mandatory Hindi Brought About by [Rajagopal]accariyar Has Been Sealed and Sacked!! Hereafter Be Ready for the Next Struggle! Heroic Tamilians! Victory is Ours!', *Kudi Arasu*, 25 May 1940, p. 9.
7. 'SILF (Justice) District Conference', and Editorial, 'Salem Conference' in *Kudi Arasu*, 2 September 1944.
8. For a background on the global 'Aryan', see Halbfass (1988); Trautmann (1997); Marchand (2009).
9. 'Opening of the Trichy Conference!' *Viduthalai*, 7 January 1955, p. 1.
10. E. V. Ramasamy, 'Public Meeting in Nakai: E.V. Ramasamy's Lecture; 5000 Persons Gathered', *Kudi Arasu*, 11 October 1931, pp. 9, 11–13.

11. From *Sunday Observer*, 20 November 1938, republished as 'The Periyar of India's Periyars', *Kudi Arasu*, 4 December 1938, pp. 5, 16.
12. For example, E. V. Ramasamy, 'Mr. Mohammad Nabi's Birthday Celebration', *Kudi Arasu*, 25 August 1929, p. 7.
13. Ramasamy, 'Public Meeting in Nakai'.
14. Editorial, 'Tamilian Conference', *Kudi Arasu*, 8 November 1925, pp. 6–7.
15. E. V. Ramasamy, 'What Is the Abolition of Brahminism? The Shyness and the Fury of Kumbakonam's "Brahmin"', *Kudi Arasu*, 19 September 1926, p. 9.
16. Editorial, 'The Simon Commission and Communal Representation', *Kudi Arasu*, 16 December 1928, pp. 10–11.
17. E.V. Ramasamy, 'The Institution of the Self-Respect Association', *Kudi Arasu*, 19 December 1926, pp. 7–8, 13.
18. Editorial, 'The Simon Commission and Communal Representation'.
19. M. S. S. Pandian suggests that attributing 'race theory' to EVR is wrong, encouraged by 'translating the Tamil word *inam* into English as race' whereas this 'dexterous Tamil word … can signify different forms of community' (Pandian, 1993, ft 18, p. 2287). My effort in this chapter is—however unwisely—to resist inhabiting the ambiguity of EVR's thought in favour of distinguishing, rather than conflating, Non-Brahmin and Dravidian. Moreover, when Pandian subsequently cites EVR's claim, 'None can divide the south Indian people into two races by means of any blood test.… [T]he fundamental difference between two different cultures, Aryan and Dravidian, cannot be refuted', published in the English daily *The Hindu* (26 January 1950), such English citations of EVR's Tamil do not clarify, but merely reproduce, the questions of translation Pandian otherwise helpfully underscores.
20. E. V. Ramasamy, 'If You Don't Become Muslims: Even Two Thousand Self-Rules Would Be Useless: Whatever Happened to Comrade M. C. Raja's Bill? Is There a Man to Struggle for You? Even If There Was Struggle, Would There Be Any Benefit? Periyar's Oration in Chennai', *Viduthalai*, 28 June 1943, p. 3.
21. 'The Kanchi Conference Event: Passed Resolutions', *Kudi Arasu*, 9 June 1940, p. 12.
22. E. V. Ramasamy, 'An Explanation of Aryan and Non-Aryan', *Kudi Arasu*, 17 September 1939, pp. 3, 4, 17–18.
23. 'Ten Figments of Shriman Chakravarti Rajagopalachariyar's Imagination', *Kudi Arasu*, 6 December 1925, pp. 9–10.
24. Editorial, 'Brahminism Trouble in the Name of Temples', *Kudi Arasu*, 13 February 1927, pp. 10–11.
25. EVR as quoted in the editorial 'Salem Conference', *Kudi Arasu*, 3 September 1944, p. 4.
26. Ceylon Em. Irajamanikkam, 'Honourable Achariyar's Dictatorial Theatrics—No Difference between Hitler's Speech and Achariyar's Speech—Both Are the Same Style!', *Kudi Arasu*, 2 October 1938, p. 5.
27. Tolar Ma. Cinkaravelu, 'Bolshevism, Fascism, and Nazism. *Polshivisam, Pasisam, Nasisam*', *Kudi Arasu*, 6 August 1933, pp. 3, 17–18.
28. Tirucci Achariyar Ke Vi Es. Vas BA (honours), 'Jean Jacques Rousseau or He Who Gave Political Rights to All: Society a Shackle—Religion a Poison', *Puratchi*, 3 June 1934, pp. 5, 15–16.
29. Dismissal of Diogenes as 'a Socrates gone mad' may encourage reapproaching prevalent analogies between EVR/Periyar and Socrates.

30. Rigorous examinations of cosmopolitanism include Cheah and Robbins (1998).
31. E. V. Ramasamy, 'Birth-Right and Its Obstacles', *Kudi Arasu*, 9 January 1927: pp. 6, 11.
32. E. V. Ramasamy, 'The First Karaikudi District Political Conference; Chairman Shriman E. V. Ramasamy Naicker's Speech', *Kudi Arasu*, 21 June 1925, pp. 4–5.
33. A Nationalist Traitor, 'Bigotry against the Institute of Indian Medicine: The Dismantling of Tamil Medicine', *Kudi Arasu*, 6 December 1931, pp. 7, 14.
34. It is tempting to insist that political projects need not insist on 'undifferentiated unity' but instead could support 'differentiation without domination' (Adorno, 2005, p. 47). For an exploration of the Non-Brahmin's effort to do this through Marxism, see Baxter (2016).
35. Editorial, 'What Does Our Country Need? Political Correction? Social Correction?', *Kudi Arasu*, 2 February 1928, pp. 10–12.
36. E. V. Ramasamy, 'Kodaikanal *Kasmapalittan* Reading Room; Opening Festivity; Mr. Soundarapandian, E. V. Ramasamy, and Their Visit; Thousands of People—Men and Women—Follow a Great Procession with Musicians', *Kudi Arasu*, 27 July 1930, pp. 8–9, 12.
37. E. V. Ramasamy, 'What Does Civilization Mean?', *Puratchi*, 31 December 1933, pp. 3, 18.
38. *Manita jivakarunyam ulaka cakotarattuvam makkal apimanam.*
39. Ramasamy, 'If You Don't Become Muslims', p. 3.
40. In lieu of further discussion, we might wonder about Non-Brahmin articulations of sensual receptivity to animate iconoclastic refusal, in contrast to cognitive attachments animating the appreciation of difference. For one related effort, see Baxter (2020).
41. Editorial, 'Brahmin Rule: What Should Be Done?' *Kudi Arasu*, 7 August 1938, p. 10.
42. 'Hitlaricamum Ariyanicamum', *Kudi Arasu*, 30 December 1944, pp. 6–8.
43. 'Ariyattinal Varum Timai: Ulakirke Apayattai Vilaivikkum', *Kudi Arasu*, 9 December 1944, pp. 12, 11.
44. Ramasamy, 'Public Meeting in Nakai'.

References

Primary Tamil Sources

Kudi Arasu (Republic, that is, 'Resident's Rule')
Puratchi (Revolution)
Viduthalai (Freedom)

Secondary Sources

Adorno, Theodor W. 2005. *Critical Models: Interventions and Catchwords*. New York: Columbia University Press.
Arendt, Hannah. 1973 (1958). *The Origins of Totalitarianism*. New York: Meridian Books.
Baxter, Matthew H. 2016. 'Bhutams of Marx and the Movement of Self-Respecters'. *History of Political Thought* 37(2): 336–359.
———. 2019. 'Two Concepts of Conversion at Meenakshipuram: Seeing Through Ambedkar's Buddhism and Being Seen in EVR's Islam'. *Comparative Studies of South Asia, Africa and the Middle East* 39(2): 264–281.

———. 2020. 'The Politics of Embrace'. *Seminar: The Untranslated in Translation* 726 (February): 25–31.
Bose, Sugata, and Kris Manjapra (eds.). 2010. *Cosmopolitan Thought Zones: South Asia and the Global Circulation of Ideas*. London: Palgrave Macmillan.
Butler, Judith. 1990. *Gender Trouble: Feminism and the Subversion of Identity*. New York: Routledge.
Chatterjee, Partha. 1986. *Nationalist Thought and the Colonial World: A Derivative Discourse?* London: Zed Books for the United Nations University.
———. 2020. 'I Am the People'. In *I Am the People: Reflections on Popular Sovereignty Today*, pp. 73–122. New York: Columbia University Press.
Cheah, Pheng. 2008. 'What Is a World? On World Literature as World-Making Activity'. *Daedalus* 137(3): 26–38.
Cheah, Pheng, and Bruce Robbins (eds.). 1998. *Cosmopolitics: Thinking and Feeling Beyond the Nation*. Minneapolis: University of Minnesota Press.
Du Bois, W. E. B. 2007. *The Souls of Black Folk*, edited by Brent Hayes Edwards. New York: Oxford University Press.
Dudley, Donald R. 1998. *A History of Cynicism from Diogenes to the 6th Century AD* (2nd edn). London: Bristol Classical Press.
Economic and Political Weekly. 1974. 'Passing of the Periyar'. *Economic and Political Weekly* 9(1–2): 13–15.
Geetha, V., and S. V. Rajadurai. 1998. *Towards a Non-Brahmin Millennium: From Iyothee Thass to Periyar*. Calcutta: Samya.
Gellner, Ernest. 1983. *Nations and Nationalism*. Ithaca: Cornell University Press.
Halbfass, Wilhelm. 1988. *India and Europe: An Essay in Understanding*. Albany: State University of New York Press.
Indian Express. 2022. 'Tamil Nadu: Periyar Statue Desecrated in Coimbatore'. 10 January.
Kant, Immanuel. 2004. *Prolegomena to Any Future Metaphysics That Will Be Able to Come Forward as Science: With Selections from the Critique of Pure Reason* (2nd edn). Edited by Gary Hatfield. Cambridge: Cambridge University Press.
Lenin, V. I., and Joseph Stalin. 1970. *Selections from V. I. Lenin and J. V. Stalin on National Colonial Question*. Calcutta: Calcutta Book House.
Marchand, Suzanne L. 2009. *German Orientalism in the Age of Empire: Religion, Race, and Scholarship* (reprint edn). Cambridge: Cambridge University Press.
Merleau-Ponty, Maurice. 2005. *Phenomenology of Perception*. New York: Routledge.
Mouffe, Chantal. 2005. *On the Political*. London: Routledge.
Nietzsche, Friedrich. 2006. *On the Genealogy of Morality* (2nd edn), translated by Carol Diethe. Cambridge: Cambridge University Press.
Nussbaum, Martha C. 1997. 'Kant and Stoic Cosmopolitanism'. *Journal of Political Philosophy* 5(1): 1–25.
Pandian, M. S. S. 1993. '"Denationalising" the Past: "Nation" in E. V. Ramasamy's Political Discourse'. *Economic and Political Weekly* 28(42): 2282–2287.
———. 2007. *Brahmin and Non-Brahmin: Genealogies of the Tamil Political Present*. Delhi: Permanent Black.
Schmitt, Carl. 2007. *The Concept of the Political* (expanded edn). Chicago: University of Chicago Press.

Shaw, George Bernard. 2013. *Saint Joan*. New Delhi: Peacock Books.
Trautmann, Thomas R. 1997. *Aryans and British India*. Berkeley: University of California Press.
Visswanathan, E. Sa. 1983. *The Political Career of E. V. Ramasami Naicker: A Study in the Politics of Tamil Nadu, 1920–1949*. Madras: Ravi & Vasanth.
Warner, Michael. 2002. 'Publics and Counterpublics'. *Public Culture* 14(1): 49–90.
Young, Iris Marion. 1990. *Justice and the Politics of Difference*. Princeton: Princeton University Press.

4
Periyar and the Forging of a Horizontal Dravidian–Tamil Solidarity

Vignesh Karthik K. R.*

A little over a hundred years after the non-Brahmin manifesto put forth by the South Indian Liberal Federation, better known as the Justice Party, in 1916 that advocated for adequate representation for non-Brahmin groups, Tamil Nadu's legislative assembly is India's most diverse in terms of caste representation (Verniers et al., 2021).

This legislative assembly's diverseness has been often attributed to the capacious Dravidian–Tamil[1] identity and its ethos, which continue to inform the politics of the Dravidian parties that have governed the state since 1967. The capaciousness of the ethos that defines the Dravidian–Tamil identity, which has allowed for horizontal solidarities across caste groups that otherwise share a hierarchical relationship, stems from the socio-economic and cultural aspirations of these groups. These horizontal solidarities and aspirations continue to derive both their legitimacy and sustainability from the ever incremental and yet radical, anti-caste episteme and activism of Periyar. This chapter is an attempt to engage with him and the way his ideas may be located or traversed both within and outside the literature of other academics, intellectuals, and scholars not just of the subcontinent but across the world. His anti-caste episteme and the vocabulary of his activism are informed by a demand for adequate representation of non-Brahmins—grounded either in their demographic weight or in a historically embedded sense of tension with Brahminical hegemony. Additionally, it embodies within itself a pluralism in identity politics, an evasion of the archaic understanding of caste by giving it a temporal and empirical context and an incorporation of a sense of self-respect as pivotal in the struggle against oppression and social degradation.

---

* I wish to sincerely thank Professor Christophe Jaffrelot and Dr Kriti Kapila for their comments and feedback on an earlier draft of this chapter. Further, I presented a version of this chapter at the Political Studies Association Conference, 2022, at the University of York in a panel titled 'Egalitarian Thought Among Indian Anti-Caste Radicals' chaired by Professor Meena Dhanda and Dr Karthick Ram Manoharan. I thank them both for organizing the panel, their comments, and feedback. My heartfelt gratitude to Jeyannathann Karunanithi, Saumya Gupta, and Raghunath Nageswaran for their help, and Laxman Pararasasingam and Meesam Ali for their support.

Self-Respect as the Engine of Anti-caste Dravidian Politics

The periodic elections in India since the latter part of the nineteenth century saw the gradual extension of electoral franchise. The Government of India Act, 1935, was an important legislation whereby around 17 per cent of the country's adult population, which included some women, was given voting rights (Metcalf and Metcalf, 2006, p. 195). The Indian National Congress that was not keen on fighting elections in the previous decade, decided to enter the electoral turf given its considerable popularity among the common public. In the Madras Presidency, the Justice Party was losing its sheen, largely owing to its weaknesses on three counts: first, it could not shed its elitist image; second, it was unable to mount a critique of the colonial government's deflationary economic policies during the Great Depression that aggravated economic suffering; and third, it failed to ameliorate that suffering despite being in power (Manikumar, 2003, pp. 166–199). The elites from Brahmin and non-Brahmin castes in the Congress and other parties garnered the support of the Depressed Classes to secure power (Baker, 1976, p. 577).

Recognizing a chance to politically mobilize the Depressed Classes in the mid-1930s, Periyar proposed a strategy that could empower them to assert their rights more effectively. On 15 March 1936, he wrote that unlike the unfettered patronage extended to Brahmins earlier, the British colonial government was courting both Brahmins and non-Brahmins taking note of the tensions between the two. Brahmins therefore were perpetuating propaganda against the government with nationalistic overtones.[2] Consequently, the Brahmins, the government, and the non-Brahmins were all seeking the support of the Depressed Classes to retain or come to power. Periyar considered this an opportune moment for the Depressed Classes to articulate their aspirations and argued that their position in the political landscape was in the ascendant as a result of the contradictions between Brahmins and non-Brahmins, and Brahmins and the government. He claimed that every group was reaching out to the Depressed Classes for their narrow political interests and not to resolve their concerns. He cautioned the Depressed Classes against the manoeuvres of the Brahmins and urged them to negotiate with the government, rather than protest, to receive social benefits, in spite of any differences of opinion and resistance they may have.[3]

Drawing from Karthick Ram Manoharan's (2022, pp. 62–63) reading of Periyar within the anarchist tradition, it can be argued that Periyar believed in and followed a systematic and relentless approach towards unsettling preexisting societal norms. He consciously held on to a rational sensibility towards issues he dealt with be it in the cultural or secular spheres. Periyar's politics could also be viewed through Nancy Fraser's (Fraser et al., 2004, pp. 375–381) triad of recognition (of particularistic grievances), redistribution (of resources), and representation (in power), the vehicle to achieve these being self-respect. In response to the lack of political agency of the lower castes, Periyar advocated the idea of *suyamariyathai* or self-respect as the prime tenet of his conception of the Dravidian–Tamil identity. Self-respect helped Periyar advance his critique of the caste system in a multipronged way by problematizing inequality between genders, lower caste-groups, and the untouchables as against a narrow framework of difference between Brahmins and the non-Brahmin Vellalas. Through the Self-Respect Movement (SRM), Periyar criticized the leaders of the Justice Party, too, for being elitist in their approach and their alienation from the masses.

The concept of self-respect was critical to Periyar's engagement with the question of caste to arrive at a horizontal Dravidian–Tamil solidarity. He rigorously went after the majority intermediate and lower castes and punctured their sense of a valorized history and self. Without a concerted effort, Periyar believed, any forged identity would merely result in a people who perpetuate the larger discriminatory ethos of Hinduism. By making Hinduism and Brahmins the outsiders and promoting a politics based on empirical socio-economic and political realities, he was able to flatten the otherwise hierarchical Dravidian–Tamil society. According to Periyar, caste was an attack on dignity and the idea of self, which were at the core of caste-based oppression and deprivation. He was thus rooting for 'suyamariyathai' as an organic and perennial solution. Thus, Periyar's characterization of the anti-caste episteme through the lens of dignity, self-respect, and oppression challenges the logic and methodology that Louis Dumont (1972), M. N. Srinivas (1952), and other scholars undertook in theorizing the caste system.

Periyar's engagement with the notion of dignity allowed him the versatility to deal with the question of mobility not just through demands for access but also by forging broader solidarities amongst various groups. This went beyond mimicking the template of hierarchy as caste unlike Dumont (1972, p. 20), or ignoring the role of religion and rituals in such struggles unlike Srinivas (1952, p. 32). Periyar's rallying cry was for creating a dent in the ossified social structure by attempting to co-opt the material and metaphysical meanings of positions of power in society. On 11 April 1964, in a speech delivered in Madras city, Periyar stated that if the hegemony of caste was to be unsettled, then one way would be to democratize opportunity and access to all occupations hitherto regarded to be hereditary. For instance, the positions of village accountant, administrative officer, local police personnel, and so on, could be opened up to the Depressed Classes and lower backward castes irrespective of lineage and family connections. This would be a blow to the arrogance that stems from caste position, thereby paving the way for coexistence and dignity. Without such vital structural changes, a rallying cry for annihilation of caste would only ring empty.[4]

The lexicon of assertion and caste association found room within Periyar's and the Justice Party's language of a Dravidian–Tamil consciousness. Caste associations helped Periyar grapple with the herculean task of galvanizing a mass movement out of socio-economic and political aspirations and transforming the idea of 'suyamariyathai' into conventional wisdom. He actively participated in various caste conferences from the mid-1920s until the late 1940s including a few Depressed Class conferences. As a result of Periyar's influence, these caste organizations extended their work towards the socio-economic and educational mobility of their members.

Unity of the Oppressed Sans Uniformity

Periyar's speeches in caste organizations after the establishment of the SRM in 1925 were instrumental in raising awareness and advocating for the upliftment of lower-caste groups. He consistently emphasized the idea that no group was inherently superior or inferior to others, a principle that was foundational to his politics of equality and social justice. This approach resonates with Ambedkar's critical analysis of the caste system which he described as thriving on the basis of relational distinctions, particularly through the concept of ritual purity (1979 [1916], p. 20). Ambedkar observed that this hierarchical structure was not only maintained by the upper castes but was also internalized by the lower castes, who, in turn, perpetuated the system to protect their own societal standing. This internalization (Ambedkar, 1935) made the caste system exceptionally resilient and deeply rooted in Indian society, contributing to the normalization of caste-based violence.

While Ambedkar recognized the importance of political action to address the tangible impacts of caste-based deprivation, such as economic and social inequalities, Periyar focused on the more complex and contentious intersections within the lower castes and the Depressed Classes. By engaging with these groups, Periyar sought to challenge the internalized hierarchies and social dynamics that sustained caste discrimination. His work aimed at dismantling the very foundations of caste-based oppression by addressing both the psychological and material aspects of the system, thereby complementing Ambedkar's broader political strategies.

In this way, Periyar's efforts can be seen as a practical application of Ambedkar's theoretical insights, focusing specifically on the intricate social interactions and conflicts within the lower strata of the caste hierarchy. By doing so, he not only amplified the voices of the most marginalized but also worked to weaken the entrenched beliefs that upheld the caste system, making his approach a critical component in the broader struggle for social justice. While Ambedkar's political action engaged with the extreme ends of the caste system, that is, the Brahmins and the Dalits, drawing from purposive compilations of Periyar's speeches and writings by journalists and activists (Thirumavelan, 2018; Subagunarajan, 2018), I argue that Periyar worked far more in the restive and warring intersections of the lower castes and Depressed Classes.

Periyar's repeated iteration of the notion of equality among lower-caste groups in his speeches both solidified the antagonism vis-à-vis the Brahmin and sought to flatten the hierarchy among the lower-caste groups, thereby rectifying a mistake that the early Dravidian identities committed. He categorically maintained that the empowerment of the Depressed Classes would be possible only through their will and action and that no other community would help them owing to the prevalent graded inequality. In a speech delivered among Adi Dravidar Youth in Erode in 1932, he called upon them to prepare for a bold revolution. Imploring them to question why they were depressed, he urged that if they thought God was responsible, then to set out and break the idols; if it was a religious order, to dismember the religion; if it was monarchy, then to destroy it; if it was through the trickery and selfishness of individuals, then to assertively declare that this could not go on.[5]

Periyar was an informed leader inclined towards forging a counter-hegemonic alliance of lower castes but not by blurring internal differences and conflicts among caste groups. Such an approach would have yielded quicker results but would subvert the ethos of social justice in a caste society. So, while engaging with both non-Brahmin lower castes and Adi Dravidars, he consciously avoided equating their struggles. He always addressed the grievances particular to each caste group without smothering the rather clear socio-economic differences. With time and concerted efforts vis-à-vis the lower and Depressed Classes, he positioned himself and other like-minded individuals not as the voices of or the representatives of the cause of the Depressed Classes but as comrades who had got together to forge an equitable society (Manoharan, 2020, p. 8). This conscious acknowledgment of the variance of grievances allowed for a more stable allyship, where no interest group had to surrender to the numerical or social might of the other or an ideology that would not yield perceivable benefits.

Periyar was acutely aware of the significant role that identities play in people's lives, particularly in the context of caste. He campaigned vigorously against the use of derogatory names for the Depressed Classes, advocating instead for terms that would reflect dignity and self-respect. For example, he supported the use of 'Adi Dravidars', a term introduced in the early 1900s, which conferred an aboriginal status on these communities in their ancestral territories. However, Periyar's advocacy for respectful nomenclature did not equate to an endorsement of names with religious or divine connotations. He was critical of such names as 'Devendra Kulathar' (formerly Pallar) and 'Arunthathiyar' (formerly Sakkiliyar) which invoked sacral or divine imagery. Periyar believed that these revised names, while avoiding derogatory labels, still perpetuated the issues inherent in a caste-based society. He was wary of any form of identity that could entrench hierarchical or parochial thinking and his focus remained on fostering agency, empowerment, rational contestation, and coexistence rather than encouraging the politics of parochial revivalism cloaked as utopia (Pandian, 1994, p.100).

Periyar proposed to identify the oppressor(s) clearly and then add the prefix of 'non-' to the oppressed people. He rationalized this effort, for it reminded people of who the oppressor was and the nature of their oppression while at the same time igniting thought and action to overcome the oppression. For instance, instead of the term Depressed Class people (Odukkappattor), he suggested the adoption of the term Non-Oppressor (Odukkinavar Alladhor; Subagunarajan, 2018, p. 37).

Because the anti-caste episteme pivots around caste groups or communities, one can argue the binary suggested by Periyar was an ambiguous construct. However, the suggested binary sought to forge a people across caste groups and inferiorized identities with a certain degree of inter-group equivalence against the oppressor(s). In other words, a plurality of grievances was accommodated without extinguishing internal differences.

Periyar abhorred the interventions of the government to create exclusionary social infrastructure like separate colonies, separate wells, and separate schools as measures which would never bring to an end the system of caste. Instead, he called upon the government to settle Depressed Class families within the traditional spatial boundaries of the village like the *agraharam*s (exclusive Brahmin quarters) and in streets where the scheduled castes were excluded. Thus, he also attacked the sources of pride from which lower-caste groups derived their social distinctiveness. For Periyar, questioning caste, mindfully acknowledging differences between communities, and advocating self-respect were not ends in themselves but ways of crafting a layered Dravidian–Tamil identity that could claim socio-economic mobility and socio-political representation for marginalized communities.

Despite Periyar's disinclination towards electoral politics, socio-political representation continued to be one of the commanding ideas in his struggle against Brahminism. He had an unusual relationship with electoral politics, where he wanted to stay away from it but appreciated its role in cementing and furthering the ideas of self-respect and social justice in the public sphere (Geetha, 2019). This disinclination never manifested into an indifference towards electoral politics and it also produced one of the most crucial alliances in Tamil politics, that between Periyar and C. N. Annadurai ('Anna') who would become his primary lieutenant in the late 1930s and 1940s. Anna's preference for the electoral path and Periyar's for social action and mobilization demonstrated the unbounded plurality and fluidity of the Dravidian–Tamil ethos. However, this alliance was not without tension, as the two leaders had differing approaches to political power—Periyar's consistent emphasis on building a robust social reform organization stood in contrast to Anna's pragmatic engagement with politics, ultimately leading to the formation of the Dravida Munnetra Kazhagam (DMK) and a breaking away from the Dravidar Kazhagam (DK) in 1949 (Venkatachalapathy, 2024, pp. 70–72). It is this unique ability where politics could mimic the altering realities of caste relations and struggle by deriving both meaning and legitimacy through sociocultural movements that allowed the Dravidian movement to remain both adaptive and deeply rooted in the aspirations of Tamil society, bridging the gap between ideological purity and practical political action, and ensuring its widespread appeal across diverse social strata in Tamil Nadu. One of the key instances where both institutional and electoral paths converged was during the protests against the imposition of Hindi. The Justice Party had suffered a humiliating defeat in the 1937 provincial elections which brought the Congress, a party that was seen to be dominated by Brahmins, to power, with C. Rajagopalachari ('Rajaji') as Premier. The compulsory study of Hindi in schools stoked a Presidency-wide furore. The policy was opposed by the Justice Party, Periyar's SRM, and many other Tamil organizations, who staged protests across the Presidency. In the wake of the protests, Periyar took over the Justice Party at the request of the party's leadership given his popularity and the need for the Justice Party to appeal to a wider populace in light of the enlargement of the electorate.

From this point, Periyar, who was dealing with the question of the socio-economic and cultural mobility of the lower sections of society, moved on to explicitly engaging with the question of language, albeit within the boundaries of his frame of self-respect and equality. Given its marginalized position in comparison to Sanskrit and Hindi, the Tamil language allowed Periyar and later Dravidianists to unite diverse interest groups under the shared Dravidian–Tamil identity. Subsequently, the Justice Party under Periyar changed its character from being a party of a few to a social reform organization of many people, transforming to the DK in 1944.

Dravidian–Tamil: Beyond Language and Territory

Christophe Jaffrelot (2000, p.107) contends that the Dravidian identity has the potential to bridge caste divisions, with language being a critical element of regional identity. However, the experience of Andhra Pradesh highlights the limitations of language as a unifying force. The creation of Andhra State in 1953, Andhra Pradesh in 1956, and its bifurcation in 2014, alongside movements such as Jai Telangana (1969) and Jai Andhra (1972), reveal how language alone could not overcome deep-seated caste and sub-regional conflicts among Telugu-speaking populations.

The modern Telugu language movement, spearheaded by Gidugu Ramamurthy in 1919 after earlier efforts by C. P. Brown, sought to avoid Sanskritization and later incorporated Western literary and Marxist influences (Ramakrishna, 1990, p. 570). However, this movement eventually diverged into two strands: one driven by communist leaders using colloquial language focused on social justice and the other by Congress elites emphasizing a more classical, nationalist approach. This split mirrored broader societal divisions and conflict, particularly within the non-Brahmin movement.

The non-Brahmin movement in the Telugu-speaking regions peaked between 1900 and 1930 but waned due to internal conflicts among the upwardly mobile non-Brahmin castes, particularly Kammas, Reddis, and Velamas (Suri, 2000, p. 3). The competition between these castes for status fragmented the movement and alienated lower castes, ultimately limiting the formation of a unified Telugu identity and instead reflecting the caste pride of dominant groups (Ramaswamy, 1949, p. 300).

Similarly, in Uttar Pradesh, efforts to create a unified identity were undermined by caste-based political mobilizations. The state, often seen as India's 'heartland', faced ongoing tensions due to the inability to forge a common identity across diverse groups, leading to its bifurcation in 2000 (Kudaisya, 2006, pp. 391–392; Tillin, 2012). These cases demonstrate the challenges of using language and regional identity to transcend caste divisions.

In contrast, K. V. Narayana Rao (1973, p. 233) notes that the 'Dravidanadu of E. V Ramasamy [Periyar] was not a province like the Andhra province but a separate autonomous unit based on self-determination.' In fact, the linguistic reorganization movement of the 1950s had a refracted existence in the Tamil-speaking regions of the Madras State. At the same time, the Tamil language served as a means to bind Tamil-speaking people, who believed in the socio-economic mobility of lower castes irrespective of their mother tongue. It is worth noting that Periyar did not prominently partake in the border contestations. In October 2021, the DMK announced that 18 July would be observed as Tamil Nadu Day, celebrating the renaming of the Madras State as Tamil Nadu[6] in 1967. Another date in question is 1 November, which signifies the implementation of the States Reorganisation Act in 1956 when the boundaries were drawn. While the DMK-led government continues to honour the activists and leaders who engaged in border contestations, 18 July is preferred over 1 November.[7] In effect, the outcome was a unique form of regionalism that was driven by a politics of the socio-economic mobility of lower castes to which language and territory were instrumental as against being markers of exclusion and nativist pride.

In other words, the Dravidian–Tamil identity as conceived by Periyar was both capacious and a regulative pivot. The binary of oppressor and non-oppressor paved the way for inclusion of people irrespective of their ascriptive identities. The identity was freed of an ancient utopia and nativist proclivities by infusion of a rational cry for empowerment vis-à-vis the present socio-economic status. Tamil served two purposes. It was a language that unified people who spoke it as against people who exclusively had it as their mother tongue. Further, Tamil rendered largely as a secular canon served as a tool to convey resistance and opened an alternative worldview to the hegemonic worldview imposed by Sanskrit[8] (Venkatachalapthy, 2006, pp. 109–110). In other words, the hyphenated term is capacious not because either of the words are empty signifiers but because in sum the term emerges as a transitive whole thereby continuously accommodating the grievances of the marginalized. The transitive element is also the regulative pivot of the Dravidian–Tamil identity that prevents dousing of internal differences. For instance, a hitherto marginalized community cannot invoke any reason to inflict suffering on another marginalized community. At the same time, once the grievances of the marginalized at the periphery have been mainstreamed, the next iteration will involve a new set of grievances of marginalized communities.

Periyar's Tryst with Communities and Particularistic Grievances

The Congress's attempt to make Hindi compulsory in schools and its indifference towards the flattening of caste hierarchies and reconciliation of diverse interest groups further augmented Periyar's scepticism regarding its outlook on nation and nationalism. In fact, Periyar in his speech in 1973 had a long list of questions that struck at the caste core of the Indian nationhood.

> You say India is a nation. You say, we are all children of the same mother. But do you treat us with love? I ask you, what is the relationship between you and me? Who are you and who am I? You say that you were born from Brahma's forehead and I from his feet. Given this irony, you compel me to be as one with you.[9]

Until his last breath, Periyar viewed the Indian nationhood as an embodiment of the hegemony of Brahmins over subalterns. Despite being termed anti-national, he not only questioned Brahminical hegemony but also the nation-building project.

The Congress's idea of nationalism vis-à-vis caste had already found sharp criticism in the non-Brahmin manifesto (1916). In the run up to the decade of the 1920s, there was an emerging shift towards politics of redistribution and welfare for addressing inequalities prevalent in societies the world over (Piketty, 2022, p. 121). The Justice Party's liberal leadership was not for agitational politics and therefore drew its hope from these developments; the 1919 Government of India Act was a welcome step towards delegation of power and subsequent welfare of the common public (Geetha and Rajadurai, 1998, p. 218). Justice Party leaders were against the Non-cooperation Movement launched by Mahatma Gandhi. Simultaneously, a range of caste associations surfaced that were engaging with the British colonial government for varied reasons. While they initially negotiated for better status within the caste hierarchy or renaming of caste groups—especially Nadars and Vanniyars—with time and the prevalence of a liberal and democratic repertoire, they were bargaining for empowerment and representation in power (Rudolph and Rudolph, 1960, p. 7). The nationalists (many of whom were also non-Brahmins) advanced the argument that the assertions for better status by non-Brahmin leaders were rooted in rivalrous pride that would only have undesirable ramifications for the forging of a unified national identity. In the same vein, caste associations of the times were regarded as hurdles and often criticized as not having even the support of their own caste people whom they claimed to represent.[10]

The limitations of the Justice Party and caste associations revolved around the inability to convert their struggles into a mass movement. A few effective and radical leaders such as W. P. A. Soundarapandian or J. S. Kannappar notwithstanding, the Justice Party could neither communicate its viewpoint beyond the upmarket urban lanes of the Madras Presidency nor fully cater to the grievances of the marginalized. Caste associations, too, could not find a frame within which to work together to mount concerted pressure whenever needed. Although Periyar did not consider the Justice Party leadership and Congress nationalists to be any different, he sympathized with and was appreciative of the legislative and welfare initiatives of the Justice Party (Geetha and Rajadurai, 1998, p. 220).

Periyar contended that caste associations and the voicing of grievances faced by various castes through organized means were legitimate as long as they strove for their empowerment and mobility in the face of Brahminical oppression. In his initial interventions, when caste conferences began to be organized in India, he consistently claimed that it was the minority group of Brahmins that had systematically subjugated large segments of society by relegating them to lower castes in order to maintain their dominance at the top of the social hierarchy. Such claims drew widespread condemnation. A section of non-Brahmins too endorsed these condemnations. Further, Periyar said that none of the castes fell for the propaganda against him and rather saw through the selfish motives of those who did not want their share in power, position, and honours to be allocated to assertive subalterns. He pointed out that every caste had awakened to the caste reality in India and started to rebel against the status quo, demanding equal rights. This led the non-Brahmins who initially opposed caste associations to support these associations, which subsequently started to express concerns regarding the improvement of their castes. He went on to expose the change in the stance of the Brahmins. The Brahmins who had at first condemned the caste associations and their conferences, sensing the imminent danger to their near monopoly on social privilege, also started to organize Brahmin caste conferences, Varnashrama Dharma conferences, and Sanatana Dharma conferences to maintain their hegemony over broader society. He appealed to non-Brahmins to engage with the nationalism question more rationally rather than falling for a farcical unification that did not promise real equality (Subagunarajan, 2018, p. 33).

Drawing from Periyar's writings, it can be argued that while questioning the Congress's stance on nationhood, he was in no way obstructing the anti-colonial struggle.[11] Instead, Periyar reflected on the ways the Brahminical order of Hinduism was inventing and reincarnating itself in the Congress's notions of nationalism.[12] These notions of nationhood and nationalism were deeply embedded within a morality indisputably similar to what Hinduism held. The Congress's nationalism was an alchemy of three crucial factors: it first advocated an imagined and forged commonality as a source of unity in nationhood; next, it rallied communities to forget or quash their differences instead of dealing with them;[13] and finally, while it argued for freedom from an exploitative British rule, it was unwilling to examine the inequalities and cruelty that constituted the sociocultural hegemony of the Indian elites vis-à-vis their caste privilege. It also upheld a certain continuity in terms of who would take over power once the British government left and thus backed Brahminical legitimacy and supremacy in the affairs of the country.[14] For Periyar, the Congress's nationalism was a self-fulfilling prophecy; adopting it to achieve self-rule and freedom from the British would ultimately ensure elite dominance through the Congress's uncontested control over the country's affairs, cloaked in an idealistic and unquestionable narrative. He feared that the Brahmins, through their structural association with the British, would transform the newly unified India into a monolithically caste-organized and Hindu country.[15]

In contrast to the Congress's concepts of nationhood, Periyar's nationalism was fiercely anti-Brahminical at the risk of often being pro-colonial. Before discussing the broader antithetical aspects of Periyar's understanding of nationalism with respect to the Congress's stand, it is important to indicate his position on the colonial government in the matter of caste and the Brahminical social order.

Aloysius has argued that Periyar articulated the transformation of the Brahminical classes from "an indolent, parasitical and merely a consumer group" (2022, p. 143) to meritorious and forward in every aspect of life under British rule, thereby making the Brahmins partners in the colonial project. Such a transformation dubbed the large working-class population as lower castes that were unworthy of higher positions and aspirations. It might seem that like Nicholas Dirks, Periyar too was blaming the British colonial administration for being responsible for the caste system. However, Dirks blamed the replacement of the local kingship in the post-1857 period as being responsible for the caste system as we know it (2002, p. 60) and somewhat absolved the pre-British era of the current conditions of the caste system. He regarded the work of M. A. Sherring, namely,

Hindu Tribes and Castes (1872) as the moment of this shift. He observed, "Gone is the ubiquitous reliance on Manu; orientalism has become empiricist rather than textual …it [has] also eclipsed earlier enthusiasms for things Indian, even if, as in the case of most early orientalists, these enthusiasms were exclusively for ancient Indian civilization …" (Dirks, 1992, pp. 66–67). In short, Dirks argued that the system of caste was Westernized. This claim is frequently echoed by proponents of Hindu nationalism today. They use it as a tool to criticize the colonial administration while simultaneously absolving the elites of their role in perpetuating the blatant discrimination inherent in the caste system in India. Of late, Dirks' argument is extended to claim that there was a glorious past where the caste system was among other things, fluid with no entry and exit barriers. However, Periyar was not absolving the Brahminical order prior to British rule of the conditions of deprivation, exclusion, and discrimination in caste; instead, he was criticizing the British for becoming complicit with such an order and worsening it.

Since Periyar's ideas on nationalism were an antithesis of the Congress's position, it also meant that the essence of discriminatory caste hierarchies that would be continued and replicated in the Congress's model of self-rule had to be challenged. In this context, the category-wise rights of subaltern communities were central to challenging the elite castes' rendition of nationalism. Periyar's idea of nationalism was an outcome of a category-wise rights movement which was in turn an extension of an anti-caste struggle for social justice based on lived and empirical realities (Aloysius, 2022, pp. 127–128).

Conclusion: A Horizontal Identity vis-à-vis Agonism and Becoming

Periyar's definition of category-rights upheld the differences between communities as a source of their uniqueness in nation-building rather than as a reason for the furthering of conflicts between them. While the Brahminical elite of the Congress were in favour of forging an identity where differences were dissolved without any true change in the lived and material realities of a large proportion of people to whom such identity was given, Periyar sought an agonistic society[16] that allowed for differences to exist and coexist through political action. He worked towards constructing an identity based on solidarity across conflicting groups on a negotiatory plane where each subaltern community had agency to assert and strive towards socio-economic and political mobility. In other words, the Dravidian–Tamil identity was a consensus-driven project and every community's aspirations within it were dealt with through contestations and mutual coexistence. He argued that a nation's unity will be stable only when empowered communities come together.[17]

According to Periyar, any category that was politicized, felt left out or oppressed due to any reason, and was asserting their dignity and mobility, had to be recognized. Thus, each subaltern category had a distinctive place in the nation. The nation was therefore a sum of these categories. In Periyar's conception of nationhood, unity—particularly cross-community solidarity—was not an inherent given but a political project that demanded active struggle and sustained commitment to advancing equal rights across diverse groups[18] (Aloysius, 2022, p. 130).

The DMK's later-day engagement with delineating society via the Tamil Nadu Backward Classes (Sattanathan) Commission (1969), the efforts to widen the backward-class lists, legislation related to the most backward class (MBC) sub-categorization, creation of the backward-class-Muslim category, legislation related to the SC-A sub-categorization,[19] and the sub-division of MBCs into three separate categories can now be understood as a natural extension of Periyar's visualization of category-wise rights. However, the larger ambitions of Periyar's politics and his motivations behind the forging of the horizontal Dravidian–Tamil solidarity can be flushed out better via the politics of becoming postulated by William Connolly. Connolly (1996, pp. 255–256) argues that a politics of becoming occurs when a community, subjugated in a given societal framework, asserts to transform itself by revisiting and revising the nature of its identity vis-à-vis the prevalent differences. Such revisions are not openly acknowledged or legitimized as they seek to unsettle the existing status quo. This predicament forces communities to engage in a persistent, experimental and, at times, militant political movement to mainstream themselves and their grievances.

Periyar's struggle against colonial power, Brahminical forces, and other forms of oppression and social degradation was not tied to one social group or just an antagonism towards Brahmins, it was also very reflective of his definition of the Dravidian–Tamil identity. The notion of self-respect, advocacy of category-based rights, an alternative perspective on nationalism, and a declaration of substantive equality were all central to Periyar's concept of the Dravidian–Tamil identity. This ethos created a conducive environment for multiple communities to assert themselves, enabling socio-economic and political mobility. As a result, it continuously opened up opportunities for those on the peripheries to follow and benefit from the movement. This capaciousness to accommodate several elements also lent it another dimension, which was somewhat of a resilience to the test of time but not without being tweaked to the empirical and contemporary realities. Not surprisingly, the transitivity that Periyar offered makes him an irritable icon to both Tamil nativists and caste supremacists who are now engaging with Hindu nationalists in Tamil Nadu. Statues of Periyar across the state of Tamil Nadu have been desecrated since the 2010s citing reasons that are often self-contradictory. However, the works of Periyar are also being widely read and discussed in the recent past on social media platforms by the youth who have been subject to anti-Periyar literature, thereby fostering another round of politicization of people. In sum, while Periyar's politics has not resonated nationally so far, the way it is etched in contemporary politics in Tamil Nadu makes the state a compelling case for other states seeking to further the ideals of constitutional-state autonomy, the federal ethos, and resilience against majoritarian waves.

Notes

1. The Dravidian–Tamil identity is a political offering synthesized since the early decades of the 1900s as a transitive construct with recognition (of particularistic grievances), redistribution (of resources and opportunities), and representation (in power) of subaltern communities as its principal pivots. Its constitution is marked by the simultaneity of bottom–up and top–down approaches. Drawing from M. S. S. Pandian (2007, p.130), I argue that such transitivity has engendered the forging of a discursive insurgence against prevalent hegemonies over time. The Brahminical value-system, primarily expressed through discriminatory social relations; constitutionally mandated asymmetric centre–state relations which were furthered to undermine regional aspirations; and the cultural exceptionalism expressed through the Sanskrit language make for examples. The term Dravidian signifies a historical territory and people marked by egalitarian values and the term Tamil refers to the oldest of the Dravidian family of languages. In the political realm, the term Dravidian emerged in the early twentieth century emanating

from Iyothee Thass and the term Tamil made its political transition in the wake of the 1937 anti-Hindi agitations. However, jointly taken the phrase Dravidian–Tamil is more than a sum of its parts, that is, it fosters a pluralist ethos aimed at the empowerment of the marginalized communities that pose and operate as interest groups. The identity can be subscribed to without any entry restrictions on the lines of gender, caste, religion, and language. Therefore, the phrase retains its essence while acquiring newer meanings as the people who wield it revise it to include newer communities and their aspirations in a steady and incremental manner.

2. 'Rival Dogs [Justice Party] Fight for the Crumbs Dropping from the Governor's Table', *Suthanthira Sangu*, 13 October 1932 in Venkatachalapathy (2006). Many such cartoons were published at the time against the Justice Party.
3. *Kudi Arasu*, 15 March 1936.
4. *Viduthalai*, 16 April 1964.
5. *Kudi Arasu*, 4 December 1932.
6. The demand for renaming the Madras Presidency was put forth by a Congress activist Sankaralinganar. He was a Gandhian who advocated for prohibition of alcohol and urged politicians to give up lavish spending. He went on an indefinite fast on 27 July 1956 with twelve demands, of which renaming Madras State as Tamizhagam (Abode of Tamils) was popular. Despite requests from leaders like C. N. Annadurai, he did not give up and as a result, died on 13 October 1956. K. Kamaraj, a fellow party member and the chief minister of the Madras State, did not pay any heed to the incident or the death, while Anna wrote an obituary in *Dravida Nadu* where he vowed to fulfil Sankaralinganar's demand. Subbu, the DMK's Madurai District Secretary, partook in organizing the funeral procession (Thirunavakkarasu, 2015: 1065–1072).
7. See 'July 18 to Be Observed as Tamil Nadu Day', https://www.thehindu.com/news/national/tamil-nadu/july-18-to-be-observed-as-tamil-nadu-day/article37247211.ece (accessed 21 August 2023).
8. Dipankar Gupta (2000, p. 21) notes that only quantitative or quantifiable concepts should be included in constructing a hierarchy and everything that is qualitative is to be regarded as a difference. The issue with this argument is that it fails to account for the complexity prevalent in society. While Gupta argues that language could not be a part of the hierarchy, it actually is a part of the hierarchy not just in terms of prejudice of power dimensions but in people's minds too, as seen in many countries like India, Sri Lanka, Spain, and so on. And hence, it is often found that while the various iterations of the Dravidian–Tamil identity recognized intra-community differences, they were always posited to challenge hegemonic identities and cultures, in this case the Sanskrit supremacy which legitimized Brahminical practices.
9. *Viduthalai*, 9 December 1973.
10. Thiru. Vi. Kalyanasundaram in *Navasakthi*, 21 May 1926.
11. *Kudi Arasu*, 4 December 1932.
12. *Kudi Arasu*, 11 October 1931.
13. *Kudi Arasu*, 23 August 1931.
14. *Kudi Arasu*, 3 May 1947.
15. *Kudi Arasu*, 13 September 1936.

16. Chantal Mouffe (2000) and Shruti Kapila (2021) have emphasized conflict as an inherent feature of democratic politics in plural societies. Kapila argues that democratic politics involves conflict and contestation, which are vital to the health and dynamism of democracy. Mouffe also sees conflict, specifically agonistic conflict, as central to democracy, where politics is understood as a struggle among diverse groups with irreconcilable differences. Both Kapila and Mouffe reject the notion that democracy should aim for consensus. They believe that striving for consensus can undermine the pluralism that is foundational to democracy. Mouffe specifically criticizes the approach that places consensus at the centre, dominant in many democratic societies, arguing it leads to a democratic deficit (2000, pp. 13–17). Kapila (2021, p. 192), by closely engaging with Ambedkar, brings out the dilemmas of a political icon invested in the socio-economic empowerment of the marginalized. She notes that by arguing against the automatic equation of majority will with popular sovereignty, Ambedkar emphasized the need for a more nuanced understanding of democratic representation that includes minority rights and perspectives (2021, p. 277). As a staunch associate of Ambedkar, Periyar too worked towards constructing an identity based on solidarity across conflicting groups on a negotiatory plane where each subaltern community had agency to assert and strive towards socio-economic and political mobility.
17. *Kudi Arasu*, 6 June 1926.
18. *Kudi Arasu*, 22 November 1925.
19. The SC-A (Scheduled Castes - A) sub-categorization refers to the internal classification within the scheduled castes to ensure a more equitable distribution of affirmative action benefits. It seeks to address disparities wherein certain communities, such as the Arunthathiyars, historically faced barriers in accessing reservations and welfare measures enjoyed by other, relatively better-off scheduled caste groups.

References

Aloysius, G. 2022. 'E. V. Ramasami Periyar on Caste-society and Category-wise Rights'. In *The Routledge Handbook of the Other Backward Classes in India: Thought, Movements and Development* (1st edn), edited by S. Somanaboina and A. Ramagoud, pp. 112–152. Oxon: Routledge. https://doi.org/10.4324/9781003152873.

Ambedkar, B. R. 1935. *Untouchables, or the Children of India's Ghetto*. https://shrigururavidasji.com/site/articles_books/files/ambedkar/48_untouchables-or-the-children-of-india.pdf. Accessed 8 October 2023.

———. 1979 (1916). 'Castes in India: Their Mechanism, Genesis and Development'. Paper presented at the Anthropology Seminar, Columbia University, New York. In *Dr. Babasaheb Ambedkar: Writings and Speeches*, vol. 1, edited by V. Moon, pp. 3–22. Bombay: Education Department, Government of Maharashtra.

Baker, C. 1976. 'The Congress at the 1937 Elections in Madras'. *Modern Asian Studies* 10(4): 557–589.

Connolly, W. 1996. 'Suffering, Justice, and the Politics of Becoming'. *Culture, Medicine and Psychiatry* 20(3): 251–277.

Dirks, N. 1992. 'Castes of Mind'. *Representations* 37: 56–78. DOI: 10.2307/2928654.

———. 2002. *Castes of Mind: Colonialism and the Making of Modern India*. Delhi: Permanent Black.
Dumont, L. 1972. *Homo Hierarchicus: The Caste System and Its Implications*. London: Paladin.
Fraser, N., Hanne Marlene Dahl, Pauline Stoltz, and Rasmus Willig. 2004. 'Recognition, Redistribution and Representation in Capitalist Global Society: An Interview with Nancy Fraser'. *Acta Sociologica* 47(4): 374–382.
Geetha, V. 2019. 'Tracing Periyar's Thinking and Struggles'. Forward Press, 24 June. https://www.forwardpress.in/2019/06/tracing-periyars-thinking-and-struggles. Accessed 28 September 2023.
Geetha V. and S. V. Rajadurai. 1998. *Towards a Non-Brahmin Millennium: From Iyothee Thass to Periyar*. Kolkata: Bhatkal & Sen.
Gupta, D. 2000. *Interrogating Caste: Understanding Hierarchy and Difference in Indian Society*. New Delhi: Penguin Books.
Jaffrelot, C. 2000. 'The Rise of the Other Backward Classes in the Hindi Belt'. *Journal of Asian Studies* 59(1): 86–108. https://doi.org/10.2307/2658585.
Kapila, S. 2021. *Violent Fraternity: Indian Political Thought in the Global Age*. Princeton: Princeton University Press.
Kudaisya, G. 2006. *Region, Nation, 'Heartland': Uttar Pradesh in India's Body Politic*. New Delhi, London: Sage.
Manikumar, K. A. 2003. *A Colonial Economy in the Great Depression, Madras (1929–1937)*. Hyderabad: Orient Longman.
Manoharan, K. R. 2020. 'In the Path of Ambedkar: Periyar and the Dalit Question'. *South Asian History and Culture* 11(2): 136–149. DOI: 10.1080/19472498.2020.1755127.
———. 2022. *Periyar: A Study in Political Atheism*. Hyderabad: Orient Blackswan.
Metcalf, B., and T. Metcalf. 2006. *A Concise History of Modern India*, 2nd edn. Cambridge: Cambridge University Press. doi:10.1017/CBO9780511812750.
Mouffe, C. 2000. 'Deliberative Democracy or Agonistic Pluralism'. Reihe Politikwissenschaft/Political Science Series 72: Stumpergasse. Vienna: Department of Political Science, Institute for Advanced Studies. Retrieved from: https://www.ihs.ac.at/publications/pol/pw_72.pdf. Accessed 25 February 2023.
Narayana Rao, K. V. 1973. *The Emergence of Andhra Pradesh*. Mumbai: Popular Prakashan.
Pandian, M. S. S. 1994. 'Notes on the Transformation of "Dravidian" Ideology: Tamilnadu, c. 1900–1940'. *Social Scientist* 22(5–6): 84–104. DOI: 10.2307/3517904.
———. 2007. *Brahmin and Non-Brahmin: Genealogies of the Tamil Political Present*. New Delhi: Permanent Black.
Piketty, T. 2022. *A Brief History of Equality*. Cambridge, London: The Belknap Press of Harvard University Press.
Ramakrishna, V. 1990. 'Modern Language Reform Movement in Telugu'. *Proceedings of the Indian History Congress* 51: 566–572.
Ramaswamy, U. 1949. 'The Belief System of the Non-Brahmin Movement in India: The Andhra Case'. *Far Eastern Survey* 18(3) (February): 290–300. DOI: https://doi.org/10.2307/264322.
Rudolph, L. I. and S. H. Rudolph. 1960. 'The Political Role of India's Caste Associations'. *Pacific Affairs* 33(1): 5–22. DOI: 10.2307/2753645.
Sherring, M. A. 1872. *Hindu Tribes and Castes as Represented in Benares*. Calcutta: Thacker, Spink & Co.
Srinivas, M. N. 1952. *Religion and Society Among the Coorgs of South India*. Oxford: Clarendon Press.

Subagunarajan, V. M. ed. 2018. *Namakku Yen Intha Izhinilai: Jaathi Maanaadukalilum Jaathi Ozhippu Maanaadukalilum Periyar*. Chennai: Kayal Kavin.

Suri, K. C. 2000. 'Non-Brahman Movement in Andhra: A Study of the Nature of Protest Against Brahmanical Order in Andhra During Colonial Times'. Dr. Garigipati Rudraya Chowdary Endowment Lecture. 25 February. East Godavari District. Andhra Pradesh

Thirumavelan, P. 2018. *Aathikka Sathigalugkku Mattume Avar Periyaraa?* Chennai: Natrinai Pathippagam.

Thirunavakkarasu, K. 2015. *Thi. Mu. Ka. Varalaaru* (Tamil) (History of DMK). Chennai: Nakkheeran Press.

Tillin, L. 2012. 'Caste, Territory and Federalism in Caste Matters'. *Seminar* 633 (May). https://www.india-seminar.com/2012/633/633_louise_tillin.htm. Accessed 6 April 2023.

Venkatachalapathy, A. R. 2006. *In Those Days There Was No Coffee: Writings in Cultural History*. New Delhi: Yoda Press.

———. 2024. 'Against the Hustings: Periyar, Elections, and Democracy'. In *Crisis of Liberal Deliberation: Facets of Indian Democracy*, edited by M. Ray, pp. 64–79. New Delhi: Primus Books.

Verniers, Gilles, Vignesh Karthik K. R., Mohit Kumar, and Neelesh Agrawal. 2021. 'Tamil Nadu's New Assembly in 33 Charts: Lowest Women Representation in 25 Years, OBCs Dominate'. Scroll.in, 10 May. https://scroll.in/article/994446/tamil-nadus-new-assembly-in-33-charts-lowest-women-representation-in-25-years-obcs-dominate. Accessed 1 January 2024.

5

The Double-Barrelled Gun

Periyar and Anna after the Split in the Dravidar Kazhagam

A. R. Venkatachalapathy

Introduction

In 1935, at a conference of Senguntha Mudaliars in Tiruppur, C. N. Annadurai (Anna, 1909–1969), then a twenty-six-year-old graduate, met E. V. Ramasamy (Periyar, 1879–1973). Impressed by the non-Brahmin youth who wanted to enter public life rather than seek a government job, Periyar was quick to take him under his wing. In less than three years, Anna was playing a major role in the Self-Respect Movement (SRM), becoming one of Periyar's chief lieutenants in the 1938–1939 anti-Hindi agitation which made the Dravidian movement a mass organization and effectively put Tamil assertion at the centre stage of politics. It was in the course of this mass-based agitation that the Justice Party was absorbed by the SRM and, in 1944, rechristened the Dravidar Kazhagam (DK). In 1949, Periyar's most brilliant protégé became his rival, breaking away to form the Dravida Munnetra Kazhagam (DMK). In 1967, the DMK dethroned the Indian National Congress (Congress). The intervening decades were marked by bitter hostility and rivalry between the DK and the DMK.

Immediately after the DMK's 1967 victory, there was a rapprochement. Since then, it has been customary to collapse the two into a unified Dravidian movement. The rivalry between the DK and the DMK has been completely elided by party ideologues, chroniclers, and historians. The three-volume edition of Periyar's collected writings compiled by V. Anaimuthu in 1974 does not include a single article from Periyar's innumerable broadsides against the DMK; the DMK does not even merit an entry in the index—an anomaly not rectified even in the vastly expanded twenty-volume edition published in 2010. Biographers and other commentators paper over this question even when this rivalry was glaringly obvious.[1]

Rather than push it under the carpet, this chapter foregrounds the rivalry and argues that the dynamics of this hostility shaped politics in Tamil Nadu in the first two decades after independence. Combining his contempt for those who left his party and his long-term strategy of working with the state to further his political and social goals, I argue that Periyar readied the political soil for the dominance of Dravidian ideology. His support of the Congress during these years rather than strengthening the Congress weakened it while the DMK with its energetic group of young leaders and members and a charismatic leader captured the imagination of politically aspirational backward castes.

Two Personalities

By 1949, in his already long political career, Periyar had never been short of talented lieutenants—but if he attracted brilliant followers, he also fell out with many. Even among this galaxy of extraordinarily gifted followers, Anna was unique. His remarkable linguistic skills, both with pen and on the podium, propelled him to fame and won him a huge following. Anna fashioned a new Tamil style, resonant to the cadence of English syntactic structure, that overturned Tamil sentence formations. By the end of the 1940s, he had added celluloid to his arsenal—scripting popular films and greatly extending his power and popularity. A voracious reader, Anna drew from a wide range of texts that not only included Tamil classical literature but contemporary and classical European works as well. A brilliant polemicist, he could milk colonial ethnography as well as modern plays for his propagandist purpose.[2]

During the anti-Hindi agitation of 1937–1939, Anna was a vital figure leading from the front. Organizationally, his first key moment came in August 1944 at the Salem conference when the Justice Party was renamed the Dravidar Kazhagam. In a resolution that came to be called the Annadurai Resolution, he skilfully refashioned the party as Indian independence became imminent. Gradually he drew significant support from within the party, becoming for all practical purposes the second in command. A generation of upwardly mobile non-Brahmin youth with education and aspiration to political power saw their leader in him. The five years following the Salem conference saw a now-open, now-invisible struggle between two strands in the party, one represented by Periyar and the other by Anna.

The fundamental difference between Periyar and Anna was in their approach to political power. While Periyar maintained a consistent position of keeping away from elections and political power, the movement he spearheaded spawned a generation of youth who sought political power and saw elections as the path to it. Anna willingly or unwillingly came to represent this strand.

Periyar and Electoral Politics

A distinguishing feature of Periyar's long and influential political career was his strong and uncompromising disavowal of electoral politics and eschewing of positions in the government—he is known to have turned down the premiership of Madras province at least twice.[3] From the time of the Non-Cooperation Movement until his death, Periyar never contested elections. During the Swarajist phase of Indian nationalist politics in the early 1920s, Periyar was an uncompromising No-Changer, refusing to run for the legislature on the ground that it would undermine the struggle for independence. After he began to adopt an anti-caste and anti-religious politics, Periyar's position on not contesting elections was only further reinforced. As mentioned earlier, the first anti-Hindi agitation had been a successful mass-based movement. Occurring as it did in the wake of the first elections under the Government of India Act, 1935, and effectively bringing the Rajaji government to its knees by giving it a dose of its own *satyagraha* medicine, it led the newly politicized generation of non-Brahmin castes into believing that political power was not out of reach. This was at odds with Periyar's stated position on electoral politics which he reiterated often.

> Dravidar Kazhagam does not enter legislatures. It does not try to form ministries. It does not contest elections. All this is known. 'How can you achieve anything without these', we are asked. I reply: 'Whoever comes [to power] it's enough if we can get things done for ourselves [through them].'[4]

Why was Periyar averse to seeking political power through elections? Periyar was clear that his radical and iconoclastic ideas alienated people and would not pass muster in elections. He therefore positioned himself as a propagandist in civil society who would try to effect social transformation by converting people through vigorous campaigns. Moreover, his public pronouncements could be provocative. While Tamil public speakers usually addressed their audience in exalted terms, taking on a demeanour of false humility, Periyar's trademark style was to chide his audience for their foolishness and superstitions. Listening to his recorded speeches and reading the transcripts now, one is amazed that audiences gave him a patient, even enthusiastic hearing. 'If someone like me develops the desire for office, can I speak on the kind of issues and words that I now speak? Can anyone who seeks to capture political power speak in this manner?' he asked with some pride.

> For example, I ask: 'Can a stone be god? Can god eat food? Does god need a wife? Why conduct the annual ritual of marriage for gods? Who benefits from all these?' Will a person who asks such questions catch many votes? But then if one does not ask such questions, will our foolish people understand a thing? Thus, one unavoidably has to speak of superstitions in this manner.[5]

Periyar arrived at this position from experience. Once, in a public election meeting in 1937, he asked: if Draupadi could have five husbands and still desire one more and if Dasharatha could have 60,000 wives and such people could be venerated 'What calamity will befall if a woman, on the death of her husband, marries another man?' Immediately the chairman of the meeting interjected saying that if one spoke like this, the party would lose votes. The speaker after him regretted Periyar's words on the same grounds.[6]

Periyar fashioned the DK as a party that campaigned in civil society and sought to change state policy by sustained public propaganda but desisted from competing for state power through elections. By the late 1940s, it was clear to him that this view did not sit well with many of his party leaders and supporters—a line of thinking represented by Anna.

> For the last ten years I [wrote Periyar] have maintained that the Dravidar Kazhagam is not a political party but a propagandist movement. In order that people should consider it to be a movement and not a party, I have been fashioning the Kazhagam as a propagandist organization. ... The Dravidar Kazhagam is not a party organization like the Congress, Communists, Socialists, Brahmin Protection Sangam, Varnashrama Swarajya Sangam, Moderates, the Muslim League, Christian Association, Scheduled Caste League [and so on]. ... Dravidar Kazhagam neither believes in the pseudo-philosophy of Swarajya nor does it pretend to aspire to win a majority and capture political power.[7]

That these words were expressed in a foreword to Anna's polemical history of the Dravidian movement, *Ilatchiya Varalaru* (1947), a few weeks before Indian independence is not without significance.

As Periyar's prime disciple, Anna was at the forefront of the espousal of his ideas. But he disagreed with Periyar on his views regarding electoral politics. Seeking power was a legitimate political exercise. Towards this end it was a consistent part of Anna's strategy to tweak Dravidian ideology, make it inclusive, and aestheticize it to accommodate a wider section of people. This was at the foundation of the split.

The Split

Even though the sparring went on for some years, the split came under peculiar circumstances. In 1949, at the age of seventy, Periyar decided to marry thirty-two-year-old Maniammai, his secretary of some years. Not only the wedding but also the manner in which Periyar went about it (it was shrouded in considerable secrecy), and the rationale that he provided for it—Periyar declared that he had no trust in his lieutenants and was therefore grooming Maniammai to take over the leadership as well as maintain the assets of the party—antagonized a large number of his followers.

Anna and his supporters attempted a variety of measures to make Periyar backtrack. But the die had been cast. Given Periyar's temperament, it could also be said that he went out of his way to provoke them by taking an intransigent position. Anna published the names of those who protested Periyar's marriage in his *Dravida Nadu* weekly. The list turned out to be a veritable who's who of the party. Titled by a subeditor as *kandana kanaikal* ('arrows of protest'), it was rephrased by Anna as *kanneer thulikal* ('teardrops'), giving it great emotional charge (Aranganal, 1988, p. 108).

Despite enormous pressure from his supporters, Anna refused to capture the party, preferring to start a new one. When the DMK was founded on 17 September 1949 (not coincidentally, Periyar's 70th birthday), the new party had walked away with an overwhelming majority of leaders and cadres. In a dramatic speech at Robinson Park in North Chennai, Anna made a final plea to Periyar. Declaring that the new party would always follow and try to realize the ideals of Periyar, in a pregnant metaphor, he called the DK–DMK a double-barrelled gun. He also declared that the chair of the *thalaivar* (president) would remain vacant until Periyar himself deemed fit to occupy it.

The DMK, while repeatedly avowing the ideals of its parent party, had to fashion itself in opposition to it in practice. This was often missed by contemporaries—for instance, the confidential fortnightly reports of the Government of Madras, which drew heavily from police intelligence reports, through the 1950s clubbed the DK and the DMK under the same rubric. Periyar was infuriated by those who bracketed the DK with the DMK and rejected this vociferously,[8] ridiculing Anna's characterization of the two parties as 'a double-barrelled gun'.[9]

Left with the rump of the party, Periyar had to rethink his strategies. The entire top and middle leadership of the party having gone with Anna, Periyar stood practically alone. The scale of the exodus from the party would have demoralized anyone. The only senior personality of any consequence behind him was the redoubtable 'Kuthoosi' S. Gurusamy (1906–1965) and even he had had a change of mind only at the last moment, as Anna needled him with relish. (By 1961, Guruswami too left the party. K. Veeramani rose to prominence in the DK in the 1960s.)[10] Periyar demonstrated extraordinary resolve in rebuilding the party and extending his ideological influence.

While the daily *Viduthalai*, the primary organ of the party, managed and edited by Guruswami, continued to be published from Chennai, Periyar shifted his operational headquarters to Trichy. Centrally located in the Tamil region, it enabled him to travel far and wide. The summer camp that used to be organized in Erode now moved to Trichy where Periyar taught a group of young activists every year.[11]

Periyar Leads the Charge

In the initial months, Periyar barely responded or even acknowledged the DMK.[12] Soon he began to make veiled remarks against the latter. Rather than mention the DMK by name, he derisively began terming DMK leaders as *kanneer thulikal* or worse, just its abbreviated form, *ka. thu. kkal*. Alluding to Hindu puranic lore, he referred to them as 'Prahaladan' (who rebelled against his father, the demon king Hiranyakashipu) and 'Vibhishanan' (the younger brother of Ravana who joined forces with Rama).[13]

Speaking at the Madras district DK conference in March 1950, initially he expressed weariness at having to start all over again. Periyar observed that in his long political career he was not new to betrayals. But while earlier only individuals had backstabbed him, now a collective had proved to be turncoats. Though he had overcome earlier treachery swiftly, he conceded that now it could take considerable time to rebuild the organization. Rather than go into retirement as planned, he expressed his determination to continue with his political life.[14] Little did he know that rest would not come any time soon; Periyar would dominate the Tamil political landscape for another quarter of a century. Ironically, it is the Periyar of the 1950s and 1960s who is deeply etched in popular memory.

Six months later, at the executive council meeting of the DK in Trichy, Periyar provided a point-by-point account of the betrayal by Anna and his followers. As this was the first meeting of an important, if depleted, body of office bearers, he gave a detailed list of how he had been backstabbed over the past decade. A summary is as follows: the renegades were selfish; Anna had launched his own journal (the *Dravida Nadu*) to rival *Kudi Arasu* and *Viduthalai*; when Periyar wanted to raise funds for the party, Anna had objected to it as unnecessary but nevertheless went on to collect a purse for the poet Bharatidasan; contrary to the party diktat, Anna had refused to wear a black shirt as a sign of the darkness engulfing the Dravidian nation; he disagreed with the characterization of 15 August as 'black day'; not only did Anna work against the Tuticorin conference (1948), he did not even attend the conference. Most importantly, Periyar alleged that Anna exulted in seeing his name in the press; remaining in Kanchipuram, he devoted much of his time to writing for films.[15] Further, he accused Anna of recruiting more and more traitors into his fold. The last straw was the Coimbatore Thirukkural conference where Anna made an unauthorized entry and created mischief by planting seeds of suspicion about Periyar's meeting with C. Rajagopalachari (Rajaji) at Thiruvannamalai in preparation for his wedding.

Periyar took on the DMK on two fronts. The first was on the ideological plane, especially criticizing its ideological shifts as the DMK strove to be a popular political party. The other was on the political front through new alliances and popular agitations.

Periyar always maintained an antagonistic attitude to the arts, especially cinema and the theatre. With the split, his criticism gained a new edge. One of the first criticisms by Periyar of the DMK was that it had now begun to embrace the nationalist poet, Subramania Bharati.[16] During his time in the Congress and in the initial phase of the SRM, Periyar had maintained a high regard for Bharati. But from the 1930s, he ran him down and debunked him as little more than a Brahmin poet. Periyar was unique in the Tamil cultural spectrum not to endorse Bharati's status as the Tamil national poet.[17] While Anna had never subscribed to this view openly, by the end of the 1940s, he was describing Bharati as 'a people's poet'. Though the pride of place went to the Dravidian poet Bharatidasan, Bharati's prime follower, the DMK did not exclude Bharati. Bharati was often invoked and DMK writings were often suffused with allusions to Bharati.[18]

Periyar especially poured scorn on the DMK's passion for films and accused it of having fully sold itself out to cinema and the theatre.[19] The DMK's argument that the media was a vehicle for ideological propaganda and a path to reform, *Viduthalai* contended, was self-serving. 'Neither Vinayaka bhakti (a reference to Gemini Studios' hugely successful *Avvaiyar* [1953]) nor rationalism could be fostered by cinema. Nothing could be achieved by inserting a few lines in the name of reform and rationalist propaganda.'[20] Instead the DK called for direct and sustained condemnation on the platform and through the press. In another editorial, *Viduthalai* blamed the DMK for making the youth addicted to cinema by turning them into fanatics of film stars and distracting them from education and employment.[21] Films were a plague from which the people needed to be saved.[22]

Pointing to Anna's earlier claim that if only he could make ten films, Dravida Nadu would be a reality, the DK taunted him by asking why a separate homeland had not materialized even after twenty, thirty films had been made by DMK scriptwriters. When Anna blamed censorship for this failure, more ridicule was in the offing. The only outcome of the DMK's foray into the film world, *Viduthalai* contended, was that the DMK ideologues had become rich. Apart from fleeting glimpses of the party flag on the screen, not an iota of ideological propaganda had been possible. It asked rhetorically: 'Did untouchability disappear after the making of *Nandanar*? Did Saivism spread due to *Thiruneelakandar*? How many became sanyasis after *Pattinathar*?'[23] *Viduthalai* concluded that films only fostered immorality while plays with rationalist themes had more effect.[24] Periyar shared the Congress leaders' contemptuous vocabulary for cinema: he employed the infamous description of DMK leaders as *koothadigal* (a pejorative term meaning 'mountebanks') used by M. Bhaktavatsalam, the Congress leader.

It is now commonplace to attribute the extraordinary reach of the DMK to the rhetorical skills of its leaders. Anna, and following him star DMK speakers such as V. R. Nedunchezhiyan, M. Karunanidhi, E. V. K. Sampath, and others, created an entirely new oratory.[25] Drawing extensively from the Tamil classical tradition, they fashioned a Tamil—*adukku mozhi*—that was alliterative and alluring. In a matter of a few years, Anna had transformed language in the Tamil public sphere, eclipsing the Indian nationalist use of Tamil—not to speak of the convoluted and turgid prose of the Communists—as a vehicle for propaganda. Even though there was criticism that rhetoric replaced substance, a whole generation was drunk on this new language and DMK speakers drew huge crowds. If the penetration of electricity led to the spread of cinema halls enabling DMK films to reach a wide audience, the easier availability of the public address system underpinned the rise of DMK public speakers.

Periyar took the challenge of the DMK speakers head on. As a public speaker from the time of the Non-Cooperation Movement, he was a seasoned orator. Even by the early 1930s, he was known to speak for hours in an earthy style yet holding his audiences in thrall. Periyar ridiculed the use of alliterative rhetoric by the DMK speakers.[26] In a conscious reaction to the DMK's adoption of a neo-classical style, he adopted a conversational tone, bristling with proverbs and parables. If DMK speakers appeared on the podium dressed in white with a flowing *thundu*, Periyar was dressed in a black shirt and a coloured lungi that was the height of informality. Rather than stand and address the crowd, he preferred to sit—by this time, he was a venerable old man and suffered ailments including a chronic hernia and a catheterized ureter. There was not a day when he did not give a talk—if not two—travelling in his custom-made van across the length and breadth of the Tamil country.

On the ideological front, the distinction that the DMK made between Brahmins and Brahminism also came in for criticism. Anna had named his party the Dravida Munnetra Kazhagam—Dravida (territory) rather than Dravidar (an ethnic people) as in Dravidar Kazhagam—to avoid any hint of racial exclusion and kept the party open to Brahmin membership (an option closed in the DK). As a contemporary journalist observed, the DMK was 'strenuously trying to live down an anti-Brahmin reputation' (Ramanujam, 1967, p. 155). Stating that it stood only against the inegalitarian ideology epitomized by Brahminism, the DMK asserted that it did not discriminate against individual Brahmins. *Parpaneeyam* is Tamil for 'Brahminism' and the DK emphasized the suffix *eeyam* to mock the DMK (*eeyam* means 'lead', an inferior metal alloying precious metals and used by alchemist conmen).[27] This was seen as a sign of selling out to the Brahmins and the developing close relationship of the DMK with Rajaji only seemed to prove this criticism (Ramanujam, 1967, p. 84).[28]

By the mid-1950s, Periyar had altered his demand for a separate Dravida Nadu. In the face of the linguistic reorganization of states that had led to a residual Madras State with only Tamil-speaking areas, he said that it was better to fight for a separate Tamil state.[29] Though this could be seen as a concession to the new territorial reality, it was also a counterpoint to the DMK's Dravida Nadu demand.

Harking back to a glorious Tamil past was a constitutive aspect of the DMK's identity politics. Periyar was rather uncomfortable with such glorification of the past. The DMK's uncritical adulation added to his fury. He reiterated his rationalistic critique of ancient Tamil literature. Did the Tamil language ever help the Tamil people to progress, he asked. In a more provocative manner, he stated that by getting bogged down with religion and god, the Tamil language had pushed the people into a barbaric state even as the whole world was making scientific advances. Tamil pandits and teachers came in for particular criticism for their antediluvian attitudes, his anger against them accentuated by the fact that an overwhelming majority of Tamil teachers tended to be pro-DMK in orientation.[30]

Twists and Turns

The battle on the political front took different turns over the two decades of the split with the most unlikely bedfellows.

During the war years and the endgame of the empire, there was little scope for popular agitation and Periyar continued with his strategy of working as a pressure group to influence state policy. Post-Independence politics was a different ballgame altogether but Periyar managed its rules rather well.

Immediately after independence he backed the Congress ministry headed by Omandur P. Ramasamy Reddiar. Considered to be honest if lethargic, Reddiar drew considerable strength from Periyar's support, especially in relation to Brahmin interests in the Congress party. (So much so that the question, 'Which Ramasamy ruled Madras, Naicker or Reddiar?', was asked.)

In the 1952 elections, Periyar supported the anti-Congress opposition combine dominated by the Communist Party of India (CPI) and vigorously campaigned for its success. Still in its swaddling clothes, the DMK did not contest elections. Instead, in a face-saving posturing, it promised to support candidates willing to sign its charter of demands. The first general elections therefore did not see any direct political confrontation between Periyar and the DMK. However, despite the Congress party not being able to garner a majority in the assembly, as the election results trickled in, Periyar said that he had wanted eight prominent Congress leaders to be defeated but thanks to the backstabbing of the DMK, two—K. Kamaraj and T. T. Krishnamachari—had managed to win.[31] Rajaji's accession to chief-ministership through the backdoor of a nomination to the upper house gave further credence to Periyar's critique of the unrepresentative character of democracy. But he backed Rajaji against the Andhra lobby and lauded what he considered welfare moves such as the removal of wartime controls. However, within less than two years, the controversial 'new modified scheme of education' introduced by Rajaji which provided for only half a day of schooling with the afternoon left free for learning the father's occupation provoked Periyar's ire.[32] Both the DK and the DMK dubbed it the *kula kalvi thittam* or 'caste-based education scheme' and were one in opposing it. The new education scheme effectively sealed Rajaji's political career and ushered in a sea change in Tamil polity and politics.

Rajaji was succeeded by Kamaraj in April 1954. Periyar welcomed Kamaraj's ascension to power on the ground that he was not arrogant—like Rajaji—and that he had a consultative approach to governance. Apart from withdrawing Rajaji's education scheme, Kamaraj had also constituted a cabinet without a single Brahmin minister for the first time in thirty years.[33] But Periyar set off a political earthquake by calling Kamaraj *pachai Tamilan* ('trueborn Tamilan') when he contested a by-election. It had been three decades since Periyar had left the Congress swearing to decimate it. But this was of a piece with his strategy of working through the government in power. Realpolitik considerations too must have played on his mind: the split had weakened him and the DMK was the Congress's inevitable rival. However, while his support for Kamaraj over the next thirteen years was unconditional, his support for the Congress was not. He maintained that he only supported Kamaraj and not the Congress party. With this new political development, the DK–DMK rivalry gained a new edge.

His support for the Kamaraj government notwithstanding, Periyar launched a series of agitations in the mid-1950s. Apart from enthusing his cadre and propagating his ideas, putting pressure on the DMK was part of the game plan. As M. Karunanidhi recollected in his autobiography:

> Seeing that the DMK's propaganda power was bearing fruit in every village and hamlet, Periyar tried to spur his movement. He was seized by a special concern that his followers should not be drawn away by the DMK. ... Periyar was not wearied by the DMK's fast growth; he opened many battlefronts to draw the attention of the people. (2000 [1975], p. 166)

In 1953, Periyar launched an agitation to break the idols of the Hindu god Pillaiyar. Two years later, he began a campaign to burn the Indian national flag to demand repeal of the status of

Hindi as a national language and for the secession of Tamil Nadu from the Indian union. In 1956 followed the movement to publicly burn pictures of the god Ram. In 1957, he commenced a movement seeking to erase the word 'Brahmin' from commercial name boards. Though these campaigns were very much in keeping with the ideology of the party, they came fast and thick. It was Periyar's strategy to expose the DMK's Achilles heel—of balancing hard rationalistic and tough political positions while striving to become a popular party. Evidently, the DMK was unnerved, if not rattled, by Periyar's agitations.

As the DMK entered electoral politics—with its inner party referendum at the Trichy conference, 1956 and its plunge into the 1957 elections—Periyar's attack gained a new stridency. The DMK's actions only proved his point that his marriage to Maniammai was only a pretext for the split: it had been motivated by the greed to swerve off the path of propaganda and gain political power.[34] To him, the DMK had sold out and he claimed that it was funded by Brahmins.[35] The decision to contest elections was a betrayal of ideology.[36] Periyar used the derisive term, *kangani*[37] to refer to the DMK's politics.[38] How would the objective of achieving a separate Dravida Nadu be attained by entering the legislature, Periyar asked in an election meeting at Kulithalai—the constituency where Karunanidhi was contesting.[39]

A *Viduthalai* editorial in early 1957 went to the extent of suggesting that the DMK intended to bring Rajaji back to the helm of affairs[40]—a prophetic forecast considering that a then down-and-out Rajaji would soon become a major player in Tamil and national politics and by 1961, the DMK and Rajaji would be on the brink of forging an alliance. If the DMK professed to champion non-Brahmin interests, why did it oppose Kamaraj, asked Periyar.[41]

Viduthalai also provided a thoroughgoing critique of the DMK's first election manifesto.[42] Its delayed release was attributed to the DMK's ideological bankruptcy. Periyar argued that it was a pipedream to hope to escape from Brahmin–Bania rule through the parliamentary route—what was actually required was a sustained mass struggle.[43] At a meeting of the Dravidian Students' Federation in Annamalai University he launched a fusillade against the DMK—the choice of forum is noteworthy as it was college students (Annamalai University was an especial seedbed of DMK activists) who were gravitating towards the DMK. Posing the question what was the DMK's philosophy, he declared: 'Objective? To make money in films. Ideology? To destroy the DK. Their prayer? That I should die soon.' He further accused the DMK of soft-pedalling the Brahmin question to gain power.[44]

In a harbinger of the future, the DMK made a creditable debut in the 1957 elections: it won 2 parliamentary seats and 15 in the state legislature. Arguing that the DMK's initial success was a fluke, Periyar said that 'even if limbs were to grow on one's back, the DMK would never succeed in forming a government ever'. In this, of course, Periyar was to be proven wrong. He questioned the DMK on its boast that the government would be put on the mat during legislative debates. What in fact happened, Periyar said, was the contrary.[45]

By 1961, it was becoming clear that the DMK was cozying up to Rajaji and the Swatantra party, united by an anti-Kamaraj and anti-Congress position. In Periyar's view, this was another example of the DMK's betrayal of non-Brahmin interests.[46] As the CPI seemed to move closer to the DMK, he condemned it as well.[47] He was also discomfited by the Indian Union Muslim League's (IUML) closeness to the DMK.[48] Remarkably, even as political forces across the spectrum were rallying against the Congress with the DMK as the centrepiece, Periyar was steadfast in his support of Kamaraj.

The DMK's continuing electoral success, Periyar saw as a sign of its further ideological fall. Following the DMK's impressive showing in the 1962 elections—it won seven parliament seats and fifty seats in the legislature—Periyar penned a hard-hitting statement titled 'Who won? Who gained?' Rajaji had won as the DMK had been divested of its ideological moorings by its alliance with Swatantra.[49]

In early 1963, following the sixteenth amendment to the Constitution of India that forbade advocating secession, the DMK dropped its separatist demand. Periyar ridiculed the party for being chicken-hearted.[50] After Anna left him, he said, he had become a coward and was clutching at Kamaraj's feet with one hand and Rajaji's with another.[51]

However, Periyar was soon on the backfoot during the anti-Hindi agitation of 1963–1965. The DMK was at the forefront of the tremendously popular agitation that was fuelled by phenomenal student activism. Periyar argued somewhat speciously that as long as Kamaraj was at the helm of affairs, there need be no fear of Hindi imposition.[52] Harking back to the days of the first anti-Hindi agitation, he said that he needed no lessons on how to oppose Hindi. The DMK was enacting a play script and he compared it to a roadside conjurer's show.[53] As the anti-Hindi agitation raged, he characterized the Tamil language as 'a nuisance' and Tamil teachers as anti-social elements.[54] The anti-Hindi agitation was only a ploy to dislodge the Kamaraj government and there need be no fear that English would be replaced by Hindi.[55] Periyar was especially harsh in condemning the violence accompanying the anti-Hindi agitation.

By the mid-1960s, Periyar probably had a sense of the general drift in favour of the DMK. When Kamaraj resigned in 1963 as chief minister (under the K-Plan—to energize the party), Periyar termed it political suicide. Periyar's was a difficult situation and his strategy of unconditionally supporting the Congress had its downside. Despite not meeting in person often, Periyar and Kamaraj shared a good relationship. The same could not be said of Kamaraj's successor, Bhaktavatsalam who nursed a resentment against Periyar and his politics. Unmindful of the government in power, Periyar continued his opposition to the DMK.

As late as in 1965, reflecting on his life's work, on his 87th birthday Periyar rued:

Amidst all this, the biggest difficulty I suffered was that all my comrades who I had recruited and groomed, after attaining full maturity, all of them—100 on 100—after gaining popular appeal turned into the henchmen of my enemies, became opponents of my work, and posed hurdles in my path. (Anaimuthu, 1974, p. 1957)

The DMK Response

Despite Karunanidhi's diplomatic assessment of Periyar's agitations in the 1950s, the DMK was far from being nonplussed. A biography of E. V. K. Sampath notes that there was much consternation in the DMK as Periyar announced one agitation after another (Vivekanandan, Sampath, and Kalpanadasan, 2013). Committed to the Dravidian ideology, the DMK could not afford to publicly decry such agitations.

The DMK too organized its own agitations. As a new movement with a youthful and aspirational cadre, the DMK's agitations were huge, popular successes, taking the party to the remote corners of the Tamil country. Government repression produced heroes and martyrs for the DMK.

While Periyar was always in the news and his agitations gained wide attention, they were often overshadowed by the DMK agitations. In response, Periyar asserted that the DMK was only aping the DK: if he launched an agitation against Rajaji's education scheme, the DMK agitated against Nehru's comment on the DMK as 'nonsense'. If the DK tarred Hindi nameboards, the DMK took up the case of giving a Marwari Dalmia's name to the Kallakudi railway station. And when the DK agitated against the Dakshina Pradesh idea, Anna campaigned against high gubernatorial salaries.[56]

Periyar's atheism proved to be a millstone around the DMK's neck and his relentless rationalist agitations were in fact so many gauntlets thrown at the DMK. As a party hoping to win the popular vote, the DMK could hardly afford to offend public sentiment. Anna had to manage this tricky issue. In the years of his meteoric rise in the DK, Anna had been second to none in professing atheism. In early 1943 he had matched wits against two respected Tamil scholars to argue that the Hindu religious texts the *Ramayana* and the *Periya Puranam* should be burnt. Anna's challenge, if he wanted to win popular electoral support, was to negotiate this minefield without appearing to compromise on the Dravidian agenda of rationalism and debunking superstition. Anna fell back on the deft use of language to extricate the DMK from the question of atheism. Drawing upon the aphoristic verse of the early medieval Tamil Saivite poet Thirumular, he appropriated a pithy line as a slogan—*Onre kulam, Oruvane Devan* ('Community is one and God too is one.'), the one-ness of God left deliberately ambiguous to accommodate all shades of opinion on religion. To Periyar's repeated taunts about not joining agitations to break Pillaiyar idols,[57] Anna famously replied, alluding to the Tamil practice of breaking coconuts as offerings to God, "I'll break neither Pillaiyar nor coconuts'. Explaining his position on why he kept off the agitation, he said, 'We do not wish to unnecessarily arouse hatred in those who will in due course be joining us'.[58]

Anna invoked the same argument when Periyar launched his agitation of burning the Indian national flag in August 1955. Burning the flag, he remarked, would create 'unnecessary animosity, unquenchable hatred and irredeemable blame', engulfing the Dravidian movement 'in a flood of enmity' and was to be avoided at all costs.[59]

Anna countered Periyar's characteristic blunt and rustic language castigating the DMK in his own style. Responding in general to Periyar's upping of the ante, Anna said: 'Shocking scandals, hair-raising agitations, amazing demonstrations that would make people gape in wonder—rather than gaining strength from [these], I greatly desire the success that can be gained from instilling our ideology among the people, especially the Dravidians in the Congress fold.'[60] Anna inventoried the other epithets that Periyar hurled at the DMK: mountebanks, speakers of alliterative language, the vulgar, money grubbers, power-seekers, speakers of lustful words, paupers, and so on.[61] While the resentment at Periyar's often intemperate language was not concealed, Anna demonstrated considerable patience and refused to repay in the same coin. Paying (sometimes backhanded) compliments to Periyar's long life of sacrifice, his criticism was frequently couched in sarcasm and innuendo.

Rather than attack Periyar directly, Anna would instead criticize Kamaraj. Often, he would target Kuthoosi Guruswami. 'Periyar has every right to be angry and impatient. For he has fought for over half a century. He is annoyed that after all his hard work the results are meagre. But do others who happen to work with him have the same right?'[62] Such criticism would be deflected to the Congress quickly and damn it effectively. Ridiculing the Congress for siding with Periyar now, Anna asked,

Does Periyar accept the Congress as a worthy political party? No! He says that Kamaraj is our man, a good man, a capable man! Not the Congress! *Khadar*? It's a superstition. The *charkha*? The device of savages. Basic education? Foolishness! Gandhism? Idiocy! Nationalism? A fraud! Sacrifice? Humbug! Religion? Stoned stupor! Brahmins? The enemies! The north? The abode of uncultured people! Nehru? An impatient and ignorant man, the scion of a rich family![63]

Anna ridiculed Periyar's support for Kamaraj in his typical style. He wondered if it was not Periyar's victory that Congressmen were now organizing meetings where Periyar expressed such views. Adverting to Periyar's withdrawal of his national-flag-burning agitation at the instance of Kamaraj, he quoted an editorial from Periyar's *Viduthalai* daily to damning effect. 'In striving to destroy the Dravidar Kazhagam, in opposing the ideals of the movement, in encouraging Brahminism, in acting as *kangani*s to the north Indians, in fanning Nehru with flywhisks, Kamaraj and Rajaji do better than each other'.[64] Anna wondered what then was the difference between the two.

In short, as late as in October 1965 a journalist was writing that Anna was still 'graciously and gratefully acknowledge[ing] his indebtedness to the Periyar in sharp contrast to the vile abuse which that old gentleman is wont to hurl on his erstwhile follower' (Ramanujam, 1967, p. 230).

If Anna, as Periyar's primary rival and prodigal son, was circumspect, drawing on carefully selected rhetorical devices to counter him, his younger lieutenants responded in different ways: while some were tactical, a few were somewhat less inhibited in their criticism.

V. R. Nedunchezhiyan, the second in command in the DMK, was civil in criticizing Periyar. Given the avowed commonality of ideology, the DMK was often confronted with the question of whether it would join Periyar's agitations, especially when the objectives were the same? Responding to a question whether the DMK would join Periyar's impending agitation against the education scheme, Nedunchezhiyan remarked that though both parties subscribed to the same ideology, they were different organizations. He reversed the question by asking if Periyar had supported the DMK's earlier *mummunai porattam*? Further, he contended that the question arose only if Periyar invited the DMK to join. Nedunchezhiyan was also critical of Periyar's call to his cadres to arm themselves with knives in self-defence. It was the DMK's contention that Periyar urged his party men to inflict violence on Brahmins—to cut the tufts of Brahmins; fill up jerry cans of petrol to burn down *agraharam*s, and so on. He contended that the DMK did not subscribe to violence of any sort against members of any community. Finally, he quoted Anna to the effect that while the DMK was not spoiling for a fight, it would not back out if an agitation was called for.[65] Like other leaders of the DMK, Nedunchezhiyan too was critical of Periyar for launching frequent agitations.[66]

N. V. Natarajan, a senior leader, wrote a regular column in his weekly *Dravidan* in the late 1950s under the pseudonym Kootharasan. Titled 'Periyar Pesugirar' (Periyar Speaks), the column was structured as an imaginary dialogue with Periyar. The burden of the column was to expose Periyar's apparent contradictory positions. His dropping of the Dravida Nadu demand in the wake of the linguistic reorganization of states came in for particular criticism, as did his support for Kamaraj.[67] Maniammai continued to be the target of criticism for ostensibly misleading Periyar and controlling the party.[68]

If leaders such as Nedunchezhiyan, Era. Chezhiyan, and Natarajan were temperate even if somewhat more forthright than Anna, Karunanidhi was less inhibited in his polemics in his weekly *Murasoli*. In his 'Kadaisi Pakkam' ('the last page'), meant for responding to readers' queries under the pseudonym *Ezhuthani* ('writing stylus'), he often took potshots at Periyar. He criticized Periyar's frequent resort to agitations. To a question what Periyar's next campaign could be about, he replied tongue in cheek: 'He may launch a door-to door agitation to force people to pay all central taxes!'[69] *Murasoli* also published a series of cartoons ridiculing Periyar's alliance with Kamaraj.[70] In one cartoon, Periyar is depicted as being seated at a table with a signboard behind him painted with the words Kamaraj Vilas Brahmin Hotel while he is being served by T. T. Krishnamachari and R. Venkatraman (both Brahmin Congress leaders) even as he calls upon everyone to boycott Brahmin hotels.[71]

By the mid-1960s the exchanges between Periyar and the DMK had settled down to a consistent pattern. As the DMK grew from strength to strength electorally, it grew in confidence and could easily afford to ignore Periyar. As Anna stated in an interview: 'We do not credit the DK with any influence whatsoever … We, in fact, consider the DK as the scout movement for the Congress … They organise receptions, etc. for Mr Kamaraj' (Ramanujam 1967, p. 258).

Conclusion

The DMK's triumph in the 1967 elections brought a new twist to the story. The party won a majority on its own. A senior journalist observed that at this crowning moment of success, Anna was 'a picture of humility and touching modesty' (Ramanujam, 1967, p. 265). That this was no journalistic platitude was demonstrated, when, in a dramatic turn, Anna made a surprise visit to Periyar in Trichy and announced that his government was dedicated to Periyar. It was an emotional reunion after a gap of two decades. Periyar was moved beyond words and graciously acknowledged the gesture.

The emotional bonds were strengthened with the tragic death of Anna of throat cancer within two years of assuming power. Periyar played an important role in Karunanidhi's succession to power. However, while maintaining his praise of Kamaraj personally—he even expressed support to him in the Nagercoil by-election in which the DMK left no stone unturned to defeat him—Periyar continued his strategy of supporting the government in power. At the same time, he also carried on his politics of organizing belligerent conferences unmindful of what embarrassment they could cause the government in power—a case in point being the superstition eradication conference in Salem in January 1971. After Periyar's death in December 1973, the DK remained a key legitimizer of the DMK. However, what concerns us here are the objective outcomes of the rivalry between the DK and the DMK from 1949 to 1967.

The trajectory of DK–DMK politics had serious consequences for the Congress. The support of Periyar accelerated the process of de-Brahminization that the Congress was undergoing. Rajaji turned out to be the last prominent Brahmin leader of the Congress. With his exit, it became an overwhelmingly non-Brahmin party. While a faction within the Congress, of the erstwhile supporters of Rajaji, detested Periyar and his politics and wanted tough action against him and the DK, overall, the party found him to be a useful ally in countering and containing the DMK.

Periyar's support gave Kamaraj the crucial legitimacy that strengthened his position and ushered in a realignment of social forces. While the wider acceptance of Kamaraj in Tamil society owed much to Periyar, the latter did not have it easy on this account. While Kamaraj evidently relished Periyar's support, he did not publicly acknowledge it.[72] By 1957, a journalist recorded that the Congress had 'adopted in thought and word' 'the principles and practices of the Dravidar Kazhagam'. All nominations to the Congress were 'Dravidar Kazhagam or special caste groups who were till recently anti-Congress' (Ramanujam, 1967, p. 114). The last Congress chief minister Bhaktavatsalam recalled bitterly, 'the bizarre, irrational relationship between EVR [E. V. Ramasamy] and some Congressmen. On platforms arranged by Congressmen, he would abuse without any inhibition Gandhiji and Nehruji' apart from raising secessionist demands, indulging in communal abuse against 'some communities', and propagating atheism. 'Another mischief' was to praise one or two Congress leaders while heaping calumnies on others. Such mischiefs accelerated after 1962, he contended, squarely blaming 'the unholy relationship' between some Congressmen and Periyar for the 1967 debacle (Bhaktavatsalam, 1971, pp. 147–148).

With the DK aligning with the Congress and the DMK growing, the Dravidian agenda came to virtually occupy the centre stage of Tamil politics. As we saw, the DMK made rapid progress on the electoral front. By 1959, the DMK had won the Madras Corporation election and captured its mayor-ship. The Communist Party which had humbled the Congress in 1952 was effectively marginalized as an also-ran, a trend that accelerated in the succeeding decades, and by the 1960s, its strength was restricted to certain pockets. (The split it suffered in 1964 added to its woes). Unlike in other parts of India where Muslims solidly backed the Congress, the IUML was comfortable under the Dravidian umbrella. Thus, by the late 1960s, the entire political space had been occupied by groups, factions, and parties that were broadly in consonance with the principles of the Dravidian movement. The Congress was weakened. The Swatantra party made a quiet exit after its loss in alliance with the Kamaraj-led Congress in the 1971 elections.

Following Anna's prescient and pregnant metaphor of 'the double-barrelled gun' to describe the DMK's relationship with the DK, the dynamics between them has precisely been that in shaping the history of Tamil politics in the twentieth century.

Notes

1. An interesting example is Pandian, Subagunarajan, and Marudhu (2009). This useful collection brings together cartoons from a range of periodicals published between the late 1950s and the late 1960s. In these cartoons, Periyar figures as a critic of Anna and the DMK but the editors do not deem it fit to comment on this. A recent series of books putting together the collected writings of Kuthoosi S. Guruswami does not include any of his columns on the DMK.
2. For instance, the 1961 split in the DMK, when E. V. K. Sampath raised the banner of revolt, was conducted through a debate on Bernard Shaw's *The Apple Cart* (1928).
3. Periyar's views on electoral politics are analysed in detail in Venkatachalapathy (2021).
4. *Viduthalai*, 15 May 1954, in Anaimuthu (1974, pp. 828–832).
5. *Viduthalai*, 23 June 1949.
6. *Dravida Nadu*, 20 June 1943, in Anaimuthu (1974, p. 440).
7. E. V. Ramasamy, 'Preface', in *Ilatchiya Varalaru* (1947).
8. *Viduthalai*, 14 November 1953.
9. *Viduthalai*, 1 August 1954; *Viduthalai*, 19 June 1955.
10. Apart from Periyar, it was 'Kuthoosi' Guruswami who took on the DMK, especially in his regular satirical column, *Palasarakku Moottai*. After his exit from the party in 1961, the column

was taken over by 'Agappaiyar' (K. Veeramani). When Guruswami's constant sniping came in for criticism, Periyar stoutly defended him. While he said he had indeed reprimanded Guruswami for going overboard in his criticism, he qualified this by blaming it on the DMK's provocation. *Viduthalai*, 10 March 1956.
11. *Viduthalai*, 12 May 1951.
12. However, *Viduthalai* occasionally published news items on and letters by DMK renegades. See for instance, the letter by A. P. Rathnasamy, *Viduthalai*, 24 January 1953.
13. Periyar continued to use these terms until the end of the conflict. See Periyar (1965).
14. *Viduthalai*, 21 March 1950.
15. *Viduthalai*, 16 September 1950.
16. *Viduthalai*, 31 October 1951.
17. See Venkatachalapathy (2018b, pp. 29–54) for a narrative and analysis of Bharati's status in the Tamil public sphere in the 1930s and after.
18. For instance, Karunanidhi's well-known autobiography, *Nenjukku Needhi* drew its title from a Bharati poem. Also see a review of the famous Sakthi edition of Bharati's collected poems in *Murasoli*, 1 June 1957. The classic DMK film *Parasakthi* included a Bharati song.
19. *Viduthalai*, 31 October 1951.
20. Editorial, *Viduthalai*, 21 May 1954. It has been argued that the Tamil Brahmin elite disdained films in the 1930s and 1940s and that it was the Dravidian movement which adopted a positive attitude to them and appropriated the art form. See Pandian (1996, pp. 950–955). Apart from the condemnation of films for propagating irrationalism, Periyar shared much of the other cultural elites' disdain for them.
21. Editorial, *Viduthalai*, 24 January 1959.
22. *Viduthalai*, 16 August 1958.
23. Editorial, *Viduthalai*, 24 January 1959.
24. *Viduthalai*, 22 July 1959. It may be recalled that Periyar had a special relationship with the maverick theatre personality M. R. Radha (1907–1979) who staged hugely successful plays with rationalist themes in the face of censorship.
25. For an ethnography of Dravidian platform rhetoric, see Bate (2009).
26. *Viduthalai*, 16 October 1958.
27. Editorial, *Viduthalai*, 5 June 1954; Editorial, *Viduthalai*, 19 August 1954.
28. By 1957, the DMK had also inducted its first Brahmin members—the lawyer V. P. Raman was the first to join.
29. *Viduthalai*, 16 October 1958. Also, *Viduthalai*, 24 September 1959 where it was contended that other south Indians would not countenance a Dravida Nadu apart from the fact that Tamils would be outnumbered in such an arrangement. Also see *Viduthalai*, 20 September 1962.
30. *Viduthalai*, 12 February 1960. Also see *Viduthalai*, 11 May 1962 where Periyar made similar comments in the presence of Kundrakudi Adigal. For a social history of Tamil pandits and their politicization, see Venkatachalapathy (2018a).
31. *Viduthalai*, 28 January 1952. Also, *Viduthalai*, 29 January 1952.
32. For a detailed analysis of the genesis and the final rollback of the scheme, see Venkatachalapathy and Veeraraghavan (2019), especially the prologue 'The Controversy in Context'.
33. *Viduthalai*, 12 May 1954.

34. Anna pre-empted criticism with the words: 'Let's continue to reiterate at length that we are contesting elections only with clean thoughts and strive in the hope that Periyar's support will be ours.' *Dravida Nadu*, 10 June 1956, in Annadurai (2002, vol. 1, p. 666).
35. *Viduthalai*, 14 November 1953.
36. *Viduthalai*, 8 December 1956. As the DMK gained support and articulated its distinct political views, the DK held these against its earlier stated positions. In a column titled 'Arasiyal Rasavadam' (political alchemy), quotes from DMK leaders from earlier times were juxtaposed with their present articulations. *Viduthalai*, 19 June 1955.
37. A *kangani* was a recruiter and supervisor of indentured labourers; *kanganis* were notorious for recruiting poor people by making false promises while ingratiating themselves with the White planters.
38. *Viduthalai*, 9 February 1957.
39. *Viduthalai*, 9 February 1957.
40. Editorial, *Viduthalai*, 11 February 1957.
41. *Viduthalai*, 19 December 1958.
42. *Viduthalai*, 13 February 1957.
43. *Viduthalai*, 2 January 1958. Also see Periyar's speech at Vellore, *Viduthalai*, 31 August 1958.
44. *Viduthalai*, 10 March 1956.
45. *Viduthalai*, 16 October 1958.
46. *Viduthalai*, 18 March 1961. Also, *Viduthalai*, 9 June 1961.
47. *Viduthalai*, 23 June 1961.
48. *Viduthalai*, 26 April 1963.
49. *Viduthalai*, 30 March 1962.
50. 'Speech at Annamalai Nagar', *Viduthalai*, 12 February 1963.
51. *Viduthalai*, 27 February 1963.
52. *Viduthalai*, 26 April 1963.
53. *Viduthalai*, 20 November 1963.
54. *Viduthalai*, 16 January 1965.
55. *Viduthalai*, 20 January 1965. Also *Viduthalai*, 21 January 1965; 22 January 1965; 1 February 1965; 6 February 1965.
56. *Viduthalai*, 10 March 1956. These views were reiterated in a *Viduthalai* (11 June 1956) editorial as well.
57. *Viduthalai*, 19 December 1958.
58. *Dravida Nadu*, 24 July 1955, in Annadurai (2002, vol. 1, p. 121).
59. *Dravida Nadu*, 7 August 1955, in Annadurai (2002, vol.1, p. 137).
60. *Dravida Nadu*, 7 August 1955, in Annadurai (2002, vol. 1, p. 137).
61. *Dravida Nadu*, 23 April 1961, in Annadurai (2002, vol. 3, p. 298).
62. *Dravida Nadu*, 19 August 1956, in Annadurai (2002, vol. 1, p. 817).
63. *Dravida Nadu*, 5 November 1961, in Annadurai (2002, vol. 4, p. 227).
64. *Dravida Nadu*, 11 March 1956, in Annadurai (2002, vol. 1, p. 485).
65. *Manram*, 15 April 1954.
66. *Manram*, 15 December 1955.
67. *Dravidan*, 18 October 1958.
68. *Dravidan*, 13 December 1958.

69. *Murasoli*, 31 May 1957. Also *Murasoli*, 11 October 1957.
70. See *Murasoli*, 1 November 1957; 8 November 1957; 22 November 1957; 29 November 1957. For more cartoons in the *Murasoli*, see Pandian, Subagunarajan, and Marudhu (2009).
71. *Murasoli*, 21 June 1957. Also see the column 'Kadaisi Pakkam' in *Murasoli*, 7 August 1957.
72. Kamaraj did not acknowledge Periyar's support publicly and in fact appeared to show discomfort. Evidently, he was embarrassed by Periyar's various provocative agitations. Even if he wanted to go soft on Periyar, his hands were pushed. Kamaraj's was not a happy situation. Recently published correspondence between Prime Minister Nehru and his chief ministers indicates that there was much pressure on Kamaraj to take action against Periyar (Nehru, 2007, p. 383; 2009, pp. 387–388).

References

Arangannal, Rama. 1988. *Ninaivukal*. Chennai: Nakkeeran Pathippagam.
Anaimuthu, V. (ed.). 1974. *Periyar Ee. Ve. Raa. Sinthanaikal*. Trichy: Sinthanaiyalar Kazhagam.
Annadurai, C. N. 2002. *Thambikku Annavin Kadithangal*, vol. 1. Chennai: Poompuhar Pathippagam.
———. 2002. *Thambikku Annavin Kadithangal*, vol. 3. Chennai: Poompuhar Pathippagam.
———. 2002. *Thambikku Annavin Kadithangal*, vol. 4. Chennai: Poompuhar Pathippagam.
Bate, Bernard. 2009. *Tamil Oratory and Dravidian Aesthetic*. New York: Columbia University Press.
Bhaktavatsalam, M. 1971. *En Ninaivugal*. Chennai: Jananayaga Seva Sangam.
Karunanidhi, M. 2000 [1975]. *Nenjukku Needhi*, 7th edn. Chennai: Thirumagal Nilayam.
Nehru, Jawaharlal. 2007. *Selected Works of Jawaharlal Nehru, Second Series*, vol. 39. New Delhi: Jawaharlal Nehru Memorial Fund.
———. 2009. *Selected Works of Jawaharlal Nehru, Second Series*, vol. 40. New Delhi: Jawaharlal Nehru Memorial Fund.
Pandian, M. S. S. 1996. 'Tamil Cultural Elites and Cinema: Outline of an Argument'. *Economic and Political Weekly* 31(15): 950–955.
Pandian, M. S. S., V. M. S. Subagunarajan, and Trostsky Marudhu (eds.). 2009. *Cartoonayanam*. Chennai: Kayal Kavin.
Ramanujam, K. S. 1967. *The Big Change*. Madras: Higginbothams.
Veeraraghavan, D. 2019. *Half a Day for Caste? Education and Politics in Tamil Nadu, 1952–54*, edited by A. R. Venkatachalapathy. New Delhi: LeftWord.
Velu, Kuruvikarambai (ed.). 2006. *Kuthoosi Gurusamy Katturaigal*, 2 vols. Chennai: Meenagopal Pathippagam.
Venkatachalapathy, A. R. 2018a. 'From Pulavar to Professor: Politics and the Professionalization of Tamil Pandits'. TRG Poverty and Education Working Paper Series. London: German Historical Institute.
———. 2018b. *Who Owns That Song? The Battle for Subramania Bharati's Copyright*. New Delhi: Juggernaut.
———. 2021. 'Against the Hustings: Periyar, Elections and Democracy'. In *State of Democracy in India: Essays on Life and Politics in Contemporary India*, edited by M. Ray. New Delhi: Primus.
Vivekanandan, N., Iniyan Sampath, and Kalpanadasan. 2013. *E. Ve. Ki. Sampathum Dravida Iyakkamum*. Chennai: Iniyan Sampath Pathippagam.

Part III
Religion, Caste, and Identity

6

The Rationale for Reason

Periyar on Religion

*Sundar Kaali**

> I am no agent to any religion; neither am I a slave to a person of any religion; I am subject to only two phenomena: love and wisdom.
>
> —Periyar (2009, vol. 4, part 1, p. 1797)

Periyar, to many in Tamil Nadu, was an atheist and iconoclast who called out belief in gods, superstitions, and rituals. He, of course, was all of that. But despite his rejection, he had a close engagement with religion and his critique was rooted in a close reading of religious texts, practices, and the values they espoused. He also creatively drew upon extant critiques of religion, Vedic and Abrahamic, and scholarly debates of his times to propound an alternative humanist ethic rooted in justice and fraternity. This chapter maps the multiple sources of his critique of religion and outlines the contours of his call for an ethical life.

There was much overlap between Periyar's thoughts and the critiques of scripturally sanctioned hierarchies of caste by spiritual and secular thinkers, both those who preceded him and those who lived in his times. Even though he was influenced by modernist critiques of religion emerging from the West, it is important to note that his views were in line with a long lineage of materialist philosophical traditions in the subcontinent.

Periyar became a militant atheist only in his forties. It was his vehement criticism of Brahminical Hinduism that led to his position of atheism. Periyar, on several occasions, observed that he was least interested in talking about God and religion. His atheism was therefore aimed at social reform and his arguments against God and religion meant only to strive for a casteless society.

---

* I wish to thank G. Aloysius, Joseph Durairaj, and Nirmal Selvamony for their useful comments on an earlier draft. I am also grateful to Rajan Kurai and S. Karmegam who suggested several inputs for editing a rather lengthy draft. Special thanks to M. Vijayabaskar for his painstaking efforts to prepare the final draft. Thanks also to Anandhi S., A. Sivasubramanian, J. Christy Femila, Mamithru Carr, S. Prince Ennares Periyar, K. Kamarasan, Pasu. Gowthaman, A. Thiruneelakandan, Prince Gajendrababu, V. M. S. Subagunarajan, G. Manikandan, P. Varadharasan, Geetha Sukumaran, Kalaivani Karunakaran, Deepa Ram, P. Padmapriya, Malavika Pavithira, and Chithiraiveethikkaran for their help in various ways in the making and shaping of this chapter. A final word of thanks to my wife, Parimalam Sundar, and my son, Niron Kaali, for their valuable support.

If caste and social hierarchy rested on God and religion, the latter had to be overturned. It was thus anti-Brahminism and anti-caste thinking that led Periyar to denounce religion. Demanding the abolition of the religious basis of communal life, he called for a reconstitution of ethical norms based on reason and justice. Periyar's strength lay in his ability to imagine and articulate the need for such norms in conjunction with a larger politics of social emancipation that resonated strongly with the people of the Tamil country.

The chapter is structured as follows. At the outset, I outline the early influences on Periyar. The section that follows maps Periyar's thoughts on the original need for religion and its subsequent evolution. The next section discusses the backdrop against which Periyar launched his critique of religion. Following this, the chapter draws parallels between Periyar's arguments for atheism and materialist traditions in the Tamil country and in the subcontinent. The chapter then turns to Periyar's call to confine religious practices to the personal sphere. Next, it explains and contextualizes Periyar's nuanced position on religious conversions. Following this, the chapter elaborates and locates Periyar's critique of the *Ramayana* in his attempts to foster a discerning and reasoning public. The final substantive section elaborates Periyar's version of reason. The core ideas of Periyar's engagement with religion are then summed up.[1]

Early Life and Views on Religion

Periyar's views on religion were rooted in his personal experience of growing up in a religious household. Born into a rich merchant family, he was exposed to religion at a very early age. Sanyasis, Bhagavatas, Puranics, and scholars of religion thronged his home. Periyar engaged in anti-Puranic debates and discussions with them from a young age. His everyday experiences during his formative years shaped his views on dominant Hindu practices. In 1902, a godman visited his native place of Erode. The younger brother of the godman had defaulted on many loans he had taken from Erode merchants. A warrant was issued to arrest him. At that time a *samaradhana* (ritual feeding of Brahmins) was underway and many Brahmins were being given a feast. Learning about the warrant, the brother of the godman tried to escape. Periyar apprehended the person and handed him over to the authorities. Later in the day, Periyar's father entered the scene and became aware of the incident. He lost his temper and thrashed Periyar. At this time Periyar was a married young man and his wife had given birth to a child which had passed away when it was five months old. Periyar decided to renounce his household life and become a *sanyasi*. He travelled to Kasi (Varanasi) and his firsthand exposure to the religious scene there left him completely disillusioned. In the meanwhile, his father located him and brought him back home (Periyar, 2017, pp. 4–10). His Kasi experience strengthened his convictions about the injustice of religious practices and caste hierarchies. His firsthand observations were bolstered by his readings on the origin and evolution of religion.

Origins of Religious Life According to Periyar

It could be argued that Periyar understood the origin of religious life in the manner of an anthropologist. He explored the history of communal living in the distant past and argued that religion as a concept needed research. The principles that governed ancient religion had gradually become distorted with the emergence of middlemen between God and people. Religion established itself when human beings started living as a community. It was a tool to structure the communal life of humans and to prevent violence between various groups. Drawing a parallel with the formation of associations or clubs in modern society, Periyar stated that such associational activity required certain codes of conduct and rules to govern it and reduce frictions that would otherwise sunder the community. Religion was also meant to curb instincts of selfishness that undermined the collective good. Periyar thus saw the origins of the concept of God in a disciplining and regulatory apparatus to ensure the functioning of human collectives (2009, vol. 1, part 5, pp. 2366–2368). He went on to point out that a close scrutiny of religious principles would show that they were based on the conditions of a particular period, geographical factors, and the mental state of the people or rather their ignorance. Further, over time, religions tended to exist merely as a set of rituals to be followed. Believers were no longer aware of the reasons for the genesis of a particular religion or why it propounded certain principles in a given space and/or time (Periyar, 2009, vol. 1, part 5, pp. 2366–2368).

Given the way it operates based on divine ordinance, religion tends to destroy one's wisdom. As a consequence, believers do not see the logical contradictions that religious beliefs and practices give rise to. The followers of every religion believe that it was God that created their respective religion and that God's actions are only in accordance with their own religious principles. This defies logic. Why then would God create separate religions for different groups of people? Why does God allow people to fight each other to establish the supremacy of one religion over another? And why does he permit degrading of other religions? (Periyar, 2009, vol. 1, part 5, pp. 2366–2368).

Another important attribute of religion is that it results in the creation of a set of agents (the priestly class) that mediate between God and believers. To Periyar, two aspects of such agents are detrimental to justice. First, believers are made to hold the words and prescriptions of the priestly classes sacrosanct even when these go against the common good. As a corollary, they are forced to suspend their reasoning abilities and are debilitated intellectually. Second, the priestly classes tend to perpetuate their power and status by claiming that salvation can only be obtained by carrying out certain sacrifices and expenditures that sustain them. Religion therefore justifies the earnings of such a class without expending any labour (Periyar, 2009, vol. 1, part 5, pp. 2366–2368). Periyar thus concluded that belief in God is blind and cannot be justified through experience or logical reasoning.

Periyar differentiated religion of all kinds from the Self-Respect Movement (SRM) he founded. The SRM sought to restore reasoning as the basis of communal life and set out to abolish any religious belief that destroyed the human intellect and self-respect, preventing people from coming together or their development or the expansion of their liberty. He however stated that the SRM is unconcerned with religious beliefs that are only meant to discipline and help people live together as a community or to help them attain salvation. When individuals choose to accept such beliefs, the SRM would not stand in the way (Periyar, 2009, vol. 1, part 4, p. 1851).

Periyar's formative views on religion can therefore be summarized as two-fold. First, religion has its genesis in a set of ethical codes to be followed for communal living. Second, over time, as it becomes organized, it tends to undermine the reasoning abilities of followers, especially through the emergence of an intermediary priestly class. The SRM, during the late 1920s and the 1930s, emphasized the irrationality of the hierarchies imposed by religion. Periyar's shift to full-blown atheism came later.

The Reason for Periyar's Religious Critique

One neglected area of Periyar's thought is that religion emerged as a binding force in human communal life. As noted earlier, he argued that during prehistoric times, human communities were formed on religious lines rather than secular ones.

On the occasion of the inauguration of *Kudi Arasu*, Periyar himself said that the purpose of launching the journal is to promote the love of our country, the love of our language, and the love of our religion (Periyar cited in Jerry, 1994, p. 152). Periyar's initial understanding of religion was that there could be religious faith but there was no place for inter-religious conflict. He was not an atheist but rather a liberal who believed in *samarasa sanmarga*—acceptance and tolerance among religions was Periyar's viewpoint (Periyar cited in Jerry, 1994, p. 152). That is the reason his publishing house brought out Swami Ramalinga Vallalar's poems in book form edited by Sami Chidambaranar in 1928 itself. It was Vallalar, a saint who lived in the Tamil region in the nineteenth century, who proposed *samarasa sanmarga* as the doctrine to be followed to create a society free of caste.

In May 1928, when the first Self-Respect wedding was performed, Periyar even offered his blessings praising the omnipotent *sakti*. Further, he went on to say that the Tamils, as real *bhakta*s, should lead the world in this regard (Periyar cited in Jerry, 1994, p. 159). However, Periyar also categorically stated that religion, which is for one purpose, and the institutions associated with it cannot be the guiding force for all times (Periyar cited in Jerry, 1994, p. 162).

> I do not say that there is no god. I do not object to your worshipping of generous and kind gods. If I am to propound my thesis, I will say that neither is there God nor is there not. …
>
> I do not object to a religion in which there is human dignity, a religion that does not subscribe to the principle of hierarchy and a god who does not demand money and other offerings from devotees. (Periyar cited in Jerry 1994: 143–144)

As Manoharan points out, for Periyar, it was impossible to be casteless and continue to be in the Hindu fold as its scriptures protect caste hierarchies. To abolish caste, it was therefore necessary to abolish the Hindu religion. The overlaps with Ambedkar's position on annihilation of caste are obvious (Manoharan, 2022, p. 82).

Further, as Manoharan puts it, if there was a central theme that ran coherently through Periyar's thoughts, it was anti-Brahminism. Anti-Brahminism to Periyar was not opposition to a single caste but a comprehensive critique of religious, cultural, political, and philosophical system(s) that were based on social hierarchy, inequality, and the denial of freedoms. Manoharan's central argument that Periyarist anti-Brahminism should be read as political atheism to counter the political theology of Brahminism therefore captures Periyar's position aptly (2022, p. 125).

A Hardcore Materialist

Periyar's belief in reason made him a lifelong materialist. He was not only a hardcore materialist but was also aware of Indian materialist traditions.[2] *Bhuta vadam, jada vadam, deha vadam, hetu vadam, ulakappatru vadam, ulakayatam, katci vadam, svabhava vadam, tarceyal vadam, brahaspati vadam, carvaka, pulan vadam, inpa vadam, vitanda vadam, inmai vadam, karpana vadam, nastika vadam, kutarka vadam*, and *prakrti vadam*[3] are other names for Indian materialist thought. As Raman (2014, p. 195) notes, such a variety of names is not available for any other philosophical thought in the world. Among the *pramanas*, which are sources of knowledge (*alavai* in Tamil), Periyar believed only in *pratyaksa pramana* (knowledge gained through the five senses as the sole source of truth) and *anumana* (inference) as the sources of right knowledge. The number of *pramanas* varies from author to author and text to text. However, a standard typology of *pramanas* emerged during the medieval period as given in Table 6.1.

Of the ten *alavai*s, Indian materialism relies only on *katci alavai* and *kandal alavai*. Periyar fell in that tradition. He did not believe in hell or heaven, any godhead, or even the concept of karma. Obviously, he refuted the idea of rebirth. In traditional Tamil logic, the *pramanas* or the means of knowledge are many. *Katci, karutal, uvamai, akamam, aruttapatti, iyalpu, ulakurai, apavam, mitci,* and *ullaneri* are the names of the different *pramanas* (*alavais*) in Tamil. Of these, Tamil Lokayata accepts only *katci* and *karutal* (*pratyaksha* and *anumana*, respectively) as the means of knowledge.[4]

Largely materialist in persuasion, Periyar and his intellectual comrades depended solely on *katci* and *karutal* as the means of knowledge. It is from this standpoint that they critiqued the Puranic materials and launched a scathing attack on the disastrous consequences that these have had in Indian society over the centuries.

While Periyar was partly influenced by Western materialism, I would argue that he was rooted in a long tradition of Indian materialism.[5] Not surprisingly, one of his booklets is named *Prakrti Vadam Allatu Materialism* (1949). Periyar employed the terms *pratyaksa pramanam, pratyaksa anubavam, pratyaksa arivu,* and *pratyaksa ulakam* in many of his speeches and writings.[6]

Given his exposure to these traditions. Periyar refused to believe in the primacy and supremacy of the Vedas as *pramanas*. Arguing that the Hindu religion is the religion of the Vedas, he questioned the ethical basis of the sacredness of the Vedas. As it is said that these are the words of God, he asked why they were not the same for people all over the world? Importantly he enquired: 'can it be such a phenomenon agreed and disagreed by a few, accessible to a few, limited to a few? Had they been

Table 6.1 Typology of *pramanas*

S. no.	Tamil term	Sanskrit	English equivalent
1	*katci*	*pratyaksa*	perception
2	*karutal*	*anumana*	inference
3	*oppumai* or *uvamai*	*upamana*	comparison
4	*urai* or *akamam*	*agama*	verbal testimony
5	*aruttapatti*	*arthapatti*	presumption
6	*iyalpu*	*svabhava*	nature or appropriateness
7	*ulakurai* or *aitikam*	*aitihya*	tradition or rumour (popular belief)
8	*inmai* or *apavam*	*abhava*	non-existence
9	*mitci*	*parisesa*	inference by elimination
10	*ullaneri* or *campavam*	*sambhava*	occurrence or inclusion

Source: Kandaswamy (2000, p. 56); see also Kandasamy (2005).

uttered by God, could that have been in only one language? If they were uttered for us, wouldn't they have been uttered in our own language?'

He further questioned the relevance of the language of the Vedas. If it was given by the gods to the people, why was it forbidden for most of the people to listen to, read, or know? Urging the need to reflect on these questions, he also asked the reader to pose similar questions to other gods and religions (Periyar, 2009, vol. 1, part 4, pp. 1799). Here, the emphasis on *katci* and *karutal* as the means to evaluate the scriptures is evident. Periyar talked further about the Vedas as the words of humans and not of gods. As they are equated with words of God, questioning or ignoring them will be read as atheism. But reading them makes it clear that that the Vedas are not the words of God but those of the (hu)man and hence should be questioned. There is no connection between God and the Vedas (Periyar, 2009, vol. 1, part 5, pp. 2396–2397).

This was to clarify the notion that the so-called divine words are in fact the words of men known as *rishi*s.

> Closely examining this, one would understand that it is not God who states, 'Vedas are the words of God' but another human being. One would never escape the truth that there are no connections between the Vedas and God …
>
> This is because none of our theist friends have ever seen God. Neither have they received any written or verbal response from God. They don't have any evidences—direct from God—to state that the Vedas are the words of God … (Periyar, 2009, vol. 1, part 5, pp. 2397–2398).

Using the same approach, Periyar questioned the notion of the soul (*atma*) in the manner of an informed materialist. To begin with he asked whether it was only the human soul that was connected with religion and God or whether the souls of plants, reptiles, birds, and aquatics too were connected to religion? If there were differences between the human soul and other souls, what would those differences be? As the human soul was expected to be reborn, he posited the following: Did the souls of plants, reptiles, aquatics, and other species also experience the outcome of their actions after the detachment of the soul from their bodies? Similarly, did human beings have any features that were exclusive and that differentiated them from the other species on earth? After posing these questions on the uniqueness of the experiences of human beings vis-a-vis other living beings, he went on to unsettle the concept of 'human beings'.

> The word 'human' in English refers to 'self'—any sensation that refers to 'I' and 'me'. How do human beings feel when they refer to themselves as 'I', 'me', and 'mine'? How did it emerge? Pondering over these will shed more light on the phenomenon of 'soul'.
>
> The term 'I' refers to which part of the body? Does it refer to the whole body? Or except the body? Up to where does this 'I' refer to? With what does 'I' disappear from the body? 'I' cannot be defined without proper answers to these questions.
>
> We scrutinize the 'self'—anything that could define 'human' or 'soul': my body, my soul, my mind, my knowledge, my wisdom, my thought, my wish, my god, my breath, and my celestial powers.

Scrutinizing these reveals that the 'self' isolates itself from all these and indulges in a dialogue with them. Hence, everything mentioned above is different from 'I'. Thus, we have to conclude that these sensations are not 'I'.

If so, for the deeds of 'I'—that is, human sensations—how could the soul or an entity or an energy, which is not 'I' face the outcomes? How could it be justified? How could it be the justice of God to punish or reward my soul for 'my' deeds? (Periyar, 2009, vol. 1, part 5, pp. 2312–2313).

Periyar's critique of religion therefore emanated from two sources. To begin with, he pointed to what religious practice meant in terms of effects on human development and social justice among believers. He then developed a critique of its assumptions based on logical reasoning and arguments derived from materialist traditions. He was however cognizant that religious principles continue to hold sway over most people. This led him to develop a nuanced position on religious practice.

Religion as a Private Affair

Though Periyar understood the origin of religion in communal life during prehistoric times, he vehemently condemned its modern forms for the presence of the caste system. As such, he had no quarrels with God or religion as long as they were confined to the private lives of individuals. This was a kind of secularization that aimed at marginalizing religion. So long as religion remained in the private sphere, it remained a phenomenon of the interior. But when religion entered the exterior as a public phenomenon, it tended to produce social injustice, particularly the caste system.[7]

Secularization therefore was the remedy that Periyar proposed. While he gave a qualified approval to Buddhism and Islam as alternatives to Hinduism and urged the Depressed Classes to convert to these faiths if they needed a religious identity (discussed subsequently in this chapter), he was also critical of these religions, particularly Islam. He claimed that the Buddha was the first philosopher of the world. In the secular society that Periyar envisaged, all religions would be treated on an equal basis and there would be a disjunction between state and religion.

Periyar made a distinction between following and worshipping in the matter of religion. For him, religion could be the private affair of an individual so long as it was not used to subjugate people:

If someone asks, 'I call love, grace, discipline and hospitality by a different name—God. Why do you object to that?' I would still say that those qualities listed as God should be something to be 'followed' and not 'worshipped'.

We don't have any objections to or conflicts with 'religion' or religious doctrines if their principles are about disciplining human behaviour towards other creatures. We don't have any conflicts with Siva, if Siva means love. I wish to call myself a Saivite. Neither do I have any conflicts with Vishnu, if that means helping other creatures and being gracious towards them. I also wish to become a Vaishnavite. We offer penance that our people should also get such 'Saivite' and 'Vaishnavite' qualities. (Periyar, 2009, vol. 1, part 4, pp. 1817–1818)

Periyar imagined a modern world with a new set of principles to regulate social life. Contending that norms should not be followed due to fear or compulsion, he argued that individual decisions such as marriage should be left to the desires of the persons concerned. The kind of control that temples and religious regulations have on people's lives is detrimental to society. Secularization of social regulation based on a set of modern norms of liberty and equality was therefore what he advocated (Periyar, 2009, vol. 1, part 4, p. 1898).

Citing the example of Western countries where enlightenment thinking had fundamentally changed the nature of religious life, he pointed to how organized religion had been relegated to the margins in these countries. According to him, 'two-thirds of the people in such countries do not go to any place of worship … They also do not seem to be practicing the worship of God in their homes. As the numbers of religious doctrines fall, so do the people following religion' (Periyar, 2009, vol. 1, part 4, p. 1899).

The Question of Conversion

Though Periyar called for confining religion to the private domain, he did engage with the issue of religious conversion at different points in his political career. While vehemently opposing religion, he upheld the rights of the lower castes to leave the fold of Hinduism to escape caste humiliation.

In 1947, when everything was set for the partition of the country, Periyar was invited to Tiruchirappalli to receive a fund collected by railway workers. Amidst a gathering of over 5,000 people, Periyar put forth his views on Islam. This speech was printed as a pamphlet and widely disseminated. The gist of the speech is as follows:

> Man cannot live without religion. The religion I am propounding does not have anything to do with *moksha*, fate, and redemption. What it is then is the respect, love, *bhakti*, *shanti*, fraternity, and unity that one person shows to the other. I am using the term religion in order to familiarize this concept. My personal conviction is to say that this is a social idea. However, if you say that this is what religion is, I wouldn't object. In fact, without such religion man cannot live in society. (Dawoodshah, 2008)

Further, as Manoharan (2022) points out, Periyar was clear about the sociocultural importance of conversion just as Ambedkar. While Periyar was committed lifelong to atheism and rationalism, he was aware and supportive of the freedoms made available to Dalits and the lower castes when they converted to other religions. He was however relatively more supportive of Islam and Buddhism in different contexts. Baxter argues that Periyar's advocacy for conversion to Islam involved 'a change of body, the somatic, where the embrace of different practices and *an alteration of how one sees the world* enables the fulfillment of democratic promise' (Baxter, 2019, p. 266, emphasis original).

Manoharan notes that Periyar's support for conversion to Islam was not because it was an ideal religion. Far from it. Rather, in a context where Brahminism and caste were widespread, conversion to Islam was a useful means to confront them (Manoharan, 2022, p. 99). Periyar urged the Depressed Classes to convert to Islam or Buddhism, if they needed a religious identity. Rather than going into the question of scripture and doctrine, Periyar called attention to the contemporary practices among believers. Unlike converts to Christianity or the Arya Samaj, conversion to Islam allowed for untouchables to get rid of their low-caste tag (Ramachandran, 2023, p. 81). While low-caste converts to Christianity or the Arya Samaj continued to be denied entry into the temple streets during the Vaikom Satyagraha, converts to Islam could walk on the streets without any restriction. He also drew attention to the persistence of caste among Christians in the Tamil region and its absence among Muslims. While other struggles to address caste-based discrimination would require effort and pain, conversion to Islam was painless and did not harm or affect anybody.

To be sure, Periyar's support for Islam was not unconditional.[8] He berated the Islamic orthodoxy for its treatment of women and called for the evolution of norms in line with the values of equality and freedom. He further questioned celebratory practices that required expenditure even by poor Muslims. Periyar was also responding to the modernizing ethos of Islam as it evolved under Kemal Pasha in Turkey in the early twentieth century. Pasha's efforts to reform outdated personal laws, introduce education and voting rights for women, and modernize the Turkish economy appealed to him. Further, as Manoharan points out, he was extremely wary of religion and the state coming together. He therefore made a strong case for the need to defeat Pakistan in the Indo-Pak war of 1965, as he feared the possibility of imposition of an Islamic state by Pakistan. In other words, he supported conversion to the extent that it expanded the degree of freedom for a lower-caste individual in their desire to escape caste oppression.

The social rationality of Buddhism too appealed to Periyar. However, he was critical of the role played by priestly intermediaries in undermining the core values of Buddhist thought, in particular, its emphasis on reasoning to arrive at ethical positions. Aloysius (2005, pp. 3–8) points to the possible influence of Dalit Buddhist thinkers like Pandit Iyothee Thass on Periyar's support for conversion to Buddhism to escape from caste oppression. Periyar also held that it was Brahmanical Hinduism that was instrumental in marginalizing Buddhism and its values in India. Buddha was the first anti-caste crusader who fought against Brahminical authority and its sanction of caste hierarchy. As to Christianity, Periyar pointed to how lower-caste converts were not treated on par with upper-caste converts (Subagunarajan, 2018, pp. 38–40). He saw this as a failure of Christianity in peninsular India and appealed to lower-caste converts to continue to struggle for their rights and not be blinded by the authority of priests.

As discussed in the previous paragraphs, Periyar's ideas on religion were shaped by both his personal experiences and his reading of relevant critical texts. Key to both were his long-term interactions and relationship with four spiritual/religious scholars who also advanced critiques of Brahminism, but from within the fold of religion.

Periyar and His Godmen Comrades

Four intellectuals who were all godmen were closely associated with Periyar: Gnaniyar Swamikal, Swami Sivananda Saraswati, Karuvur Ilatthu Adikal, and Kaivalya Swamiyar.

When Periyar launched the weekly *Kudi Arasu* in 1925, he invited Sivashanmuga Meygnana Sivacharya Swamikal, popularly known as Gnaniyar Swamigal, to inaugurate the event.[9] Speaking on the occasion Gnaniyar Swamigal appealed to Periyar to reform the world of religion also. Periyar's address at the time has been noted in the preceding discussion.

Another godman closely associated with Periyar was Swami Sivananda Saraswati. His book, *Gnana Suriyan*, first published in 1928, saw sixteen editions until 1982. In the book, Sivananda Saraswati exposed the fallacies of the Vedas, Upanishads, Agamas, Smritis, and Puranas. With eloquent endorsements by the nationalist leader V. O. Chidambaram Pillai and the Saivaite and Tamil scholars K. Subramania Pillai and Maraimalai Adikal, the text, written in a lucid style, demystified many Brahminical discourses. This was largely due to the deep knowledge of Sanskrit texts that Swami Sivananda Saraswati possessed. Here is an instance of his humorous critique of Brahminical greed:

> A south Indian aristocrat, disturbed by misfortunes and deaths in his family, summoned a Brahmin scholar to help him escape from this bad phase of his life. The Brahmin looked into the aristocrat's horoscope and said that the afflictions were caused by the fury of Yama's buffalo and required a *yagna* to be performed. The Brahmin also demanded a donation of female buffaloes with horns and hoofs covered with gold and other gifts. A few days later, as the *yagna* was being performed, a traveller, also a Brahmin scholar, heard about it and came to the appointed place expecting to receive certain gifts. When he reached the place, to his surprise, he saw a performance which was quite different from any of the prescribed rites found in the Sanskrit texts. Afraid of being found out by the newcomer, the Brahmin introduced a new 'mantra' to indicate to the latter that the gifts could be shared if he kept silent. (Swami Sivananda Saraswati, 1961 [1928], pp. 143–144)

Karuvur Ilatthu Sivananda Adikal served as the second-in-command in the first anti-Hindi agitation of 1937. He wrote two seminal works deconstructing Puranic materials. The first, *Hindu Matam Tamilar Matama?* (Is the Hindu Faith a Religion of the Tamils? [2009]) exposed the politics of Brahminical Hinduism in suppressing the work of Tirunavukkarasar, the only non-Brahmin among the four prime *Camayak Kuravar*s. It also offered a critique of the story of Candesvara Nayanar, another Saiva saint who belonged to that class.

Ilatthu Adikal's second work, *Periyapurana Araychi* (2013 [1941]) is a much more detailed study of the politics of fanatic Saiva devotion found in the Tamil Puranic hagiography, the *Periya Puranam*, depicting the legendary life stories of the sixty-three Nayanars. Periyar characterized the *purana*s as a major exercise in cultural deceit and debauchery. His critique of the Puranas, particularly Tamil Puranas like the *Periya Puranam* and *Kanda Puranam*, was based on such deconstructive logic.

Of all the godmen associated with Periyar, it was Kaivalya Swamiyar who was his closest confidant (see more in chapter 7). Kaivalya Swamiyar got his name from his expertise in Tamil Vedanta, particularly the fifteenth-century text, the *Kaivalya Navanitam*. First published in 1931, his collection entitled *Kaivalyam Allatu Kalakkiyanam* contained articles published in *Kudi Arasu* consisting of intense discussions on the Vedas, the Shastras, the Smritis, and the Puranas.

A vehement critic of Brahminical Hinduism, Kaivalya Swamiyar used to travel all over the western Tamil region and counter the religious discourses put forth by various godmen belonging to the Brahminical Hindu fold. His main targets were the *Parasara Smriti* and *Manu Smriti*. As mentioned previously, at an early age, Periyar used to engage in arguments regarding religion with scholars and *bhagavata*s. Particularly, he engaged in debates on the Puranas. One day in 1903, Kaivalya Swamiyar visited Periyar's home and from then on, they met frequently. This was a lasting relationship that influenced Periyar's later political engagements.

Periyar and the *Ramayana*

We now enter the significant phase of intervention by Periyar in the world of religious texts. Paula Richman's analysis of Periyar's reading of the *Ramayana* attempts 'to demonstrate the pivotal role that [his] attack on the Ramayana played in fusing religious texts and political issues in Madras during the middle third of the twentieth century' (1991, p. 176). Richman locates the positive reception of such an interpretation in the Tamil country in the way the Dravidian movement appealed to the people, the relationship between the Brahmins and elite non-Brahmins, and the role played by print in the intellectual life of Madras (1991, p, 178).

Richman delineates the manner in which this was accomplished in the Tamil country, particularly through print that was expanding rapidly at the time. Full-length books would have been too expensive for most people; moreover, reading such lengthy texts also required time that may not have been possible for many, especially the literate professionals. Short and inexpensive pamphlets on the other hand could reach a wider audience. Periyar wrote critical and short pieces on the *Ramayana* in a way that was simple and appealing. His humour-laced rhetorical style, written and spoken, easily captured the imagination of his audiences (Richman, 1991, p. 180).

Richman argues that through this mode of mobilization, Periyar attempted to demythologize Tamil texts. While admitting Periyar's continuity with the long tradition of Tamil polemics, she nevertheless locates his interpretation as an exhilarated literal reading of the texts that was in line with the popular discourse of the second half of the nineteenth century (Richman, 1991, p. 190). Arguing that Periyar's reading of the *Ramayana* was 'a hyperliteral reading of a mythic text', she contends that he used this technique to discredit and desacralize the *Ramayana*. Richman then goes on to trace the genealogy of such critical readings of the *Ramayana* to P. Sundaram Pillai, T. Ponnambalam Pillai, and M. S. Purnalingam Pillai in the nineteenth century.

Richman comments on Periyar's strategies of exegesis and argues that 'He anachronizes the text, condemning customs from centuries earlier on the basis of modern norms. He literalizes the text, subjecting mythic material to scientific analysis in order to "prove" that such events could not have occurred' (1991, p. 192). In short, she argues that Periyar's analysis of the Puranas was governed by his audience: 'E. V. R. intended his exegesis as a way of expounding Dravidian ideology to the popular reader, not to scholars' (Richman, 1991, p. 192). Finally, Richman observes that 'reassessing the traditional characters and incidents of the epic with polemical flamboyance, he created a rhetoric of political opposition that shaped public discourse for a group much larger than his relatively small band of followers' (1991, p. 195).

Periyar's most important critiques of the *Ramayana* are contained in two books, *Ramayanap Pattirankal* (2012 [1944]) and *Ramayanak Kurippukal* (2015 [1964]). Moreover, Periyar and the SRM attacked the *Ramayana* from various angles. For instance, Chakravarthy Nainar considered the issue from a Jaina viewpoint. Also, Periyar had in his collection of books one by C. R. Srinivasa Aiyankar (1928), which talks about Jaina, Buddhist, Graeco-Roman, and Christian *Ramayanas*. Further, P. V. Manicka Naicker (2018 [1955]) compared Kampan and Valmiki in his work *Kampan Pulukum Valmiki Vaymaiyum* (Kampan's Lies and Valmiki's Truth), where he exposed Kampan's fallacies.

This in fact is what contributed to a hitherto unprecedented culture-debating public in the Tamil country. While Richman's argument about the emergence of public discussion is highly relevant, her discrediting of Periyar's deconstruction of the Puranas as a literalization and an anachronization of materials is debatable. I turn to this question in the section that follows.

Periyar's Version of Reason

While reason (*pagutharivu*) was central to Periyar's thought, we need to bear in mind Manoharan's pointer towards an important dimension of Periyar's argumentative tradition. Periyar's *pagutharivu* needs to be *differentiated* from the Socratic *logos*. While *logos* is based on *a priori* concepts, that is, the idea that justice, virtue, good, beauty, and so on, are pre-existing notions and that the task of the rational mind is to discover the universal forms or definitions of these concepts, Periyar's *pagutharivu* was closer to empiricism, that is, a concept is true only if it can be verified by experience or experiment, and historicism, the view that value suited for one age will not be suited for another (Manoharan, 2022, p. 27).

Periyar's concept of rationality stemmed from his idea of a Tamil enlightenment. While it is commonly believed that Periyar was a militant atheist who lashed out against all forms of religious life from a rational viewpoint, I would venture to argue that his approach to religion was a much more nuanced and complex phenomenon. His denial of and opposition to religion were based largely on his anti-caste ideology. This is the reason why he opposed Brahminical Hinduism on which the caste system is premised. For him annihilation of caste was coeval with annihilation of religion, particularly the Brahminical Hindu version. Periyar, therefore, addressed the question of religion not just as an atheist in the Western sense, but as one who was deeply aware of the complex realities of socio-religious life in India.

Engaging in a debate to establish one's faith or other phenomena has a fairly long history in the Tamil country. In *Purananuru*, an anthology of poems belonging to the Sangam corpus (300 BCE–300 CE), the earliest extant literary tradition in Tamil, we find a poem in which a wealthy Brahmin by name Kavuniyan Vinnantayan engages in debates with scholars of other faiths. The debating tradition in Tamil could be classified into three categories: *Vivadam*, *Vadam*, and *Khandanam*. An exemplary phenomenon belonging to the first category is the chapter which shows the heroine of the second-century Tamil epic *Manimekalai* listening to scholars of many different faiths. She does not argue any particular position, but opts for Buddhism at the end. This mode of debate is then more of a dialogue and discussion and, therefore, I name it *Vivadam*. The second mode, *Vadam*, represents an argumentative tradition where persons belonging to two parties stridently put forth their contentions. Swami Ramalinga Vallalar's debate with the Brahma Samajist Pagadala Narasimhalu Naidu is an instance of this kind. The debate between Arumuga Navalar, the great proponent of Tamil Saivism, and the Christian scholar Karol Viswanatham Pillai also belongs to this category. In this form of debate, one party wins over the other and in many instances, the one who loses the battle becomes the follower of the victor. The third class of debate is *Khandanam*, characterized by an outright condemnation of the other party's viewpoint. The tract warfare that continued for a very long time between Christian missionaries and Tamil Saivites is an apt example of this category.[10] It is important to note that the first two modalities of debate were public events. Periyar drew upon these traditions for his discursive reasoning.

Periyar believed that in a religious community, when members are unable to locate the origin of the world and occurences in society, they tend to believe in God and his deeds. However, when those people understand the mechanisms behind such phenomena, they will likely experience a change in their minds (Periyar cited in Jerry, 1994, pp. 130–131). In short, the religious phenomena that people believe in gradually come to an end when they understand the mechanisms causing different occurences (Periyar cited in Jerry, 1994, p. 132). When human beings get rid of their superstitions and tread the path of reason, religion and God will cease to be active in their lives (Periyar cited in Jerry, 1994, p. 138).

Periyar condemned the priests and Brahmins who enslave us in the name of religion and urged the people to shake off this enslavement. The priests and Brahmins are as cruel and selfish as corrupt politicians and nationalists who betray the people in the name of fighting for a larger political cause. Using religion to divide people, they appropriate hard-earned wealth, destroy society and one's self-respect, and leave the masses as walking corpses. (Periyar, 2009, vol. 1, part 4, p. 1797).

For Periyar the materialist, God and religion were among the most artificial phenomena in human life. They were part of wild human imagination bordering on fanciful thinking:

> For religious persons, no matter which religion they belong to, God is artificial. I explain what is natural and artificial. Natural refers to something like eating, defecating, seeing, listening, breathing, speaking, experiencing pain, feeling hungry, sleeping, staying awake, feeling the emotions like lust, sorrows and happiness, sun and the moon, light and darkness and the five elements. All these are common for everyone and none can deny them. Apart from these, any God without such qualities, religion, salvation, heaven, hell, reward, condemnation, wealth, pride, humiliation, devotion, prayers and Vedas are mere imaginations… (Periyar, 2009, vol 1, part 5, pp. 2351–2353)

Periyar stated that belief in God and religion is quite difficult after an enquiry into the mechanisms that underlie such phenomena:

> We give an image to 'God' who has no physical form, who is invisible and who is not even an entity. Thus, God is an entity invisible and incomprehensible. 'Soul' is also given a similar definition. It is not an entity, not even an energy and it doesn't have a form and so we define it as a celestial phenomenon, which is invisible and incomprehensible to the mind and cannot be proved logically. However, one has to believe the existence of such phenomena—which is difficult after a detailed enquiry into logic and reason. (Periyar, 2009, vol 1, part 5, pp. 2351–2353)

Periyar firmly believed that this is an age of science and enlightenment where people would gradually lose faith in religion and start thinking in a rational fashion (1949, p. 10).

Conclusions

Periyar's thoughts on religion can be summarized as follows. Its origins lay in the need for a moral order in prehistoric times that made it essential for communal life, but it morphed into a set of ossified codes. People who practice them are seldom aware of the rationale for these codes, and in fact, religious authority prevents them from evaluating the basis of these codes, which turn out to be regressive. The rise of an intermediary priestly class is key to perpetuating this veil of non-reason, as such non-reason is critical to sustaining its power and wealth. Rather than an ethic rooted in an immutable scriptural authority, Periyar demanded an ethical reason that was capable of responding to historical changes and one that was based on equality and fraternity. He consistently highlighted the need for reason to be the basis for evaluation of all norms including religious ones.

While he was critical of unjust practices in all religions, Periyar was particularly interested in exposing the basis of caste injustice in Brahminical Hinduism as it was the dominant religious paradigm shaping everyday life on the subcontinent. Caste divisions and caste hierarchies are the primary obstacles to the realization of social fraternity, critical to the building of a modern and just society. His earlier efforts to engage with reforming religion gave way to an atheistic position as he found it impossible to reconcile the forging of an inclusive democratic republic with the caste society norms approved by Vedic Hinduism. He continued to support temple entry movements and struggles by the lower castes. The chapter points out how he drew upon materialist traditions in Indian philosophy and the argumentative traditions of nineteenth- and twentieth-century anti-caste spiritual leaders in the Tamil country to develop his critique of Brahminical religion. A materialist and atheist himself, he however acknowledged the importance of faith in people's lives. This faith must be personal and a part of one's interior self, but acknowledge the equality of all practices. He was strongly against its exteriorization in the form of social organization and the ordering of religious life by a priestly class. More importantly, he was opposed to the alliance of religion with the state.

While acknowledging the reformist egalitarian traditions in the Hindu religion, Periyar was open to the idea of conversion of lower castes to other religions to free themselves from the stigma of their low status. Again, his opinions on this were very context-specific and instrumental in terms of its aid in liberating lower castes. To him Islam was capable of erasing caste identities. He was especially appreciative of the reforms as regards women's rights undertaken in Turkey under Kemal Pasha. Holding Buddhism above other religions for its appeal to reason and its fight for caste equality, he supported Ambedkar's decision to convert to Buddhism. He was however critical of regressive practices in other religions, such as the treatment of women by Islamic conservatives. He also pointed to the failure of Christianity to erase caste distinctions.

The bulk of his political attention was however devoted to exposing the inconsistencies and regressive social norms that undergird the popular epics and myths constituting the corpus of Brahminical Hinduism such as the *Ramayana*. He inverted the accepted axis of good and evil in the epic by celebrating Ravana's wisdom and valour and criticizing Rama for upholding caste and gender hierarchies. To him, such critiques were important political tasks for fostering a modern republic and a fraternal society.

Notes

1. Unless otherwise stated, all quotations in this chapter are from the volumes on Periyar's thoughts edited by Anaimuthu (2009).
2. This is not to say that Periyar and his comrades were unaware and ignorant of Western atheism and agnosticism. Bertrand Russell's *Why I Am Not a Christian?* was translated and published by the SRM. Similarly, Robert Ingersoll's work, *Great Speeches of Col. R. G. Ingersoll* was translated as early as 1934. Another of his works had been translated as *Matam Enral Enna? (What is Religion?)* in 1933. Further, the famous French Catholic priest Jean Meslier's *Testament: Memoir of the Thoughts and Sentiments of Jean Meslier*, which promoted atheism and materialism, was

translated into Tamil in 1935. It is also worth noting in this connection that the revolutionary Bhagat Singh's *Why I Am an Atheist?* was translated by P. Jeevanandam in 1934.

3. Kamarasan (2021, pp. 9–11) is of the opinion that the term *prakrti vadam*, used by Periyar to denote materialism, is more appropriate than *porulmuthal vadam* employed in Marxist discourse.
4. *Anumana Vilakkam,* written by Narayana Iyengar (1935), principal of the Madurai Tamil Sangam College, was a textbook during those times. However, the scholarly nature of the book makes it a significant work on the *pramanas*.
5. See Muppaalmani (2012, 2013) for a serious study of Tamil Lokayata and a comparison with various other philosophical systems in India.
6. The term *pratyaksa* also occurs in several places in Periyar's work *Thatthuva Vilakkam* (2018). See, particularly, pp. 10, 17, and 24.
7. Sivasubramanian observes that Periyar viewed the Hindu temple as a public space and therefore emphasized the right to temple entry for the untouchables. See Sivasubramanian (2021, 2022) for a detailed discussion of the subject.
8. On Periyar's views on Islam, see Aloysius (2004).
9. On the life and work of Gnaniyar Swamikal, see Sundara Shanmuganar (1993) and Chinnak Kuthoosi (n.d.).
10. For a detailed discussion of debating in the Tamil scholarly and religious world, see A. R. Venkatachalapathy's foreword to Saravanan (2014, pp. 17–47).

References

Adikal, Karuvur Illatu. 2009. *Hindu Matam Tamilar Matama?* Chennai: V. O. C. Noolakam.
———. 2013 [1941]. *Periyapurana Araychi*. Chennai: Periyar Suyamariyathai Prachara Niruvana Veliyeedu.
Aiyankar, C. R. Srinivasa. 2007. *Itara Ramayanankal*. Chennai: Dravidar Kazhahaka Veliyeedu.
Aloysius, G. trans. and ed. 2004. *Periyar on Islam*. New Delhi: Critical Quest.
———. trans. and ed. 2005. *Periyar on Buddhism*. New Delhi: Critical Quest.
Anaimuthu, V. ed. 2009. *Periyar E. Ve. Ra. Chinthanaigal* (Thoughts of Periyar E.V.R.), 20 vols. Chennai: Periyar E. Ve. Ramasamy–Nagammai Kalvi, Araychi Arakkattalai.
Baxter, Matthew H. 2019. 'Two Concepts of Conversion at Meenakshipuram: Seeing Through Ambedkar's Buddhism and Being Seen in EVR's Islam'. *Comparative Studies of South Asia, Africa and the Middle East* 39(2): 264–281.
Dawoodshah, P. 2008 (1929). 'Suyamariyathai Vazhve Suyarajya Vaazhvu'. In *Dravidan Malar*. Chennai: Aavanak Kaappaka Veliyeedu.
Ingersoll, R. G. 1933. *Matam Enral Enna?* Translated by Lakshmirathan Bharati. Erode: Pakuttarivu Noorpatippuk Kazhakam.
———. 1934. *Naan Samsayavadi Aanaten?* Erode: Pakuttarivu Noorpatippuk Kazhakam.
Iyengar, Narayana. 1935. *Anumana Vilakkam*. Madurai: Madurai Tamil Sangam.
Jerry. 1994. *Manitham: Thanthai E. Ve. Ramasamy Periyarin Mata Ethirppu Nilaippaatu: Or Arasiyal Seyalpatu*. Dindigul: Vaikarai Pathippakam.
Kaali, Sundar. 2014. 'Adiyum Lingamum: Thonmankalaik Kattutaippattil Tattuva Vivesiniyin Palveru Anukumuraikal'. *Matruveli* (March): 139–156.

Kaivalya, Swamiyar. 1983 (1931). *Kaivalyam Allatu Kalakkiyanam*. Chennai: Periyar Suyamariyathai Prachara Niruvana Veliyeedu.

Kamarasan, K. 2021. *Periyarum Sila Tatthuva Visaranaikalum*. Thanjavur: Revolt.

Kandasamy, S. N. 2000. *Indian Epistemology as Expounded in Tamil Classics*. Chennai: International Institute of Tamil Studies.

———. 2005. *Tatthuva Nokkil Tamil Ilakkiyam*. Chidambaram: Meyyappan Pathippakam.

Kuthoosi, Chinnak. n. d. 'Tamil Valartha Gnaniyar Adikal'. N.p.

Manoharan, Karthick Ram. 2022. *Periyar: A Study in Political Atheism*. Hyderabad: Orient Black Swan.

Meslier, Jean. 1980 (1935). *Kattholikka Mataguru Marana Sasanam*, translated by S. Gurusamy, 3 vols. Chennai: Periyar Suyamariyathai Prachara Niruvana Veliyeedu.

Muppaalmani, K. 2012 (2009). *Tamilaka Tatthuva Chinthanai Marapukal*. Chennai: New Century Book House.

———. 2013. *Tamilaka Tatthuvam Ulakayatam*. Chennai: New Century Book House.

Naicker, V. Manicka. 2018 (1955). *Kampan Pulukum Valmiki Vaymaiyum*. Chennai: Dravidar Kazhahaka Veliyeedu.

Periyar. 1949. *Prakrti Vadam Allatu Materialism*. Erode: Kudi Arasu Pathippakam.

———. 2009. *Periyar E. Ve. Ra. Chinthanaikal*, compiled and edited by V. Anaimuthu, 20 vols. Trichy: Periyar E. Ve. Ramasamy–Nagammai Kalvi, Araychi Arakkattalai.

———. 2015 (1964). *Ramayanak Kurippukal*. Chennai: Suyamariyathai Prachara Niruvanam.

———. 2017 (1993). *Thanthai Periyare Ezhuthiya Suyacharitai*. Chennai: Dravidar Kalaga Veliyeedu.

———. 2018 (1947). *Thatthuva Vilakkam*. Chennai: Periyar Suyamariyathai Prachara Niruvana Veliyeedu.

———. 2020 (1977). *Manithanum Matamum*. Chennai: Periyar Suyamariyathai Prachara Niruvana Veliyeedu.

———. 2021 (1944). *Ramayanap Pattirankal: Periyar Suyamariyathai Prachara Niruvana Niruvanam*.

Ramachandran, A. B. ed. 2023. *Islam Patri Periyar*. Chennai: Seermai.

Raman, R. 2014. 'Ulakayatamum Manimekalai Punaiyum Ulakayatamum'. In *Manimekalayil Samayamum Meyyiyalum*, edited by R. Srinivasan and K. Kamarasan, pp. 195–240. Chennai: Tamil Nadu Buddha Sangam and Mettha Pathippakam.

Richman, Paula. 1991. *Many Ramayanas: The Diversity of a Narrative Tradition in South Asia*. New Delhi: Oxford University Press.

Russell, Bertrand. 1979 (1968). *Naan En Christavan Alla?* (Why I Am Not a Christian?), translated by S. Gurusamy. Chennai: Periyar Suyamariyathai Prachara Niruvana Veliyeedu.

Shanmuganar, Sundara. 1993. *Gnaniyar Adikal*. Chidambaram: Manivasagar Pathippakam.

Singh, Bhagat. 1979 (1934). *Naan Naathikan - En?* (Why I Am an Atheist?), translated by P. Jeevanandam. Chennai: Periyar Suyamariyathai Prachara Niruvana Veliyeedu.

Sivananda Saraswathi (Swami). 1961 [1928]. *Gnana Suriyan*. Erode: Kudi Aarsu Pathippakam.

Sivasubramanian, A. 2021. 'Kovil Panpadum Periyarum'. In *Sathiyum Samayamum*, pp. 17–30. Chennai: Parisal Books.

———. 2022. *Periyarum Kovil Panpadum*. Chennai: Nimir Publications.

Subagunarajan, V. M. S. ed. 2018. *Namakku En Intha Izhinilai?* Chennai: Kayal Kavin Books.

Venkatachalapathy, A. R. 2014 (2010). 'Introduction: Tamilil Khandana Ilakkiyam'. In *Arutpa Marutpa Khandanat Tirattu*, by P. Saravanan, pp. 17–48. Nagercoil: Kalachuvadu Publications.

7

Periyar's Anti-Aryanism

A Genealogy, a Synopsis, and a Critique*

Karthick Ram Manoharan

'Periyar had hatred towards the Brahmins and preached violence against them.' 'Periyar favoured the powerful among the non-Brahmin castes.' 'Periyar sidelined the Dalits.' These are the three main accusations against Periyar by his critics on the issue of caste. In an earlier paper (Manoharan, 2020), I have questioned the last two criticisms. In this chapter, I will address the first. Periyar was opposed to casteism in all its forms. In India, he identified the dominant form of casteism to be Brahminism, a ritual birth-based social hierarchy that derived legitimacy from scriptures, practices, traditions, and values associated with Hinduism and had material consequences. This led Periyar to be vehement in his criticism of the castes that were scripturally considered the highest, the Brahmins, and most sympathetic to the castes that were considered to be the lowest, the 'untouchables'. He understood that caste had a secular–material dimension as well, which was interconnected to the ideological–ritual dimension.

Working in the historical context that he did in Tamil Nadu, Periyar's approach to caste identified three broad social categories—the Brahmins, the Dalits,[1] and the 'Shudras'. His primary target of criticism was the first, the Brahmins. This led to counter-accusations that he was unfairly targeting only one community for casteism. But as I have discussed earlier (Manoharan, 2022), he often challenged the non-Brahmins for internalizing casteism, for subscribing to notions of hierarchy over others, and for the lack of an egalitarian spirit. Building on my earlier work and engaging with new material, this chapter attempts to present Periyar's approach to the Brahmins. This is best seen by engaging with Periyar's anti-Aryanism. I contend that anti-Brahminism was a consistent thematic concern in Periyar's political career. And anti-Brahminism for Periyar was interlinked with anti-Aryanism, that is, an opposition to notions of racial-caste supremacy.

---

* An earlier version of this chapter was presented at the Center for South Asia, Stanford University (2023), and I benefitted from interaction with the participants. I thank Nithin Seelan for drawing attention to the 'Dravidian connection' in the works of Africanist thinkers. A. R. Venkatachalapathy and Vilasini Ramani went through the first draft and helped finetune it. I am grateful to Professor A. Ramasamy for helping with the translation of A. V. Nayakkar's verses. I am also thankful to Valasa Vallavan for sending me the works of Nayakkar and Vidiyal Rajaram for sending me the works of Kaivalya Swamiyar.

I begin this chapter with an overview of Aryanism and anti-Aryanism in modern Indian thought. I then provide a genealogy of anti-Brahmin critique in Tamil Nadu, highlighting (neglected) thinkers in the region in whose intellectual lineage Periyar may be placed. Next, I give a synopsis of Periyar's approach to the Brahmin question, drawing from his own writings. I conclude with a critique of Periyar's anti-Brahminism.

Aryanism and Anti-Aryanism

In 'Anti-Casteist Casteism?' (Manoharan, 2017), I attempted a Fanonist critique of Periyar's approach to caste. The title of the article was a spinoff from Jean-Paul Sartre's (1965) famous polemical description of the Negritude movement as 'anti-racist racism'. To be clear, anti-racist racism is not what is popularly caricatured as reverse racism. In Sartre's usage, the term refers not to a feeling of racial supremacy, but a racial consciousness and assertion among the colonized Black people (Irele, 1964). Likewise, when I speak of Periyar's 'anti-casteist casteism' (also polemically), it does not indicate a 'reverse casteism' towards the Brahmins. It refers to Periyar's attempts to create an anti-caste political consciousness among non-Brahmins by challenging Brahmin dominance as well as caste-based divisions within the whole non-Brahmin bloc—Periyar also discourages *any* caste consciousness or caste assertion *except* that of the scheduled castes. The main criticisms I offered of Periyar's approach, deriving from a Fanonist understanding, are that, first, it does not adequately unsettle identities of communities seen as oppressor and oppressed. Second, relatedly, the identities of emancipation that Periyar proposes revolve around *not being* a Brahmin. That is, the Brahmin still constitutes the identity of the subjects to be emancipated, albeit negatively.[2]

Periyar sought to rally the non-Brahmin under the banner of the 'Dravidian' who was different from and opposed to the 'Aryan' Brahmin. Who was the Dravidian? This term does not find mention in ancient or medieval Tamil texts. It is however used in the *Manu Smriti* to refer to a community of fallen Kshatriyas, the warrior class. The idea of the 'Dravidian' as a linguistic–racial group different from the Aryan became popular as a rallying point of politics in the Madras Presidency only with colonial modernity, when a discourse of Aryan invasion and Aryan racial–cultural superiority grew to be dominant. More specifically, Robert Caldwell's *A Comparative Grammar of the Dravidian or South Indian Family of Languages* published in 1856 identified Brahmin–Aryan–Sanskrit as interlinked and as outsiders to the Dravidian land of the south. Further, Caldwell also endorsed the idea that the Brahmin introduced caste to the Dravidians. Soon after, the idea of Brahmin–Aryan–Sanskrit as different from and inimical to non-Brahmin–Dravidian–Tamil was promoted by Tamil Saivites, Buddhists, and secularists. These included intellectuals from elite non-Brahmin castes such as the Vellalars, intermediate castes such as the Vanniyars, and Dalit castes such as the Paraiyars. The notion that Aryan–Brahmin and Dravidian–Tamil–non-Brahmin constituted hostile racial groups, the latter having been subjugated by the former around two millennia earlier, gained political and intellectual influence even before Periyar arrived on the scene. He used these binaries to bolster his anti-caste movement. *The Dravidian was not only not Aryan, but was opposed to Aryanism.*

Recent writings (Joseph, 2018; Thapar, 2019) suggest that there was no Aryan invasion but only waves of migration. Joseph claims that the Aryans did not introduce the caste system on their arrival, but much later, when caste emerged as a new powerful ideology and was imposed on society (2018, p. 212). Traditionally, 'Aryan' meant a person of status and nobility (both material and cultural) and it is only in nineteenth-century narratives, strongly influenced by the colonial atmosphere, that the Aryan as a central figure of Indian history emerged (Thapar, 2019, p. 35). Others note 'Aryanism's pre-colonial iterations' and draw attention to a 'more entangled, temporally expansive examination of Aryanism' which reveals 'the interconnections between different "morphologies of domination", expressly that of Sanskrit Brahmanism and British colonialism' (Birkvad, 2020, p. 74).

The critics who are quick to discount the Dravidian identity as mythical or separatist, rarely take into account how Caucasians and Indian upper-castes of the nineteenth and twentieth centuries saw the Aryan identity. Trautmann discusses the 'racial theory of Indian civilization' where British Sanskrit scholars sought to read in the Vedas evidence of conflict between the 'fair-skinned civilized Aryan' and 'the dark-skinned savage' (1997, p. 206). Figueira highlights a number of influential European thinkers who glorified the Vedic Aryans, in a racial sense, to bolster their own racist anti-Semitic theories. She argues that 'a fictive India and fictional Aryan ancestors were constructed in the West to provide answers for questions regarding European identity' (2015, p. 16). These narratives travelled to India where they received an anti-colonial makeover. Hindu nationalists developed a vision of 'Aryan superiority' which was linked with 'India's regeneration' and 'Faith in the Aryan past thus became a tool in the fight against foreign oppression' (Figueira 2015, p. 140). Thapar alerts us to the works of Tilak, who saw the European Aryans as inferior and the Aryans who settled in India as superior, and also to the writings of Dayanand Saraswati, Madame Blavatsky, and Colonel Olcott, all of whom greatly contributed to the myth of Aryan racial and cultural superiority (2019, pp. 50–53).

The situation in the Tamil south was not much different. G. Subramania Iyer, one of the founders of *The Hindu*, wrote a text in 1888 called *Arya Jana Ikiyam Allathu Congress Mahasabhai*—Unity of the Aryan People or the Congress Party—which strongly endorsed the idea of the Aryan as the ideal Indian (Pandian, 2007, p. 52). In his work *Tamil Studies*, M. Srinivasa Aiyangar (1914, p. 42), who saw the Brahmins as Aryans, urged the readers of Caldwell to acknowledge that 'the earliest grammarians of Tamil were Brahmans, their first spiritual instructors were Brahmans, and their first teachers of philosophy were also Brahmans'. One R. Swaminatha Iyer, writing in *The Hindu* in 1924, claimed that Dravidian languages and civilization were but the creations of the Aryans (Irschick, 1969, pp. 298–299). In a 1927 text, Sarvepalli Radhakrishnan (2018, p. 2), the philosopher who would later become the second Indian president, wrote that in ancient India, the Aryan culture marched southward and dominated the earlier Dravidian culture. He was further of the opinion that 'Caste, on its racial side, is the affirmation of the infinite diversity of human groups' (2018, p. 69). In 1949, Sir T. Vijayaraghava Acharya addressed a Brahmana conference where he derided the Dravidian movement and claimed that 'The bond which binds all Hindus together, wherever we live, is the Sanskrit language and the Sanskrit culture which comes down to us from a period long anterior to the dawn of recorded history'.[3] Later, the eminent historian K. A. Nilakanta Sastri (2018, p. 169), perhaps disturbed by the repeated accusations of casteism against the Aryans, made a fabulous claim in a 1958 article in *The Hindu* that the pre-Aryan people of India were the ones responsible for the system of hereditary castes. He praised the 'Indo-Aryan founders' for bringing religion and philosophy to affirm the 'fundamental purity and nobility of the human soul', adding for good measure that Sanskrit and sacred Hindu shrines preserved Indian national unity. These were the considered positions, not of fringe elements, but well-educated thinkers in the political and intellectual mainstream with great influence and following.

The Dravidian response to Aryanism was to be expected. It cannot simply be dismissed as a colonial creation. It was a movement grounded in secular ideas of citizenship which challenged a caste-and-religion-inspired nationalism. If it used racialist vocabulary, it did so because that was the available vocabulary at the time to contest Aryan racialism promoted by influential Brahmin and European thinkers, and when it did, it was in an 'anti-racist racist' way.[4]

There were others in India who also responded to the Aryan racialism. In Maharashtra, Jyotirao Phule (2008, pp. 24–25) read Hindu myths to argue that the Aryans were foreign conquerors who devised the caste system to rule and oppress the natives. He prayed to God and appealed to the British government to liberate the oppressed castes from 'the psychological slavery of the Brahmans' (2008, p. 20). Like the Periyarists who came later, he identified the Shudra–Atishudra castes as the indigenous people of India and the Brahmins as Aryan invaders.[5] Recent research alerts us to a nineteenth-century Marathi text *Jatibhed Viveksar* by Tukaram Padwal who presented the Shudras 'as indigenous heroes who were vanquished by the Aryan invasion' (Jaywant, 2023, p. 381). Reading Aryans as oppressors of the Shudras, therefore, was hardly limited to Tamil Nadu and went back a few decades before Periyar.

Genealogy

From the mid-nineteenth century, many reformist Saivites and Buddhists in the Tamil region were opposed to Brahmin dominance, which they also viewed as Aryan racialism (see Introducing an Iconoclast). While they were definitely predecessors *in time* to Periyar, they were not necessarily predecessors *in thought*. Ramalinga Swamigal (1823–1874), more popularly known as Vallalar, was a Tamil saint whose egalitarian spirituality stressed love and universal fraternity. His thoughts greatly influenced Tamil cultural–spiritual assertion and socio-religious reformation from the late nineteenth century onwards. Vallalar had followers across caste and class, took a strong pro-poor and anti-caste stance, and also challenged the conservative Saivite establishment (Weiss, 2019, p. 21). Srilata Raman (2022), noting the long influence of Vallalar's ideas on Dravidian and Dalit thinkers who succeeded him, points out that the Self-Respecters under Periyar saw Vallalar as their intellectual forerunner and placed him 'squarely within a progressive and distinctly Tamil historical teleology' (2022, p. 310). Post-Vallalar thinkers such as Iyothee Thass and Maraimalai Adigal, who were additionally influenced by the impact of Caldwell's work, incorporated a criticism of the Aryan–Brahmin in their anti-caste discourse. Thass for instance declared that 'the category "Hindu" is a fantasy invented by the invasive Aryans who live by casteism' (Ayyathurai 2023, p. 22).

While Periyar did share with these thinkers an opposition to caste and/or a criticism of Brahmin dominance and also acknowledged their contributions to egalitarian thought, he did not find a solution to the problem of caste in religious reform or conversion, even though he was willing to engage with those promoting these ideas. Further, as Sibley (2024) notes, 'Unlike Neo-Saivas and Thass's Adi Dravida Movement, Ramasamy's vision of ancient Dravidian society does not affiliate itself with any particular religious tradition.' Periyar was a political atheist (Manoharan, 2022a) who challenged the irrationality behind both religion and nation and held *pagutharivu*, rationalism, as an idea to be followed and propagated. His criticisms of the Brahmins were rooted in his commitment to a secular rationalism and to his understanding that Brahminism influenced different forms of oppression in India. A work of intellectual history would trace Periyar's philosophical legacy to thinkers who held similar opinions, like the Madras Secular Society that was active for about a decade from the late 1870s.[6]

The Madras Secular Society, originally called the Hindu Freethought Union, was a group of intellectuals who identified as secularists, freethinkers, and atheists.[7] They published two journals, the *Thathuvavivesini* in Tamil and *The Thinker* in English.[8] Greatly influenced by the European Enlightenment, these journals published articles introducing thinkers such as Giordano Bruno, Voltaire, David Hume, Benedict Spinoza, Thomas Paine, P. B. Shelley, and Robert Ingersoll. They were particularly inspired by the English atheist Charles Bradlaugh, founder of the National Secular Society in England and the name, the Madras Secular Society is testimony to the same. The names of Charles Darwin and Thomas Malthus also appeared frequently in their pages. Diverse topics were covered including atheism, religion, secularism, science, philosophy, caste, and women's empowerment. Several articles supported widow remarriage and condemned the orthodox for opposing this. Religious myths, especially from Hinduism and Christianity, were subjected to interrogation and even ridicule.

Some of the contributors were openly critical of the Brahmins. An unsigned article in *The Thinker* (17 December 1882) condemned caste as a system of injustice which privileges the Brahmins at the expense of others: 'Caste is not merely the outward symbol of the Hindu religion, but it is its fortress … The system of caste in its very nature enforces the superiority of one class of Hindus and the inferiority of another' (Arasu, 2012f, p. 25). In an article on 2 November 1884, a contributor signing himself as 'Challenger' accused the Brahmins of exploiting the masses through spirituality. 'These people who live a rich life at the expense of others are supposed to be the mediators between the lower classes of the Hindus and their god or gods' (Arasu, 2012e, pp. 261–262). The contributor further lampooned the Hindu religion. In another critique, an author with the same pseudonym challenged 'objectionable opinions' of 'Aryan morality' (Arasu, 2012f, p. 214). In an article on 17 January 1886, M. Masilamani Mudaliar referred to the Brahmin–Shudra divide and to how this was validated by texts like the *Manu Smriti* (Arasu, 2012c, pp. 271–273). Masilamani, a key intellectual contributing to Buddhist revivalism in Madras, was also the author of *Varna Bedha Surukkam*, a booklet condemning the varna system, which was later republished by Iyothee Thass.[9] An excerpt published in the *Thathuvavivesini* shows the author criticizing Brahminical practices for contributing to the oppression of women and Shudras (Arasu, 2012a, pp. 43–44). A series of articles were written in favour of an atheist *weltanschauung* (Arasu, 2012b) and opposing superstition (Arasu, 2012d).

An important personality in this collective was Athipakkam Venkatachala Nayakkar (1799?–1897). Nayakkar belonged to the socio-economically backward Vanniyar caste, but was from a relatively affluent background. Well educated, he was at ease both in English and Tamil and demonstrated a consummate command of the Hindu scriptures. He published at least two books in his lifetime, *Payakkarigalikkum Mirasudarargalukkum Undayirukkira Vivaatham* (2014a [1872]) and *Hindu Matha Aachara Aabasa Dharsini* (2014b [1882]).[10] The first was a defence of peasant cultivators and highlighted the oppressions they faced under landlords—a longtime concern of Nayakkar. In 1863, he had written to the *Madras Times*, complaining about the 'gross partiality … shown [by the colonial government] to the Mirassidars from their being Brahmins, whilst the actual cultivators, the Poyakkaries and Sugavasis ha[d] been trodden down, and unreservedly made over to the tender mercies of their hard hearted and cruel task-masters' (2014a, p. 178). He noted how the 'right-hand' castes like the Vellalars and Agamudaiyars joined with the Brahmins to oppress other castes (2014a, p. 87). This 1872 book also condemned superstitions, irrational rituals, and the ill-treatment of widows (2014a, pp. 89–90).

Hindu Matha Aachara Aabasa Dharsini (which may be loosely translated as 'Light on the Obscenities in Hindu Traditions'), was a frontal attack on the practices associated with Hinduism. Written entirely in verse, it discussed the origins of the varna system, caste differences, Brahmin hegemony, the oppression of women, religious myths, irrational practices, and the need for rationalism. Some examples of the verses in the book are:

> With evil in their hearts, the kings and Brahmins conspired together to create the caste system,
> Placing the Shudras at the bottom, and the Brahmins, Kshatriyas and Vaishyas above them, claiming
> That they came from the head, shoulder and thigh of Brahma, and Shudras from the feet
> O listen to how the Shudras were made to carry out lower occupations on the basis of birth.
> (Nayakkar, 2014b, p. 119)

> Those who are called Shudras were made to serve the other three
> Dutybound to do all that those above wanted to be done
> The Shastras, the Vedas, and any form of education
> They were prevented from learning or even hearing (Nayakkar, 2014b, p. 119)

> Posing as gods from a different world, the Brahmins who came from the north
> Said that their language was the language of the gods, and duped
> Those in the south, and to continue this fraud they wore
> New guises and spoke new ideas, all of which are lies (Nayakkar, 2014b, p. 126)

> They say that they are twice-born, the Brahmins, who would perform rituals
> Give blessings, act as preceptors, curse those who had done wrong,
> And guide those who were born lower to them; they also made others believe
> They created new castes by mingling with animals and birds (Nayakkar, 2014b, p. 183)

Periyar was presented a copy of this text in 1946 by his comrade K. Ramalingam. In his commentary, Periyar praised the author for anticipating his propagation of rationalism by more than sixty years and identified him as a predecessor in time and thought of the ideas of the Self-Respect Movement (SRM); he soon arranged for the republication of the text (Ramasamy 2014, pp. 29–31).

Kaivalya Swamiyar (1877–1953) was an important personal influence on Periyar. Born as Ponnusami in a Sozhiya Vellalar family in Kozhikode, he was drawn to Saivite spirituality and theology at an early age. In honour of his expertise on the medieval Vedanta text *Kaivalya Navaneetham*, he was named Kaivalya Swamiyar. Periyar's biographer Chidambaranar identifies

Marudhaiya Pillai, an Erode-based rationalist Tamil scholar and Kaivalya Swamiyar as the key personalities who shaped Periyar's approach to caste and religion (2016, p. 92).

Kaivalya Swamiyar was a frequent contributor to *Kudi Arasu*. Compilations of his articles have been produced since the 1930s, with the most recent and most comprehensive being published in 2022.[11] In his foreword to a 1931 compilation, Periyar notes his friendship with Kaivalya Swamiyar from as early as in 1903 and how they would argue with each other, and also praises his commitment to social reform and rationalism (Ramasamy, 2022, pp. 15–19).

In an article in *Kudi Arasu* in 1926 titled 'Why Do We Blame the Brahmins?', Kaivalya Swamiyar stated that 'The upper-castes did not spread education to the lower-castes but they undertook all efforts to gain knowledge for themselves, to keep their homes flourishing and to show to the Europeans that they were high-class people' (2022, p. 31). In a follow-up, he defended *Kudi Arasu's* criticism of the Brahmins, arguing that just as it is impossible not to criticize the colonialists until independence is achieved, similarly it is impossible not to criticize the Brahmins till a casteless society is achieved (2022, p. 68). He lambasted Hindu orthodox leaders such as the Shankaracharya for their views on women and caste (2022, pp. 227–230) and asserted that the priestly class was a hurdle to the spread of knowledge in society (2022, pp. 389–393).

Kaivalya Swamiyar opposed the scriptures as they described the Shudras as slaves of the Brahmins (2022, p. 395). Though a renouncer himself, he criticized God, the Shastras, and common ignorance for contributing to the state of the Shudras (2022, p. 397). He asked rhetorically: 'Let the Brahmins read English and advance in the professional services despite the injunctions of the Shastras, we do not care about that, but should they still see themselves as Brahmins and the rest as inferiors and as Shudras?' (2022, p. 407). He further noted that all the rules and restrictions of the Shastras were suspended when it came to the Brahmins, while they were enforced to prevent the progress of the Shudras. He also pointed to the 'sins' of the non-Brahmins, in ill-treating the lower castes among them and in not cultivating a common spirit of humanity (2022, p. 615). Calling strongly for the abolition of untouchability and advocating a revolution based on 'truth, equality, and unity', he asserted that radical changes are a component of human history (2022, p. 818).

The criticism of Brahmin privilege by the Madras Secular Society, Venkatachala Nayakkar, and Kaivalya Swamiyar, besides being rooted in concern for a casteless society, was also based on an understanding and appreciation of secular rationalism. This greatly influenced Periyar's approach.

Synopsis

Writing in 1925, Periyar questioned why the *poonool* (sacred thread worn by Brahmins) should be a marker of identity. Criticizing reformers who sought to conduct the *poonool* ceremony for non-Brahmins as well so as to elevate them to the status of Brahmins, Periyar observed that this marker only served to strengthen notions of high and low between humans and added that abolition of ideas that glorify the *poonool* and its wearers is as important as the abolition of untouchability (2011, pp. 33–36). In 1926, he explained that the opposition to Brahminism was because of the Brahmins' unequal treatment of the rest of the population. Referring to Brahmin overrepresentation in government jobs by which they exercised dominance over the rest, he argued that non-Brahmins must take-over these jobs. But he also added that he was not promoting jealousy against Brahmins with respect to such positions—he wanted non-Brahmins to shake off their belief in the ritual and cultural superiority of Brahmins (2011, p. 43).

Periyar questioned if there was any point in political freedom without the destruction of the caste system. He argued that a majority of the people had been denied economic progress by virtue of caste (2011, p. 218). In a tirade against the *Bhagavad Gita* in 1933, Periyar claimed that all except the Brahmins were lower castes, of which about 25 per cent (referring to the Dalits) were in slave-like conditions (2011, p. 269). Would the mere removal of the British remove Brahmin privilege as well? 'A self-rule [swaraj] that does not remove the insults and humiliations that a human being faces, is only a duplicitous rule and not a just rule' (2011, p. 270). He further stated that if self-rule could promise a society free of caste divisions, atrocities, and discrimination, he would support it, while expressing his doubts about the commitment of Brahmin leaders to the same (2011, p. 275).

By the late 1920s, Periyar, who started his political career as a Congress leader, had become its strongest opponent. Dravidian activists inspired by Periyar began subjecting the Hindu scriptures to criticism. A public burning of the *Manu Smriti* was organized by J. S. Kannappar, editor of *Dravidan*, in June 1928 (Visswanathan, 1983, p. 76). As a response to the fledgling SRM, Brahmins organized conferences in 1929 and 1930 where they lamented the growing anti-religion and anti-Brahmin discourse and passed resolutions 'reaffirming their faith in the validity of the *varnashrama dharma* and in the sanctions against the scheduled castes' (Visswanathan, 1983, pp. 103–104).

While he was open to dialogue with Hindu reformist saints, Periyar was convinced that one could not annihilate caste without becoming an atheist (2011b, p. 1). In a 1936 article, he spoke highly of Ambedkar's idea of leaving Hinduism (2011b, p. 4) and opined that 'If Brahmins are gone, caste, religion and God will also go. If caste, religion and God are gone, Brahmins will also go. If caste is gone, Brahmins will also be gone' (2011b, p. 4). One can infer here that what Periyar is talking about is annihilation of caste as a system, which both requires and results in the disappearance of the 'Brahmin' identity that is fundamentally based on ritual superiority over other identities. This is far from a call for annihilation of Brahmins as individuals or a social group, but rather for a radical social change where the identity of 'Brahmin' as high-caste ceases to have social relevance. A question can arise on why Periyar focused *only* on Brahmins and not others. We will return to this in the concluding section of the chapter.

Periyar saw the Aryan and non-Aryan conflict as stretching over two millennia. The Aryans came from outside and imposed the caste system on the native Tamils or Dravidians and thus ruled over them. To substantiate this, he cited scholars such as R. C. Dutt and R. C. Majumdar (2011b, pp. 56–69). In a move reminiscent of Phule, he racialized caste and viewed Brahmins as the Aryan race and their ideology as Aryanism, which is the same as Brahminism, a social perspective of racial-caste supremacy. For the non-Brahmin Tamils who subscribed to this ideology, it meant a loss of self-respect and personhood. In a 1941 article, he argued that Dravidians were not Hindus and that it was incumbent on the non-Brahmin Tamils to work for their own liberation. The Brahmins would not engage with this because 'they have inherited privileges on the basis of birth. They will therefore try to stop change. Thus, in the struggle to abolish birth-based caste differentiation, we and the Brahmins end-up becoming enemies and combatants' (2011b, p. 136). That Brahmins will not commit to reform is a sentiment also found in Ambedkar's *Annihilation of*

Caste, where he argues that even secular Brahmins will not challenge the caste system because 'the break-up of the Caste system is bound to affect adversely the Brahmin Caste' and further that 'it is useless to make a distinction between the secular Brahmins and priestly Brahmins'. The significance of the focused criticism of the Brahmins is because they form 'the intellectual class of the Hindus' and are seen as 'Gods on earth'. When such a powerful community has its interests against reform, then reform itself becomes 'very, very remote'. To Ambedkar, caste was 'nothing but Brahminism incarnate' (Ambedkar, 2014, pp. 70, 71, 77).

Given Periyar's emphatic disclaimer that he harboured no personal enmity against Brahmins (2011b, p. 204), how do we understand the idea of enmity that he claimed exists between the Brahmins and non-Brahmins, as discussed in the previous paragraph? Periyar's politics was Schmittian in the sense that it had a conception of the 'absolute enemy' in the Brahmin Other; as a person claiming the absence of rights in the Brahminical order, we can say that he sought 'justice in enmity' (Schmitt, 2004, p. 65). A key difference however is that in a Schmittian imagination, the Friend–Enemy conceptualization of politics entails a potential existential elimination of the enemy. Periyar's notion of 'caste annihilation', like Ambedkar's, was not about the elimination of a particular group of people belonging to a particular caste, but about the elimination of a mentality and of privileges that they believed were inherent to the Brahmin identity. For instance, at a public meeting in 1949, Periyar appealed to the Brahmins to leave attachment to orthodoxy and to embrace rationalism and see themselves as equals of all others (2011c, p. 115). 'The goal of the Dravidar Kazhagam [DK] will not cause even the mildest harm to Brahmins in a personal way' (2011c, p. 116). And the work of the DK would continue as long as Brahminism existed. Again, at a public meeting in Karur in 1950, he reiterated that 'We want the Aryan culture, that is, Brahminism, which is responsible for caste hierarchy to be destroyed. We oppose Brahminism and not the Brahmins' (2011c, p. 176).

In a 1950 article in *The Hindu*, Periyar said that he did not subscribe to a race theory like Hitler and that south Indians could not be divided racially on the basis of a blood test; to him, Aryanism and Dravidianism were differences of sociocultural values and the purpose of the Dravidian movement was to 'reconstruct society on a human and rational basis'.[12] Reiterating this, in a 1953 speech in Dharmapuri, Periyar stated that the Aryan–Dravidian difference is not one of blood, but of culture and beliefs. Here, he gave his understanding of Aryans as 'Those who think of themselves as Brahmins, and by virtue of that, think of themselves as superior castes' and Dravidians as 'Those who have been marked as the fourth caste, lower caste, Shudras by Brahmins and their gods, religions, Shastras and Puranas' (2010a, p.10). We can see here that Periyar was not rigid about the racialist understanding of caste or Aryan and Dravidian. When he used racialist vocabulary, it was *only* to oppose the supremacy of Aryanism. Periyar consistently identified Aryanism with Brahminism and saw them as political and cultural systems of racial and caste supremacy, injustice, and inequality. His attacks on these systems involved polemics against those he saw as the greatest beneficiaries, the Brahmins.

At times, the polemic did become extreme. On one occasion, Periyar alleged that the Brahmins were controlling all political parties and were working concertedly to the detriment of the Dravidians (2010a, p. 11). 'No matter what party they are in, when it comes to issues regarding Brahmin society, all Brahmins are in the same camp' (2010a, p. 27). Claiming that the Dravidians could not progress in any field when the Brahmins were hegemonic, he said that it was necessary to raise the slogan of 'Brahmins leave!' (2010a, p.12). But he tempered this slogan by adding that Brahmins who wanted to stay could stay, but not as 'Brahmins', rather as humans, equal to all (2010a, p.12). Later he compared the 'Brahmins leave!' slogan to the 'Quit India!' slogan of the Congress (2010a, p. 70).

In 1957, Periyar made many offensive remarks against the Brahmins, which have been interpreted by his critics as calls to violence. In a statement in April 1957, he accused the Brahmins of monopolizing religious spaces and of also not allowing representation for non-Brahmins in secular occupations. To fight for non-Brahmin rights, he said, one should 'remove and destroy the Brahmin' (2010a, p. 212). October 1957 saw controversial speeches and articles from Periyar calling on his followers to burn copies of the Indian Constitution, alleging that it protected caste, and demanding a confrontational approach towards Brahmins (2011d, pp. 15–48). In one speech, he said: 'The first goal of the Dravidar Kazhagam is to annihilate caste' (2011d, p. 19) and urged his followers to take a pledge to 'Break Gandhi statues and annihilate Brahmins' (2011d, p. 21). His reasoning was that Brahmins profited from caste and that Gandhi defended the caste system, an opinion found even more strongly in Ambedkar.[13]

Periyar's provocative statements, especially his incendiary language, prompted a national reaction. Prime Minister Nehru condemned him in the harshest of terms urging Chief Minister K. Kamaraj to take action. Local Congressmen were also perturbed by the friendship between Kamaraj and Periyar. A *Times of India* editorial referred to Periyar and his followers as 'hate-mongers' and called on the Congress to take stern action against him, besides ridding itself of the Periyar sympathizers in its ranks.[14] The Madras Assembly passed the Prevention of Insults to National Honour Bill in November 1957, which criminalized any form of desecration of the Indian Constitution, the national flag, and images of Mahatma Gandhi. The Madras Home Minister M. Bhaktavatsalam justified this measure reasoning that 'the Government had to resort to such legislation when there were men who indulged in eccentric activities'.[15] The bill was passed without much opposition, the exception being the Dravida Munnetra Kazhagam (DMK), whose leader C. N. Annadurai called it 'totalitarian' and wondered if 'mere criticism of the Constitution' might also be seen as an offence.[16] On 26 November 1957, over 200 DK activists were arrested for attempting to burn the Constitution and Periyar himself was detained. Periyar was later sentenced to six months simple imprisonment for his anti-Brahmin comments.[17] Given his ill-health, he spent most part of his sentence in a hospital. Ram Manohar Lohia, who met Periyar during his detention, praised him for being a 'man of action' and for his 'burning sense of resistance to injustice'; Lohia agreed with the idea of 'destruction of symbols of caste', disagreeing, however, with disrespect of the Indian flag and Constitution.[18]

Periyar himself was unfazed and unapologetic. He criticized his opponents for not responding to his calls to annihilate caste and instead picking on his language (2011d, p. 55). He called on the intelligent among the Brahmins to declare that there is no caste and to oppose scriptures that legitimize caste (2011d, p. 58). He welcomed arrest, claiming that he and his followers were ready to sacrifice for the cause of annihilation of caste. But on the eve of his detention, he instructed his followers that there should be no violence whatsoever against any Brahmin individual. 'It is true that I have said use weapons and burn the *agraharams*. But not now. The time has not come for that. It is my desire that the time for it will not come' (2011d, p. 80). If the measures for eradicating caste fail, such violence could become a reality in the future (2011d, pp. 80–81). On the receipt of news of a few stray cases where the sacred threads of Brahmins were cut, he condemned those who were involved in such activities (2011d, p. 95). While calling for a social boycott of Brahmins, he strictly warned that any of his comrades getting involved in violence would be his enemy (2011d, p. 152). To critics who highlighted his choice of words, he pointed out that no violence had followed his speeches. Not only did he not believe in violence, he was even opposed to the unruliness in Gandhian politics: 'I am a person who stops even if a policeman gestures with his eyes. Someone who follows the law' (2011d, p. 174). Much later, in 1969, he reasserted his commitment to non-violence and said, 'In our country, except our movement, anyone else who protests is involved in violence. Only our movement [has] conducted several agitations without violence' (2006a, p. 88).

More explanations can be given for why Periyar's provocative statements did not result in anti-Brahmin violence. Barnett views such statements not as calls for violence against individual Brahmins but 'as metaphoric devices meant to encapsulate the complex ideas of the movement for mass appeal' (1976, p.71). Narendra Subramanian, pointing out that the DK's 'heretical gestures' did not lead to serious violence against the Brahmins, notes that the occasional attacks, with no loss of life or any major injury, occurred only in times when the DK was weak, like in the late 1950s. But it was not owing to fear of punishment that the DK avoided attacking Brahmins, rather 'The DK's anti-Brahmin propaganda was evidently meant to protest "Brahmin dominance" rather than to evoke massive attacks against Brahmins' (Subramanian, 1999, p. 120). Even when they saw Brahmins as outsiders or Aryans, this was not to expel them or deprive them of their civil rights, but only to contest their power. Subramanian, otherwise a critic of Periyar's politics, notes that calling the DK 'fascist' would be erroneous because while the fascists had an understanding of state power which they used with lethal effect against disempowered minorities, 'Periyar lacked a clear conception of state power and a strategy to acquire it and exercise it, the demand for Dravida Nadu notwithstanding' (1999, p. 120). Also, Periyar's polemical words and political actions did not always match. For instance, 1957, the year when Periyar launched some of his harshest anti-Brahmin polemics, was also the year of the Indian general elections, when Periyar campaigned for the candidature of T. T. Krishnamachari, a Brahmin (Karunanandam, 2013, p. 285).

But apart from these explanations, can such vocabulary nevertheless be seen as hate speech? In a recent article in *Frontline* (2024, pp. 55–58), I argued that Periyar's anti-Brahmin speeches were undoubtedly offensive and uncivil—the last speech he gave on 19 December 1973 had a generous dose of expletives (2006b, pp. 345–365)—but to call it hate speech, especially one that had actual consequences, is an untenable argument. Bonotti and Seglow make an important observation about hate speech that it 'successfully attacks individuals as *group members*' but to be effective and count as hate speech 'it must exploit a pattern or structure of prior injustices … it cannot be employed against members of majority or privileged groups' (2021, p. 33, emphasis original). Giving examples of offensive anti-White statements, they further note

> the desire to rid society of white people or deprive them of equal civic status, though logically coherent, gains no purchase in a majority-white population, or even in one where whites constitute an advantaged minority, as in apartheid South Africa (Bonotti and Seglow, 2021, p. 34).

Black militants fighting racism in the United States and apartheid in South Africa did make anti-White statements that were seen as extreme and offensive. If these were to be compared with Periyar's anti-Brahmin statements, Periyar seems moderate. One need not excuse and may genuinely be critical of Periyar's uncivil language. But it was not hate speech because it did not target an underprivileged group, it did not instigate physical violence against that group, it did not deprive them of civic status, and it was not upholding historical injustice. Offensive as it may be, Periyar's anti-Brahminism was rooted in an idea of social justice, a struggle against discourses of Aryan racial-caste supremacy.

Critique

Criticisms of Periyar's uncivil language apart, there have been bizarre claims of persecution of Tamil Brahmins. For instance, the writer Ashokamitran, a Brahmin, made 'scathing attacks against the Dravidian movement' and claimed in 2005 that the Tamil Brahmins felt castrated and their situation was like that of the Jews in the 1930s (Mangai, 2017). That he said this without any irony at a time when Jayalalithaa was ruling the state of Tamil Nadu was not a problem to the writer known for the 'streak of irony' in his writings. J. Jayalalithaa, six-time chief minister of Tamil Nadu and leader of the All-India Anna Dravida Munnetra Kazhagam (AIADMK), was a Brahmin. Neither did this affect her popularity in Tamil Nadu, nor did it prevent Periyarists from supporting her. The DK under K. Veeramani honoured Jayalalithaa by conferring on her the title, 'Protector of Social Justice'. Jayalalithaa also regularly attended Periyar's anniversary functions—the last in September 2016, three months before she died. Other progressive Brahmin intellectuals, writers, and celebrities have defended Periyar's legacy as well.

A. S. Krishnamachari Iyengar, or A. S. K., as he was known to his comrades, was a contemporary of Periyar and was a prominent communist and labour leader. Drawn to Periyar's thoughts in 1937, in later years, he dropped his caste title, 'Iyengar' from his name following the ideals of the SRM. Soon after Periyar's demise, A. S. K. authored *Pagutharivin Sigaram Periyar E. Ve. Ra.* (1974)—The Pinnacle of Rationalism: Periyar E.V.R.—where he argued that Periyar was not just an atheist, but an important rationalist and materialist in the Indian tradition (1974, p. 55). Sharply dismissive of those who accused Periyar of hatred towards the Brahmins and terming it as slander (1974, p. i), he argued that Periyar's rationalist convictions led him to oppose Brahminism. The book opens with a poetic tribute to Periyar, praising him as a patriot who loved humanity and hated caste.

Other empirically grounded research puts paid to claims of persecution of Brahmins in Tamil Nadu. C. J. Fuller and Haripriya Narasimhan's work *Tamil Brahmans* (2014) notes how the Brahmins' 'privileged status within a hierarchical society' is perpetuated despite changes in society and politics (2014, p. 4). Though powerful non-Brahmins replaced the Brahmins in the villages, it was for the most part the Brahmins who voluntarily moved to the city in search of better opportunities (2014, p. 38). This was no traumatic flight because 'Brahmans do not identify themselves with the majority of the local population and the *agraharam*'s physical separation from the rest of the village has itself been a constitutive factor in the caste's social separation' (2014, p. 47). Further, having no attachment to land facilitated an easy move to the city and transformation into an urban middle-class caste (2014, pp. 51–54). Many also found lucrative careers in the West. There is a 'cumulative upward mobility' among Tamil Brahmins of both rich and poor backgrounds, while 'downward mobility' among them is unheard of (2014, pp. 84–86). But, according to the authors, the rural-to-urban shift or economic mobility did not necessarily bring about a change in mentality.

They argue that notions of Brahmin superiority were not only attractive to the traditionalists, but are also accepted by the modern urban middle-class Brahmins (2014, p. 200). Further, the Tamil Brahmins 'customarily regarded "vernacular" Tamil as inferior to Sanskrit' (2014, p. 228). That Periyar, who consistently sought to dismantle claims to the superiority of Brahmins as a caste and Sanskrit as a language, continues to be an irritant should come as no surprise.

But while Periyar directed more criticisms towards the Brahmins, they were not singled out for his censure. Periyar viewed caste as providing social privilege and social capital by birth. In a 1941 article, he identified 'birth capitalists', the Brahmins following Aryan ideology, and 'birth labourers', who should follow Dravidian ideals to liberate themselves (2011b, pp. 149–151). In this article, he also criticized leaders from the Mudaliar and Chettiar communities for being 'small capitalists' who were not doing enough to abolish the system of oppression. Elsewhere, rebuking non-Brahmin elites, he said 'Tamil zamindars copy those who are above them, speak in a Brahmin language, and treat their servants and the poor like Shudras, and seek approval from the higher castes' (2011b, p. 236). Thirty years later, he expressed similar opinions when he said that 'Before we can take joy in the end of Brahmin domination, an equally oppressive and vile zamindar domination has risen its head. All the evils of Brahmin domination continue in zamindar domination' (2010b, p. 175). He noted that the zamindars, like the Brahmins, enjoy birth privileges, are favoured by the ruling class, and are responsible for the misery of the poor (2010b, p. 176). For why he blamed the Brahmins more, he had a rationale:

> I am aware of the criticism that while the non-Brahmins are bitter about the superiority complex of the Brahmins, they themselves do not grant equality to those below them in the infamous caste hierarchy. There is much truth in this criticism. My only reply is that the Brahmins have to take the greatest blame, because their forebears have been the authors of caste and it is they who have meticulously striven to preserve the system. (Ramasamy 1998, p. 16)

Greatest, not sole, blame. Periyar located the Brahmin agent at the centre of an ideological system that maintained social hierarchy. He was aware of 'the pervasive nature of caste consciousness among all castes' and made every effort to challenge this, including when he was invited to speak at specific caste gatherings (Venkatachalapathy, 2020). While other castes below the Brahmin were also complicit in the preservation of this hierarchy, it was the discourse of Brahminism which needed to be challenged for any social reform to be effective.

Periyar's anti-Brahmin statements taken in isolation might sound extreme. Seen in comparison with the vocabularies of movements for social justice across the world, a different reading can be made. There is no shortage of rhetoric of 'violence' in the speeches of anti-colonial and anti-racist militants the world over. Maharashtra's Dalit Panthers used aggressive language. Radical feminists in the West coined slogans like 'kill all men'. One radical feminist group called the Society for Cutting up Men, which was active in the 1960s in the United States, had a manifesto which called for the elimination of the male sex. Provocative though such slogans were, these groups cannot be called 'reverse sexist' or be accused of persecuting men.

In the Kurdish movement led by the Kurdistan Workers' Party and its affiliates, the idea of 'killing the male' is very popular and it is argued that 'the concept of "killing the male" is key to the Kurdish women's movement's everyday practices, as it encourages personal reflections about internalized power structures and their origins ... it constitutes a call for both men and women to unlearn patriarchy and build a more balanced society' (Al-Ali and Käser, 2020, p. 26). Periyar's anti-Brahmin statements, seen in this light, can be read not as calls for violence, but a part of unlearning casteism—among both Brahmins and non-Brahmins—and building an egalitarian society, moving towards the goals of *samathuvam* (equality), *jaathi ozhippu* (annihilation of caste), and *penn viduthalai* (liberation of women).

For Periyar, 'Aryanism gives no space for change. Dravidianism gives space for change' (2010c, 255). Periyarism can also change for the times, reaching out to broader audiences beyond the boundaries of Tamil Nadu and moving beyond the binaries of Brahmin and non-Brahmin.

Notes

1. The vocabulary of 'Dalit' was not available in Periyar's times. He used terms such as Panchamar, Adi Dravidar, and Thazhthappattor (the depressed) interchangeably. In this chapter, I will consistently use 'Dalit' to refer only to those scheduled caste (SC) communities that identify as such, acknowledging exceptions like the scheduled caste group, the Devendra Kula Vellalars who refuse to do so.
2. This reading of Periyar is challenged by Abhimanyu Arni (2024), who makes a strong case for approaching Periyar's Dravidian politics as universalist.
3. *The Hindu*, 20 February 1949.
4. Incidentally, Leopold Sedar Senghor, one of the founders of the Negritude movement, saw Dravidians as belonging to 'Negro blood' (Senghor 1956, p. 64) while earlier, the African–American thinker W. E. B. Du Bois had credited the 'Dravidian Negroes' with laying the foundations of Indian culture in ancient times (Du Bois, 2007, p. 113).
5. Chairez-Garza (2021, p. 11) notes correctly that 'Ambedkar vehemently rejected the Aryan race theory of caste and linked its popularity to the desire of both colonial rulers and upper caste Hindus, particularly Brahmins, to justify their political dominance'. Ambedkar however identified two basic races in India, the Aryans and the Nagas, and argued that the Nagas and the Dravidians were the same people (Ambedkar 2020, p. 300).
6. Sundar Kaali (2018) elucidates on the pre-Periyar thinkers who contributed to the making of a 'new public sphere' in Tamil Nadu. He also notes the similarities in the concerns of the Madras Secular Society, Athipakkam Venkatachala Nayakkar, Kaivalya Swamiyar, and Periyar.
7. *Frontline*, 16 October 2013.
8. The articles from *Thathuvavivesini* and *The Thinker* have been published in separate compilations by V. Anaimuthu and V. Arasu. For this chapter, I refer solely to Arasu's compilations published by New Century Book House.
9. *Frontline*, 16 October 2013.
10. These two books, along with a selection of Nayakkar's articles, were published by V. Anaimuthu's Periyar Nool Veliyittagam in 2014. The biographical information about Nayakkar is also taken from Anaimuthu's forewords to these books.
11. This collection titled *Kaivalya Swamiyar Katturaigal*, edited and compiled by Valasa Vallavan and published by Vidiyal Pathippagam, contains 216 articles by Kaivalya Swamiyar featured originally in *Kudi Arasu*.

12. *The Hindu*, 26 January 1950.
13. See for instance Ambedkar's *What Congress and Gandhi Have Done to the Untouchables* (1945).
14. *Times of India*, 28 October 1957.
15. *Times of India*, 12 November 1957.
16. *Times of India*, 12 November 1957.
17. *Times of India*, 15 December 1957.
18. *Times of India*, 25 January 1958.

References

Aiyangar, M. Srinivasa. 1914. *Tamil Studies*. Madras: Guardian Press.
Al-Ali, Nadje and Isabel Käser. 2020. 'Beyond Feminism? Jineolojî and the Kurdish Women's Freedom Movement.' *Politics and Gender* 18(1): 1–32. doi:10.1017/s1743923x20000501
Ambedkar, B. R. 1945. *What Congress and Gandhi Have Done to the Untouchables*. Bombay: Thacker & Co.
———. 2014. *Dr. Babasaheb Ambedkar: Writings and Speeches*, vol. 1, first reprint. New Delhi: Dr. Ambedkar Foundation.
———. 2020. *Dr. Babasaheb Ambedkar: Writings and Speeches*, vol 7, third reprint. New Delhi: Dr. Ambedkar Foundation.
Arasu, V. ed. 2012a. *Chennai Laukika Sangam (1878–1888)*, vol. 1. Chennai: New Century Book House.
———. 2012b. *Thathuvam-Kadavul-Nathigam: Chennai Laukika Sangam*, vol. 2. Chennai: New Century Book House.
———. 2012c. *Saathi-Pengal-Samayam: Chennai Laukika Sangam*, vol. 3. Chennai: New Century Book House.
———. 2012d. *Kaalaniyam-Vignanam-Moodanambikkai: Chennai Laukika Sangam*, vol 4. Chennai: New Century Book House.
———. 2012e. *Atheism and Theism: Madras Secular Society*, vol. 5. Chennai: New Century Book House.
———. 2012f. *Woman-Culture and Poverty: Madras Secular Society*, vol. 6. Chennai: New Century Book House.
Arni, A. 2024. 'Taking Periyarism Seriously: The Dravidian Identity as a Universality.' *Global Intellectual History*: 1–22. https://doi.org/10.1080/23801883.2024.2386600
A.S.K. 1974. *Pagutharivin Sigaram Periyar E. Ve. Ra*. Chennai: Bhagat House Publications.
Ayyathurai, Gajendran. 2023. 'Memory, History, and Casteless Consciousness: Tamil Buddhists in Modern South India'. *South Asian History and Culture* 14(1): 9–26.
Barnett, Marguerite Ross. 1976. *The Politics of Cultural Nationalism in South India*. Princeton: Princeton University Press.
Birkvad, Ida Roland. 2020. 'The Ambivalence of Aryanism: A Genealogical Reading of India–Europe Connection'. *Millennium* 49(1): 58–79.
Bonotti, Matteo, and Jonathan Seglow. 2021. *Free Speech*. Cambridge: Polity Press.
Caldwell, Robert. 1875. *A Comparative Grammar of the Dravidian or South Indian Family of Languages*, 2nd edition. London: Trubner & Co.

Cháirez-Garza, Jesús F. 2021. 'Moving Untouched: B. R. Ambedkar and the Racialization of Untouchability'. *Ethnic and Racial Studies* 45(2): 216–234. DOI: 10.1080/01419870.2021.1924393.

Chidambaranar, Sami. 2016 [1938]. *Periyar: Vaazhkai Varalaru*. Chennai: Neer Veliyeedu.

Du Bois, W. E. B. 2007. *The World and Africa*. New York: Oxford University Press.

Figueira, Dorothy M. 2015. *Aryans, Jews, Brahmins: Theorizing Authority Through Myths of Identity*. New Delhi: Navayana.

Fuller, C. J. and Haripriya Narasimhan. 2015. *Tamil Brahmans: The Making of a Middle-Class Caste*. New Delhi: Social Science Press.

Irele, Abiola. 1964. 'A Defence of Negritude'. *Transition* 13: 9–11.

Irschick, Eugene F. 1969. *Politics and Social Conflict in South India: The Non-Brahman Movement and Tamil Separatism, 1916–1929*. Bombay: Oxford University Press.

Jaywant, Ketaki. 2023. 'Reshaping the Figure of the Shudra: Tukaram Padwal's Jatibhed Viveksar (Reflections on the Institution of Caste)'. *Modern Asian Studies* 57(2): 380–408.

Joseph, Tony. 2018. *Early Indians: The Story of Our Ancestors and Where We Came From*. New Delhi: Juggernaut.

Kaali, Sundar. 2018. 'Making of a New Public Sphere'. *Seminar* 708 (August): 45–48.

Kaivalya Swamiyar. 2022. *Kaivalya Swamiyar Katturaigal*, edited by Valasa Vallavan. Coimbatore: Vidiyal Pathippagam

Karunanandam, Kavignar. 2013. *Thanthai Periyar: Muzhu Muthal Vazhkkai Varalaaru*, 4th edn. Chennai: VOC Noolagam.

Mangai, A. 2017. 'Ashokamitran: A Not-So-Simple Writer Who Inspired Not-So-Easy Affection'. *The Wire*, 26 March. https://thewire.in/books/asokamitran-a-not-so-simple-writer-who-inspired-not-so-easy-affection. Accessed 18 May 2024.

Manoharan, Karthick Ram. 2017. '"Anti-Casteist Casteism?" A Fanonist Critique of Ramasamy's Discourse on Caste'. *Interventions: International Journal of Postcolonial Studies* 19(1): 73–90.

———. 2020. 'In the Path of Ambedkar: Periyar and the Dalit Question'. *South Asian History and Culture* 11(2): 136–149.

———. 2022. 'Sudras and the Nation: Periyarist Explorations'. *Economic and Political Weekly* 57(44–45). https://www.epw.in/engage/article/sudras-and-nation-periyarist-explorations. Accessed 26 April 2024.

———. 2022a. *Periyar: A Study in Political Atheism*. Hyderabad: Orient BlackSwan.

———. 2024. 'Did Periyar Call for a Genocide of Brahmins?' *Frontline* 41(7): 55–58.

Nayakkar, Athippakkam Venkatachala. 2014a. *Payakkarigalikkum Mirasudarargalukkum Undayirukkira Vivaatham*, edited by V. Anaimuthu. Chennai: Periyar Nool Veliyittagam.

———. 2014b. *Hindu Matha Aachara Aabasa Dharsini*, edited by V. Anaimuthu. Chennai: Periyar Nool Veliyittagam.

Pandian, M. S. S. 2007. *Brahmin and Non-Brahmin: Genealogies of the Tamil Political Present*. Delhi: Permanent Black.

Phule, Jyotirao. 2008. *Slavery*, translated by Maya Pundit. New Delhi: Critical Quest.

Radhakrishnan, S. 2018. *The Hindu View of Life*. Noida: HarperCollins.

Raman, Srilata. 2022. *The Transformation of Tamil Religion: Ramalinga Swamigal (1823–1874) and Modern Dravidian Sainthood*. London: Routledge.

Ramasamy, (Periyar) E. V. 1998. *Social Reform or Social Revolution*, translated by A. M. Dharmalingam. Chennai: Dravidar Kazhagam.

———2006a. *Periyar Kalanjiyam 18: Jaathi-Theendaamai*, Paagam (12), 1st edition. Chennai: Periyar Suyamariyathai Prachaara Niruvanam.

———. 2006b. *Periyar Kalanjiyam 21: Jaathi-Theendaamai*, Paagam (15), 1st edition. Chennai: Periyar Suyamariyathai Prachaara Niruvanam.

———. 2010a. *Periyar Kalanjiyam 10: Jaathi-Theendaamai*, Paagam (4), 2nd edition. Chennai: Periyar Suyamariyathai Prachaara Niruvanam.

———. 2010b. *Periyar Kalanjiyam 19: Jaathi-Theendaamai*, Paagam (13), 2nd edition. Chennai: Periyar Suyamariyathai Prachaara Niruvanam.

———. 2010c. *Periyar Kalanjiyam 20: Jaathi-Theendaamai*, Paagam (14), 2nd edition. Chennai: Periyar Suyamariyathai Prachaara Niruvanam.

———. 2011a. *Periyar Kalanjiyam 7: Jaathi-Theendaamai*, Paagam (1), 2nd edition. Chennai: Periyar Suyamariyathai Prachaara Niruvanam.

———. 2011b. *Periyar Kalanjiyam 8: Jaathi-Theendaamai*, Paagam (2), 2nd edition. Chennai: Periyar Suyamariyathai Prachaara Niruvanam.

———. 2011c. *Periyar Kalanjiyam 9: Jaathi-Theendaamai*, Paagam (3), 2nd edition. Chennai: Periyar Suyamariyathai Prachaara Niruvanam.

———. 2011d. *Periyar Kalanjiyam 11: Jaathi-Theendaamai*, Paagam (5), 2nd edition. Chennai: Periyar Suyamariyathai Prachaara Niruvanam.

———. 2014. 'Dravida Naatu Thalaivar E. Ve. Ra. Avargal'. Introduction to Athipakkam Venkatachala Nayakkar, *Hindu Matha Aachara Aabasa Dharsini*, edited by V. Anaimuthu, pp. 29–31. Chennai: Periyar Nool Veliyittagam.

———. 2022. 'Mugavurai'. In Kaivalya Swamiyar, *Kaivalya Swamiyar Katturaigal*, edited by Valasa Vallavan, pp. 15–19. Coimbatore: Vidiyal Pathippagam.

Sartre, Jean-Paul. 1965. 'Black Orpheus', translated by John MacCombie. *Massachusetts Review* 6(1): 13–52.

Sastri, K. A. Nilakanta. 2018. *K. A. Nilakanta Sastri: Writings in The Hindu*. Chennai: The Hindu Group.

Schmitt, Carl. 2004. *Theory of the Partisan: A Commentary/Remark on the Concept of the Political*, translated by A. C. Goodson. East Lansing: Michigan State University Press.

Senghor, L. S. 1956. 'The Spirit of Civilization, or the Laws of African Negro Culture'. *Presence Africaine: Cultural Journal of the Negro World* (8–10): 51–64.

Sibley, Collin. 2024. 'Social Progress and the Dravidian "Race" in Tamil Social Thought'. *Genealogy* 8(1). https://doi.org/10.3390/genealogy8010006.

Subramanian, Narendra. 1999. *Ethnicity and Populist Mobilization: Political Parties, Citizens and Democracy in South India*. Delhi: Oxford University Press.

Thapar, Romila. 2019. 'Multiple Theories About the Aryans'. In *Which of Us Are Aryans? Rethinking the Concept of Our Origins* by Romila Thapar, Michael Witzel, Jaya Menon, Kai Friese, and Razib Khan, pp. 30–93. New Delhi: Aleph.

Trautmann, Thomas R. 1997. *Aryans and British India*. Berkeley and Los Angeles: University of California Press.

Venkatachalapathy, A. R. 2020. 'Periyar E. V. Ramasamy'. In *Oxford Research Encyclopedia of Asian History*. 28 February. https://oxfordre.com/asianhistory/view/10.1093/acrefore/9780190277727.001.0001/acrefore-9780190277727-e-340. Accessed 18 May 2024.

Visswanathan, E. Sa. 1983. *The Political Career of E. V. Ramasamy Naicker: A Study in the Politics of Tamil Nadu, 1920–1949*. Madras: Ravi & Vasanth.

Weiss, Richard S. 2019. *The Emergence of Modern Hinduism: Religion on the Margins of Colonialism*. Oakland: University of California Press.

8

Periyar in Singapore

Transnationalism and Decolonization

Darinee Alagirisamy

Ideologue, reformer, feminist, firebrand secessionist: these are some of the many things E. V. Ramasamy Periyar has been called. If there is one strand of Periyar's thought that runs through all these titles and the politics that informed them, it would be his clarion call for self-respect. Not one to stop at dismantling the hegemonic power structures that he saw around him in India, Periyar was committed to the cause of reform in and for the Tamil diaspora as well. His views on nationhood thus 'constantly violated the certitude about boundaries, identities, agents of change, and went beyond the territoriality of the nation' (Pandian, 1993, p. 2282). Periyar emphasized that foreign settlement could enable the regeneration of Tamil society abroad, unfettered by India's oppressive traditions. Moreover, he saw the diaspora as an important source of financial support for the Dravidian movement. To this end, Self-Respect literature often asserted that Tamil people everywhere were bound by obligations of mutual assistance and reciprocity (Alagirisamy, 2016). Periyar visited British Malaya and Singapore twice in his lifetime: once in 1929–1930 and again in 1954–1955. Both visits were pivotal in aiding the development of a *settled* Tamil political consciousness in Singapore.

Scholars of the Indian Ocean world continue to trace the comings and goings of sojourners and settlers, privileging the ocean itself as a key agent of change (Moorthy and Jamal, 2010; Amrith, 2013; Menon et al., 2022). Yet, settlement also brought with it a sea-change in the lived presents and anticipated futures of migrant communities that aspired to citizenship. Traditional approaches to Indian politics in Malaya focused on elite motivations and actions in the domain of formal politics, often to the detriment of grassroots Tamil activism, dismissed as a 'sub-communal' pressure that impeded Indian mobilization (Stenson, 1980, pp. 73–75; Sandhu and Mani, 1993).[1] Subsequent scholarship has shown that these pressures were in fact instrumental in influencing the character of (post)colonial Malayan Indian representative politics, and hence, the very nature of Singapore Indian society (Solomon, 2016). As a historically interconnected region, the Bay of Bengal presents us with a unique opportunity to consider the impact of intertwining mobilities that were concerned with such difficult but critical questions as the relationship between ethnicity and nationhood. Crucially, it offers the possibility of tracing the contours and impact of these mobilities from the vantage point of the transnational movements that traversed the ocean along with sojourners, settlers, and itinerant reformers.

While flows and exchanges of all kinds serve as entry points to the study of transnationalism, which, by definition, unsettles the assumed centrality of the nation-state, Periyar's second visit engendered a brand of transnationalism that helped to reinforce the Tamil position in Singapore's emerging nation-state instead. The visit brought about an intensive engagement by the diaspora with the leader and his ideas in a short period of time. It presented Tamils with a versatile ethnic idiom of reform that facilitated the development of a settled consciousness ahead of decolonization. Inasmuch as transnationalism entails multiple imaginaries and articulations of belonging, the language of Self-Respect in 1950s Singapore simultaneously emphasized solidarity with a transnational Tamil community and patriotism to the emerging nation-state. The ensuing negotiations of identity were manifested most viscerally in the realm of language and literature, both of which became indispensable agents of mobilizing, or more accurately—*settling*—Tamil public opinion in Singapore in the lead up to independence.

Negotiating a space between being a minority migrant community and becoming part of a community of citizens informed Tamil cultural–linguistic assertion in Singapore in the 1950s, a context characterized by the development of nationalism and progress towards decolonization. Relatedly, this period laid the groundwork for far-reaching postcolonial developments in such matters as citizenship and national language policy. Between the late eighteenth and mid-twentieth centuries, the states of the Malay Peninsula and Singapore had been brought under British imperial control through a combination of direct and indirect rule. The hotchpotch of territories and systems of administration that together made-up British Malaya included the Federated and Unfederated Malay States, along with Singapore as part of the Straits Settlements, the latter under direct Crown control. With the end of empire in India and changed political circumstances in postwar Malaya that proved fortuitous to the spread of nationalism, the stage was set for decolonization in the region. Singapore achieved independence from the British as part of the Federation of Malaya in 1957 and gained internal self-governance in 1959. Following a short-lived merger that eventually fell apart owing to disagreements over Malaysia's stance of Malaysia for Malays foremost, and Singapore's stance of Malaysia for all Malaysians regardless of race, the Chinese-majority country became fully independent in 1965. The question of the Tamil position in Singapore thus became especially politicized in a context wherein the transition to independence hinged on the question of the community's place in the nation.

Sumathi Ramaswamy has traced the strands of Tamil devotion, *tamilpparru*, and its centrality to the emergence of a distinct 'imagined community' in the Tamil south (Ramaswamy, 1997; Anderson, 1983). This imagined community that Ramaswamy references was not limited to the Madras Presidency in India, or even south Asia. Instead, it was at least as vast as the flow of Self-Respect ideas that connected the philosophies of the Dravidian movement with Tamil populations settled across the Bay of Bengal. It has been argued elsewhere that Indian politics in Singapore had entered its post-Dravidian phase by the time of Periyar's second visit. Although Tamil reform organizations in Singapore articulated a Tamil identity that was 'progressive, egalitarian and casteless', they apparently stood in contrast with the politicization of caste in Tamil Nadu in this reading (Solomon, 2016, pp. 175–176).

The argument of a 'post-Dravidian' phase, however, seems to stem largely from concerns that conceding engagement with the movement would be irreconcilable with Singapore's political development in the 1950s and 1960s. It seems to be based, in other words, in concerns that Dravidian transnationalism would be incompatible with nationalism. Aside from the fact that it would be odd to expect the same outcome across two such markedly different contexts as India and Singapore, the notion of a post-Dravidian phase is further rendered untenable considering the imprint of Self-Respect discourse on the linguistic–literary imaginings of Tamil identity that had such an important bearing on the community's mobilization in this period. Catalysed by Periyar's second visit, Tamils in Singapore often (re)invented devotion to the Tamil language in ways that were strikingly similar to the original, yet uniquely reflective of their particular circumstances of settlement. Unfortunately, the erstwhile scholarly attention to the centrality of Tamil newspapers as instruments of change has come at the expense of the less tangible but more crucial role of the uses to which the Tamil language itself was put in bridging belonging to the community with belonging to the nation. Responding to an uncertain future with a rational vision of progress was the essence of Periyar's message to the community during his visits. To this message and its reception, we shall now turn.

Periyar's First Visit to Malaya: Mutual Assistance, Solidarity, and Tamil Pride

Periyar's overseas travels were significant in that they evidenced the global dimensions of his commitment to reform. Periyar first visited Malaya in 1929, in a colonial context wherein he was fast emerging as the public face of a movement that sought to rewrite the rules of the relationship that prevailed between politics and caste: the Dravidian movement. Moreover, the visit came just four short years following his inauguration of the Self-Respect Movement (*suyamariyatai iyakkam*; SRM) as the cultural arm of the Dravidian movement. The SRM had originated in a milieu of acute political struggle with which it remained deeply concerned throughout its development. Following his disillusionment with the Indian National Congress (Congress), Periyar started the SRM in 1925 determined that there ought to be 'no God; no religion; no Gandhi; no Congress; and no Brahmins'.[2] The anti-caste movement that he envisioned was radical in its advocacy of comprehensive reform; it demanded women's emancipation, deplored superstition, and emphasized rationality.

Transnational reform networks had enabled Periyar's first visit. In particular, the Tamil language press had served as a bidirectional conduit for the exchange of ideas and news relating to Self-Respect. In a letter to the newspaper *Kudi Arasu* in 1927, a Self-Respecter from Ipoh applauded the movement's success as prayers for the Hindu fire-walking religious observance of *tīmiti* had been offered without Brahmin priests that year.[3] Just a month before Periyar's visit, a Kuala Lumpur magistrate's refusal to recognize a Self-Respect wedding had caused an uproar within the community.[4] There was palpable anticipation and enthusiasm in the region ahead of Periyar's visit.

The empowering message of caste eradication, promotion of equality, and social uplift that the SRM propagated, resonated with the circumstances that the majority of Tamils in the diaspora found themselves grappling with. It has been argued that living in diaspora is not an issue of 'naturally felt roots but of specific political circumstances that suggest the mobilisation of a transnational imagined community' (Sökefeld, 2006, p. 280). We may see Periyar's visits as simultaneously being part of the specific political circumstances that shaped diasporic consciousness and as an outcrop of Malayan Tamil mobilization. Working-class migrants drawn from Adi-Dravidar communities, who comprised the majority within the diaspora, found to their dismay that caste-based discrimination had survived migration. Moreover, the community found itself at the bottom of the racial hierarchy that presented in Malaya's multiracial society. A pressing lack of political representation added to their woes. Tamils in Malaya looked to developments in India, and in Madras in particular, as a source of hope and support in navigating the uncertainty that settlement had brought with it.

However, support for Periyar and his SRM was far from universal. Upper-caste resistance to Periyar's visit had, in fact, almost prevented it from happening. Prior to his departure, Periyar received a telegram alerting him to strong opposition in Penang to his visit. The chief editor of the *Penang Gazette*, who was Brahmin, had tried to dissuade its readers from attending Periyar's speeches, while the Brahmin-owned *Tamil Nesan* had warned readers about the SRM as a subversive movement. The Penang Hindu Society even petitioned the Malayan government to stop Periyar's visit (Veeramani, 2012, p. 66). Varying shades of resistance persisted throughout Periyar's visit, underscoring the polarization the SRM caused in the diaspora.

On 15 December 1929, Periyar and his group set sail for Malaya from the port of Nagapattinam. Large crowds gathered to welcome them in Penang, while numerous Indian associations catered to the travellers' needs during their month-long stay. Periyar's visit not only attracted the attention of Tamils, ranging from teachers and journalists to labourers, but was followed with interest by other Indian communities as well. He spoke at numerous conferences and was engaged in public meetings every day. Prior to his departure from Madras, Periyar had promised his followers that he would refrain from broaching politics during his trip. However, his Malayan message constituted nothing short of a political commentary. His speeches evidenced an international view of progress, scathing criticism of conditions in India, and concern for Indian rights in Malaya. Whilst Periyar advanced a brand of modernity that frequently transcended political boundaries, the object of these efforts was always 'local', the parameters of which variously encompassed the Madras Presidency, India, and Malaya.

Periyar often made deliberate comparisons between Malayan Indian society and the land that the diaspora had left. During a speech in Singapore, he spoke about the Congress, emphasizing that in spite of its initial good intentions, the nationalist party had fallen prey to the personal ambitions of its elite leadership. As the audience cheered in agreement, he added that the Malayan India Association should be careful not to follow in the Congress's footsteps. At another meeting, when an audience member asked whether Katherine Mayo's then-recent damning critique was justified, Periyar replied that it was a clarion call to 'clean up' Indian society (Veeramani, 2012, pp. 35–36). Such exchanges constructed India as a site for social and political reform in Malaya, thus bridging the diaspora's worlds of belonging.

Malayan Tamil engagements with Periyar's visit likewise reflected a Janus-faced orientation that simultaneously looked to developments in India and Malaya in articulating a vision for the diaspora's future. Community leaders drafted several resolutions in his presence that sought social reform in alignment with Self-Respect values. Significantly, several of these sought change along the lines of reforms that had recently been introduced in India. The Tamils' Conference in Ipoh endorsed the (Sarda) Child Marriage Restraint Act, 1929, for recommendation to the Malayan government. An informal decision was reached to legalize widow remarriage in the Federated Malay States, while the legitimacy of Self-Respect weddings was affirmed. Moreover, the community's unity was reaffirmed under the banner of the Tamil language (Veeramani, 2012, pp. 23–24).

At the same time, Periyar despaired that the movement's repeated emphasis on rationality appeared to fall on deaf ears, where religion—or superstition, as he would call it—was concerned. His memoirs recount incidents wherein large groups of labourers kissed the ground that he walked on and threw flowers and fruits to show their devotion. In one such incident, a woman had demanded that Periyar bless her daughter with the boon of childbirth. A reluctant Periyar finally had to oblige in order to send her away (Veeramani, 2012, pp. 38–39).

Periyar's visit not only evidenced a keen engagement on the part of his Malayan Tamil audience with the realities of living abroad, but equally, a willingness to emulate 'modern' societies all over the world. In Ipoh, the president of the Tamils' Conference likened the impact of the SRM on Indian society to Mustapha Kemal Pasha's reforms in Turkey. The Tamils' Conference ended with the hoisting of the British flag, followed by the joint unveiling of a portrait of King George V and a photograph of Periyar. Performances of loyalty that positioned reform firmly within the ambit of politics, such aspects of the visit show that the diaspora's engagement with Self-Respect extended beyond India and Malaya, to posit a global vision of modernity.

The SRM opened up new avenues for the further development of transnational networks of allegiance in the aftermath of Periyar's visit. The anti-Hindi-imposition protests in the Tamil districts of the Madras Presidency in the 1930s became an especially emotive site of diasporic engagement. Tamils in Singapore and Malaya collected funds for, and enlisted as volunteer brigades against, language imposition in Tamil south India. Developments in the Madras Presidency spurred many in the diaspora into action as they presented an alarming premonition of what might happen in Malaya too in the near future. This was especially so as they came in the wake of events that were inherently threatening to the Tamil position in the region. For instance, there were grave concerns at that time that Tamil students in Malaya lacked basic knowledge of the language, owing to a severe lack of facilities and a widespread notion that Tamil language education was impractical. Flows of Self-Respect volunteers, donations to aid the movement, and coverage of these events by the Tamil press in Malaya together constituted a dynamic sphere of engagement that fused emotion and activism to create a radical brand of transnational reform (Alagirisamy, 2016). Periyar breathed life into this particular brand of reformist politics: one in which Tamil devotion emerged as the very antidote to Brahmanical domination over politics and society.

Periyar's Second Visit: Consolidating the Tamil Position Between Community and Nation

'We must have united communities before we can have united nations, and united nations before we can have a united earth.' A local English press that interviewed Periyar during his second Malayan visit quoted him thus, although it prefaced the piece with a caption that seemed strangely at odds with its contents: 'Periyar E. V. Ramasamy, Prime Agitator for an Independent Tamil State'.[5] Of course, the reporters' cynicism stemmed from a conviction in the nation-state's presumed infallibility, of which Periyar had emerged as a powerful critic in India. The Dravidian movement's iconoclastic leader had raised the demand for Dravida Nadu in the lead up to Indian independence as he was certain that Congress nationalism and the nation-state that it was paving the way for would be inimical to non-Brahmin cultures, interests, and livelihoods. Politics in the Madras State had boiled over in the early 1950s; C. Rajagopalachari's Congress government had introduced policies like a scheme to educate children in their parents' vocations and the promotion of Hindi as the national language that appeared contemptuous of non-Brahmin Tamil sensibilities (Hardgrave, 1965).

Periyar's second visit to Singapore and Malaya took place seven years after Indian independence. It came in a markedly changed context. Periyar was now the leader of an established movement in Tamil Nadu. The circumstances of settlement had also shifted for the Malayan Tamil diaspora. From formerly navigating the transition between migration and settlement, the community was now facing the vicissitudes of settlement as issues like citizenship loomed ahead. Coming in this context, Periyar's visit lasted three weeks, during which time he spoke at several public meetings. He and his wife, Maniammai, had left Madras harbour for Rangoon on 5 December 1954. Arriving in Rangoon first, Periyar attended the World Buddhist Conference as an invitee. Periyar would later remind his Malayan audience that he had always been emphasizing the importance of 'one community and one god' as the 'Christians and Muslims believe'.[6] Buddhism, Christianity, and Islam all received his endorsement as they had no place for caste, at least in theory. At any rate, the reformer set sail from Rangoon harbour for Malaya on 11 December 1954. Reception committees had been set up to make all the necessary arrangements for his stay. Singapore's Periyar Reception Committee was headed by A. C. Suppiah and G. Sarangapany. The committee decided that there would be a public meeting in Singapore and a tea party reception to which leaders of other communities would be invited so that they could learn about Periyar's contributions to the progress and welfare of south Indians. To this end, three sub-committees were formed to oversee various aspects of the visit. An English newspaper[7] reported the scene of Periyar's arrival in Penang thus:

> The moment the ship, *SS Sangola* was sighted, a wave of enthusiasm and exhilaration swept over the mass of Tamils assembled at the Penang harbour. As the ship neared the harbour and the old venerable Periyar made his appearance, cries of 'Long Live Periyar' rent the air and a large number of them, overwhelmed with joy, shed tears! With his face adorned with a broad, understanding smile and the distinguishing grey beard and his black, short and old familiar walking-stick, Periyar Ramasamy sent a thrill among those gathered round him, only to sober them with his kind, soft and affectionate words.

Strong emotion was equally evident during Periyar's addresses to his Malayan Tamil audience. He gave an address later that day itself at a public meeting arranged by the Penang Municipal Labour Union at the Kampong Java Padang, attended by over 5,000 Indians. He also gave speeches in Penang in the towns of Butterworth and Perai, where he emphasized, in a voice 'choked with emotion' that he had not come to Malaya to preach against God, or religion, or the priesthood, but instead to see his 'beloved Tamils' after a gap of twenty-five years.[8] From Penang, Periyar visited Kuala Lumpur, Seremban, Malacca, and Johor before reaching Singapore by train from Kluang on 2 January 1955. Periyar's stay in Singapore included a reception meeting at Happy World Stadium where he addressed an estimated 5,000–7,000 people.[9] Like Periyar, many in the audience came attired in black shirts to hear his speech on the evils of caste and the urgency of acquiring a good education.[10] Besides meeting with representatives of the English press,

Periyar also met correspondents from a wide cross-section of the vernacular Malayan press, including from Chinese, Malay, and Malayalam newspapers. Having concluded his tour, he left Malaya for Madras on 9 January 1955.

During his visit, Periyar addressed large groups of Tamils, particularly labourers. Discernible in his speeches is an abiding commitment to the eradication of poverty and backwardness and a concomitant emphasis on progress through unity in a transnational, multicultural context. Akin to the matryoshka doll, his Malayan speeches evidence intertwining and overlapping identities, with each idea relating to one identity nested within another. The crux of Periyar's message to Tamils in Singapore and Malaya was that the community needed to be strengthened in association with, and in service to, the nation. Simultaneously, he stressed that the nation depended on social uplift movements, the onus for initiating which rested with its constituent communities. For instance, he told estate labourers near Klang that they should return to India, 'even if it means begging in the streets there' in the event that they were unable to give their children an education in Malaya.[11] The point here was not to encourage Tamils to return to India but to challenge them to strive for progress in Malaya, whatever the cost. His pointed comment was motivated by an abiding concern that 'only the strong and the equal can cooperate'.[12] Periyar saw the nation as a chain that was only as strong as its weakest link. In a context wherein the emerging Malayan nation was comprised of different races that were cleaved along distinct lines of social class, communities needed to prioritize self-strengthening as a precursor to national unity and cooperation. In his view, 'the Chinese, Tamils and others should strive to become strong links in the chain of the Malayan nation.' Inasmuch as the Chinese in China and the Chinese in Malaya were links in an international bond, the national bond, Periyar emphasized, should always come first. His message was thus strikingly similar to Jawaharlal Nehru's emphasis on Indian unity in Malaya. However, when the latter had visited Malaya in 1950, he had reminded the diaspora that they alone were responsible for their future; India had its own problems to take care of (Brown, 1981).

If Periyar's visit came at a time of great upheaval for south Indian politics, it also coincided with a charged context for Tamils living in Singapore and Malaya. It took place when the diaspora showed great interest in the Dravidian movement. The various Dravidian organizations in Malaya had been centralized in 1947 into the All-Malaya Central Dravidar Kazhagam. The community was spearheading numerous efforts to promote the Tamil language, culture, and identity, many of which were initiated from Singapore. The *Tamil Murasu* newspaper, which, since its beginnings in the 1930s had functioned as the press mouthpiece of the Dravidian movement in Malaya, was published from Singapore. G. Sarangapany, who wore many hats as the *Murasu*'s editor, Periyar's close comrade, and leader of the movement in this region, was also widely respected as the leader of Singapore's Tamil community. Singapore, in fact, became the site for the establishment in 1951 of the Tamils' Representative Council under Sarangapany's leadership. In September 1951, 1,500 people gathered to celebrate Periyar's birthday, with Sarangapany explaining that Periyar would be remembered more than anything else for his fight to 'wipe out the slur cast on Tamils'.[13] These events had been followed by the enthusiastic launch of the Tamils' Festival (*Tamizhar Thirunaal*) a year later in 1952. An annual event, it sought to replace landmark Hindu festivals as Aryan impositions on the Malayan Tamil identity and emphasized pan-Tamil solidarity in their place. The festival may be thought of as a transnational performance of Dravidian ideals that was similar to the Self-Respect wedding in its symbolic significance. The key distinguishing factor was that it was concerned with the projection of overlapping community identities: the festival envisioned a reformist Dravidian community as an inextricable part of an emergent national community.

The year 1952 also marked a significant milestone for Tamil cultural–linguistic assertion in Singapore and Malaya owing to a prominent dispute that had broken out over the right of representation in Malayan Indian media. The Tamils demanded that the Radio Malaya Tamil section's incumbent leader should be replaced. In early November, a reader, S. Moganam, wrote to the *Murasu* complaining that the leader of the Tamil section had allotted thirty-five minutes daily to broadcasting Hindi songs, asking why Hindi songs should be featured in the first place when the community saw no reason for them. Another reader demanded that all who professed to be Tamil without knowing the Tamil language should leave the section along with the defamed leader.[14] Following comments from English newspapers denouncing the incident as 'petty parochialism', the newspaper published another letter. Duraisamy wrote that the Radio Malaya Tamil section's leadership was a matter that only Tamils had the right to decide.[15] In the same year, the newspaper published commentaries on the widespread usage of the Malay word, 'kling,' a derogatory slur referring to south Indians. Readers expressed deep anguish that the 'great Tamil race' had had to thus endure insult from Malaya's other communities.[16]

Shortly thereafter, recommendations to install a Sanskrit Chair at the University of Malaya sparked a furore, with Tamil publications vehemently condemning the blatant disrespect for the Tamil language and people that the proposal seemed to suggest. This particular incident motivated G. Sarangapany to initiate the Tamil-Our-Life Fund to finance a rival bid to replace Sanskrit with Tamil. The petition to the university was accompanied by a pact that was signed by Malayan supporters of the SRM to defend the status of Tamil in the country, no matter the cost of such an endeavour. Much of the 1950s thus witnessed radical Tamil cultural–linguistic assertion. The Tamils Representative Council took the lead in resisting the notion that Tamils, on the basis of their being Indian, should look to the Malayan Indian Congress (MIC) for representation. Tamil opposition to the MIC became startlingly apparent in 1954 when the community threatened to withhold support for the MIC's planned entry into a political alliance between the dominant nationalist political parties that championed Malay and Chinese interests respectively, the United Malays National Organization (UMNO) and the Malayan Chinese Association (MCA). The MIC needed to prove its credentials first by securing the national position of the Tamil language.

In the period in question, Indians were a minority in Singapore and Malaya, with Tamil speakers dominating the Indian ethnic bracket. A substantial proportion of Tamils were from working-class backgrounds. The demands of Malaya's plantation economy had necessitated an enormous influx of south Indian labourers into Malaya, many of whom were from Dalit communities. Indian society in Malaya was rapidly acquiring a more settled character than before, with the vast majority of Tamils being first-generation settlers. Coming in this context, the MIC's decision in 1947 to introduce Hindi as the language of Indian unity in Malaya frustrated the Tamils (Stenson, 1980). A branch of the MIC, the Singapore Regional Indian Congress (SRIC) did not seem to be any more representative of Tamil interests in Singapore. Tamil assertion thus gained ground among the diaspora as there were important parallels between the Tamil situation in the Malayan peninsula and that in India.

The community was in the unique place of simultaneously being in a position of strength and weakness: strength in that it commanded the numbers and weakness in that there were overwhelming problems of poverty and lack of representation that had to be addressed and overcome.

In circumstances wherein the Tamils were mostly either illiterate or Tamil-literate and vastly outnumbered the other Indian communities, they had every interest in ensuring that the Tamil language be the unifying Indian language in Singapore and Malaya. As in India, however, the transition to independence seemed imminently threatening to Tamils in this region as politics did not provide any safeguard for the Tamil identity, at least to begin with. The Tamil people in Singapore increasingly found themselves subsumed within an Indian communal bracket that, as in India, appeared to be defined by north Indian hegemony. This challenge had been at least partly responsible for the MIC's 'Tamilization', which was most markedly symbolized by the accession to its presidency of V. T. Sambanthan, the Tamil leader from a rural background, in 1955. Upon assuming power as the MIC's president, Sambanthan initiated a party reshuffle through which he replaced north Indians in key leadership positions with Tamils. Dravidian ideology thus provided the language through which the leaders of the Tamil community challenged the entrenched leadership as elitist and oppressive. Periyar was well aware of these circumstances when he addressed Tamils in Malaya. One to emphasize rational thinking over superstition and dogma of any kind, he was speaking precisely to these challenges when he advocated communal self-strengthening and national unity.

The Idiom of Self-Respect and the Development of a Settled Tamil Consciousness in the Aftermath of Periyar's Visit

'Although she would previously balk at the idea, my grandmother would now wear a saree blouse. As times change, we must be willing and prepared to change too! People will change as they improve their level of education and gain experience. No one can stop this!' Periyar said in his speech at Singapore's Happy World Stadium on 3 January 1955.[17] Malayan Tamil newspapers covered every aspect of the leader's visit, often drawing the reader's attention to issues that he discussed as being of particular relevance to Malaya. Ramaswamy's (1997) argument that language devotion transcended the colonial space that it inhabited in India, provides us with a lens to explore the dexterity with which Malayan 'devotees' of the Tamil language negotiated the parameters of identity, a negotiation that became especially important in the aftermath of Periyar's second visit in the mid-1950s. By then, Malaya was making rapid strides towards self-rule. The idiom of Self-Respect and the Tamil language itself emerged as foremost agents of change in this context of transnational exchange, one in which the worlds of belonging that the Tamil diaspora in this part of the globe invoked and the meanings of belonging that they attached to them, were undergoing profound transformation.

Malayan Tamil newspapers reported minute aspects of key literary developments in India, such as the activities of the Madurai Tamil Sangam (Madurai Tamil Academy), poet and writers' conventions, and *Tirukkural* movements, and reprinted the works of Dravidian writers based in India (Sathisan, 2009). The main audience for Tamil writing came from the middle and lower strata of Tamil society. Owing to the nexus that was thus established between the Dravidian movement and the *Tamil Murasu*, social uplift formed the newspaper's main thrust. In fact, Tamil labourers seem to have subscribed to Tamil publications on a regular basis; the *Murasu* not only lowered its price with the stated aim of easing the financial burden on labourers, but also launched a weekly feature, 'Labourer's Page',[18] that was dedicated to developments pertinent to them. However, in the aftermath of Periyar's second visit to Malaya, a more obvious and distinctive engagement with the Tamil language and specifically, the characteristic idiom of Self-Respect, emerged in the *Murasu*.

As compared to Periyar's first visit, the aftermath of the second visit also engendered deliberate assertions of loyalty to the Malayan nation, reflecting the context of decolonization that framed Tamil engagements with Self-Respect values and ideals in this period.

Although there was a long history of engagement with Dravidian ideology among the Tamil people of Singapore and Malaya, Periyar's second visit aided the development of a settled identity in the community at a time when the end of empire loomed large in Malaya. As with previous negotiations of identity, the Tamil press played a crucial role in the construction and dissemination of a transnational idiom of Self-Respect. Tamil literary writings in this period drew upon the imaginative resources afforded them by the Dravidian movement, although they simultaneously evidenced a keen engagement with circumstances that were unique to the community in Singapore and Malaya. There was no wholesale exportation of ideology here. Nor, as we shall see, was there an undiscerning importation of Self-Respect ideas by the community that attended Periyar's speeches and meetings, often in the thousands.

The *Murasu* featured an outpouring of Tamil literary writings from readers and professional writers in the 1950s that reveal selection, interpretation, and application of those aspects of the movement that aligned closely with the community's most pressing needs. During his visit, Periyar had emphasized that 'he only wanted to see his beloved Tamils living in Malaya and advise them to live united' adding that the community was still 'disintegrated', which would lead to a worsening of the situation should things fail to improve.[19] Reflecting this call for solidarity and unity, the writing of this period often foregrounded '*inam*' and, less commonly, '*kulam*'. One poem set out that 'when your language is in danger, when others ridicule and curse your *inam*, do not think that it is wrong to get angry; arise'[20] *Inam* denotes race while *kulam* is more accurately understood as community, a subset of racial belonging. Ramaswamy has described these terms as 'ethnic idioms' that constructed 'the Tamil community as a distinctive and autonomous racial and political entity (*inam*), the sacral center of which is occupied solely by the Tamil language from which all members claim shared descent' (1993, p. 704). The use of these idioms was enormously significant in that it revealed the extent of the SRM's influence on imaginings of Tamil identity. By investing supreme authority in the *inam*, these works posited a distinctive Tamil community in Singapore and Malaya in place of the homogenizing Indian racial category that had been imposed by the colonial state. Indeed, Malayan conceptualizations of *inam* conveyed a particular sentiment of belonging, the limits of which were forged at the intersections of ethnicity and nationality. Poems exhorted courageous Tamil men to 'hasten to protect our *kulam*' and to work to enable the community's return to a state of former glory (Subramanian, 1997). As used in the Malayan Tamil literature of this period, notions of Tamil identity were often presented as inextricably entwined with imaginings of a resurgent masculinity and tied to a distinctly racialized construct of belonging. They referred not to Tamil-speaking individuals *per se*, but to the community that the people and language were imagined as forming together.

The writings that the *Murasu* published in the aftermath of Periyar's second visit were aimed at inspiring in its readers a sense of loyalty and pride in this identity. Akin to the rhetoric of the Dravidian movement in India, they referenced a Tamil history defined by greatness. An English newspaper commentary set out that Periyar had provided 'the right example' to all visiting dignitaries to Malaya 'to leave all their politics, controversies and revolutionary slogans behind' and 'to give just such advice as is needed for the people here'.[21] Whereas previously the community had celebrated Periyar by commemorating his birthday or by naming cherished institutions, like the EVR Samadharma (lit., equality for all) Tamil School, after him, the effect of seeing him on Malayan soil appears to have come as an enormous boost to the Tamil morale. The literature of this period reflects not just pride and hope, but also an emphasis on the historic glory of the Tamil people. It often exhorted readers 'to heed history to know who the Tamil people are; to know who ruled; roar with pride!' (Subramanian, 1997, p. 454) Such literary writings thus looked to the past in imagining a proud transnational Tamil identity.

At the same time, however, the writings of this period evidence a growing concern that complacency was setting in. In 1956, the poet N. Pazhanivelu (Subramanian, 1997) wrote mocking those who asked,

> Reform and reform-oriented unions for *Tamils*?
> How have we declined?
> From a [tradition] praised by the world have we come;
> Those who speak thus of our community's life
> are those who would deny the wound that festers beneath
> We who live here have alone become ridiculed,
> We have become a moth-eaten race!

implying that merely claiming a glorious past would not be enough if Tamils in Singapore and Malaya refused to do anything to help the weakest members of their community. If Periyar had spoken about the community's self-strengthening as a necessary prerequisite for national self-strengthening, Malayan Tamil writers often demanded that the *inam* take stock of its circumstances in order to ensure its future progress. To this end, the writing of this period also criticized existing social divisions amongst the Tamil people. Such works questioned the community's seeming fixation with divisive representative organizations: 'What will happen to us if we are to form a union for every ten people?' (Mugilan, 1954, p. 457). They were also concerned with the importance of projecting a united front to other communities. The fact that Tamils were keenly aware of their social standing relative to the Chinese and Malays was thus closely reflected in the literary writing of this period, which emphasized the urgency of forging a cohesive identity so that the community could be recognized as an equal among equals.

Perhaps the most interesting aspect of the Tamil identity as it took shape in the literary outpouring of the 1950s and early 1960s was its sheer geographical scope. The projected identity was supposed to be universal in its embrace of Tamils. To this end, these writings called for the Tamil people in Singapore and Malaya to show empathy for their kin settled elsewhere, and indeed, everywhere. References to the shared immigrant experience were made explicit through the theme of a people who had contributed to their respective countries with 'tears and blood', only to have their livelihoods threatened after achieving nationhood.[22] In a situation of impending decolonization, it can be surmised that such writings were equally representative of Malayan Tamil anxieties arising from political transition. A poem lamenting the sufferings of Tamils in what was then Burma asked, 'who did they harm, my Tamil people in Burma? A people with such a great ancestry reduced to this state? Can we bear to see this?' (Subramanian, 1997, p. 361). Inspired by the forced exodus of Indians from Burma in 1962, the poem's emotional tone, reminiscent of Periyar's reference to Tamils in Singapore as his kin, established a familial bond between its subjects and its audience. Parallels were thus drawn between the sufferings of Burma's Tamil people and the circumstances of the Tamil people in Singapore, emphasizing mutual solidarity and kinship.

Poems, especially those depicting the labourer's condition, also alluded to the socio-economic differences between Tamil settlers in Malaya who had come from India and those who hailed from what was then Ceylon. K. Perumal bemoaned the iron-grip of the '*krani* (clerk), the god of death', the 'heartless slave driver' who, he wrote, had no sympathy to spare for his brother, the labourer (Subramanian, 1997, p. 400). The Ceylon Tamils in fact dominated clerical positions on the Malayan plantations, while Indian Tamils were largely employed as their subordinates; as labourers. Indeed, the Ceylon Tamils were generally worlds removed from their working-class Indian counterparts. Ceylon Tamils were also estranged from their Indian counterparts as they sought separate political representation for themselves, principally through the establishment of the Ceylon Federation of Malaya.

Periyar's message to the Malayan Tamil community and the discourse of the SRM appear to have provided a powerful fillip to Tamil assertion in that they enabled the community to rally around an aspect of Tamil settlement in Malaya that was generally considered a weakness, and turn it into a proud and resilient emblem of strength instead. The economic importance of labourers and by extension their political value, had been noted as early as in 1939 by the Singapore Indian Association's K. M. Kannampilly, when he complained that Indian organizations did not realize that the labourer was the community's 'greatest force and the strongest weapon' in its political fight (Stenson, 1980). The 1940s had been a decade of trade unionism. In 1948, however, the start of the Malayan Emergency—a twelve-year period of Communist insurgency—brought about the curtailment of the space allowed for trade unionism. Another type of labour politicization nevertheless began in the 1950s with the coolie at the vanguard of the Malayan Tamil identity. Most of Periyar's speeches during his visit had engaged with the socio-economic conditions of labourers and the importance of education for children from working-class families. Likewise, in the aftermath of the visit, the labourer became the focal point of the community's demand for increased political rights and representation. In the writings of this period, the labourer became symbolic of the diaspora; a people who sought to establish their contributions and hence prove their loyalty to their adopted homeland. To this end, literary musings depicted the Tamil labourer's toil as indispensable to the country's riches; the labourer, who, like 'the beneficent sky protects the people, all whilst denying himself of any comfort'.[23] Tamil cultural–linguistic activism in this period thus demanded that labourers' toil should be honoured. Through the trope of the labourer, writings of the period emphasized the value of the Tamil 'race' to Malaya.

Since the labourer's condition was posited as indicative of the condition of the Tamil race, the Malayan Tamil identity was structured around recommendations to help the community, beginning with the labourer. As in his first Malayan trip, Periyar focused on the social problems confronting the Tamil diaspora in Singapore and Malaya, a list that alcoholism topped. Addressing an audience of 1,000 people who had come to see him at Malacca's Kubu Stadium, he exhorted labourers in particular to shun toddy as it would 'ruin' them.[24] A crucial link was established between alcoholism, which was rife among labourers, and the community's overall progress in a poem that asked, 'how can we achieve progress when you yearn for alcohol daily in a hovel, shrouded in darkness?

Alcohol is responsible for our state of sorrow, friend!'[25] The implication was that labourers owed it to the community to put an end to habits that were not only destructive at a personal level, but were likewise hurting the community's standing within the nation. Equally importantly, literary writings in this period held the wealthy responsible for social uplift when they charged, 'what good have the Tamil people done when they remain indifferent? What good are they even if they number in the millions in this country?' (Mugilan, 1954, p. 314).

Malayan Tamil literature in this period also emphasized that the Tamil language should not be ignored in the community's pursuit of progress. Poems pointedly asked why labourers, whose children primarily attended Tamil schools, gave whatever they could to aid the cause of Tamil education in Singapore and Malaya when those who had the means in society to make a difference refused to get involved.[26] A poem that was published in the inaugural magazine of a Tamil school in 1958 enquired, 'will the Tamil school not grow and flourish to elevate the condition of the Tamil people of the Malayan nation?' thus equating the progress of the Tamil 'race' with the state of its language, and specifically, the state of Tamil language education (Subramanian, 1997, p. 315). Those who refused to repay 'the Tamil school's debt' were criticized as 'unmanly cowards'. Given that representative political organizations in this period appeared to be unconcerned about Tamil interests, such writings and poems constituted as much a political critique as a social one on class divisions within the Tamil community. In keeping with the established tradition of supporting Tamil education, G. Sarangapany raised funds for the Umar Pulavar Tamil High School in the 1960s, aided in his efforts by the publication of weekly advertisements in the *Murasu* to gather contributions for the endeavour.

One of the main differences between Tamil identity politics in the aftermath of Periyar's visit in 1929 and that which developed in the mid-1950s was that the latter pivoted around the clear articulation of Singapore and Malaya, and indeed, Singapore within Malaya, as the diaspora's home. Although articulations of Tamil identity posited a sense of cultural community that transcended national boundaries to emphasize kinship and solidarity with Tamils living elsewhere, they equally posited the centrality of a Malayan political community to which Tamils were to owe their foremost loyalty. While the desirability of dual citizenship was debated in this period, it was not so much a manifestation of loyalty to India, as it was of the desire to secure a political safety net for the Tamil position in Malaya (Sandhu and Mani, 1993). Even as the umbilical cords were being severed by the Indian homeland, Tamils in the Malay peninsula were developing a distinct national consciousness. A candid poem[27] on the Malayanization of the Tamil identity and indeed, of the Tamil language set out:

Shall we go *jalan jalan* [stroll around]?
I will *dukar* [pawn] the jewellery.
Krani [clerk] gave salary.

Please *tolong* [show mercy] sir.
I told *dukaan* [shop] to make a chair.
What is this *gila* [mad] Tamil?

Such writings show that Tamils in Singapore and Malaya were culturally as well as politically becoming Malayan in outlook, thus reflecting the essence of Periyar's message to the community.

The writings produced in the period in question would reveal that the Malayan Tamil identity was centered on establishing Malaya as the community's home and nation. For one, they emphasized a pan-Malayan consciousness. Poets in Singapore wrote extensively about the condition of 'Malayan Tamils' while those based in the mainland mourned the poverty of Singapore's Tamil schools as the woe of all Tamil people in Malaya (Mugilan, 1954). In a context wherein political developments were shaping up towards independence for Singapore as part of Malaysia, Tamil writings stressed political and emotional attachment to the notion of a pan-Malaysian identity. Indeed, they also emphasized the necessity of adapting to sociopolitical realities as a means of demonstrating the community's loyalty. Several of these works imagined 'Malaya's son' as living and toiling alongside the Chinese and Malays.[28] Implicit here was the desire for equality for all races on the basis of their being bound by familial ties to the emerging nation.

Hence, Tamil cultural–linguistic assertion in the diaspora was very much attuned to the context in which it unfolded. The literature of the period stressed that the assertion of a distinct Tamil identity should not come at the expense of jeopardizing the already tenuous national position of the Tamils. Instead, Tamil writings underscored that this identity, could—and indeed, must—be realized within the limits of loyalty to the nation. What was demanded was activism, not separatism. Periyar had exhorted Tamils to accept Malayan citizenship and owe their loyalties to their country of settlement in 1954.[29] The Singapore Citizenship Ordinance of 1957 offered Singapore citizenship to all who had been born in Singapore and those who had lived in the country for ten years or more. Sarangapany and advocates of Self-Respect reform in Singapore would prove influential in rallying Tamil support for the People's Action Party (PAP), which rose to power in 1959 and has formed the ruling government ever since. The PAP in turn courted Tamil support, as the largest community within the Indian ethnic bracket, through the partnership that was forged with Sarangapany and other leaders of the Tamil community. It was due to the convergence of fortuitous political circumstances and Tamil cultural–linguistic activism that the Tamil language eventually secured the status of being one of Singapore's four official languages.

Reflecting on Periyar's Relevance in Singapore

Today, the Tamil language is one among Singapore's four official languages. Indian communities speaking Indo-Aryan languages, despite their long history in the city-state, have historically constituted a demographic minority within the Indian ethnic bracket in Singapore, which remains dominated by Tamil-speaking south Indians. Since the 1990s, a third wave of migration has brought a linguistically and culturally diverse group of south Asians to Singapore. Whilst Tamils, comprising more than 50 per cent of Indians, still form the majority, this state of affairs occasionally gives rise to certain confusions. In 2019, a market put up an announcement in what it thought to be the country's four official languages. The only problem was that one of those languages was Hindi, not Tamil. Responding to this error, a Tamil netizen took to social media with the comment, 'I think you need more people who can read and write Tamil. What language is that? Please remove the person from your team if they don't know our very own official languages!'[30] The response constituted but the latest episode of Tamil assertion in the country.

Tensions between migration and settlement thus remain relevant to articulations of Tamil identity in contemporary Singapore. Although they are similar in some ways to the negotiations that played out over and through language in the 1950s, they differ in important ways as well. We have seen from this chapter that Tamil assertion in Singapore has had a long history, strengthened as it was at pivotal moments of the community's story of settlement by the Dravidian SRM. Direct transnational linkages were forged between Tamils in Singapore and Malaya and the SRM when Periyar visited in the 1930s and 1950s. Given the context of impending nationhood that confronted Tamils in Singapore and Malaya in the aftermath of his second visit, the Tamil language itself became the foremost instrument of change, as a veritable literary revolution took place. This crucial subset of Tamil cultural–linguistic assertion in Singapore, which was catalysed by Periyar's visit, in turn mobilized Tamil public opinion and aided the development of a *settled* Tamil consciousness.

Communalism and nationalism are often viewed as being mutually irreconcilable. Whereas the latter is valorized—as is the nation-state that it is expected to culminate in—the former is vilified owing to its potential to produce divisive, fissiparous tendencies that threaten the nation-state's integrity. Communalism, in other words, is dismissed as counting for nothing more than chauvinism. History and contemporary developments alike bear testimony to the violent potential of communalism, although much the same can be said about nationalism as well. In contrast, the SRM developed as a critique of the nation-state's totalizing tendencies in India. More importantly, it helped to orientate Tamil linguistic communalism towards Malayan nationhood in Singapore and Malaya. Self-Respect provided an immensely persuasive language of empowerment through which a community that was associated with the working-class profile of its people, pulled itself up from associations of poverty and backwardness to instead lay claim to the national community as an equal among equals. In tandem with efforts at social uplift that were being spearheaded by Tamil associational life in Singapore and aided by a context that proved favourable to the political position of the Tamil people on the eve of Malayan independence, this aspect of cultural–linguistic activism helped to cement Tamil's national position as an official language in Singapore. Communalism engendered parity, not chauvinism, in this context. Periyar himself played a pivotal role in calling upon the Tamils to prioritize community self-strengthening in service to the Malayan nation and not to Tamil Nadu. If anything, this aspect of the SRM's transnational career and application shows that the cultural and instrumental values of minority languages are inextricably intertwined with each other. In drawing upon Self-Respect ideas and ideals, and in adapting them to address their circumstances of settlement, Tamils in Singapore showed critical engagement with Periyar's thought. They negotiated the Tamil position, with its emphasis on the welfare of the labourer, between their communal identity and nationality. In the process, the SRM was thoroughly Malayanized. Here was no deification of Periyar. Instead, there was a critical engagement with his ideas insofar as they addressed the community's most pressing needs. This is perhaps the best tribute the diaspora could have given a man who challenged the world to prioritize the continual pursuit of reform premised upon rationality.

Notes

1. For works that buck this trend, see Arasaratnam (1970).
2. *Kudi Arasu*, 2 May 1925.
3. *Kudi Arasu*, 3 April 1927.
4. *Malacca Guardian*, 23 December 1929.

5. 'Periyar E.V. Ramasamy, Prime Agitator for an Independent Tamil State', *Straits Times*, 9 January 1955, p. 11.
6. 'After 25 Years', *Indian Daily Mail*, 30 December 1954, p. 1. See also Arasaratnam (1970).
7. *Indian Daily Mail*, 16 December 1954, p. 1.
8. 'Periyar's Plea for Unity Among All Sections of Indians!', *Indian Daily Mail*, 19 December 1954, p. 12.
9. English newspapers estimate an attendance of 5,000 people whilst the *Tamil Murasu* places this figure at 7,000. The actual attendance is likely to have been between these figures. The author has translated all the Tamil textual references cited in this chapter.
10. 'Happy World Stadiathil 7,000 per! [7,000 people in Happy World Stadium]', *Tamil Murasu*, 6 January 1955, p. 5.
11. *Singapore Free Press and Mercantile Advertiser*, 28 December 1954, p. 5.
12. 'Call for National Unity', *Straits Times*, 9 January 1955, p. 11.
13. 'Periyar E. V. R. Removed the Slur Cast on Tamils', *Indian Daily Mail*, 21 September 1954, p. 1.
14. 'Neyargal Abiprayangal: Tamilariyathavar thaguthiyillai [Reader's opinions: Those who do not know Tamil are not qualified]', *Tamil Murasu*, 10 November 1952, p. 5; 'Neyargal Abiprayangal: Ellorum Ethirparthathu [Reader's opinions: What everyone expected]', *Tamil Murasu*, 9 November 1952, p. 7.
15. 'Neyargal Abiprayangal: Radio Malayavin Tamil pirivum, Tamil sanga pradhinithithuva sabaiyum [Reader's opinions: Radio Malaya's Tamil section and the Tamils Representative Council]', *Tamil Murasu*, 16 November 1952, p. 2.
16. 'Neyargal Abiprayangal: Vetrikku vilakkam [Reader's opinions: An explanation for victory]', *Tamil Murasu*, 2 November 1952, p. 10.
17. 'Periyar kooriyathil rasamanavai sila [Some interesting aspects of Periyar's speech]', *Tamil Murasu*, 3 January 1955, p. 8.
18. The newspaper launched this column in 1952.
19. 'After 25 Years', *Indian Daily Mail*, 30 December 1954, p. 1.
20. 'Somasanma, Aaruvathu sinam endru ennathae! Aanmayudan ezhunthu vaa! [Do not think that it is wrong to be angry! With manliness arise!]', *Tamil Murasu*, 4 November 1956, p. 5.
21. 'Notes and Comments', *Indian Daily Mail*, 18 December 1954, p. 2.
22. 'Service kallathirkerpa sambalamum iyalbaga uyarum murai vendum [Salary should increase in tandem with service length]', *Tamil Murasu*, 7 January 1954, p. 2.
23. A. Muthaiyanar, 'Malainadu Petra Magan [Malaya's son]', *Tamil Murasu*, 25 April 1960, p. 5.
24. 'Indians are Told: Don't Drink Toddy', *Straits Budget*, 30 December 1954, p. 15.
25. 'Ilaventhan, Thalai Nimirvom! [We will stand tall]', *Tamil Murasu*, 17 July 1960, p. 6.
26. 'Thillaidasan, Thuraimugatthozhilaazhar [Dock labourers]', *Tamil Murasu*, 20 November 1962, p. 7. See also *Indian Daily Mail* (1954).
27. 'Tamizhan, Ithuvum Tamizha? [Is this Tamil?]', *Tamil Murasu*, 20 November 1954, p. 4.
28. A. Muthaiyanar, 'Malainadu Petra Magan [Malaya's son]', *Tamil Murasu*, 25 April 1960, p. 6.
29. 'After 25 Years', *Indian Daily Mail*, 30 December 1954, p. 5.
30. 'Wet Market Operator Apologises for Flyers Carrying Hindi Instead of Tamil Translation', *Straits Times*, 23 March 2019.

References

Alagirisamy, D. 2016. 'The Self-Respect Movement and Tamil Politics of Belonging in Interwar British Malaya, 1929–1939'. *Modern Asian Studies* 50(5): 1547–1575.

Amrith, S. S. 2013. *Crossing the Bay of Bengal: The Furies of Nature and the Fortunes of Migrants.* Cambridge, MA: Harvard University Press.

Anderson, B. 1983. *Imagined Communities: Reflections on the Origin and Spread of Nationalism.* London: Verso.

Arasaratnam, S. 1970. *Indians in Malaysia and Singapore.* Oxford: Oxford University Press.

Brown, R. A. 1981. *Indian Minority and Political Change in Malaya, 1945–1957.* Oxford: Oxford University Press.

Hardgrave, R. L. 1965. *The Dravidian Movement.* Bombay: Popular Prakashan.

Indian Daily Mail. 1954. 'Give Your Children an Education: Periyar's Fervent Appeal to Malayan Tamil Labourers'. 28 December.

Mahajani, U. 1960. *The Role of Indian Minorities in Burma and Malaya.* New York: Vora.

Menon, D. M., N. Zaidi, S. Malhotra, and S. Jappie. 2022. *Ocean as Method: Thinking With the Maritime.* New Delhi: Routledge.

Moorthy, S. and A. Jamal. eds. 2010. *Indian Ocean Studies: Cultural, Social, and Political Perspectives.* New Delhi: Routledge.

Mugilan, S. 1954. *Thudikkum Ullam* (Beating Heart). Singapore: R. Nagaiyan.

Pandian, M. S. S. 1993. '"Denationalising" the Past: "Nation" in E V Ramasamy's Political Discourse'. *Economic and Political Weekly* 28(42): 2282–2287.

Ramaswamy, S. 1993. 'En/gendering Language: The Poetics of Tamil Identity'. *Comparative Studies in Society and History* 35(4): 683–725.

———. 1997. *Passions of the Tongue: Language Devotion in Tamil India, 1891–1970.* Berkeley: University of California Press.

Sandhu K. S. and A. Mani. eds. 1993. *Indian Communities in Southeast Asia.* Brisbane: ISEAS and Times Academic Press.

Sathisan, D. 2009. 'Speaking for the Diaspora: Tamil Newspapers in Malaya and Singapore as Instruments of Modernity, Protection, Reform and Change, 1930–1940'. *Heritage Journal* 4: 74–96.

Sökefeld, M. 2006. 'Mobilising in Transnational Space: A Social Movement Approach to the Formation of Diaspora'. *Global Networks* 6(3): 265–284.

Solomon, J. 2016. *A Subaltern History of the Indian Diaspora in Singapore: The Gradual Disappearance of Untouchability, 1872–1965.* New York: Routledge.

Stenson, M. 1980. *Class, Race, and Colonialism in West Malaysia: The Indian Case.* Brisbane: University of Queensland Press.

Subramanian, R. ed. 1997. *Maleciyat Tamizh kavithaik kalanciyam, 1887–1987* (Anthology of Malaysian Tamil Poems, 1887–1987). Kuala Lumpur: Arulmathiyam Publications.

Veeramani, K. 2012. *Maleciya Sinkappuril Periyar* (Periyar in Malaysia and Singapore). Chennai: Periyar Self-Respect Propaganda Institute.

Part IV
Women and Culture

9

Periyar, the Women's Question, and Maniammai*

Karthick Ram Manoharan and Vilasini Ramani

Periyar's writings on women were at the heart of his commitment to a radical concept of freedom. Periyar is known most not only for his atheism and radical critique of religion (Manoharan, 2022a) but also for his commitment and contribution to anti-caste thought and politics (Manoharan, 2020; 2022b). However, crucial, perhaps even central, to Periyar's politics of Self-Respect was his approach to the women's question. In this chapter, we discuss how Periyar's approach to the women's question was grounded not only in a rights-based discourse, but also in a freedom-based discourse; not just freedom from patriarchy, but also sexual freedom in a radically libertarian sense. More importantly, Periyar argued that freedom for women took priority over freedom from colonialism, and challenged patriarchal tendencies within Indian nationalism.

Scholars engaged with feminist politics have looked at the critical importance given to the women's question and gender in the Self-Respect Movement (SRM). In their readings on gender politics in India, Anandhi and Velayuthan (2010) highlight the 'limitations in theory itself in dealing with diversities and subalternity' and argue that in a scenario where gender intersects with caste and class, the theory and methods used 'should generate knowledge from the margins'. While feminist scholars such as Uma Chakravarti (2018) and Sharmila Rege (2013) have discussed the intersections of caste and patriarchy, others who have studied the Periyarist politics of gender—Anandhi (1991), Geetha (1998), and Hodges (2005)—have meticulously captured what we very broadly call Self-Respect perspectives and made important contributions to the study of women's politics of and from the margins of Tamil Nadu.

In her essay 'Women's Question in the Dravidian Movement', Anandhi provides a concise account of Periyar's ideas regarding women, perhaps the first of its kind in the English-speaking academia, and records the participation and reception of women in the SRM and the eventual dilution of the radical politics of Periyarism once Dravidian political parties became formalized.

---

* Parts of this chapter were published on Open Research Europe in 2021 under the title 'Radical Freedom: Periyar and Women' authored by Karthick Ram Manoharan. The authors would like to thank K. Bhaskaran for sending copies of Professor Saraswathi's books on request. The authors benefitted from conversations with S. Anandhi, Meena Dhanda, Nrithya Pillai, and Davesh Soneji.

She says 'According to Periyar, while marriage and chastity were key patriarchal institutions, patriarchy as such was ubiquitous, pervading spheres like language, literature and gender-based socialization' (1991, p. 26). Geetha, writing about the resistance of Periyar's thoughts to quotidian politics, argues that 'experiences of the Self-Respect Movement help in theorising the position of those feminists who are critical of and do not wish to ground identity in family and community, and who look to a comradeship to root a new and radical female subjectivity' (1998, p. WS15). Hodges provides an account of how the SRM revolutionized to some extent ideas on family in twentieth-century Tamil Nadu, arguing that apart from its activism, 'the Self Respect movement also based its campaign for transforming society at a key site of its production: the family and its domestic spaces' (2005, p. 257). There is a consensus among these three scholars that family was one of the main targets of critique by Periyar and his followers. In other words, Periyar politicized the personal.

This chapter builds on the work produced by these feminist academics and also taps into recently published collections of Periyar writings on the women's question. For long, the primary sources for scholars seeking to understand Periyar's gender politics were the three volumes of Periyar's selected works published by V. Anaimuthu and Periyar's booklet *Penn Yen Adimaiyanal?* (Why Were Women Enslaved?). We will be drawing on G. Aloysius' translation of the latter, titled *Women Enslaved*. We will also rely on the five volumes on *Pennurimai* (Women's rights) published as part of Periyar's collected works in the *Periyar Kalanjiyam*. The first two volumes of compilations were published earlier in 1981 and 1991, while the last three volumes were published in 2007. Together, they comprise 1,349 pages of Periyar's writings on women and cover a period from 1926 to 1973, providing new material that could aid in arriving at a more comprehensive picture of Periyar's 'feminist' politics.

In Tamil Nadu, Periyar was too radical for his contemporaries. His successors also either diluted or plainly ignored his emphasis on women's liberation. This seems rather ironical, given that E. V. Ramasamy was formally conferred the title of 'Periyar' in 1938 at a women's conference. While Periyar is considered the *Thanthai*, or father, of the Dravidian movement, the feminist concerns of this father figure are often brushed aside in popular public discussions, but for the rare academic or activist concerned with gender justice. The omission does this thinker much injustice because, as we argue, his conception of freedom cannot be grasped in its totality without engaging with his ideas on the women's question.

It is quite remarkable that Periyar, a man who was born in a socially conservative background in the family of an intermediate trading caste and operated in the patriarchal socio-historical context of a colonized 'Third World' country, should develop a radical position as regards the women's question which anticipated in many ways the ideas of Western feminists such as Simone de Beauvoir and Shulamith Firestone. It is hard to identify a singular source of inspiration for Periyar's approach to the women's question. The primary sources available do not indicate his familiarity with leading feminist thinkers of the West. One can reasonably speculate that his travels to Europe and the Soviet Union in 1931–1932 exposed him to radical ideas on women's liberation, and he does hold up the Soviet model positively in many of his references. But his *Women Enslaved* was written before these travels. Saraswathi, in her significant study of Periyar's Self-Respect 'philosophy', argues that Periyar's approach to the women's question 'was based on extensive and intensive observation of Western countries and a good deal of study of the historical past', adding that to him 'the liberation of women was as necessary as the removal of untouchability to become fit for self-government'

(1994, p. 194). Diehl notes that Periyar's 'ethical structure' was based in a social concern for equality and justice and rooted in secular life (1978, p. 47). Alongside, it could be argued that Periyar's commitment to rationalism, together with his critique of religion and caste, led him to advocate freedom for women.

In 2002, a selection of political writings of women affiliated to the SRM, covering the period 1931–1934, edited by Mu. Valarmathi, was published under the title *Suyamariyathai Iyakka Veeranganaigal* (2002)—Heroines of the Self-Respect Movement. The volume included writings by prominent women activists like Kunjitham Gurusamy, Neelavathi Ramasubramaniam, Sivakami Chidambaranar, M. Maragathavalli, R. Annapooraniammal, K. A. Janaki, and others. These writings reflected on equal rights for women, social reform, critique of religion, labour, and caste and untouchability. Some of these writers and others feature in *The Other Half of the Coconut: Women Writing Self-Respect History* (2003), edited and translated by K. Srilata. Anandhi's paper on Muthulakshmi Reddy (2020) and Sriharan's paper on Moovalur Ramamirtha Ammal (2021) give insights on the views of these social reformers who played a key role in Devadasi abolition. These works cover the dominant concerns for women activists in south India in the early twentieth century and provide a sense of the intellectual context in which Periyar was advocating his thoughts in the colonial period. However, regarding debates on 'Devadasi' abolition, Davesh Soneji (2012) and Nrithya Pillai (2022) capture the complicated social histories of hereditary performance artists, which many reformers in their zeal elided over, to the disadvantage of women from these communities.

Periyar's personal context is also significant. Nagammai was Periyar's wife for thirty-five years. His biographer Kavignar Karunanandam notes that even before Periyar entered political life, he convinced his wife to reject rituals, stop wearing the *thaali* (auspicious thread worn by married Hindu women), and avoid going to temples (2013, pp. 48–51). Sami Chidambaranar's 1939 biography of Periyar, *Tamilar Thalaivar*, provides a more intimate account of the Periyar–Nagammai relationship. Nagammai would later join Periyar in his political endeavours and played a prominent role in the Vaikom Satyagraha, also courting arrest on occasion. She helmed the *Kudi Arasu* in his absence. When she died in November 1933, Periyar, in his obituary, while noting her comradeship, wrote with great introspection and emotion that he hardly practiced at home the principles of women's liberation he preached outside. In 1949, he married Maniammai, his personal assistant and the daughter of a Justice Party activist. This marriage was the subject of great controversy, as he was seventy years old at the time and she thirty-two. Critics of Periyar continue to use this to attack him (and at times, abuse them both) even today. Defending the agency of Maniammai, who was a political activist in her own right, is not the concern of this chapter, but we would like to approach her as not just Periyar's co-traveller, but a serious political activist in the Dravidian movement. While Nagammai's writings, if any, have not been available to researchers till now, Maniammai was a regular contributor to the papers run by the Dravidar Kazhagam (DK). Her works, however, have rarely been referred to in academic literature.

In what follows, we provide a brief account of caste and the women's question. Then we discuss in detail Periyar's *Women Enslaved* and the important themes it covers. Next, we proceed to highlight how Periyar saw the question of women's freedom and how this was an important concern for him in his political career, referring to his works from the *Periyar Kalanjiyam*. We conclude with a discussion of Maniammai and her contributions to the DK. For this, we rely on the volume *Annai Maniammaiyarin Sinthanai Muthukkal* (2012), first published in 1987 and edited by K. Veeramani.

Caste and the Women's Question

In India, sex and caste are so deeply intertwined that it is hard to analyse one without considering the other. Even in contemporary India, popular matrimonial sites and pages routinely advertise for brides and grooms based on caste. In fact, the institution of arranged marriage in the country is grounded on caste. Apart from a few liberal spaces, transgression of caste endogamy is generally frowned upon, at times resulting in violence termed dubiously as 'honour killings'.

The historian Suvira Jaiswal argues that endogamy *alone* is not the root of the caste system, and it was 'the emergence of a class society in which patriarchal control played an important role in securing the rights and privileges of the elite on a hereditary basis' (2016, p. 5). Endogamy was not necessarily the cause, but definitely a central component of the caste system, with strict punishments prescribed for transgressors. Jaiswal identifies two key features of the caste system: 'the subordination of women' and 'its capacity to reinvent itself in changing social formations in the service of the powerful and the dominant' (2016, p. 58). And for the dominant castes and castes aspiring to be dominant, guarding the chastity of their women from men of other castes, especially those lower down the hierarchy, was important to preserve the purity of their caste (2016, p. 118).

Uma Chakravarti observes that 'Each caste is a closed and bounded group, and all social relations are represented in terms of bounded groups'—crucially, the relation of marriage (2018, p. 10). The notion of purity of the socially powerful castes made them try to posit it as a universal hierarchical principle and claim that it had the consent of all the castes. To understand the intersection of caste and gender in India, it is important to consider how reproduction is organized, who controls female sexuality, and the ideologies that sanction this (2018, p. 25). Caste needs endogamy to reproduce itself as a system and endogamy is a tool for both caste and subordination of women. Endogamy, she argues, 'is a necessary feature of a society *stratified on the basis of birth*, as different strata would not be able to maintain their distinctive identities without it' (2018, p. 28). Chakravarti then gives a succinct definition of the ideology that links caste and gender, making them interdependent and prescribing rules to govern society:

> brahminical patriarchy … is a structure unique to Hinduism and the caste order … It is a set of rules and institutions in which caste and gender are linked, each shaping the other and where women are crucial in maintaining the boundaries between castes. (2018, pp. 32–33)

Two important concepts of Brahminical patriarchy were *pativrata* (devotion to one's husband) and *stridharma* (duties of a woman). Brahminical law-givers like Manu and Yajnavalkya, not to mention the Hindu epics and Puranas, provided detailed prescriptions, and descriptions, of rules and regulations for the high-caste woman based on these concepts. The ancient texts feared the *strisvabhava*, the essential nature of woman, and believed that it had to be tamed by *stridharma* (2018, p. 69). However, these prescriptions were largely for the high-caste woman, while lower-caste women were seen as loose, immoral, and sexually available for upper-caste men. The practical result of this was that any caste which sought social mobility within the caste system needed to adopt *stridharma* and place stronger restrictions on its women, their movement, and their choices.

As we shall see in the following sections, Periyar called on women of all castes to break not just notions of chastity and honour, but all forms of community-based restrictions; not only to fight caste, but equally to emerge as free individuals.

Women Enslaved

From his entry into political activism in the 1920s, Periyar was acutely conscious of involving women in politics and social reform, not as mere subordinates, but as comrades. In the Vaikom Satyagraha, he encouraged the mass participation of women, and both his wife Nagammai and his sister Kannammal played an important role in it. He recognized that his peers in the Congress party and the Justice Party did not give adequate importance to the women's question and at times, sought to sideline it. To Periyar, however, women's liberation was key to ending oppression in society. In the Chengalpet Self-Respect conference held on 17–18 February 1929, Periyar and the Self-Respecters passed resolutions demanding equal rights to property for women, widow remarriage, abolition of child marriage, and freedom to choose spouses defying caste and community norms, besides encouraging women to enter professions of their choice. These resolutions rattled not just the Congress, but also many in the Justice Party. As Anandhi rightly notes, 'Periyar's commitment to the cause of women's emancipation often led him to be critical of his own political comrades' and he frequently challenged the Justice Party on their approach to the women's question (1991, p. 27). The articles that comprise *Women Enslaved* were written in this context.

Women Enslaved is composed of what can be called Periyar's 'early writings', and contains ten essays he wrote on the women's question between 1926 and 1931. These essays were compiled and published as a booklet in 1934, perhaps the first work of Periyar to be published in book form, under the title *Penn Yen Adimaiyanal?* This booklet provides a general introduction on Periyar's approach to the women's question, his analysis of the cause of their oppression, and his suggestions for change, and has been an important reference on the subject. In his preface to a 1942 reprint, Periyar wrote that the aim of the booklet was to 'demonstrate the different factors by which women were enslaved and continue to be so enslaved, and also the different ways and means by which they could emancipate themselves and live as free people'. He further added that the booklet was written for both men and women, and for 'people of all religions, societies and nations' (2009, p. 19). One may be tempted to draw parallels between this work and Frederick Engels' *The Origin of Family, Private Property and State*. Echoing Engels, Periyar noted that 'the philosophy of private property' was at the foundation of marriage (2016, p. 178). But where Engels located the oppression of women in political economy, Periyar located it in culture, primarily the 'Aryan' and Brahminical, but he did not spare Tamil culture either. In 1930, in a speech at Kozhikode, while arraigning the Hindu epics and Puranas for the oppression of women, Periyar said that Dravidian *dharma*, Jainism, or celebrated ancient Tamil thinkers like Thiruvalluvar also did not fare well on the women's question (2011, pp. 86–87).

Periyar challenged the value that conservative Tamil society placed on *karpu*, which can be loosely translated as chastity, as a social hypocrisy that limited the freedom of women while placing no such limits on men. He wondered why this was the case and called out both Hindu religious texts and Tamil secular texts like the *Thirukkural* for engendering oppression. Criticisms of Hindu religious and moral texts for prescribing rigid and caste-based notions of chastity are well known now. Ancient Tamil poets like Thiruvalluvar, Ilanko Adigal, and Auvaiyar also eulogized the virtues of chastity. These ancient poets were not only central to the modern political imagination of the Tamil nationalists in the colonial period, but the latter also invoked them to oppose Aryan–Hindi–Brahminical supremacy. The fervent ideologues of Tamil nationalism projected the notion of chastity and purity onto a secularized, but desexualized, *Tamilttay* (Mother Tamil), who stood for a feminized, pure, chaste, and virgin Tamil language to be protected from a corrupting outside influence (Ramaswamy, 1998, pp. 114–126).

While Periyar was critical of Indian anti-colonialism, which he felt to be coloured by Brahminism and patriarchy, he was equally an uncomfortable presence for the Tamil nationalists. Not only did he mock the romanticization of the Tamil language, he also did not excuse classical Tamil poets, thinkers, and saints for what he thought were their condescending views on women. Condemning Thiruvalluvar for promoting 'ideas of slavishness', he asked if the poet would have written the same thing had he been a woman (2009, p. 10). Arguing that the *Thirukkural* 'does not advocate uniform morality for both the sexes', Periyar said that morality and chastity, if they were valid at all, should be seen as equal for both women and men (2009, p. 16). Viewing chastity as a device of oppression coded by religion, Periyar ultimately wanted women to be liberated from the clutches of this concept. It is of interest to note that in 1929, Virginia Woolf wrote in *A Room of One's Own* that 'Chastity had then, it has even now, a religious importance in a woman's life, and has so wrapped itself round with nerves and instincts that to cut it free and bring it to the light of day demands courage of the rarest' (2009, p. 11). While there is no evidence to suggest that Periyar was aware of Woolf's work, he could perhaps be credited for demonstrating that rare courage.

Periyar recognized the pervasiveness of patriarchal ideology and noted that the concept of chastity makes women complicit in their own oppression. And though he expressed a qualified sympathy for Islam in other places, in *Women Enslaved*, he condemned the practices of veiling and polygamy that restricted the movement of women while allowing men multiple partners (2009, p. 16). Alhaj Subako, a Muslim woman who reviewed *Women Enslaved* in 1934, remarked: 'May Muslim men and Muslim parents shed their prejudiced views about women! May they arrive at a rationalist understanding of the problems that beset women!' (2003, n.p.) Periyar expressed similar opinions in 1947, when he wrote that 'Muslim youth should break the shackles of slavery of their community's women. They shouldn't just criticize other religions. They must also remove the evils in their own community' (2016, pp. 124–125). Periyar argued that 'If women are to be truly liberated, this gender-biased and enforced practice of chastity [ha]s to be abolished and in its place [a] gender-neutral, egalitarian and voluntary practice of chastity [ha]s to be established', and called for the abolition of marriages, laws, and religions that forced women to remain subservient to men (2009, p. 11).

Periyar then proceeded to attack the idea of 'love' as traditionally understood. It is notable here that ideal forms of love were greatly eulogized in ancient Sangam Tamil poetry. For instance, the *Ainkurunuru*, an anthology compiled roughly in the second–third centuries AD, consists of 500 poems dedicated exclusively to love. What is significant about this poetry is that it is located in the secular, where gods rarely figure. Again, while such poetry was celebrated by Tamil nationalists, Periyar dismissed it for providing rigid, essentialized notions of the sexes. Periyar revolted against the ancient, and he found the ancient revolting. He believed that ancient notions of love and undying commitments had no place in a rational, modern society. He called out such advocates of love as being 'ignorant of general natural dispositions' (2009, p. 17). He believed that the biological urge and the freedom to choose should be the criteria for partnership, not culture or pressures from family or society. He argued that the idealization of love or the family relationship would force couples to live in 'perennial dissatisfaction and harassment' (2009, p. 20). Instead of idealizing love, Periyar sought to view it in a utilitarian way, as a private emotion that should contribute to the wellness and pleasure of individuals and not a norm imposed by society that compels people to remain bonded in unjust and unhappy relationships. Periyar opposed the idea that 'people's expressions of love and desire must be brought within certain discipline and they ought to be expressed between particular individuals, in a particular way only' (2009, p. 27). In other words, disciplined and idealized notions of love chained women to their oppression and caste.

If love was attacked, marriage could not be far behind. Periyar said that the philosophy of marriage in India was an atrocity committed on women, 'which leads to the enslavement of women by men' (2009, p. 21). He believed that the idea of the sacredness of marriage was but part of the patriarchal ideology to cheat women into accepting their own enslavement. He was of the view that across the world, marriage functioned as a cruel institution; but while conditions had relaxed in the West, especially in the Soviet Union as a consequence of the socialist revolution, India '[wa]s doggedly holding on to the same old practices' (2009, p. 22). He argued that legal provisions to annul marriages and approve of remarriages alone could guarantee the freedom of men and women. The progress of women was not possible without creating the space for the cancellation of marriages (2009, pp. 22–23). Marriage was but a 'contractual agreement entered into by a couple for the purpose of their own life-comfort' (2009, p. 24).

Periyar viewed love and sexual desire as fundamental freedoms that should not be regulated by social and cultural institutions and advocated that the freedoms that exist for men should exist for women as well. However, prohibitions against adultery and the social derogation of women who had more than one sex partner were values that sought to force women to conform to notions of chastity. Periyar noted how a woman who had multiple sex partners was derogatorily called a *vibachaari* (adulteress or prostitute) but a man who did the same was not called a *vibachaaran* (2009, p. 29). He observed how the notion of the purity of women is closely connected to the purity of the caste and clan, as a result of which the 'adulteress' is thrown out of the caste and ostracized, while the philandering man takes pride in his 'trophies'.

Periyar believed that India could not achieve full freedom without women and the untouchable castes attaining their freedoms and equal rights. Without foregrounding this, he argued, 'to hand over the responsibility of such depressed people's freedom and welfare to us is equivalent to handing over the sheep to the butcher' (2009, p. 39). Women and the untouchable castes needed to understand the true meaning of liberty and freedom for themselves and not rely on others to give it to them. He said that it was evident from the manner they treated women and the untouchable castes that Indians had no sense of freedom at all. One step towards enhancing the freedom of women was to ensure that they had an equal right to hereditary property, educational training, and economic independence (2009, p. 41). The other was contraception.

Periyar noted that contraception had been advocated by others for the sake of women's or children's health or for maintaining a small family, but the SRM wanted to advocate it for the 'liberation and autonomy of women' (2009, p. 42). Pregnancy was 'positively harmful to the autonomy of women' and he saw it as the root cause of 'women's frequent illnesses, premature aging and early death' (2009, p. 43). Women, if they were to enjoy freedom, had to stop bearing children. Contraception, thus, was not to be advocated only for health reasons, but also because it was a step towards the freedom of women. He argued that there must be wide propaganda in favour of contraception through books, theatre, and cinema. While the absence of childrearing and childbearing responsibilities would enhance the freedom of both men and women, he firmly believed that only women could be the agents of their own liberation. Rhetorically he asked if mice could expect cats to give them liberation, adding that just as Brahmins would not liberate non-Brahmins, neither would men liberate women.

The booklet concludes with the assertion that 'masculinity' must be destroyed if women are to be liberated. *Aanmai*, which is the Tamil word corresponding to masculinity, is a positive term that also denotes virility, courage, and straightforwardness in a man. On the other hand, *penmai*, or femininity, is associated with docility and purity of character and body. Periyar argued that the concept of masculinity was socially and culturally constructed so as to elevate men at the expense of women, and, thus, without demolishing the idea of masculinity and the virtues associated with it, the freedom of women could not be achieved. Further, he said that masculinity prescribed certain oppressive roles to femininity, most notably that of motherhood, often by appeals to biological nature. Periyar however rejected this appeal to biological nature saying that to be human was to be 'against nature' and that one should not worry if as a result of the abolition of childbearing, humanity did not expand—according to him, it was an unjust argument to speak of the propagation of humanity at the expense of women (2009, p. 46).

Like the Canadian feminist Shulamith Firestone (1972), Periyar located the oppression of women in (what a male-dominated society relegated as) their biological functions, namely the bearing and rearing of children. Noting that masculine norms imposed unfair standards of love and chastity on women through institutions like family and marriage, he argued that these needed to be discarded for the creation of a truly egalitarian society. Finally, he noted that anti-colonial nationalism would not address, but brush aside the women's question. American journalist Katherine Mayo published *Mother India* in 1927, calling for the prolonging of British colonial rule since Indians could not be trusted to safeguard the rights of lower castes and women. Unsurprisingly, the book saw strong opposition from Indian nationalists. The Self-Respecters however welcomed it: not because they agreed with the author that British colonialism ought to continue, but rather because if at all the promise of 'freedom' of the anti-colonialists were to be taken seriously, then the caste question and the women's question had to be addressed in the proper spirit. Periyar saw the caste problem as predating the colonial problem, and the problem of women's oppression as predating both. He provocatively thanked the 'White man' without whom, 'in the name of religion and tradition, women would have been burnt along with their dead husbands. It was only the White man's law that changed this' (2007c, p. 130) Periyar had no faith in the Indian nationalist project or in local Tamil nationalist imaginations to secure liberation for women. If anything, he viewed them as movements that reinforced patriarchy and misogyny which were inherent in Hindu society. In a 1975 interview, Simone de Beauvoir opined that women's oppression was not solved by communist, anti-colonialist, or anti-racist approaches alone and that it needed its separate attention. For most of Periyar's political career, he strongly held a very similar opinion. He thus advocated freedom in its most radical sense, as both a means and an end, for women.

The Centrality of Women's Freedom

Periyar called the conventional marriage system, which requires the woman to stay with the man even if there is mutual incompatibility, a form of slavery (2007a, p. 11). In particular, he opposed the Brahminical rituals in marriage and saw Hindu customs and practices as evidence of the oppression of women. Traditional marriage was an institution that maintained caste purity, and he argued that marriages should take place without the influence of caste, religion, God, traditions, or rituals, as these practices legitimized the enslavement of woman to man (2007a, p. 43). Accepting Brahminical marriage rituals not only degraded women, but also non-Brahmin men as they consented to being inferior to the priests officiating such rituals (2007a, p. 74).

Speaking at a wedding function in April 1943, Periyar criticized the idea of *pativrata* for contributing to the slavery of women, further asking how a woman without economic independence, liberty, and equality could progress (2016, p. 56). It is of interest to note that several of Periyar's speeches on the problems of the conventional marriage were delivered at wedding functions. While weddings have for long been social, communal affairs, leaders speaking politics at such functions was a new practice, and pointed to the emergence of new publics. Periyar used these events to speak out against marriage itself. For instance, at a wedding event in February 1968, Periyar criticized the traditional marriage and asked when women could not choose their own partners, how could one say that this was a free country. 'If women have to progress, the system of marriage should be banned just like Sati. Only then can women be free and contribute to society' (2007b, p. 107). On a similar note, speaking at a marriage ceremony in Ambur in August 1969, he stated that he supported the abolition of marriage, reasoning that just as polygamy, which was permissible in the past, had been made illegal, it was possible to speculate and even desire that marriage could be made illegal in the future (2007c, pp. 64–67).

As an alternative, he promoted Self-Respect marriages[1] based on friendship, equality, and respect. The fundamental requirement for a Self-Respect marriage was the absence of a priest and rituals. It is important to note that certain communities in Tamil Nadu also practiced weddings without Brahmin priests and Sanskrit slokas, wherein a community elder or priest would recite verses in Tamil and bless the couple. This practice was hailed by Tamil enthusiasts as an alternative to the 'Aryan' wedding, which had a Brahmin as the officiating priest and involved recitation of Sanskrit slokas. Periyar, however, was sceptical about this. Speaking at one such wedding (of his friend's daughter) in 1940, Periyar differentiated between the Tamil marriage and the Self-Respect marriage—'Tamil marriage is based on community sentiment. Self-Respect marriage is based on rationalist enquiry' (2016, pp. 47–48). He felt that such Tamil marriages only replaced Brahmin priests with Saivite priests, and Sanskrit with Tamil, but as such were not rooted in ideas of self-respect and social reform. 'If I oppose Aryanism, it is only its practices, and not the Aryans. Claiming that Aryans and Tamils are different while following Aryan practices is not even a bit rational' (2016, p. 49). Avoiding employing Brahmin priests at such weddings was not enough; marriages between castes were to be promoted and all superstitions were to be avoided. 'Those having genuine concern and courage for a social revolution will only have an inter-caste marriage' he said (2016, p. 186).

Periyar wanted Self-Respect marriages to be based on secular contract. In this contract between a man and a woman, neither divinity nor social restrictions would interfere (2011, p. 208). Such a system would also encourage remarriage of widows and not frown upon divorce. Periyar saw Self-Respect marriages as a form of companionship that could and should be dissolved if either of the partners so desired. This liberty to walk out of an unhappy—or even just boring—marriage was important to women's freedom. He also believed that marriage would become unnecessary in the future. In 1961, he speculated a future where 'human society' with its biological family bonding would cease to exist, and machines would play an increasingly important role (2007a, pp. 39–40).

Periyar rejected looking to the past for moral instruction in the present. 'We are new humans. Our ancestors were barbarians. They held barbaric opinions' (2007a, p. 11). Appeals to the past were but excuses for oppressive practices in the present. In the 1960s, at a time when the figure of Kannagi, the key character of the Tamil epic-poem *Silappadikaram*, was celebrated as a symbol of Tamil civilization, he called the work a 'dustbin' that re-enforced ridiculous concepts of chastity of women and called on the thinking public to not pay heed to such literature (2007a, p. 66). He said that classic literature eulogized the beauty of women only so that they would remain objects of sexual fantasy for men, and, thus, urged women to stop beautifying themselves and focus instead on scientific learning (2007a, p. 217). He also advocated for women to take over 50 per cent of the jobs so as to ensure their economic independence (2007a, p. 221). He criticized the inherent hypocrisy in the sexual economy in India where a man could have multiple sexual partners but a woman was forbidden from pursuing her desires. He attacked the customs that required women to repress their sexual pleasure. He said that women should also have multiple sexual partners like men. He called on women to strike back at men who physically abused them and retaliate against those who verbally abused them. If a marriage could not recognize this freedom to retaliate, it should be dissolved!

At an Adi Dravidar meeting, Periyar said that the oppression of women was worse than the oppression of the 'lower' castes, workers, and peasants (2018, p. 177). 'A wife is an unpaid servant for a man. Even a servant cannot be beaten or kicked around. But a wife can be beaten or kicked and others will not interfere' (2007a, pp. 109–111). The oppression of women operated in dual ways: one economic, which treated them as unpaid labourers at home and thrust upon them the burden of housework including the bearing and rearing of children; and the other, cultural, the moral codes of Brahminism which legitimized their oppression, glorified it, and made them complicit in it. He said that for 3,000 years, the oppression of women went unchallenged because 'men thought it right to give respect and pay obeisance to Brahminism' (2007a, p. 102). Brahminism provided a system of values to justify patriarchy and the degraded position of women and, as Uma Chakravarti puts it, *brahmana women must consent to brahmana ideology for it to be effective* (2018, p. 20). Periyar put it more bluntly: 'In this country whichever women remained foolish slaves, those women were called *pativrata*s by the Brahmins' (2007a, p. 102). Periyar, of course, was not just talking about Brahmin women here, but women as such. He believed that Brahminism and patriarchy interacted in convenient ways to restrict the liberties of women in general. While recognizing Aryan-Brahminism as a fundamental doctrine of inequality, he did not spare Tamil patriarchal traditions, which he thought collaborated with Brahminism to create a native system of gender inequality.

In a 1932 article, Periyar said that a progressive mind would think that 'Women should be encouraged to be fit and be given training in weapons. They should have all the means and strength to protect themselves from savage men who are sexual predators. If needed, they should also join the army to fight enemies' (2011, p. 182). The women's question needed a total revolution, like what had occurred in the Soviet Union. Periyar praised the Union of Soviet Socialist Republics (USSR), not just for equal property rights, but also for the freedom of women to pursue the occupations they desired. He noted that women in Russia functioned very efficiently in the police and that this was the model for India to follow (2016, p. 117). By glorifying subservient women from mythology, society curtailed the freedom of women and prevented the birth of revolutionaries like

Sophia Perovskaya, the anarchist who assassinated Tsar Alexander II! Calling for greater representation of women in state services while hailing an anti-statist revolutionary and supporting Self-Respect and inter-caste marriages while calling for the abolition of marriage as such, are but some of the apparently contradictory positions Periyar took. Read in context, they nevertheless highlight the centrality of freedom for women in his political thought.

It would require a separate paper to explore the reception of such radical and provocative thoughts among Periyar's diverse audiences. While we hope that this chapter would inspire future research on these topics, we would like to conclude with a discussion of the role of E. V. R. Maniammai,[2] Periyar's successor, as the leader of the DK.

E. V. R. Maniammai (1917–1978)

Gandhimathi, born in 1917 to Kanagasabai Mudaliar, a supporter of the Justice Party, took an interest in non-Brahmin politics from her teenage years and named herself 'Arasiyal' (political) Mani. She met Periyar for the first time at a wedding in 1936. Soon she was drawn to his movement and began taking an active part from the early 1940s. In 1944, the year when the Justice Party was disbanded to form the DK, she was introduced as a member of the organization and was now known as Maniammai—'ammai' being an honorific suffix. She joined Periyar in his travels in north India in the following months. In 1946, she took on a key editorial role in the DK party paper *Viduthalai*. She was arrested in 1948 for taking part in anti-Hindi agitations. Besides growing into an indispensable member of the DK, she greatly assisted Periyar in his public and private life. In Maniammai, Periyar saw a trustworthy companion who had the potential to run the DK after his time. Against stiff opposition from within the organization, they were married in a civil ceremony in 1949. The marriage caused a split in the party, leading to an exodus of party leaders and members who formed the Dravida Munnetra Kazhagam (DMK; see Chapter 5).

Defending the marriage in a speech in October 1949, Periyar lashed out at critics who had accused him of immorality (Ramasamy 1974, pp. 2028–2035). He noted Maniammai's several contributions to the organization and identified her as a mature and seasoned activist. The marriage was not for the purposes of family, but to ensure that the assets of the party went into the right hands, especially because he did not trust many of his followers whom he saw as opportunists. He trusted Maniammai to handle the affairs of the DK diligently. Additionally, he said that given that this was no traditional wedding, if she felt like it, she was free to walk out or marry someone else.

In 1952, the Periyar Suyamariyathai Prachara Niruvanam started to publish and propagate the DK's ideas, with Maniammai as secretary. Even as she began taking more organizational responsibilities within the DK, she also participated in public protests against caste and Hindi imposition. On Periyar's demise in 1973, Maniammai succeeded him as leader of the DK—she is regarded as 'Tamil Nadu's first woman political leader'.[3]

Maniammai saw criticism of religion as a democratic right and believed that the state should be secular. In 1974, she wrote a letter to Prime Minister Indira Gandhi urging her not to attend Ramleela celebrations in Delhi, to which Mrs Gandhi responded asking her not to politicize the event.[4] As a further act of protest, Maniammai organized a 'Ravanaleela', where effigies of Rama were burnt. She was arrested for a short period for this. Later, she vocally opposed the Emergency.

Despite severe political repression, she was involved in protests against Mrs Gandhi. Through all her political activities, she ensured that the DK's interests were safeguarded. When Maniammai died in 1978, the DK's position in Tamil Nadu was secure.

In 1944–1945, Maniammai wrote four articles in *Kudi Arasu* on what she felt were objectionable aspects in the Hindu religion. She criticized the religion for claiming to have high philosophical concepts but ill-treating humans in practice (Maniammaiyar, 2012, p. 16). She shared the Periyarist notion that religion was a tool of oppression and liberation had to be sought outside of religion. Urging women not to live domesticated lives, she called on them to engage in public activities, with rationalist thinking (2012, p. 42). Foregrounding women's rights and liberation, she encouraged women to participate in agitations against north Indian domination (2012, pp. 39–40). Maniammai did not see the fight for the state's rights and women's rights as separate, but interlinked. She was also firm in her commitment to the idea of annihilation of caste and opposition to scriptures that justified caste (2012, p. 91).

Under Maniammai, the DK expanded its work into founding more educational institutions. In particular, she believed that it was important for girls to have a technical education. Maniammai wanted Periyar's death anniversary to be observed as women's day, acknowledging her predecessor's contributions to and concern for the women's question (2012, p. 72). Speaking in Vaikom at the golden jubilee celebrations of the Vaikom struggle, Maniammai called on women to come forward to work as agents of their own liberation (2012, p. 187). She criticized social mores that restricted women's liberty and emphasized on equal access to education and employment. Further, she demanded that 50 per cent of the seats in the legislature be reserved for women (2012, p. 194). Soon after emergency was declared, Maniammai issued a protest statement which concluded thus: 'Instead of living as cowards, we must take an oath to steady ourselves for the progress of humanity' (2012, p. 205). Both Periyar and Maniammai strongly felt that humanity would not progress without the liberation of women.

Conclusion

The women's question saw Periyar at his most radical. Periyar did not approach women's issues as peripheral to his politics, but placed them at its core. A *textual* reading of Periyar reveals that this was not an interest over a phase, but a central concern throughout his public life and could provide a frame for understanding how a conception of 'radical freedom' informed his politics. A *contextual* reading of Periyar with his contemporaries in India or the broader colonized world that was transitioning to political independence would reveal not only his almost unrivalled radicalism on the women's question, but also the significance of his pithy criticisms of simplistic anti-colonial nationalisms regarding how they obstructed genuine women's empowerment. Reading him in relation to Marxist, anarchist, libertarian, radical feminist, anti-colonial, and other approaches to women's liberation would be a productive exercise in comparative political theory. As mentioned in the introduction to this volume ('Introducing an Iconoclast'), Periyar's thoughts on women's liberation deserve a book of their own, with a greater focus on his co-travellers like Nagammai, Maniammai, and other women leaders and thinkers of the SRM. That apart, echoing concerns raised by scholars like Soneji and Pillai, voices of women from communities of hereditary performing artists also need to be foregrounded more, to provide alternative critical approaches to reforms of the national as well as the Dravidian movement.

How far Dravidian electoral parties have actually imbibed Periyar's perspectives on this issue has been legitimately held up as a criticism against them. Leaving aside his more radical opinions, even the relatively simple demand of 50 per cent representation of women in the legislature has not been met. If anything, women's representation in higher positions in these parties leaves much to be desired. J. Jayalalithaa's domineering leadership in the All-India Anna Dravida Munnetra Kazhagam (AIADMK) did not make it a feminist party nor did it secure more positions for women on her passing. Notwithstanding leaders like Kanimozhi Karunanidhi who use their political platform to articulate Periyarist views, the DMK has been criticized for being predominantly a male bastion. Studies in political economy such as S. Narayan's *The Dravidian Years* (2018) and A. Kalaiyarasan and M. Vijayabaskar's *The Dravidian Model* (2021) do record the significant structural improvement in the lives of women under Dravidian rule, especially owing to several inclusive welfare policies. While appreciating this, it is important to note that Periyar saw women's liberation as interlinked to sociocultural, political, economic, ideological, as well as biological issues. A transformation on these fronts would require not only reform according to Periyar, but a revolution.

Notes

1. Self-Respect marriages were legalized after the DMK came to power in 1967 through the Hindu Marriage (Tamil Nadu Amendment) Act of 1967, which added section 7A to the Hindu Marriage Act of 1955. However, this act is applicable only in the state of Tamil Nadu and is valid only for couples from a Hindu background.
2. Much of the biographical information on Maniammai presented here is sourced from *Annai Maniammaiyarin Sinthanai Muthukkal* (2012).
3. *Scroll.in*, 8 March 2017.
4. *Times of India*, 27 October 1974.

References

Anandhi, S. 1991. 'Women's Question in the Dravidian Movement, c. 1925–1948'. *Social Scientist* 19(5–6): 24–41.

———. 2020. 'The Manifesto and the Modern Self: Reading the Autobiography of Muthulakshmi Reddy'. In *Rethinking Social Justice*, edited by S. Anandhi, Karthick Ram Manoharan, M. Vijayabaskar, and A. Kalaiyarasan, pp. 15–30. New Delhi: Orient BlackSwan.

Anandhi, S., and Meera Velayudhan. 2010. 'Rethinking Feminist Methodologies'. *Economic and Political Weekly* 45(44–45): 39–41.

Chakravarti, Uma. 2018. *Gendering Caste: Through a Feminist Lens*. New Delhi: Sage.

Chidambaranar, Sami. 1983. *Tamilar Thalaivar*, 8th edition. Chennai: Periyar Suyamariyadhai Prachara Niruvana Veliyeedu.

Diehl, Anita. 1978. *Periyar E. V. Ramaswami: A Study of the Influence of a Personality in Contemporary South India*. New Delhi: B.I. Publications.

Engels, Frederick. 2010. *The Origin of Family, Private Property and State*. London: Penguin.

Firestone, Shulamith. 1972. *The Dialectic of Sex: The Case for Feminist Revolution*. New York: Bantam Books.

Geetha, V. 1998. 'Periyar, Women and an Ethic of Citizenship'. *Economic and Political Weekly* 33(17): WS9–WS15.

Hodges, Sarah. 2005. 'Revolutionary Family Life and the Self Respect Movement in Tamil South India, 1926–49'. *Contributions to Indian Sociology* 39(2): 251–277.

Jaiswal, Suvira. 2016. *The Making of Brahmanic Hegemony: Studies in Caste, Gender and Vaisnava Theology*. New Delhi: Tulika.

Kalaiyarasan, A., and M. Vijayabaskar. 2021. *The Dravidian Model: Interpreting the Political Economy of Tamil Nadu*. Cambridge: Cambridge University Press.

Karunanandam, Kavignar. 2013. *Thanthai Periyar: Muzhu Muthal Vazhkkai Varalaaru*, 4th edition. Chennai: VOC Noolagam.

Maniammaiyar, E. V. R. 2012. *Annai Maniammaiyarin Sinthanai Muthukkal*. Chennai: Periyar Suyamariyathai Prachara Niruvanam.

Manoharan, Karthick Ram. 2020. 'In the Path of Ambedkar: Periyar and the Dalit Question'. *South Asian History and Culture* 11(2): 136–149.

———. 2022a. *Periyar: A Study in Political Atheism*. Hyderabad: Orient BlackSwan.

———. 2022b. 'Sudras and the Nation: Periyarist Explorations'. *Economic and Political Weekly* 57 (44–45). https://www.epw.in/engage/article/sudras-and-nation-periyarist-explorations. Accessed 26 April 2024.

Mayo, Katherine. 2000. *Mother India: Selections from the Controversial 1927 Text*. Ann Arbor: University of Michigan Press.

Narayan, S. 2018. *The Dravidian Years: Politics and Welfare in Tamil Nadu*. New Delhi: Oxford University Press.

Pillai, Nrithya. 2022. 'Re-Casteing the Narrative of Bharatanatyam'. *Economic and Political Weekly* 57(9). https://www.epw.in/engage/article/re-casteing-narrative-bharatanatyam. Accessed 26 April 2024.

Ramasami, Periyar E.V. 2009. *Women Enslaved*, translated by G. Aloysius. New Delhi: Critical Quest.

Ramasamy, Periyar E. V. 1974. *Periyar Ee. Ve. Ra. Chinthanaigal: Thoguthi 3*, edited by V. Anaimuthu. Trichy: Sinthanaiyaalar Kazhagam.

———. 2007a. *Periyar Kalanjiyam 22: Pennurimai*, Pagam (3). Chennai: Periyar Suyamariyathai Prachara Niruvanam.

———. 2007b. *Periyar Kalanjiyam 23: Pennurimai*, Pagam (4). Chennai: Periyar Suyamariyathai Prachara Niruvanam.

———. 2007c. *Periyar Kalanjiyam 24: Pennurimai*, Pagam (5). Chennai: Periyar Suyamariyathai Prachara Niruvanam.

———. 2011. *Periyar Kalanjiyam 5: Pennurimai*, Paagam (1), 4th edn. Chennai: Periyar Suyamariyathai Prachaara Niruvanam.

———. 2016. *Periyar Kalanjiyam 6: Pennurimai*, Paagam (2), 3rd edn. Chennai: Periyar Suyamariyathai Prachaara Niruvanam.

———. 2018. *Namakku Yen Intha Izhinilai? Jaathi Manadugalilum Jaathi Ozhippu Maanadugalilum Periyar*, edited by V. M. Subagunarajan. Chennai: Kayal Kavin.

Ramaswamy, Sumathi. 1998. *Passions of the Tongue: Language Devotion in Tamil Nadu, 1891–1970*. New Delhi: Munshiram Manoharlal.

Rege, Sharmila. 2013. *Against the Madness of Manu: B.R. Ambedkar's Writings on Brahminical Patriarchy*. New Delhi: Navayana.

Saraswathi, S. 1994. *Towards Self-Respect: Periyar E.V.R on a New World*. Madras: Institute of South Indian Studies.

Soneji, Davesh. 2012. *Unfinished Gestures: Devadasis, Memory, and Modernity in South India*. Chicago and London: University of Chicago Press.

Sriharan, Sitharthan. 2021. 'Counter-hegemonic Visions of Self-Respect in a Novel: Ramamirthammal's Challenge to Indian Nationalism'. *ANTYAJAA: Indian Journal of Women and Social Change* 5(2): 119–131.

Srilata, K. (ed.). 2003. *The Other Half of the Coconut: Women Writing Self-Respect History*. New Delhi: Zubaan. Ebook.

Subako, Alhaj. 2003. 'Why Was Woman Enslaved? Muslim Women Are Slaves Too! The Plight of Muslim Widows'. In *The Other Half of the Coconut: Women Writing Self-Respect History*, edited by K. Srilata. New Delhi: Zubaan. Ebook.

Valarmathi, Mu. (ed.). 2002. *Suyamariyathai Iyakka Veeranganaigal*. Chennai: Karuppu Pradhigal.

Woolf, Virginia. 2009. *Liberty*. London: Vintage.

10

Periyar's Engagement with Literature

Antony Arul Valan*

> Yes, EVR is an enemy of literature, an opponent to the way of religion; to be precise: he is an enemy of everything that is good about this country.[1]
>
> —Sivagnanam (1994 [1951])

In his 1951 essay *Ilakkiyathin Ethirigal* (Enemies of Literature, 1994 [1951]), Ma. Po. Sivagnanam (1906–1995; hereafter, Ma. Po. Si.) identifies two major problems in Periyar's engagement with literary criticism: (*a*) Periyar does not understand the fundamental unity of a text—that is, a text's core and how events, characters, and techniques converge to expand on that core—and why it is important for a reading to revolve around that essential theme; and (*b*) Periyar is unable to fathom the depths or purchase of the literary imagination, essentially calling him a hyper-literal reader. Even if the essay was written over seven decades ago, the force of that criticism of Periyar's literary engagement is emblematic of the persistent animosity to his reading strategy and is continuously summoned in contemporary state and national politics (Ansgar, 2023; Singh, 2023). Ma. Po. Si.'s scathing dismissal is indicative of how Periyar's political project was perceived in relation to literature. Here was a prolific writer who was committed to tearing down venerable classics of the long Tamil literary tradition, and in the articulation of the commentator, Periyar's treatment of these texts betrays an enmity with the literary enterprise, which metonymically extends to religion and thereafter the nation.

This rhetorical slippage is not accidental, since it comes from a very illustrious quarter of the Tamil intelligentsia. Besides being a freedom fighter and a legislator, Ma. Po. Si. founded the Tamil Arasu Kazhagam (Association for Tamil Autonomy), a pressure group within the Congress that advocated for the formation of an autonomous Tamil state within the Indian union. Despite being a school dropout who began life as a compositor in a printing press, this autodidact was an influential scholar and popular orator. He has to his credit critical works on the ancient epic the *Silappadikaram*, the *Tirukkural*, and the twentieth-century poet Subramania Bharati, besides biographies of freedom

---

* I would like to thank Amrita Sekhar, Samayita Banerjee, Madhavi Sethupathi, Dr M. A. Muthusethupathi, and the editors of this volume for reading a draft of this chapter and giving me their feedback.

fighters V. O. Chidambaram and Veerapandiya Kattabomman. This chapter will use the crucial problems identified by Ma. Po. Si. in his essay as a counterpoint to introduce readers to the nature of Periyar's engagement with literary artefacts and to investigate how it fit in his political activism. I present a general overview of Periyar's thoughts on three texts in ascending order of the frequency of his engagement: his scathing attack on the gendered social underpinnings of the *Silappadikaram*, his staunch opposition to reading the *Ramayana* as a textual model of discipline and governance, and his ambivalent take on the didactic *Tirukkural* for which he went as far as organizing a two-day scholarly conference. In the process, I will delineate an understudied strategy of reading that Periyar handled quite effectively, one that foregrounded an irreverent and playful—and, counterintuitively, serious and enduring—engagement with literature.

Periyar and the *Silappadikaram*

Composed around the second half of the first millennium CE (Parthasarathy, 2004 [1993], pp. 5–6), and set during the third century CE, the story of the epic *Silappadikaram* by Ilango Adigal is as follows. A young Kannagi is married to Kovalan, both of whom belong to the merchant community in the port city of Poompuhar in the Chola kingdom. Kovalan watches the performance of a dancer named Madhavi, is smitten by her beauty, and moves in with her. After a period of time and after squandering his wealth on her, Kovalan leaves Madhavi following a disagreement and returns to Kannagi. Kannagi and Kovalan leave Poompuhar and journey to the Pandya kingdom to start a new life. They reach Madurai, the capital city. Kovalan enters Madurai with one of Kannagi's *silambu*s (anklets) and intending to sell it, approaches a goldsmith. The goldsmith, who had just stolen the queen's anklet, asks him to wait and hatches a plan to foist his crime on this outsider. The goldsmith presents himself to the king and informs him of having found the thief who has stolen the queen's anklet. The king immediately orders the execution of the thief. The waiting Kovalan is killed by swordsmen who accompany the goldsmith on his way back from the palace. Kannagi hears of this, rushes to the place where her husband's body lies, and then wails and marches to the Pandya palace seeking justice. She argues her case with incontrovertible evidence. Realizing his mistake, the king dies. The queen also dies in sorrow. Kannagi tears away her left breast, throws it at the city and curses it: Madurai is destroyed in a fire that ensues. Kannagi then walks to the mountainous borders of the Pandya kingdom and ascends to the heavens along with Kovalan. Some forest-dwellers who witness her ascension convey the news to the Chera king, Senguttuvan, whose younger brother commits to writing down the story of Kannagi on the insistence of another poet, Sattanaar. Senguttuvan is moved by the story and resolves to build a temple for her. He marches northward, defeats northern kings along the way, and brings back a rock from the Himalayas that is used to sculpt her image.

Since the narrative moves across the three Tamil kingdoms, weaves in various belief systems of the time, demonstrates different styles of composition, and places at its centre a commoner couple (as against nobility), the epic is markedly different from those within the Sanskrit tradition. As A. K. Ramanujan observes, this epic is distinct as it does not depict the descent of God, but the ascent of man, since Kannagi is apotheosized at the end (Elder, 1970, p. 105). Ever since the discovery of manuscripts of the epic in the late nineteenth century, Tamil scholarship has hailed it as an exemplary text that marks out the region and its people as having a rich and separate culture.

A translator of the epic R. Parthasarathy explains why Kannagi's story has a lingering presence in the Tamil cultural imagination:

> A language and nation remember themselves best in a poem. The Cilappatikaram is the well of Tamil undefiled to which the Tamils return to witness their language and identity most vigorously asserted. (Parthasarathy, 2004, p. 362)

Periyar delivered a speech in 1951 at a meeting in Kangeyam presided over by the Self-Respecter Maniammai, who was also his wife. Titled 'Servility of Women in Marriage' (Periyar, 1951), the speech goes from talking about the oppressed status of the working classes (the Shudras) to questioning why Bhakti literature does not directly address this sorry state of affairs. He then proceeds to describe the evils of the caste system; the harmful nature of the Puranas and the depravity of the deities and their role in perpetuating caste; and the contemporary political establishment under the Congress that advocated for such literature and gods. He emphasizes that the *Silappadikaram* depicted a woman who is married to a man to whom she is a slave, and argues that it is a vehicle for Aryan and Brahmanical values: the solemnization of Kannagi and Kovalan's wedding in Brahmin presence and according to Aryan rituals, the portrayal of a Tamil king as a fool who would hastily believe the words of a goldsmith, and Kannagi's directive to Agni to burn Madurai but spare the Brahmins living within the city. What is also interesting is how he structures his rhetoric. With carefully calibrated language he refers to a conference that was organized to discuss the merits of the *Silappadikaram*, and asks a barbed question that bears significance for what he sets up immediately after: 'Let me say it as it is: Will any true Dravidian—any Tamil son—organize a conference for the *Silappadikaram*?' (Periyar, 1951) He points out that as a result of the Self-Respect Movement's (SRM's) successful campaign against the Hindu epics and the Puranas, such organizers do not convene conferences on the *Ramayana* and *Bhagavad Gita* any more, and have instead begun celebrating the *Silappadikaram* as a text about the Tamil region by a Tamil person, with the intention of deceiving Tamilians. He firmly grounds himself in an argumentative position averring that the problems incumbent in literature were not merely confined to the Sanskrit–Tamil divide or the Brahmin–non-Brahmin divide, calling instead for a precedence of the social over the singularly defined notion of 'literary merit' when assessing a work of art:

> Consider an excellent painting, beautiful to behold, one that inspires awe in people. If that painting depicts a Shudra trampled under the feet of someone, with his eyes popped out, his tongue loosely hanging about, can we celebrate it? For the artistry that brims in it? That is how it is with the *Silappadikaram*. If it is artistic, let it be. Why should we let our lives grow dark? (Periyar, 1951)

While subjecting oneself to live by Aryan norms would no doubt render one's Dravidian life dark, Periyar argues that the subjection to a position of uncritical acceptance simply because one is told that they are in the presence of literary genius is far worse. To illustrate his point, he raises simple questions that his audiences would relate to: Is Kannagi not a fool to keep sending money to her husband who has abandoned her for another woman? Can a city erupt in flames if she wrenches her breast and throws it? Is it just to kill so many innocent people of Madurai for the atrocity committed by their king? Is this *karpu*?[2] The speech, in fact, begins with a caveat: he asks his audience to not trust everything he says. He asks them to forget that he is the speaker and to only focus on the ideas he presents, so each and every one of them can apply their mind to assess the accuracy of what he says so they may ignore his mistakes and accept what they feel is right. But, more importantly, he invites his audiences to trust their judgement that there could be mistakes in what he says ('There may be errors in what I say; you may perceive mistakes in them'). This set of phrases preface many of his speeches across the years, and their rhetorical import is crucial to consider, especially when one is confronted with provocative oratory.

While we cannot be sure of the reaction of his listening public, there was an angry response from a redoubtable scholar who was given the title 'Lord of the Silambu' in recognition of his services to the literary exegesis of the epic: Ma. Po. Si. In an essay titled 'The Leader of the Blackshirts Who Blames Kannagi', Ma. Po. Si. (Sivagnanam, 1951) cites a laudatory preface that Periyar had written for M. Ilanchezhian's 'The War that the Tamilian Fought', which dealt with Senguttuvan's campaign against the northern kings, and a speech by C. Ilakkuvanar in praise of the epic that was published by the SRM's own weekly, *Viduthalai*. He rebuts Periyar's claim that the epic traffics Aryan norms into the Tamil region by presenting verbatim the central arguments of a *Viduthalai* article written by Sami Chidambaranar. Ma. Po. Si. is unable to fathom how such contradictory and opposing views, between teacher and student (Sami Chidambaranar looked up to Periyar as his mentor and was also his biographer) and members of the same political movement, could be published within days of each other in the same magazine. Further, he insinuates that Periyar confuses Kannagi for his wife, Maniammai, and remarks that it was Kannagi's intelligence and deep love for her husband that led her to choose chastity over entering into a marriage of convenience. What Ma. Po. Si. found faulty in the SRM's apparent lack of consistency and unanimity of critique, informed no doubt by literary conventions—Tamil or otherwise—that insisted on the reading of a text for a false notion of unity, seems to have left the ideologues of the SRM unbothered. Their method, after all, predicated on picking and choosing instances from within any text to ask how it corresponds to problems plaguing the whole of society.

There was no direct response from Periyar. But in July of the same year, he delivered a speech (very similar to the one delivered earlier) in Salem where he indirectly accuses the Tamil Arasu Kazhagam of exploiting a rhetoric of Tamil pride to line their pockets. In a cheeky move, he uses alliteration to characterize the organizers of Ma. Po. Si.'s conference. In translation it reads: 'But those conference organizers! Those chameleons have their palms greased by green currency bills paid by Brahmins for whom they campaign' (Periyar, 2013 [1951], p. 194).

It is also important to note that Periyar had already spoken against the epic at least as early as in 1943 in the essay 'Is Kannagi's Story Literature?' (Periyar, 1981 [1943]). He notes having watched the film *Kannagi* (1942, directed by R. S. Mani) and then having sought out the book to acquaint himself with the epic. Expressing repugnance towards the epic noting that a temple was built for a 'crazy woman', he shows how it is incompatible with rationality by singling out the episode where Kannagi narrates the life stories of seven chaste women from her hometown. He leaves it to the reader to decide if the portrayal can be construed as anything close to reality and urges them to think what such impossible standards of chastity actually demand of women. If Periyar's engagement with the epic begins with watching a film, as the aforementioned 1943 article suggests, over twenty years later, another film on the classic, helmed by his protégés, appears on the Tamil screen. *Poompuhar* (1964, directed by P. Neelakantan and scripted by M. Karunanidhi) made several changes (of commission and omission), bending the epic to attest to Self-Respect ideology besides incorporating other political concerns of the fledgling electoral party (the Dravida Munnetra Kazhagam [DMK]) which funded, wrote, and promoted it. Resonances of Periyar's critique of the epic can be found in this later adaptation.

Periyar and Hindu Texts

In a 1949 essay titled 'What Has to be Done to Develop Tamil?', Periyar begins by identifying what he perceived as the primary problem with teaching Tamil literature in schools:

> If Tamil has to develop to be able to be listed among the languages of the world, it must be separated from religion. The relationship between Tamil and God must also be kept apart. A secular person finds it very difficult to find relevant literature in Tamil. Even Tamil grammatical texts are always read in relation to religion. … What are the literary texts taught to children in schools? What other texts but those offensive treatises such as *Kambaramayanam*, *Bharatam*, *Bhagavatam*, *Periya Puranam*, *Tevaram*, and *Tiruvaymozhi* that propound religious doctrines and a particular brand of Aryan religious philosophy that leave people bereft of self-dignity are being taught? (Periyar, 2010 [1949])

While it is apparent from this excerpt that Periyar was railing against the shifts in the pedagogical instruction of the time, he was also directly pointing to a turn in the nationalistic discourse spearheaded by Gandhi and, at the regional level, by his trusted lieutenant, C. Rajagopalachari. As V. Geetha and S. V. Rajadurai observe, the *Ramayana* was singled out by Congress nationalists to signify 'all that was wise and valorous in ancient India' (1998, pp. 334–349). Gandhi mobilized the literary idea of *Ramrajya* as his model for governance in independent India and in turn, Periyar and other Self-Respecters engaged in a systematic deconstruction of the model by pointing out its inherent biases, flaws, and inconsistencies. As Karthick Ram Manoharan shows (2022, pp. 73–87), Periyar's anti-hegemonic politics and his opposition to Brahmanical political theology informed his reading of Hindu texts. Periyar was unsparing of both *dharmic* (such as the *Manusmriti*) and Puranic (such as the *Ramayana* and the Puranas) literature. He politicized these texts by demythologizing them and contemporized them by offering spirited, humorous, and even satirical comments. His objective was two-fold: to identify and isolate the casteist impulses within these texts, and subject them to ridicule on rationalist grounds. His method? To work within the parameters set by the discourse around these texts.

For instance, a typical Periyar argument would be: If it is the heroic code to face an opponent in battle with courage, why did Rama attack Vali from behind? (Richman, 1995) Periyar published two books devoted to the problems he found with the *Ramayana*: *Ramayanap Pattirankal* (Characters in the *Ramayana*) and *Ramayanak Kurippukal* (Points About the *Ramayana*). Paula Richman describes in careful detail the various ways in which Periyar politicizes the epic in 'Characters in the *Ramayana*': first, he demythologizes the epic by reading it as a text of the political domination of 'Aryan' north Indians over 'Dravidian' south Indians and sees 'Rama's greed for power and desire to dominate' as the prime mover of the text' (1991, p. 176). Second, by employing a 'rhetoric of empowerment' oriented towards liberating south Indians from the inferiority they had been made to feel because of the values espoused in the epic, Periyar re-signifies his intellectual exercise as a social intervention.

Finally, in perfecting the contemporaneous technique of hyper-literal readings of sacred religious texts to discredit assumptions in the orthodoxy of a religion, Periyar desacralizes the epic and its hero and renders them accessible for popular consumption and thereby critique by those who did not have access to or interest in academic scholarship. While Richman sees this depriviliging of literary imagination in favour of a hyper-literal reading as a technique that was meant to empower his listeners/readers, it is also impossible to miss out the immediate and affective impact of such a reading: it would instigate anger, trigger defence, and instil doubt in his audiences. Periyar was cognizant of this effect. What Ma. Po. Si. identified as the second flaw in Periyar's critical reading—that is, Periyar does not understand literary imagination and undertakes a hyper-literal reading—seems to have been a carefully curated set of strategies to elicit one response or the other.

While these are attempts at decentring the near-scriptural authority of a text by drawing attention to the lack of a fundamental unity, that is, a centrality of purpose and universality in application, Periyar also worked towards dismantling the discourse by encouraging the production of alternative literary sources. Richman (1995) highlights the attendant material conditions of the time in her comparison of the interpretive treatments of the epic by Periyar and Rajaji. While Rajaji made effective use of print and the radio, Periyar's engagement was theatrical in at least two senses of the word: he organized a much-advertised public burning of Rama's pictures, and influenced a cheeky stage production by Thiruvarur K. Tangarasu (Richman, 1995, p. 640) that played with the ridiculousness of the epic's characters. This play was panned and subjected to much ridicule in the nationalistic press of the time, with reviewers turning its original title 'Ramayana' into the disparaging 'Keemayana' which was the name it was remembered by for quite some time. Another significant play that was influenced and patronized by Periyar was the fiery poet Bharatidasan's creative reimagination of the Hiranyakashipu episode from the *Vishnu Purana* titled *Iraniyan Allathu Inayatra Veeran* (Hiranyan or the Peerless Warrior, 1934). Periyar had the following to say as a critique of the aesthetic choices made in the play:

> Not only did the play help us get a grasp of the heroic fervour, the cunning, and the self-respect inherent in the story of Hiranya, this play was also a feast to the rationalist's mind. However, we could also see a few explorations in the play as a subversion of the incidents in the story and a few harsh words. A reform-oriented play ought to have change embedded in it. Only if there are words that are necessary for this revision and serve as an effective retort will there be opportunity for the old to transform. In the absence of such words, the required change will not take effect. (*Pagutharivu*, 16 September 1934; quoted in Iramasami, 2019)

In terms of style, Periyar was a journalist who had founded and edited several journals, such as *Kudi Arasu*, *Revolt*, *Pagutharivu*, *Viduthalai*, and *Unmai*, and his writing therefore carried the hallmark of journalistic prose. It is remarkable for its brevity and sharpness, for taking alternative opinions on board, and for providing his readership with easy access to new and innovative explorations that influenced his thinking. Presenting summaries of research by scholars of religion, he would explain their basic argument for the benefit of his readership who would otherwise not have had access to such literature. He also drew links from the Puranas to the *dharmic* texts and emphasized that the Puranic texts were all meant to be illustrative of the theories set forth in the *dharmic* texts. In an essay titled '*Ramayanam is Manudharma*' (Periyar, 2008 [1966]), which summarized his speeches at multiple venues in 1966, he reports the views of two contemporary advocates of the epic, K. M. Munshi and the Shankaracharya, and shows how their views align with the preservation of Brahmanical hegemony.

Another literary exegetical strategy that Periyar employed was the constant reference to these mythological stories as *purattu* (a spin or lie). He identified these as materials produced to put a spin on political conflicts facing vested interests. In an essay titled 'What Saivite and Vaishnavite Authorities Say' (Periyar, 2007a [1943]), he begins by presenting evidence from the *Ramayana* to illustrate how the deities Siva and Parvati were humiliatingly portrayed and from the much later *Kanchi Puranam* to show how Saivites struck back at the Vaishnavites by degrading Vishnu, their highest deity.[3]

Yet another literary technique Periyar employs to read sacred texts was his mode of argumentation. In many cases, his literary engagement was limited to mere assemblages of viewpoints, or pithy one-line summaries. For instance, while Richman does a reading of 'Characters in the *Ramayana*', the much more incendiary 'Points about the *Ramayana*' is just that: points about the *Ramayana*. The force of its provocative rhetoric is gathered in the bare simplicity of the prose and numbering of the points. The introduction, for instance, opens with a very concise argument that the *Ramayana* depicts a conflict between the Aryans who regarded themselves as the devas, rishis, and saints, and the Dravidians whom they regarded as the *rakshasa*s. Quickly following this are twenty-six points intend to summarize the entire book of twenty-one short chapters. Each chapter includes a list of quotes from at least three translations of the epic: Periyar primarily quotes from the translation by C. R. Srinivasa Iyengar, and at times corroborates those with quotes from translations by Desika Acharya and S. M. Natesa Sastri. In many chapters Periyar restricts his commentary to only a few lines and lets the assembled archive of quotes from these Brahmanical authorities speak for itself.

Periyar follows the same method when he points out the inherent Brahmanism in a text central to the Saivite Bhakti tradition: the *Periya Puranam*, a hagiographical account of the sixty-three Nayanmar saints who lived between the sixth and eighth centuries CE (Periyar, 2007c [1950]). He begins the essay by mentioning that the *Periyapuranam* talks about the lives of the sixty-three great Saivite Nayanmar saints and immediately follows it with two statements within double quotes: 'They did good karma and attained Kailash' and 'God directly appeared in front of several of them and granted them Mukti'. He then asks what was the good karma they did, and lists brief summaries of the lives of ten of the Nayanmar saints, along the way drawing attention to instances of humiliation or assault to impress on his readers that karma was fundamentally not tied with what is right in the moment, but what is convenient to the Brahmanical authority.

As we close our engagement with Periyar's treatment of religious literature, it is imperative to address concerns among contemporary right-wing commentators on how the SRM, and Periyar specifically, were fascist and caused an exodus or facilitated a genocide (loaded terms used interchangeably) of Brahmins from Tamil Nadu. While there is no evidence for either, the subject of fascist leanings of the SRM (or its successor, the Dravidian movement) has been addressed by Narendra Subramanian (1999, pp. 119–121). In a subsection titled 'The Tamil Variant of Fascism?' he takes up the debates around the comparison of the Dravidian movement to European fascism, and shows that the so-called ideological similarities with fascism hardly included ethnic antagonism; moreover, Periyar did not aspire to capture state power, while the electoral party, the DMK, took a populist turn (see Chapter 5). Further Subramanian emphasizes the cordial relationships Periyar maintained with Brahmins despite his routine criticisms of them.

What enabled Periyar to sustain a friendship with Rajaji even while he critiqued the latter's interpretations of the *Ramayana* and his state policy? In an essay on the origins of the SRM, Periyar articulates his earliest experiences of engaging with religious texts.

> So, finally, my studies at that school were stopped … and I was asked to help around with the family business. … Although I have neither read the Puranas nor any sacred books, my house was steeped in Saivite and Vaishnavite myths and histories, because they were regularly being narrated in the form of stories by devotees and pandits belonging to those traditions. … My mother would devoutly listen to any yarn these fellows spun and my father was proud and content with these developments at home. Without much effort I began getting to know about religion and the Puranas. … I would ask them (those *bhakt*s and pandits) a lot of questions which they struggled to answer, and when they did, their answers would vary quite a bit from each other. All of this excited me a lot, and I began to be identified as a 'brilliant boy' in the neighbourhood. Though my father would get angry at my incessant questioning, deep inside he felt delighted that his son was brilliant. (Periyar, 2019 [1937])

This autobiographical note is interesting for a few reasons. Despite being recalled fifty years after these events occurred, it gives us a glimpse of how Periyar began his engagement with religious texts. Even as a boy Periyar was being a provocateur; of course it is a different matter that youth guaranteed a level of indulgence he would not receive in his half-century long activism. Also, he enters this world of myths and legends at the level of oral discourse, and not through written texts. His literary training or practice as a critic, if we may call it that, was shaped by the form of articulation: questions, rebuttals, and a yearning for responses. Finally, Periyar seems to have enjoyed engaging with these texts even from an early age. He was excited by his method of argumentation with scholars, even if his logic was characterized as specious in return. Not only did the young Periyar receive acknowledgement and appreciation from his neighbours, even his father is remembered as having been proud of his brilliance. When one reads his books and speeches on the *Ramayana* and the Puranas, one cannot help but come away with the feeling that even when he investigates their dangerous effects— for instance, oppression of women, humiliation and subjugation of the Shudras to Brahmanism, or the lyrical and moving instruction on immoral conduct—he seems to have carried this playful irreverence to what may be set apart as the sacred. This playful political activism is also crucial to understanding the fascist slip that never happened, and his persistent and powerful relevance in Tamil religious and social politics today.

Periyar and the *Tirukkural*

In multiple instances, Periyar (2015b [1944]; 2015c [1948]; 2015d [1948]) makes it clear how this kind of playful engagement with a revered work such as the *Tirukkural* (or *Kural*) was crucial to how he began viewing the text. The *Kural* is a collection of 1,330 aphoristic verses that were non-denominational and had a didactic purpose. If the Puranas discussed in the previous section featured venerable gods and saints, the text of the *Kural* is venerated for its teachings on three axes of human engagement with the world: virtue, wealth, and love. As the pre-eminent secular treatise on ethics and morality, the work has been commented upon by numerous scholars in the past millennia and translated into a number of global and Indian languages in the past two centuries. However, Periyar's engagement with the text comes with his characteristic argumentative and literary playfulness:

> My friend (the late) P. V. Manicka Naicker was the one responsible for instilling a taste for the *Kural* in me. Even when he would talk jovially with me, he would use the *Kural* so well. As I began poking fun at Brahmins and Aryanism, I began to slowly understand what the *Kural* meant. But, then, just as I critique the faults of Aryan Puranas and *itihasa*s in Saivism and Vaishnavism, I would point out a lot of flaws in the *Kural* too. I would passionately debate my friend Manicka Naicker about the problems with the *Kural*. The reason? I assumed that the commentaries on the *Kural* written by Aryans and those religious commentators with Aryan leanings were true. (Periyar, 2015b [1944], p. 107)

Since the *Kural* had the significant advantage of being powerfully quoted in speeches and writings, its style seems to have endeared itself to Periyar even before he started the SRM. In the excerpt above, besides remarking on the caste leanings of the commentaries he had access to, Periyar also draws attention to the demand a spirited confrontation makes: the inspiration to question the assumptions of writers or interpreters. As mentioned already, Periyar would consistently warn his audiences not to accept everything he says simply because they respect him. He would find a kindred spirit in the *Tirukkural*'s author, whose verses he would often cite in his exhortations:

> To discern the truth in everything, by whomsoever spoken, is wisdom. (*Kural* 423, Tiruvalluvar, 1982 [1886], p. 85)

> The mark of wisdom is to see the reality
> Behind each appearance. (*Kural* 355, Tiruvalluvar, 1982 [1886], p. 72)

In quoting these verses he would urge his supporters to follow the 'path of the *Kural*' (*kural neri*) and the moral conduct it espoused, which, according to him, primarily depended upon the unceasing pursuit of reason and knowledge. He would repeatedly single out these *kural*s and explain in various registers how every fundamental aspect of our lives should be questioned: 'Whatever it is, whoever says it is as it is, ask the question: What is the merit of that meaning?' (Periyar, 2015j [1951], p. 217) 'If a ball of dung is deemed to be God, wouldn't a ball of human faeces also not be God? How should a god exist?' (Periyar, 2015g [1949], p. 152) 'What is good? What is bad? What is fictitious in that? What is the actual reality?' (Periyar, 2015h [1949], p.166) He would refer to *Kural* 1062 to pursue his critique of the entrenched trust people had in the notion that a deity hovered above solely for the welfare of humans:

> If the Creator of the world has decreed even begging as a means of livelihood, may he too go abegging and perish. (Tiruvalluvar, 1982 [1886], p. 128)

His quoting and glossing of this *kural* was almost always a direct critique of the nationalist poet Subramania Bharati's notion of *veeram* (valour), espoused in the poem *Bharatha*

Samuthayam (Indian Society), in particular the phrase: 'We will destroy the world if even one man goes hungry'. Periyar asks why those who extol Bharati as a socialist would subscribe to such *veeram*, which would in effect be mass suicide. Would it not be more useful to turn our ire against the belief we hold in a deity, since he is supposed to protect us from poverty? Would it not make sense to destroy the idea of a god who is benevolent and yet inaccessible instead of embracing a hatred for the entire world from which we cannot, in effect, escape? (Periyar, 2015c [1948], p. 38) He would also offer an alternative reading of the term *oozh*, which earlier commentators had equated to the Brahmanical concept of *vithi* or fate. He glossed it instead as the character or nature one is born with. Even if Periyar agrees that the *Kural* supposes an intransigence for most such inherent traits, he shifts the focus from belief in a pre-destined closure to human action to an openness to diversity and inclusion, and illustrates it with examples (Periyar, 2015b [1944], p.117–118). As is evident from the archives of his speeches and writings, Periyar spoke at various *Tirukkural* conferences; he even organized a two-day conference in Chennai in 1949 celebrating the text.

However, Periyar also made sure to qualify his extensive use of the various *kurals*, anticipating in effect a reading of his appreciation as blind praise for the work. Referencing one of Tiruvalluvar's monikers—*deiva pulavar* (divine poet)—he says that he does not believe that there can be any attribute in a human that is essentially divine, and locates this ascription of divinity as a Brahmanical ploy to erase the genius of a non-Brahmin person (Periyar, 2015c [1948], pp. 22–23). Concomitantly, Periyar argues that a hallowed work which cannot be subjected to intense questioning cannot be authoritative. He places himself alongside the author of the *Kural* when he says:

> Don't ask me why I do some things my way when the *Kural* advises against it. I advocate for the *Kural* only insofar as what I say is there in it too! (Periyar, 2015i [1950], pp. 184–185)

He goes on to mention that he disagrees entirely with the *Kural*'s proscription of meat-eating, as he believes that it is impossible in this day and age to live without eating meat. He argues that the text is dated, understandably so, and that his audiences would have to choose those instructions from the text that they have thought over and decided are right. He goes further in another instance (Periyar, 2015g [1949], p. 131) when he says that the audience he was addressing is more knowledgeable than Tiruvalluvar, simply by virtue of being born two thousand years after him. Pointing to the scientific and technological accomplishments they are privy to, he prods them to follow Tiruvalluvar's method of reason. He points out that he does not intend to disparage Tiruvalluvar: he was indeed a wise man, perhaps the wisest of all wise men of his time, a prophet who had profound knowledge about the world of his time. It was precisely this situatedness in the world, Periyar says, that does not enable the *Tirukkural* to transcend its time and make it completely and perfectly relevant for the contemporary world that has seen electricity, the telephone, and the atom bomb. Periyar refers to this as Tiruvalluvar's 'experiential truth' (2015 [1950a], p. 174). Even if he does not explain how he arrives at this notion of truth with respect to Tiruvalluvar (especially because of the incredible range of topics covered in the work), he draws a fundamental link between sensory perception and knowledge, delinking it from sophisticated intellectual endeavour. He illustrates this later in the same speech when he cites the example of *Kural* 20, and notes the interpretive approach of Brahamanical commentators who explain that Tiruvalluvar pointed to the lack of religious discipline (that is, of ritual observances) as the metaphysical *cause* behind drought.

Periyar notes that Tiruvalluvar's acute observation was in fact contrary to that interpretation: the lack of discipline and order among the people is a social *effect* of drought (2007b [1950], p. 177). That is why Periyar goes as far as suggesting that his readers had to read the original text without concern for authoritative commentaries, since he is convinced that the *Kural* was written for commoners to understand (2015a [1928], p. 3).

If these were attempts at making a text that was perceived at the time to be the pinnacle of Tamil literary achievement accessible to the masses, Periyar also attacked the hallowed position of the *Kural* directly insofar as it was read by commentators as professing faith in god. He did this through a close reading and alternative interpretation of what was and continues to be perceived as an invocatory chapter to god, that is, *kadavul vazhthu* (in praise of God) (Periyar, 2015f [1949]; 2015l [1959], pp. 283–88; 2015m [1960], pp. 296–301),[4] and by presenting the Brahmanical bases of the folklore that surrounds the origin story of Tiruvalluvar.[5] He substantiates this by pointing out multiple instances where the *Kural* does not endorse a hierarchy that is predicated on caste (Periyar, 2015c [1948], p. 28; 2015g [1949], p. 139; 2007b [1950], p. 177; 2015i [1950], p. 192; 2015j [1951], p. 220). He also urges his Muslim and Christian audiences to take up reading the *Kural* and states that the philosophy of the text is not very different from that of the Bible and the Quran, even if he maintains in the same breath that Tiruvalluvar does not lay any claim to divine infallibility (Periyar, 2015k [1956], pp. 255–256). He would repeatedly draw parallels to the teachings of the Buddha and argued that Tiruvalluvar was an atheist and Buddhist.[6] What is also crucial is that Periyar does not seem to have delved into discussions of how Tiruvalluvar may have been Jain; but as late as 1960 he states that there are no instances in the verses of the *Kural* that prove that Tiruvalluvar was Jain (2015m [1960], p. 297). In fact, at a juncture, Periyar urges his followers to declare when asked for their religion that they followed *Kural neri* (the way of the Kural; 2015e [1948], p. 82) pointing to his conscious choice of the word *neri* (conduct) instead of the Tamil word for religion, *matham*, which brought with it the baggage of ritual (2015c [1948], p. 32).

However, even Periyar uses the religious term 'bhakti' to refer to his engagement with the *Tirukkural* in response to an allegation of misreading. In an essay titled 'Karpu' (Chastity), written in 1928 under the pseudonym Chithiraputhiran, Periyar (2015a [1928]) denounces the Tamil literary insistence on chastity as an attribute peculiar to women. He traces the literary and linguistic roots of this ascription of chastity to women and calls out Tiruvalluvar, specifically chapters 6 and 91, for advocating a slavish position for women. In response to this article, P. R. Paramasiva Mudaliar, an indignant reader, writes an essay extolling the essential differences between men and women (and arguing that therefore their rights would be different owing to their different needs), and cites the medieval poetess Avvaiyar and her thoughts on women ('Don't listen to women' and 'Ignorance is an adornment for women'),[7] wondering why Chithiraputhiran would take issue with a revered intellectual who was also a woman. He advises Chithiraputhiran to be a bit tentative and account for doubts when he argues his position, especially when he challenges literary giants. Periyar responds to this by reading the biases inherent in the very same stanzas that his interlocutor had quoted, and shows how focusing on biological differences do not automatically disqualify women from acquiring attributes conventionally associated with men. He concedes that Tiruvalluvar and Avvaiyar were great, but it is precisely because they are great that their thoughts and words would have immense effect (he uses the imagery of a destructive weapon) and therefore need to be vetted for such major philosophical mistakes.

It is at this juncture that Periyar humbly submits that his devotion (*bhakti*) to the *Kural* is no less than his interlocutor's. His devotion to the text, however, is marked by rigour, not blind reverence, and does not preclude condemnation for its mistakes.

While some contemporary detractors cite Periyar calling Tamil a 'barbarian language' as evidence of his anti-Tamil views, a reading of the vast corpus of his writings on Tamil literature and the reason for his scorn at the literature will explain why he persisted in such hyperbole. There have also been explanations seeking to clarify the context and reason for such utterances of Periyar. But what has not been addressed is what Periyar already warned us about—that his rhetoric is not free of slippages and that it would not always pass his own test of rigorous reason. For instance, when he writes about cultivated ignorance of one's own depraved state as a Shudra, he illustrates it with the problematic example of how 'sanitary workers are immune to the smell of human faeces' (2015c [1948], p. 39). The simile works only in one's limited imagination.

Conclusion

As V. Geetha and S. V. Rajadurai show in their magisterial work on the non-Brahmin movement over a century, Self-Respecters worked towards a social utopia that was grounded in the notion of *samadharma*. This cultural alternative to *manudharma* required a constantly evolving, and therefore at times inconsistent and contradictory, method of borrowing, critique, and imagining that sought a new set of norms that would subvert the caste order. These repetitive acts of defiance and redefinition in effect were intended to 'cultivate and nurture a new structure of feeling' (Geetha and Rajadurai, 1998, p. 420). This chapter is an attempt at presenting the various methods adopted by one such Self-Respecter, Periyar, as he evoked and articulated a range of affects that would contribute to this new structure of feeling. In a speech delivered at the annual function of the literary club of a school in 1969, Periyar has this to say about what he thinks of the great classics:

> What I mean to say is people's perceptions have to be infused with the new. He is constantly being thrust into the obsolete. And wherever the thought is ancient, his awareness is shoved into it. People are forced to give the bygones a lot of respect. No one has taught people to think for themselves. (2020 [1969])

Periyar's criticism of these texts was in search of the new, not merely because the old was obsolete, which it was, but also because he was responding to contemporary attempts at recruitment into service of those old ideals in the garb of nationalism or tradition. He was abrasively critical of these texts, not only because he wanted to make his criticism pointed and piercing, but also to model for his audiences a way of being that eschewed respect in favour of self-respect. He was not merely teaching people to think, he was also showing them how to enjoy a literary text even if one were confronted with a call for it to be burnt.

Notes

1. All translations are mine unless otherwise stated.
2. 'Karpu' is the Tamil concept of chastity developed and defended in the *Silappadikaram*. For a brief note on the concept of *karpu*, see Valan (2020).

3. The history of the SRM's conflicted engagement with the Saivite elites of Tamil Nadu has been addressed by A. R. Venkatachalapathy (1995). He shows how even if a large number of professed Saiva Vellalar elites were part of the SRM, the Self-Respecters constantly engaged in rationalist critiques of the Saivite epics and stood firm in their criticism even if they had to make tactical compromises as they came together to protest against Brahminical state policies of the time.
4. In his in-depth study of the interpretive manoeuvres of Parimelazhagar, the most prominent Brahmanical commentator on the *Tirukkural*, Norman Cutler (1992) shows that Pulavar Kuzhantai, a younger contemporary and follower of Periyar, had published in 1949 a commentary on the *Tirukkural* much on the same lines as Periyar's critique here. Periyar does not mention his name in any of the three essays. However, Pulavar Kuzhantai was very much part of the two-day Tirukkural Conference that Periyar had organized earlier that year.
5. In his detailed study of the various legends surrounding the *Tirukkural*, Stuart Blackburn (2000) points out that the *Tirukkural* was at the centre of a millennium-long debate on the comparative status of Tamil versus the learning of Sanskrit and acquiring of Brahmanical knowledge systems, and the social relations between Brahmins and 'untouchables'. He notes a particularly vocal critic in the Dravidianist M. S. Purnalingam Pillai who published a rebuttal of the legend by pointing to its Brahmanical bias in 1904. Periyar does not cite his name.
6. As Stuart Blackburn notes, the claim for Tiruvalluvar's Buddhist identity was first argued by the Dalit activist and journalist Iyothee Thass Panditar much before Periyar seems to have done so in print (2000, p. 467). However, in my reading I have not come across any instance where Periyar has mentioned Iyothee Thass in his essays or speeches with reference to Tiruvalluvar's Buddhist identity.
7. These phrases are from Meena Kandasamy's translation of Periyar's *Penn Yen Adimaiyanal?* (Ramasamy, 2007 [1942], pp. 1–13).

References

Ansgar, R. 2023. 'Silappatikaram patri Periyar sonnathenna? Muthalil athai padiyungal sagothari: Medayil seeriya Annamalai' ('What Did Periyar Say about Silappatikaram? First Read That, Sister!' Fumes Annamalai on Stage). *AsianetNews Tamil*, 12 August. https://tamil.asianetnews.com/tamilnadu/mp-kanimozhi-must-read-what-periyar-said-about-silapathikaram-k-annamalai-heated-speech-rza02o. Accessed 30 October 2023.

Blackburn, Stuart. 2000. 'Corruption and Redemption: The Legend of Valluvar and Tamil Literary History'. *Modern Asian Studies* 34(2): 449–482.

Cutler, Norman. 1992. 'Interpreting Tirukkuṛaḷ: The Role of Commentary in the Creation of a Text'. *Journal of the American Oriental Society* 112(4): 549–566.

Elder, Joseph W. (ed.). 1970. *Lectures in Indian Civilization*. Dubuque, Iowa: Kendall/Hunt Publishing.

Geetha, V., and S. V. Rajadurai. 1998. *Towards a Non-Brahmin Millennium: From Iyothee Thass to Periyar*. Calcutta: Samya.

Iramasami, Ve. 2019. 'Isai Nadagath thuraigalil Periyar Iyakkathin Kalagangal (2)' (Disruptions in the Fields of Music and Drama by Periyar's Movement). *Keetru*, 19 September. https://www.keetru.com/index.php/2016-10-05-08-08-14/nimirvom-aug19/38087-2. Accessed 23 October 2023.

Manoharan, Karthick Ram. 2022. *Periyar: A Study in Political Atheism*. Hyderabad: Orient BlackSwan.

Parthasarathy, R. 2004 [1993]. 'Introduction' in *The Cilappatikaram* by Ilanko Atikal, translated by R. Parthasarathy, pp. 1–18. New Delhi: Penguin.

Periyar, E. V. R. 1951. 'Pennadimai Thirumanam' (Marriage that Enslaves Women). Speech delivered on 30 March 1951. *Viduthalai*, 3 April. https://periyarpesukirar.blogspot.com/2011/10/blog-post_22.html. Accessed 24 January 2024.

———. 1981 [1943]. 'Kannagi kathai ilakkiyama?' (Is Kannagi's Story Literature?). *Viduthalai*, 16 June 1943. In *Periyar Kalanjiyam*, vol. 6 (*Pennurimai*: Part 2), edited by K. Veeramani, pp. 48–51. Chennai: Periyar Self-Respect Propaganda Institution.

———. 2007a [1943]. 'Saiva vaisnava aadharangal solluvathu' (What Shaivite and Vaishnavite Sources Say). *Kudi Arasu*, 30 October 1943. In *Periyar Kalanjiyam*, vol. 27 (*Matham*: Part 3), edited by K. Veeramani, pp. 314–318. Chennai: Periyar Self-Respect Propaganda Institution.

———. 2007b [1950]. 'Dravidar kazhagap paniyin maaperum vetrigal' (The Great Triumphs of the Work of the Dravidian Movement). Speech delivered at the Dravida Kazhagam conference organized in Dharavi, Mumbai, on 12 February 1950. *Viduthalai*, 20 February 1950. In *Periyar Kalanjiyam*, vol. 37 (*Tirukkural–Periyar*), edited by K. Veeramani, pp. 170–181. Chennai: Periyar Self-Respect Propaganda Institution.

———. 2007c [1950]. 'Nayanmar Mukti Petra Vitham' (The Way the Nayanmar's Gained Mukthi), *Viduthalai*, 6 May 1950. In *Periyar Kalanjiyam*, vol. 28 (*Matham*: Part 4), edited by K. Veeramani, pp. 179–181. Chennai: Periyar Self-Respect Propaganda Institution.

———. 2008 [1966]. 'Ramayanam: Manu adharmame!' (Ramayana: Nothing but Manu Adharma!). *Viduthalai*, 22 May 1966. In *Periyar Kalanjiyam*, volume 30 (*Matham*: Part 6), edited by K. Veeramani, pp. 143–150. Chennai: Periyar Self-Respect Propaganda Institution.

———. 2010 [1949]. 'Thamizh munnetram adaya enna seyya vendum' (What Should Be Done to Improve Tamil). *Viduthalai*, 1 May 1949. In *Keetru*, 1 March. https://www.keetru.com/index.php/homepage/2009-10-07-11-18-55/periyar-muzhakkam-apr18/4423-2018-04-26-14-41-15. Accessed 23 October 2023.

———. 2013 [1951]. 'Speech Delivered at a Meeting Held in Salem on 22 July 1951'. *Viduthalai*, 27 July 1951. In *Periyar Kalanjiyam*, vol. 33 (*Pagutharivu*: Part 1), edited by K. Veeramani, pp. 191–196. Chennai: Periyar Self-Respect Propaganda Institution.

———. 2015a [1928]. 'Karpu (Chithiraputhiran)'. *Kudi Arasu*, 8 January 1928. In *Periyar Kalanjiyam*, vol. 37 (*Tirukkural–Periyar*), edited by K. Veeramani, pp. 1–5. Chennai: Periyar Self-Respect Propaganda Institution.

———. 2015b [1944]. 'Kural Patri Periyar' (Periyar on Kural). *Kudi Arasu*, 7 May 1944. In *Periyar Kalanjiyam*, vol. 37 (*Tirukkural–Periyar*), edited by K. Veeramani, pp. 106–128. Chennai: Periyar Self-Respect Propaganda Institution.

———. 2015c [1948]. 'Tirukkuralum Manudharmamum' (Tirukkural and Manudharma). *Viduthalai*, 25 March 1948. In *Periyar Kalanjiyam*, vol. 37 (*Tirukkural–Periyar*), edited by K. Veeramani, pp. 21–40. Chennai: Periyar Self-Respect Propaganda Institution.

———. 2015d [1948]. 'Kural', *Viduthalai*, 27 November 1948. In *Periyar Kalanjiyam*, vol. 37 (*Tirukkural–Periyar*), edited by K. Veeramani, pp. 59–62. Chennai: Periyar Self-Respect Propaganda Institution.

———. 2015e [1948]. 'Neri enakkettal kural neri enbeer' (If You Are Asked What Your Morality Is, You Say the Morality of the Kural). *Viduthalai*, 31 December 1948. In *Periyar Kalanjiyam*, vol. 37 (*Tirukkural–Periyar*), edited by K. Veeramani, pp. 75–84. Chennai: Periyar Self-Respect Propaganda Institution.

———. 2015f [1949]. 'Kural: Araichi katturai' (Kural: A Research Essay). *Viduthalai*, 2 February 1949. In *Periyar Kalanjiyam*, vol. 37 (*Tirukkural–Periyar*), edited by K. Veeramani, pp. 96–101. Chennai: Periyar Self-Respect Propaganda Institution.

———. 2015g [1949]. 'Samuthaya pani, matham, arasiyal, anaithilum thodarpudaya kural' (Kural, Which Relates to Social Work, Religion and Politics). *Viduthalai*, 8, 9, 10, and 11 November 1949. In *Periyar Kalanjiyam*, vol. 37 (*Tirukkural–Periyar*), edited by K. Veeramani, pp. 128–160. Chennai: Periyar Self-Respect Propaganda Institution.

———. 2015h [1949]. 'Matha iyale kuruttu nambikkaigalukku adippadai' (Religion Is the Basis of Superstition). *Viduthalai*, 5 December 1949. In *Periyar Kalanjiyam*, vol. 37 (*Tirukkural–Periyar*), edited by K. Veeramani, pp. 160–169. Chennai: Periyar Self-Respect Propaganda Institution.

———. 2015i [1950]. 'Arivali, aaraichikkaarar antha naal moodappazhakkathai saadiyavar valluvar' (An Intellectual and a Researcher, Valluvar Criticized the Superstitions of His Day). *Viduthalai*, 27, 29, 30, and 31 May 1950. In *Periyar Kalanjiyam*, vol. 37 (*Tirukkural–Periyar*), edited by K. Veeramani, pp. 182–199. Chennai: Periyar Self-Respect Propaganda Institution.

———. 2015j [1951]. 'Moodanambikkayai ozhikkave "meipporul kaanbatharivu" engirathu kural' (The Kural Says 'It Is Knowledgeable to Seek the Truth' to Uproot Superstition). *Viduthalai*, 11 and 12 September 1951. In *Periyar Kalanjiyam*, vol. 37 (*Tirukkural–Periyar*), edited by K. Veeramani, pp. 214–233. Chennai: Periyar Self-Respect Propaganda Institution.

———. 2015k [1956]. 'Muhammadhu Nabiyum valluvap periyarum' (Muhammad Nabi and the Revered Valluvar), *Viduthalai*, 18 August 1956. In *Periyar Kalanjiyam*, vol. 37 (*Tirukkural–Periyar*), edited by K. Veeramani pp. 251–256. Chennai: Periyar Self-Respect Propaganda Institution.

———. 2015l [1959]. 'Ariyarin poikootrugalai maruthu thondriyathe kural!' (The Kural Emerged to Refute the Lies of the Aryans). *Viduthalai*, 18 and 19 January 1959. In *Periyar Kalanjiyam*, vol. 37 (*Tirukkural–Periyar*), edited by K. Veeramani, pp. 265–289. Chennai: Periyar Self-Respect Propaganda Institution.

———. 2015m [1960]. 'Nalvazhkaikku vazhikattiye valluvar vaguththa kural' (The Kural, Which Was Composed by Valluvar Who Showed Us the Way to a Moral Life). *Viduthalai*, 22 March 1960. In *Periyar Kalanjiyam*, vol. 37 (*Tirukkural–Periyar*), edited by K. Veeramani, pp. 290–304. Chennai: Periyar Self-Respect Propaganda Institution.

———. 2019 [1937]. 'Suyamariyathai iyakkam' (Self-Respect Movement). *Navamani*, 18 July 1937. *Keetru*, September. https://www.keetru.com/index.php/2016-10-05-08-08-14/nimirvom-sep19/38200-2019-09-26-06-23-26 (30 October 2023).

———. 2020 [1969]. 'Speech delivered at Annavasal School in Pudukkottai Taluk on 5 March 1969'. In *Ilakiyam Valarchiku Uthava Vendama?*. Chennai: Dravidar Viduthalai Kazhagam.

Ramasamy, E. V. 2007 [1942]. *Why Were Women Enslaved?*, translated by Meena Kandasamy. Chennai: Periyar Self-Respect Propaganda Institution.

Richman, Paula. 1991. 'E. V. Ramasami's Reading of the Ramayana'. In *Many Ramayanas: The Diversity of a Narrative Tradition in South Asia*, edited by Paula Richman, pp. 175–196. Berkeley: University of California Press.

———. 1995. 'Epic and State: Contesting Interpretations of the *Ramayana*'. *Public Culture* 7(3): 631–654.

Singh, Rishika. 2023. 'Row Over Sanatan Dharma: The History of DMK's Anti-religion, Anti-caste Origins'. *Indian Express*, 6 September. https://indianexpress.com/article/explained/explained-politics/sanatan-dharma-history-dmk-periyar-8923906. Accessed 30 October 2023.

Sivagnanam, Ma. Po. 1951. 'Kanagiyai Periyar pazhikkalama?' (Can Periyar blame Kannagi?). *Thamizhmurasu*, April. https://tamilthesiyan.wordpress.com/2018/07/10/கண்ணகியைப்-பெரியார்-பழிக/. Accessed 25 October 2023.

———.1994 [1951]. *Ilakkiyathin Ethirigal* (Enemies of Literature). Chennai: Inbanilayam; first published in *Tamil Murasu*, April 1951. https://www.projectmadurai.org/pm_etexts/utf8/pmuni0327.html. Accessed 21 October 2023.

Subramanian, Narendra. 1999. *Ethnicity and Populist Mobilization: Political Parties, Citizens and Democracy in South India*. New Delhi: Oxford University Press.

Tiruvalluvar. 1982 [1886]. *Tirukkural*, translated and with a commentary by Rev Dr G. U. Pope, Rev W. H. Drew, Rev. John Lazarus, and Mr F. W. Ellis. Tinnevelly, Madras: The South India Saiva Siddhantha Works Publishing Society. https://www.projectmadurai.org/pm_etexts/pdf/pm0153.pdf. Accessed 23 October 2023.

Valan, Antony Arul. 2020. 'Karpu' in *Keywords for India: A Conceptual Lexicon for the Twenty-first Century*, edited by Rukmini Bhaya Nair and Peter Ronald deSouza, pp. 318–319. London: Bloomsbury Academic.

Venkatachalapathy, A. R. 1995. 'Dravidian Movement and Saivites: 1927–1944'. *Economic and Political Weekly* 30(14) (8 April): 761–768.

11

Periyar, Art, and Cinema

Swarnavel Eswaran

This chapter focuses on Periyar and Tamil cinema, particularly early Tamil cinema of the 1930s and the cinema of the Dravidian ideologues whom he mentored. The purpose is to engage with what has generally remained a contested terrain because of the common perception of Periyar's aversion to mainstream cinema vis-á-vis the penchant of his chief lieutenants like C. N. Annadurai (Anna) and M. Karunanidhi for it. One of the main reasons for the split of his protegees from the party he founded, the Dravidar Kazhagam (Federation of Dravidians; DK), to form the Dravida Munnetra Kazhagam (Federation for the Progress of Dravidians; DMK) was their investment in electoral politics. Periyar, being a social reformer, who was preoccupied with the upliftment of the people on the fringes, oppressed by the systemic entrenchment of caste, religion, and gender, had his priority on questioning the status quo and challenging reactionary and regressive forces. Therefore, electoral ambitions predicated on consensual or concessional politics and opportunistic coalitions were anathema to him (Venkatachalapathy, 2021). Conversely, the Dravidian ideologues of the split faction veered towards electoral politics and believed in the potential of popular cinema for disseminating Dravidian ideology as filtered through the lens of mass appeal to mobilize people with the resultant electoral gains in terms of votes. Thus, the fascination of commercial cinema was, one could argue, at the root of the contention between the leader and his close and trusted disciples.

Periyar's ideology regarding the challenging and subversion of the construct of caste hierarchy and oppression and its intricate ties to religion had its foundation in rationality and the interrogation and rejection of blind faith. He was understandably suspicious of cinema and its putative potential for social change because of the ubiquity of the mythological, particularly in early Tamil films. The 1940s, the period when there was tumult within the party (see Chapter 5), was also a period when the transition to the socials—films focused on social themes—was only gradually taking place, and mythological and folkloric fantasies were still the order of the day. Nonetheless, Annadurai, the founder of the DMK, went on to engage with Tamil cinema as a writer, followed by M. Karunanidhi and other talented writers like A. V. P. Aasai Thambi and Murasoli Maran, to mention only a few. There were other equally skilled collaborators like Udumalai Narayana Kavi, the lyricist, and actors such as K. R. Ramasamy and S. S. Rajendran, who worked in the initial films of the Dravidian ideologues (Paavendhan and Subagunarajan, 2013). Although primarily a left sympathizer, 'Kalaivanar' N. S. Krishnan, the unparalleled comedian of Tamil cinema, known for his propagation of progressive ideas, was also a supporter of Dravidian ideology and its egalitarian ideals. There was an array of lyricists too including the iconic Bharathidasan, who overcame his early reluctance to write for cinema. The celebrated lyricist Kannadasan was also a DK sympathizer in his early years. Similarly, a retinue of top stars were later involved with Dravidian cinema, including Sivaji Ganesan, M. G. Ramachandran (MGR), M. R. Radha, and C. R. Vijayakumari.

However, Periyar's views on art as a whole are yet to find their analyst. Without knowing his overall perspective on art, we cannot understand his aversion to cinema. While canonical films like *Velaikkari* (1949) and *Parasakthi* (1952) exemplify Dravidian ideology propelled by Periyar's resistance to Aryan or north Indian thought, what is even more important is to make visible the lesser known but focused and sustained rhetoric of Periyar against the literal brainwashing of people and their induction into regressive ideas through art driven by religion and the corpus of literature surrounding it. Periyar found cinema an assault on the sensibilities and the dignity of Dravidians, particularly the early Tamil cinema of the 1930s, as detailed in this chapter. It is in this backdrop that the cinema of the Dravidian ideologues stands out as revolutionary and pathbreaking. More importantly, it is essential for us to know Periyar's views on art and cinema to trace the convergences and divergences of the Dravidian ideologues, who made a mark in cinema and were instrumental in the evolution and entrenchment of a genre unique to Tamil cinema—Dravidian cinema (Sivathamby, 1981). One could argue for its categorization as a subgenre at the intersection of melodrama and propaganda or political or subversive cinema.

Nonetheless, as this chapter will show, the corpus of critically acclaimed and commercially successful films and their continuing influence undoubtedly justify labelling it as a genre specific to Tamil cinema. Dravidian cinema played a central role in taking Periyar's sociopolitical thoughts regarding resisting the hegemony of the north and casteist oppression and exclusion and subverting faith in religion to Tamils not only in India but across national borders in the diaspora. However, as this chapter argues, Periyar's progressive ideas regarding women's empowerment, the dismantling of patriarchy at the very base of its institutions like marriage, and censoring concepts like chastity were disavowed by his protegees in their films. Their investment in appealing to the masses in a way affirmed Periyar's disenchantment with cinema as a medium driving consumption of palatable ideas and entrenching stereotypes of women as subservient to and serving men. In analysing some key sequences relevant to Periyar's discourse on cinema, this chapter begins with Periyar's apprehensions and unsparing critique of art and cinema and details the convergences of his thoughts with Dravidian cinema, followed by the divergences that validate his premise.

Periyar: Art and Cinema

In Periyar's view there were two groups of people in society: 'the ones who really believe [in] and work towards reform and the others who will use the label [of change and progress] to maintain the status quo' and will obstruct any progressive move (Periyar, 2011, p. 7). The former were generally poor, while the latter, including those involved in the production of art, had all the resources, but they would try to seek personal benefit from such hypocrisy (Periyar, 2011). In an editorial in *Kudi Arasu* (22 January 1944), Periyar (2011) observed that he had expressed these thoughts in 1928 in his keynote address at a conference on social reform. Most of Periyar's ideas, particularly on art, are a continuation of his sustained rhetoric as a social reformer who genuinely cared for change in a generally complacent and conservative Tamil society and expressed this publicly from the 1920s. Periyar was most apprehensive about the mainstream culture industry's propensity to educate and reform, believing instead that it focused on entertaining and making money. However, his pungent rhetoric against regressive media took the print form much later. This segment, therefore, looks at Tamil cinema of the 1930s and Periyar's thoughts on art that he had been expounding from an earlier period though they could find space in his editorials only much later since much of the 1930s was spent in focusing on his anti-Brahmanical stance, entrenching the ideology of his party, the DK.

Periyar's steadfast rejection of things that would hinder the progress of humanity explains his strong aversion to not only cinema but any art form that was primarily intended to entertain. Additionally, when such a culture industry relied on religious epics, mythology, and folkloric fantasies as sources for its narratives, it was especially abhorrent. For Periyar, Tamil cinema was thus regressive as it took its audiences 'a thousand years back' instead of taking them forward with progressive ideas and representing the reality around them (Anaimuthu, 1974, p. 437). Other art forms like painting, theatre, and even *kathakalatchepam*s (musical discourse on mythological stories) also came under his critical lens. It would be productive for us to know how he was protesting against any form of art that he felt was regressive since it all added up when it came to cinema which is a mélange. When attacked for his criticism of vulgarity in temple art, he pointed out how the arousal of carnal instincts in devotees persisted through obscene paintings (and sculptures) in temples (Anaimuthu, 1974, p. 432). People belonging to the Self-Respect Movement (SRM) were criticized by popular magazines for trying to destroy the ancient arts when the defenders had no logical answers to explain the impropriety of religious art or depictions in temples. When Periyar reproved the obscenity of the Puranas or epics, they pointed out that art had to be preserved even while apparently agreeing with him. Periyar particularly rebuked the invocation of Kamban's poetic finesse and Chekkizar's literary excellence (Anaimuthu, 1974, p. 432) in defending the Puranas, which according to him, not only bordered on pornography but also reinforced the Aryan or north Indian hegemony.

His detailed critique of the *Ramayana* in his pamphlet, 'Characters in the *Ramayana*', is well known.

> … EVR vehemently attacks the respect with which Tamilians have traditionally viewed the *Ramayana*, arguing that the story is both an account of and a continuing vehicle for northern cultural domination. Reversing the conventional understandings of villain and hero, he also calls upon readers to abandon their 'superstitious' beliefs and embrace a desacralised view of the world. (Richman, 2018)

As Paula Richman further points out, Periyar's imperatives in deconstructing the sacredness surrounding the *Ramayana*, which was inextricably tied to the Hindu religion, were not only to question the superiority of the heroes from the north but to invert the irrational claims regarding racial superiority. Periyar's scathing attack on the concept of art for art's sake had its provenance in his disavowal of Kamban's finesse with the Tamil language and poesy. For him, art had meaning only in the context of its contribution to the progress of humanity and a socially just and egalitarian society. He was not one to be enamoured of language or its descriptive power. If art was going to wean people away from rationality and be retrogressive in entrenching superstitions in the name of religion and caste, it had no value for him as such works undid the efforts of reformers like himself who were already faced with an uphill task of awakening a society that was in deep slumber and felt at home with its inhumane values and barbaric lifestyle.

Following Periyar, Annadurai wrote *Kambarasam*, which detailed Rama, the protagonist, as a characterless man who, despite his own debauched behaviour, questioned Sita's chastity. Periyar wanted to inform the Dravidians how 'they have been deluded by northern propaganda into believing that Rama was exemplary as well as divine'. Additionally, he inverted the equation by arguing for the greatness of Ravana and other characters rendered as villains by Valmiki (for instance, Kaikeyi). Periyar's perspective on the *Ramayana* is pivotal to our discussion given the centrality of the *Ramayana* and *Mahabharata* to Indian films. The first Tamil (silent) film, *Keechaka Vadham* (dir. R. Nataraja Mudaliyar, 1917) drew from the *Mahabharata*. Scholars like Vijay Mishra (2002) have convincingly argued that all the narratives in Indian cinema could be traced back to sources in these two epics. Filmmakers as diverse as Mani Kaul and Peter Brooks have been inspired by and adapted the *Mahabharata* in their own ways and engaged with writers of epics like Kalidasa (*Ashad Ka Ek Din*, 1971). Periyar's critique of the *Ramayana*, for which he spent time reading its many versions apart from those by Valmiki and Kamban, is vital to our understanding of his criticism of Tamil cinema, which was obsessed with many different narrative renderings of the epic on the screen, particularly in the 1930s when sound entered cinema.

Periyar also lambasted Indian paintings as they mainly drew from the Puranas and rarely depicted nature. For him,

> ninety percent of them are unnatural as they are generally about bestiality and anthropomorphism wherein an animal face is transplanted on a human body ... The paintings revolve around flying animals carrying a heavy load of people on them, birds carrying people, people flying with four hands and one, two, three, four, five, six faces ... a woman standing on a lotus ... (Anaimuthu, 1974, pp. 432–433)

Periyar criticized the impossible and unnatural situations portrayed in such paintings and contrasted them with Western painting, the realism of which made one wonder whether it was a painting or reality. He also argued that, unlike Indian paintings, Western art educated us about nature, time, space, action, and so on. Western paintings were also easily comprehensible being about quotidian life and did not demand rituals like pujas and offerings (*naivaithiyam*) to approach; nor did they take a toll on one's time and commonsense (Anaimuthu, 1975, p. 433).

Periyar's Resonance: Tamil Cinema of the 1930s

Reviewing *Radha Kalayanam* (1935), the Tamil film critic P. S. Chettiar (2020 [1935], p. 49) took the film to task for its crassness. When Vishnu leaves his spouse Lakshmi in heaven and sets up a family on earth with Virajai and has seven children, the neighbouring childless couple is jealous. When the husband points to the fertility of Virajai in delivering a child every six months, the wife retorts with his being macho only in appearance. When the astrologer intervenes and talks about propitiating the planets, the wife cuts him short by saying that such *shanthi* was already done twenty years earlier (when they were married; Chettiar, 2020 [1935], p. 49). Chettiar was reviewing the film prior to its release and expressed his dismay, hoping that the scene would be cut. Furthermore, Chettiar also pointed to the scene where the child Krishna's mouth was to reveal the entire universe to his mother Yashodha when she wanted to search for the butter that had disappeared from the pot. Instead, in the film, the child Krishna's mouth is empty—a failure of special effects—without any image, and Yashodha and Radha simply look at the empty space outside and sing in praise of Krishna (Chettiar, 1935, p. 50). If the beginning of *Radha Kalyanam* exemplified Periyar's concern over religion and mythology being vessels to peddle vulgar narratives, the scene described thereafter emblematized the irrational narrative surrounding Krishna and the unskilful rendering of such illogical imagery.

Kalki's review of *Prahladhan Charithiram* under the pseudonym Karnatakam in his popular column, 'Aadal Paadal [Dance and Songs]', in *Ananda Vikatan* (1933, p. 25), drew attention to Periyar's critique of the Puranas as far removed from the reality of ordinary life and as only providing fodder for blind faith and the numbing of common sense. Kalki pointed to how Iraniyan (Hiranya), a popular and dark mythological character because of his intentions to destroy his pious son, Prahladhan, waits patiently for his turn to act even during an intensely dramatic moment: Iraniyan waits for a song patiently until it climaxes with Prahladhan's encounter with the divine, when he announces, 'Naan Kandukoden [I have seen].' At this point, Iraniyan, who has a strong aversion to his son's devotion to God, suddenly knocks him down. In a humorous vein, Kalki (1933) added that Iraniyan, who patiently heard his son's unduly long song, could have waited a few more seconds till Prahladhan mentioned the name of the divine figure he had seen: 'Narayana'. More significantly, Kalki detailed the scene wherein, after thousands of years, when Iraniyan is engulfed by fire because of the intensity of his penance, Brahma appears to appease him and bring the fire under control. Brahma, however, appears with only one head and seems to have forgotten to wear his other three. Kalki quipped that he might have hidden the rest due to his fear of the obstinate Iraniyan. When Brahma's arrival quenches the heat and the flames subside, Iraniyan is seen with his long beard. Framing the review as a conversation between friends, Kalki wondered how the beard did not get burnt in such a conflagration. The friend responds by saying that the beard was acceptable when the body could be intact. Nonetheless, the dyed and neatly kempt beard stood out like a sore, Kalki retorts (1933, p. 27). Thus, one could argue that not only the texts but also the paintings that could have inspired such films did not stand up to any reasoning, even after taking into account the liberties available for jumping logic within a mythological or fantasy universe. Kalki's criticism of the illogical intrusion of a song during a dramatic moment and a beard that survives a mammoth fire reflects Periyar's meditation on religious or mythological paintings, particularly in the context of affirming irrationality or blind faith.

Besides, films like *Radha Kalyanam* bring to mind how even prior to Independence, Periyar castigated what was happening in the name of art in his article in *Kudi Arasu* (1944), which was a transcription of his speech. 'The Aryan-ideology-driven religious epics like the *Ramayanam*,

[Maha]*bharatham*, *Kanda Puranam*, [and] *Periya Puranam* are depicted as artworks for the Tamils. Those who are working towards protecting such art in the name of *kalai valarchi, kalai pathukappu* (advancement and protection of art) are indeed involved in deceit. How can one not feel revulsed at their shameless and mindless actions when the damage they do is palpable,' asked Periyar (2011, p. 4). Consider, for instance, a review of *Rama Rajyam*, which was the dubbed version of the Hindi film seen by Mahatma Gandhi. In the magazine *Kadhal*, the reviewing team said, 'While watching the film, we forget Rajaraman [King Rama]. Only Seetharaman and his heartfelt love for his wife fills our mind. For this reason, youngsters and elderly people should watch the film to forget their worries at least for a few hours.' (2020 [1947], p. 214). Such uncritical reviews, which focused on (irrational) love rather than logic in the content, in popular magazines like *Kadhal*, vindicated Periyar's concerns regarding the hegemony of the north flooding the south with narratives foregrounding the Aryans as heroes. Moreover, what is pertinent here is also the juxtaposition of the Sanskritic Tamil with the Aryan characters, as exemplified by the film *Seetha Kalyanam*, detailed and criticized by Kalki in his review (1934, p. 25):

(A dialogue sequence between Kaikeyi and Rama)

Kaikeyi: Dear! Some [sweet] news!

Rama: What? Please hurry as I have to leave.

Kaikeyi: Rama! A bride for you…

Rama: Why tease me! Father [Dasarathar] will be looking for one.

(At this point, Dasarathar enters.)

Dasarathar: What a tease [you Kaikeyi!]

Kaikeyi: Shouldn't we get our darling [son] married?

Dasarathar: Yes, we should. But Rama's *vivaham* [marriage] is *Rajanga kariyam* [the State's affair]. We have to do it in consultation with the *kulaguru* [guru of the clan] and the minister[s].

Here, the italicized words demonstrate how Tamil cinema, particularly in the 1930s, acted as a vehicle for Aryan ideology and reinforced Sanskritized Tamil as a superior form spoken by kings and royalty.

Periyar's trenchant rhetoric against such a move to preserve the *inamaanam* (racial dignity) of the Dravidians or Tamils is vindicated when one considers any mythological film (the leading and overwhelming genre of Tamil films in the 1930s): 'Along with art, does not man need knowledge, dignity, and racial affinity? Is money the primary concern? The wealth earned through art, if not used for the sake of fellow Dravidians, at least must not be used for harming them' (Periyar, 2011, p. 13). Periyar's critical focus on the way the epics were retooled to evoke erotic pleasures and instrumentalize emotions as commodities by appealing to the baser instincts of (young) audiences, as exemplified by references to youth (*Rama Rajya*) and marriage (*Seetha Kalayanam*), was portentous.

Music too did not escape Periyar's discerning criticism. Drawing attention to the costly tickets for classical concerts, he questioned their utility for most audiences who may not be well versed in the grammar of music or acquainted with its nuances: 'They are enthralled by the divinity of Murugan, Raman, and Krishnan. Therefore, these music concerts, if not propaganda to make Dravidians worship Murugan, Raman, and Krishnan, [are] what else, I ask?' (2011, pp. 14–16).

Instances of love scenes featuring religious figures recall Periyar's critique of eroticism in religious-themed films. Listing cinema among the five gravest sins, *panchamaa paathagangal*, Periyar admonished those who critiqued the government for its five-year economic plans, unnecessary spending, and superfluous taxes but kept visiting the cinemas (Anaimuthu, 1974, p. 429). His focus shifted from taxes paid to the money collected at the box office. 'Investors in cinema capitalize on people's idiocy and barbaric nature' (Anaimuthu, 1974, p. 430). They invested in lakhs and tried to reap in crores. The money thus looted from the public was spent unproductively on wine and women, without any use for humanity. Cinema was thus damaging and destructive. The onscreen obscenity spread outside the diegesis, one could argue; or it mirrored or was an extension of activities off-screen.

> When a man and a woman unite and kiss, whether it is in the form of gods or lumpen elements, there will be no dearth of crowds or box-office collection. That too, with actors and beauties, who are already known for their expertise in *srungara rasam* [erotic aesthetics], it will be a wonder if people do not rush to see them. But those aware of human nature and instincts will not say that such a (huge) audience was because of *bhakti* [devotion]. The reason for more number of shows of films in Tamil Nadu than in other states is because investment in devotion has dwindled whereas interest in the (embodied) emotion of *srungaram* [eroticism] has flourished. (Anaimuthu, 1974, p. 445)

Periyar further condemned the government for allowing and depending on the advertisements and publicity of cinema. According to him, the media also worked against society by relying on the advertisements of films (Anaimuthu, 1974, p. 445). He deplored the ubiquity of distasteful posters: 'Everywhere you see, walls are filled with posters of men and women in intimate postures, focusing on voluptuousness.' With 'money, propaganda, and publicity', one could (mis)direct the people any which way one wanted. Before the release of a film, the media targeted the audience through titillating scenes and dialogues revolving around sex and obscenity. When hundreds of magazines continuously published lakhs of copies, in hundreds of different ways, and kept focusing on cinema, why would cinema not prosper, he asked? (Anaimuthu, 1974, p. 446). Thus, Periyar was much ahead of his time in pointing to the centrality of commoditizing romance and sex, even or especially in narratives revolving around the epics or Puranas. Nonetheless, he expressed hope regarding the possibilities of cinema, particularly when he got an opportunity to felicitate great artists of Tamil cinema like M. R. Radha and Sivaji Ganesan. He eloquently praised M. R. Radha when he honoured the latter on stage after watching his famous play *Ratha Kanneer* (Tears of Blood), written by Thiruvarur K. Thangaraj. In the transcription published in *Viduthalai* (18 January 1966), the felicitation of M.R. Radha, he said, 'We need plays that reform people and not embellish the outdated' (Anaimuthu, 1974, p. 439). Periyar extolled those actors who worked for an ideal, like N. S. Krishnan and M. R. Radha for courageously interpolating their narratives with social reformist ideas. In particular, he lauded the conscientiousness of Nadigavel (masterful actor) M. R. Radha.

Periyar acknowledged that he had endorsed M. R. Radha's work for over a decade (Anaimuthu, 1974, p. 440), particularly because 'since Kalaivanar N. S. Krishnan's passing away, it is Radha alone who undauntedly foregrounds progressive ideas regarding change and explains them in his plays.' Periyar also clarified that his appreciation of a play depended on its utility to the people. 'The narrative chosen must shed light on the ills in society while focusing on what is needed for the future. Only such things must be depicted.' (Anaimuthu, 1974, p. 440). There was no need to draw from religion and gods and Shastras (scriptures), while there was a lot to inform the people about regarding what was lacking in society and the need for transformation. While complimenting Radha as a non-commercial actor driven by ideals, Periyar also approved of theatre as a superior medium that could reform the audience. Music and dance provided a feast for the ears and eyes but not food for thought, unlike plays, which could provide all three (Anaimuthu, 1974, p. 441). 'Theatre can be used to promulgate a regressive or progressive idea. People should follow Radha's example' (Anaimuthu, 1974, p. 441).

In contrast, Periyar admonished Sivaji Ganesan for not provoking people's thoughts through his play (Anaimuthu, 1974, p. 439). In his appraisal of the play *Kaalam Kanda Kavignan* ('The Poet Who Witnessed Valour', written by Tanjaivanan), he said, Sivaji Ganesan's play 'had expensive scenes, production design, and settings … whereas in Radha's play, there was nothing extravagant regarding the art direction. A few painted scenic backdrops were used … I appreciated Sivaji's acting … [but] the theatre must cater to the needs of the people.' Additionally, it should address today's issues (Anaimuthu, 1974, p. 439). 'These thousands of people, when they return home [after watching the play], will keep talking about the finesse of the acting and settings but not about [the theme or] what they have learned from the play' (Anaimuthu, 1974, p. 439). He was scathing in his critique of MGR too. In 1968, while approving Annadurai's rationality (*pagutharivu*), Periyar praised MGR for his skills but not his service: 'Having earned enough (through cinema), he should now focus on inculcating knowledge in people' (Karunanandam, 2013, p. 485). In his editorial, 'Advice to MGR', he acknowledged that he knew the actors M. R. Radha and Sivaji Ganesan well (Karunanandam, 2013, p. 311)—the former was praised for his social commitment, and the latter for his talents but criticized for irrational (mythological) films. Periyar, however, confessed that he did not know MGR well. After the split, when MGR's candidate won the May 1973 by-election, Periyar castigated the media for favouring MGR and his fans in Dindigul for their blind adulation and 'insanity' that extended to 'drinking soda from the bottle MGR [had] sipped' (Karunanandam, 2013, p. 633). Such incidents only confirmed Periyar's contention that cinema was a 'disease' (Karunanandam, 2013, p. 337).

Periyar and Dravidian Cinema

> Therefore, [as] young people like you begin your journey—for this war to revolutionize art— [I request all of you] even if you do not provide help, at least do not trouble us. Wherever you see the murder or decimation of the [Tamil or Dravidian] race, self-respect, knowledge, or individual thinking, and the artists are but the lackeys of the Aryans and obstruct progress, chase them away.
> —*Kudi Arasu*, 5 August 1944 in Periyar (2011, pp. 15–16)

This call of Periyar, mainly addressing young Dravidian ideologues, was chiefly responsible for the late 1940s and the 1950s being an eventful period for Tamil cinema. Though Hindi and other regional cinemas too felt energized, the decade following Indian independence could be argued as unparalleled in the history of Tamil cinema for many reasons. One of the primary reasons was the success of Dravidian-ideology-driven films like *Velaikkari* (Maid Servant; dir. A. S. A. Samy, written by C. N. Annadurai, 1949) and *Parasakthi* (Goddess; Krishnan and Panju, written by M. Karunanidhi, 1952), which laid the foundation for and set in motion elements that would define the specificity of Dravidian cinema. For instance, the melodramatic style combined frontality and florid and alliterative dialogues with profoundly political implications, through the court scenes in a social film or in the royal court in a period costume drama, and songs directly addressing social issues and contemporary politics. Consider, for instance, the songs in *Nallathambi* (dirs Krishnan and Panju, 1947), which drew from Periyar's ideology regarding looking forward to the future with rationality and science and shedding light on the evils of the caste system and working towards its decimation. *Nallathambi* also drew from the background of N. S. Krishnan as an accomplished folk musician of the Villupattu (bow music) genre and framed him frontally addressing the audience.

Arguably, Annadurai's most famous film as a writer remains *Velaikkari*. One of the reasons is the film's engagement with Dravidian ideology as foregrounded by Periyar: *Velaikkari* exposes a fake godman and how he cheats the public, as we see in the anecdote by Periyar revolving around a donkey.[1] More importantly, it reveals the oppression and hegemony of caste and juxtaposes it with class when Vedachalam Mudaliyar (D. Balasubramaniam), the feudal landlord around whom the plot revolves, disapproves of his son Murthy (M. N. Nambiar) falling in love with and getting married to his servant's daughter, Amirtham (M. V. Rajamma). The main plot is about Anandan (K. R. Ramasamy) who tries to settle scores with Vedachalam, the latter being responsible for his father's death. *Velaikkari* also sheds light on the criminality of wealthy people—the central theme of many of Annadurai's works. In a rush of blood, when Anandan wants to kill Vedachalam and his friend Mani (T. S. Balaiah) says, *Kaththiyai theettathey! Buddhiyai theettu* (sharpen your brain, not your knife), Annadurai had put the words of his mentor Periyar regarding rationality concisely, and it became a viral dialogue, quoted widely by the Tamil public. Similarly, when Anandan is dismayed at the Goddess Kali for not heeding his just request regarding punishing Vedachalam, he vents his anger on her in an emotional scene questioning her silence.

> Your devotee has arrived late, missing the time of the puja. Are you wondering why? Hey, Kali, how could you forsake me who has steadfastly trusted you? How could you reduce me to this state [of helplessness] when I believed that even when men deceive, the Mother will safeguard me? How could you bless a man whose conspiracy and treachery have led to the ruin of my family? Is it just? How many families has he [Vedachalam] ruined? He killed my innocent father; how could you be his saviour? How did your conscience agree to it? Mother, look at me, look at this poor man, look at the one who has worked himself to death! I trusted in you alone, and look at my sorry state now!

One could argue that these lines of Anandan in *Velaikkari* prefigured those of Gunasekaran in *Parasakthi*. This is the beginning of a long tirade Anandan directs at Kali inside the temple premises wherein, towards the end, he throws the venerated materials away in a fury. He tears the garland away and kicks the sacred puja objects, and concludes, 'When the rich beat the poor, the way the poor remain silent, you are too!' Such dialogues resonated with the audiences due to the balance Annadurai could achieve between the highly stylized and alliterative words and the lived reality of the audiences. They not only carried the message of Periyar's atheism but foregrounded the irrationality of leaving the responsibility for solving one's problems to a divine entity. Nonetheless, *Velaikkari* also marked the departure of Annadurai from his mentor Periyar when the film ended with the slogan, 'Ondre Kulam, Oruvane Devan' (One Community, One God)! It invoked a common god by drawing from Thirumoolar's mystical and poetic Siddha treatise, *Thirumanthiram*, which is a part of the *Thirumurai*—a canonical text of Saiva Siddhantha (see Chapter 5).

The discourse surrounding atheism and the challenge thrown at blind faith by directly staging a crucial sequence inside the sanctum sanctorum of a temple continued in *Parasakthi*, which was a phenomenal success. It ran for at least fifty days in all the sixty-two theatres where it was released in Tamil Nadu and 175 days at the Mailan theatre in Sri Lanka. *Parasakthi* engaged with the theme of subnationalism, both through its opening song by Bharathidasan, invoking Periyar's aspirations regarding Dravida Nadu and its critique of the then Chief Minister C. Rajagopalachari (Rajaji) beseeching the people to appease the rain god, Varuna, to extricate the state from drought. While the politics of challenging the state is not unusual in parallel or art cinema, Tamil cinema's singularity lies in its preoccupation with such themes in the mainstream.

As M. S. S. Pandian notes in his seminal essay on *Parasakthi*, Gunasekaran's sustained lamentation in the film delineates the exploitation of subjects by the state (1991, p. 760). *Parasakthi* was remarkably inspired by Periyar's ideology and addresses issues regarding class; gender; at least rhetorically, the state (police) hounding the helpless and the hungry; the (Congress) government's apathy regarding necessities and basic amenities like water; and most importantly, north Indian or Aryan hegemony. The most crucial aspect of *Parasakthi* is its detailing of the grief of Kalyani who goes through a series of unfortunate losses, like the sudden death of her husband and her old father, to be left alone with her infant son to fend for herself in a world where most men are debauched and characterless, their true nature revealing itself when they encounter a helpless and despairing woman like her. Simultaneous to this despondent narrative is the predicament of her brother Gunasekaran, who was coming to participate in her wedding and is desperately trying to reach her, having been delayed in his arrival via ship from Rangoon due to Second World War bombings, even as she is getting continuously displaced. Kalyani's desolateness reaches its apotheosis when finding no way to survive in an indifferent and inhumane society, she decides to end her life. Her misfortune does not leave her even at this point. She throws her son from a bridge and tries to jump into the water when the police arrest her on charges of infanticide. Thereafter, she is produced in court.

In one of the most iconic court scenes, Kalyani recounts her unending misery and tries to justify her act of killing her son. She invokes Nallathangal, 'not as emblematizing a glorious past but as a vestige of the continual sufferings of young Tamil women—mothers who have been forsaken' (Eswaran, 2015, p. 172). Listening to her hardships, the judge, who is in fact her eldest brother Chandrasekaran, having migrated due to the bombing of Rangoon, faints after realizing that she is his sister. Her other brother Gunasekaran, charged with trying to attack the priest who molested her, takes the stand next. In what is arguably the most discussed and quoted court scene in the history of Indian cinema, Gunasekaran spiritedly defends his sister and his own act of attacking the priest. In so doing, he lays bare how the temple has become a den of criminals.

Keeping with Periyar's ideology, the film highlighted the way religion exploits the helpless, particularly women. It resonates with contemporary Indian society when we think of the number of cases against godmen for trapping and molesting or raping women (Tharoor, 2017). At the same time, however, the film's critique of religion was diluted by shifting the blame onto the individual pujari or priest, thus keeping open the DMK's drive towards inclusion and success in electoral politics. Therefore, this crucial scene marked the convergences and divergences of the Dravidian ideologues with their leader. *Parasakthi* was based on a popular play written by Pavalar Balasundaram; Karunanidhi as the screenplay and dialogue writer retained the emotional narrative regarding the separation of a family and their final reunion, a staple of Indian cinema, and added the political dimension as a Dravidian ideologue, criticizing the depravity and debauchery of the priest and shedding light on social ills to delineate the government's inefficiency.

Thereafter, in 1953, Karunanidhi wrote for *Panam, Naam, Thirumbi Paar,* and *Raja Rani*. Of these, *Thirumbi Paar* was remarkable for its subversive politics, with an anti-hero driving the plot. It is unparalleled in Indian cinema for having as its main character an anti-hero who has all the shades of what one can possibly imagine as the utmost evil or criminal. Karunanidhi's acumen as a screenwriter lay in organizing the darkness surrounding Parandhaman for his Dravidian imperatives.

> *Thirumbippaar* mocks Nehru's response of 'nonsense' to the secession and autonomy of *Dravida Nadu* [the Dravidian Nation]: the hero Parandhaman not only wears the Nehru coat … but also keeps responding with a curt 'nonsense' repeatedly during significant moments in the film. (Eswaran, 2021a)

Such mockery of a prime minister is unthinkable now and resonated with Periyar's reproach of Aryan or north Indian hegemony. However, at the same time, unlike Periyar's disavowal of the past and rebuke of the classics, *Thirumbi Paar* drew its (secondary) plot from the myths surrounding Arunagirinathar's and Indra's narratives.

Among the other significant films of Dravidian cinema were *Sorgavaasal* and *Rangoon Radha*. From a Periyarist perspective, MGR's successful films like *Rajakumari* (1947), for which Karunanidhi collaborated on the script with the director A. S. A. Sami, and *Sarvadhikari* (1951), written by the young Dravidian ideologue A. V. P. Asai Thambi were less significant as they were about intrigues surrounding kings and kingdoms, even if they extolled egalitarianism towards the climax and thus did carry traces of Periyar's vision. But the subtext of a glorious Tamil past undermined their future outlook. *Sorgavaasal* (The gate to heaven), written by Annadurai, was propagandistic and didactic, arguing for the goals of the DMK. The film was a critique of the legend surrounding 'Vaikuntha Vaathiyar Street' in Madras City, where 'an orthodox Brahmin priest of th[e] area used to perform certain rituals and bless people on their deathbed to ensure they reached heaven [Vaikuntam] fast! Obviously, he was in great demand' (Guy, 2010). Annadurai recycled the myth in the form of the villain, 'the ritualistic guru (Balasubramaniam) who plans to build his "sorgavaasal"' (Guy, 2010). The guru wields power over the king and creates obstacles for the protagonists and their love affair. Here, Annadurai reversed the trend of invoking history to address the present. Instead, he drew from the present for the plot of a period story.

Later, *Manohara* (dir. L. V. Prasad, 1954), written by Karunanidhi, engaged with a sensuous vamp figure: Vasantha Senai (Endearing spring) could be read as a metaphor for the north or Aryan who tempts Purushottaman (the righteous king). Padmavati, the queen, is steadfast in her conservative beliefs, remaining subservient to her debauched and unfeeling husband, and restrains her virtuous and upright son, who wants to question and seek justice against his immoral father, until the end. Such a characterization of Padmavati, however, went against Periyar's spirit of challenging regressive values and the empowerment of women.

Thereafter, *Rangoon Radha* (dir. A. Kasilingam, 1956) was notable for its departure from the other significant Dravidian films discussed in the previous paragraphs. Annadurai was a fan of Hollywood cinema. If *Nallathambi* was a loose adaptation of *Mr Deeds Goes to Town* (dir. Frank Capra, 1936), *Rangoon Radha* was more perceptibly influenced by *Gaslight* (dir. George Cukor, 1944). The protagonist Kottaiyur Dharmalinga Mudaliyar could be read as an extension of Parandhaman of *Thirumbi Paar*. However, the focus on his wife Rangam and his womanizing ways, extending his arms to enfold her sister Thangam by marrying her as his second wife punctuates his avarice in usurping the entire property of his father-in-law. The parallels to *Gaslight* can be seen in Dharmalingam projecting and victimizing his wife Rangam as insane. However, unlike in *Gaslight*, the local comes into play in the bigamy that Dharmalingam is invested in and the fake (religious) rituals conducted in the name of exorcizing the ghost that has supposedly possessed the seemingly unstable and deranged Rangam. She is violently thrashed with archetypal objects like neem leaves that symbolize traditional beliefs. Thus, Periyar's discourse surrounding the potential for appropriation and criminality of rituals predicated on religion informs the script, along with his critique of marriage and family as institutions that enslave women.

Poompuhar (dir. P. Neelakantan, 1964), written by Karunanidhi, was an adaptation of the Tamil epic, the *Silappadikaram*, one of the *aimperunkappiyam* (five great epics). Though *Poompuhar* had Karunanidhi's flourish, particularly during the scene in the royal court when Kannagi is seeking justice, her persona when questioning the king on behalf of her wayward husband affirms the status quo and the stereotype of the ideal wife, who will go any lengths to defend her husband. The divergences from Periyar's investment in the subversion of traditional values lead us to the next segment.

Periyar and Dravidian Cinema: The Women's Question

Periyar's perspicuous and unassailable critique of *karpu* or chastity, as detailed in his *Penn Yen Adimaiyanal* (Why Were Women Enslaved), is eternally valid for Tamil culture, as one could argue much classical literature and cinema of the last century revolved around the idea of *karpu*, even if Periyar had made some of his most strident critiques of it in the 1920s itself (see Chapter 9). The Dravidian ideologues, too, were not free of the patriarchal web surrounding the enslavement of women even if, as seen in the preceding discussion, they were at one with their mentor Periyar on the retrogression due to irrationality and religion and his progressive objective regarding an egalitarian society. Nonetheless, gender equity, which was paramount for Periyar, was left out. *Poompuhar* is a classic example of a plot revolving around the chastity of Kannagi (C. R. Vijayakumari), wherein her mythical *karpu* is invoked as having the power to bring the unjust Pandya King Nedunchezhiyan (O. A. K. Thevar) to his knees and burn Madurai as well, but the philandering and unchaste husband Kovalan's (S. S. Rajendran) character is unaccounted for.

One could argue that *karpu* is a spectre that haunts Dravidian cinema. In her compelling book, *Tamil Cinemavil Pengal* (Women in Tamil Cinema), K. Bharathi (2013) details the stereotypical representation of women in the otherwise progressive Dravidian cinema. She criticizes the portrayal of women as bereft of any agency, particularly in films like *Ore Iravu* (One Night; dir. P. Neelakantan, 1951) and *Rangoon Radha*, by astutely reading the changes in the adaptations and arguing how they are unconditionally patriarchal, male-centric, and regressive. *Ore Iravu* was based on a play by Annadurai, and he adapted it for the screen along with its director. The protagonist Karunakara Thevar (T. K. Shanmugam), abandons his lover Sornam (B. S. Saroja), citing her lower caste status and class. Bharathi delineates the stark and crucial difference between the play and the film.

> We must also pay attention to the changes made to the realistic play of Annadurai by the producer A. V. Meiyappa Chettiar and the director Pa. Neelakantan. In the play, Sornam, after being abandoned by Karunakara Thevar, lives as the concubine of a landlord and bears a male child. However, in the film, Sornam lives as a chaste woman and meets Karunakara Thevar twenty years later. (2013, pp. 41– 42)

Since Annadurai was credited as the screenwriter, one could argue the leading Dravidian ideologue tempered his progressive agenda and compromised when it came to the representation of women by extolling their chastity. Similarly, Bharathi details the conscious changes in the adaption of *Rangoon Radha*, wherein Annadurai and Karunanidhi were both involved as novelist and screenwriter, respectively: after the endless torture inflicted on Rangam (P. Bhanumathi), she goes away to Rangoon. While in Annadurai's novel, having run away to Rangoon to escape her lascivious husband's torture, Rangam lives with Burma Naidu and has a female child (the eponymous 'Rangoon Radha') with him, Karunanidhi's adapted screenplay was primarily concerned with safeguarding the chastity of Rangam, who lives in virtue and defends it when it is attacked (on her return to India). Ultimately, she is transformed into a character who defends and eulogizes her undeserving husband as God (Bharathi, 2013, p. 50).

Since *Rangoon Radha* was produced under the banner of Mekala Pictures, associated with Karunanidhi, one could argue that the regressive representation of a chaste woman was deliberate and dictated by the need to cater to conservative audiences (voters). Nonetheless, committed actresses like Chandrakantha, A. Sakunthala, and C. R. Vijayakumari, among others, contributed immensely by acting in the plays of the Dravidian ideologues, supporting the image of women as not subjugated and having agency through specific roles. This reaffirmed their Tamil lineage of independent and robust women from Sangam poetry, where a mother is more concerned about whether her son died valorously while fighting on the battlefield. But one particular actress topped the list when it came to Dravidian cinema—Madhuri Devi. Though she did not belong to the constellation of 'Dravidian' artists, one could argue that she left the most lasting impression when we talk about the golden era of Dravidian cinema—the decade after Independence—whether crossdressing and singing a romantic song with her own sister in search of the king, her lost brother-in-law in *Aayiram Thalai Vaangi Apoorva Chinthamani* (Unique Chintamani, Who Took a Thousand Lives; dir. T. R. Sundaram, and writer Bharathidasan [uncredited], 1947) or playing the sensual lover Poongothai in *Ponmudi* (dir. Ellis. R. Dungan, 1951), written by Karunanidhi, based on Bharathidasan's *Ethirpaaraatha Muththam* (Unexpected Kiss). Nevertheless, what made news were the bold love scenes between Madhuri Devi and Narsimha Bharathi. Madhuri Devi's uninhibited and captivating performance and her chemistry with

Narasimha Bharathi were the main reasons for the film's success, apart from Karunanidhi's dialogues and Dungan's direction.

However, Madhuri Devi's iconic role was in *Manthiri Kumari* (dirs. Ellis R. Dungan and T. R. Sundaram, 1950), wherein she played the titular minister's daughter. Rising above the stereotypical script and its contrived happy ending, Madhuri Devi, in her body language and gestures, could be expressive about her desire, signifying the independent woman in the Periyarist mode. Madhuri Devi as Manthiri Kumari is thus unparalleled in Tamil or Indian cinema for not only taking on the might of her evil husband, who is planning to kill her and marry the princess but pre-empting his plot through the ritual of paying respect and turning patriarchy on its head by pushing him over a cliff. Because of the way she is eulogized through the song at the end, her persona is further entrenched as a woman with her own mind who plays up the traditional role only to subvert it. Her behaviour recalls Periyar's idea that 'the concept of chastity that deals a different justice to each sex must be destroyed'. In *Manthiri Kumari*, as in *Aayiram Thalai Vaangi Apoorva Chinthamani* and *Kanniyin Kathali* (Maiden's Lover; dir. K. Ramnoth, 1949), an adaption of Shakespeare's *Twelfth Night*, Madhuri Devi's penchant for crossdressing continued. Indeed, Madhuri Devi, through her many significant roles, shed light on gender as a societal and cultural construct.

In *Devaki* (dir. R. S. Mani, 1951), written by Karunanidhi, Madhuri Devi again played a dynamic and progressive woman, Leela, who returns after studying abroad to find her beloved sister Devaki (V. N. Janaki) in the traditional role of a subjugated wife, suffering silently at the hands of her belligerent and unchaste husband, Durai (N. N. Kannappa). He forgets all the hardships Devaki has endured, from running small tea shops to a modest café when he had an accident and was rendered invalid. Back again in wealth, he philanders and tortures his chaste wife, who, prefiguring the *abalaippen* (the desolate woman) Kalyani decides to commit suicide by jumping from a bridge. At the opportune moment, Leela intervenes, saves her sister, confronts her brother-in-law, and brings him to his senses. From a Periyarist perspective, *Devaki* is one of the rare Indian films where a foreign-returned character is treated with dignity, as they are generally ridiculed and dismissed as superficial. More importantly, despite her orthodox sister's disapproval, Leela confronts her wayward brother-in-law exposing his unconscionable behaviour and threatening him with legal consequences. Thus, Madhuri Devi successfully challenged the trope of the *abalaippen*, a helpless woman who needs to be saved by a man—a staple of Tamil and more broadly, Indian cinema.

Nonetheless, the trope of the *abalaippen* continued to be used and reached its apotheosis with *Annayin Aanai* (Mother's Command; dir. Ch. Narayanamurthy, 1958), written by Murasoli Maran. Its revenge plot revolves around a pledge given by Ganesh (Sivaji Ganesan) to his mother (Pandari Bai) that he will avenge the murder of his father by Paropakaram (S. V. Rangarao). It takes a dark twist when Ganesh marries Prema (Savithri), the daughter of Paropakaram, and holds his father-in-law captive in the basement of his house in his mission of vendetta. Prema, the helpless woman, is caught between her husband and father and has to pay the heaviest price. She could be seen as an extension of Devaki and Kalyani—a trope Periyar certainly would not have approved of.

Conclusion

From the foregoing sections we can see that there were convergences between the Dravidian ideologues and Periyar's philosophy when it came to the progressive content of the narratives in

Dravidian cinema. However, the divergences too were clear as regards the representation of women. Nevertheless, Periyar's vision as to empowering women and building an egalitarian society free of irrationality and religious and caste oppression will always remain a guide for meaningful cinema in Tamil Nadu and elsewhere.

More importantly, unlike in the West, where melodrama is perceived as replacing the binary of good and evil with the Manichean binary conflict of the modern post-sacral world regarding love and violence predicated on the family and quotidian life, the eminent scholar Ira Bhaskar has convincingly argued for the persistence of the 'traditional sacred' in contemporary films in India (Brooks, 1976; Bhaskar, 2009). One could claim that the centrality of melodrama is still the marker of Tamil cinema, which has disavowed nuanced engagement with social, cultural, and political issues by its aversion to art films. In such a scenario, as Karthick Ram Manoharan astutely observes, the *Ramayana*'s influence across the spectrum has to be questioned, mainly its potential for appropriation:

> For instance, Gandhi, Rajaji, and the Rashtriya Swayamsevak Sangh (RSS) chief M. S. Golwalkar, though they belonged to different political persuasions, saw in the *Ramayana* not just a pure literary text, but a guide to political morality. It thus became imperative for counter-hegemonic voices like those of Ambedkar and Periyar to question religious texts like the *Ramayana* using a political critique. (2022, pp. 78–79)

Mainstream cinema has the potential to disseminate political thought, as in the case of the Dravidian ideologues, but also be appropriated for regressive agendas like reaffirming caste hierarchy, masculinity, and the subservience of women by invoking the Puranas and the myths, as exemplified by much contemporary cinema, particularly the blockbusters. Periyar's critique of art and cinema, therefore, remains as relevant today as in the times he spoke or wrote about them.

Note

1. Periyar invokes a play he saw in Russia, in which a son assures a father how he can continue exploiting people's blind faith in worshipping a donkey through its foal, keeping the superstition alive across generations in the name of religion.

References

Aanaimuthu, V. 1974. *Periyar Ee. Ve. Ra. Chinthanaigal* (Thoughts of Periyar E. V. R.). Tiruchirappalli: Thinker's Forum.
Baskaran, Theodore S. 2013. *The Eye of the Serpent*. Chennai: Tranquebar Press. eBook.
Bharathi, K. 2013. *Tamil Cinemavil Pengal* (Women in Tamil Cinema). Chennai: Vikatan Prasuram.
Bhaskar, Ira. 2009. 'The Limits of Desire'. *Seminar* 598. https://www.india-seminar.com/2009/598/598_ira_bhaskar.htm. Accessed 9 June 2022.
Brooks, Peter. 1976. *The Melodramatic Imagination: Balzac, Henry James, Melodrama, and the Mode of Excess*. New Haven: Yale University Press.
Chettiar, P. S. 2020 [1935]. 'Review: Radha Kalyanam'. *Cinema Ulagam*, 17 November 1935. In *Tamil Cinema Vimarsanangal (1931–1960): Oli Vanthapin Oliththidum Panmugakuralgal* (Tamil

Cinema Reviews [1931–1960]: The Multiplicity of Voices After the Arrival of Sound), edited by Swarnavel Eswaran and P. Thirunavukkarasu, pp. 49–51. Chennai: Nizhal Pathippakam.

Eswaran, Swarnavel. 2015. *Madras Studios: Narrative, Genre, and Ideology*. New Delhi: Sage.

———. 2021a. 'Periyar, Dravidian Ideologues, and Tamil Cinema'. *Periyar Project*, 4 January. https://theperiyarproject.com/tag/swarnavel-eswaran. Accessed 9 June 2022.

———. 2021b. 'The Pioneer, Thespian, and Special Effects'. *Muse India* 98 (July–August). https://museindia.com/Home/ViewContentData?arttype=feature&issid=98&menuid=9668. Accessed 9 June 2022.

———. 2022. 'Trajectory of Tamil in Cinema'. In *The Oxford Handbook of Dravidian Languages*, edited by Amritavalli Raghavachari and Bhuvana Narasimhan. Oxford: Oxford University Press. https://doi.org/10.1093/oxfordhb/9780197610411.013.25.

Eswaran, Swarnavel, and P. Thirunavukkarasu. eds. 2020. *Tamil Cinema Vimarsanangal (1931–1960): Oli Vanthapin Oliththidum Panmugakuralgal* (Tamil Cinema Reviews [1931–1960]: The Multiplicity of Voices After the Arrival of Sound). Chennai: Nizhal Pathippakam.

Guy, Randor. 2010. 'Sorgavaasal 1954'. *The Hindu*, 4 February. https://www.thehindu.com/features/cinema/Sorgavaasal-1954/article15448137.ece. Accessed 9 June 2022.

Kaadhal. 2020 [1947]. 'Review: Rama Rajyam'. *Kaadhal*, November 1947. In *Tamil Cinema Vimarsanangal (1931–1960): Oli Vanthapin Oliththidum Panmugakuralgal* (Tamil Cinema Reviews [1931–1960]: The Multiplicity of Voices After the Arrival of Sound), edited by Swarnavel Eswaran and P. Thirunavukkarasu, pp. 213–214. Chennai: Nizhal Pathippakam.

Kalki (Krishnamurthy). 2020 [1931]. 'Kalidas'. *Ananda Vikatan*, 16 November 1931. In *Tamil Cinema Vimarsangal (1931–1960): Oli Vanthapin Oliththidum Panmugakuralgal* (Tamil Cinema Reviews [1931–1960]: The Multiplicity of Voices After the Arrival of Sound), edited by Swarnavel Eswaran and P. Thirunavukkarasu, pp. 21–24. Chennai: Nizhal Pathippakam.

——— (Karnatakam). 1933. 'Aaadal Padal'. *Ananda Vikatan* 8(30; 26 November): 25–29.

——— (Karnatakam). 1934. 'Aaadal Padal'. *Ananda Vikatan* 9(13; 1 April): 19–25.

Karunanandam, Kavingar. 2013. *Periyar: Muzhumaiyana Varalaaru* (Periyar: The Complete History). Chennai: V.O.C. Noolagam.

Manoharan, Karthick Ram. 2022. *Periyar: A Study in Political Atheism*. Hyderabad: Orient BlackSwan.

Mishra, Vijay. 2002. *Bollywood Cinema: Temples of Desire*. New York; London: Routledge.

Paavendhan, Ra. and V. M. S. Subagunarajan. 2013. *Dravida Cinema*. Chennai: Kayal Kavin.

Pandian, M. S. S. 1991. 'Parasakthi: Life and Times of a DMK Film'. *Economic and Political Weekly* 26(11–12): 759–770.

Periyar. 2007 [1942]. *Penn Yen Adimaiyanal?* (Why Were Women Enslaved?), translated by Meena Kandasamy. Chennai: Periyar Self-Respect Propaganda Institute.

———. 2011. *Ithuva Kalai Valarchi* (Is it the Development of Art?) Chennai: Periyar Suyamariyathai Prachara Niruvanam.

Richman, Paula. 2018. 'Why Periyar Was Critical of the Ramayana (and Rama)'. *Scroll*, 9 March. https://scroll.in/article/871237/part-and-parcel-of-the-north-indian-worldview-why-periyar-was-critical-of-the-ramayana-and-rama. Accessed 9 June 2022.

Sivathamby, Karthigesu. 1981. *The Tamil Film as a Medium for Political Communication*. Madras: New Century Book House.

Tharoor, Sashi. 2017. 'The Harsh Truth about India's Godmen'. Project-syndicate.org, 8 September. https://www.project-syndicate.org/commentary/singh-rape-conviction-protest-riots-by-shashi-tharoor-2017-09. Accessed 1 May 2025.

Venkatachalapathy, A. R. 2021. 'Against the Hustings: Periyar, Elections, and Democracy'. In *Crisis of Liberal Deliberation: Facets of Indian Democracy*, edited by Manas Ray, pp. 64–79. New Delhi: Primus Books.

Part V

Labour and Dignity

12

The Social Subsumes the Economic

Periyar's Reading of Economic Power in Caste Society

M. Vijayabaskar

> Our first task is to address the social, and not the political.
> —Periyar (Anaimuthu, 1974, vol. 3, p. 1639)

Periyar's reading of social injustice was rooted in a set of conceptual insights on how power shapes economic relations in caste society. A proponent of socialism (*samadharmam*), he was however critical of the political priorities of mainstream left parties. To him, they failed to recognize the scope of caste-based power in shaping the economy. His insights on the nature of this power continue to unsettle and challenge more popular narratives of justice. Through a close reading of his own work and secondary sources, this chapter maps how Periyar's original conceptualization of power in India fed into his interpretation of the economic domain. Periyar held that status-based stratification and ideological hegemony exercised by caste elites fundamentally shape economic outcomes. The ritually sanctified division between mental and manual labour and their hierarchizing were particularly important to him. Periyar believed that economic justice can therefore be secured only through waging a counter-hegemonic struggle against caste-sanctioned hierarchies and the ideological apparatus that upholds such status-based stratification. The primary contention that the chapter makes is that in Periyar's political imaginary, the 'economic' was a sub-set of the 'social'. Redistribution of economic power could not be sustained without addressing the social institutions that help reproduce economic hierarchies and concentrate economic power.

The chapter therefore makes a case for how Periyar's privileging of status inequality resonates with arguments made by B. R. Ambedkar and anticipated Thomas Piketty's recent insights on relationship between ideology and economic inequality (2020). Cognizant of the emergence of new domains of power in colonial India, Periyar argued that redistribution of power derived through access to modern education, the economy, the judiciary, and the bureaucracy is more critical than that emanating from ownership of physical assets like land. Through such a reading, Periyar also advanced a spatial perspective on inequality and hence emancipation. He held that mobility of lower castes out of caste-ridden rural spaces and traditional occupations into urban and modern spaces of education and employment is crucial to securing social justice. He also emphasized the spatial scale of economic domination by the Brahmin–Baniya elites, derived from their access to pan-Indian networks as well as proximity to the nationalist movement. Periyar argued for decentring of political power to counter their hegemony (Ganeshwar, 2022). By illuminating the positional bias of the economic programmes advanced by the nationalist and socialist movements, his propositions help imagine an alternative model of social and economic emancipation.

Periyar's ideas transformed over time in line with his political trajectory that began with his association with the Indian National Congress (Congress) and the Gandhian nationalist movement. His discomfort with Gandhi's persistent upholding of the varnashrama dharma and the silence of Congress leaders on the demand for representation of lower castes within the party and in political offices influenced his subsequent ideological shift. Even as he developed a critique of the Gandhian model of economic reconstruction, some ideas that he imbibed during his association with Gandhi continued to inform his thoughts on the economic dynamic in India. Important among them were his lifelong support for cooperative production and his aversion for 'wasteful or unproductive expenditure'. His celebration of Andhanarpettai, a village in the Cauvery delta region, where handloom weavers had organized to produce and market on a cooperative basis is a good illustration of this position.[1] He built on this rationale for cooperative production over his subsequent political career. When he argued for the modernization of agriculture later, he highlighted the importance of cooperative institutions that could help farmers access input and output markets and eliminate the moneylender and trader intermediaries. A related idea that he consistently upheld was the necessity for workers to get a share of the profits being made apart from wages. His insights on expenditure became more incisive over time and helped him articulate a new axis of power.

'Imitative Consumption' as Impoverishing

Periyar's condemnation of 'wasteful expenditure' can be dated back to his affiliation with the Gandhian movement, but the scope of his critique extended beyond the ecological imperative of consumption that Gandhi upheld. Earlier, Periyar believed in Gandhian economic nationalism that sought to pitch an alternative Indian modern rooted in the revival of labour-intensive, native forms of production and an accompanying consumption ethic. He held that diffusion of *khadi* (handspun and handwoven cloth) was the route to building economic self-reliance. He however contrasted the cooperative handloom model with the cooperative funding model adopted by the Nattukottai Chettiars (a mercantile caste) in the Chettinad region where they pooled funds to create amenities (that he labelled 'Western') such as street lights, ice, and so on. To him, such cooperation would not help nation-building as it relied on imports and met only the needs of the rich.[2] Such consumption by the colonialists was probably justified because it was backed by improvements in productivity and overall standards of living, but such imitative consumption by Indian elites merely contributed to economic drain. Cooperative production of *khadi* on the other hand, could create a self-sustaining and independent local economy that could build the country's economic resilience as it also promoted consumption of locally produced goods.

Periyar's visit to the Union of Soviet Socialist Republics (USSR) helped him further extend the liberatory potential of cooperatives, especially when production was based on modern technologies and saved resources (Anaimuthu 1974, vol. 3, pp. 1651–1653). Based on his observations of the Soviet experience, he questioned the losses incurred by confining the scale of food production to that of the household. Food was a major source of pollution in caste society and inter-dining across castes was taboo.[3] Among other factors, food as a source of pollution was a major driver of households relying on home-cooked food. Periyar questioned the efficacy of this arrangement citing the example of social kitchens that served large numbers of people in socialist USSR. To him, getting a person to cook for four or five people in an exclusive kitchen was a waste of both human and infrastructure resources apart from the higher possibility of wastage of food (Anaimuthu 1974, vol. 3, p. 1651). This was yet another dimension of unproductive utilization of resources in caste society.

Following his disenchantment with the Gandhian ideal, his critique of wasteful consumption expanded to address expenditure on festivals, rituals, and life-cycle events in Hindu society. All life-cycle events such as birth, attainment of puberty, marriage, and death involve expenses. Additionally, many festivals demand expenditure. Writing about Deepavali, he pointed out that the festival was invariably an occasion when the rich displayed their wealth by adorning themselves with expensive clothes. This in turn generated incentives among the poor as well to indulge in similar celebrations, forcing them to borrow from usurious moneylenders. This Sanskritization of consumption, taking place as it did in colonial India, also meant a drain of wealth from the country as the producers of such clothing were in England. The expenditure during Deepavali was only an illustration of how Hindu rituals in general involve unproductive utilization of resources (Anaimuthu 1974, vol. 3, pp.1637–1638). An article in the English magazine *Revolt* launched by the Self-Respect Movement (SRM) best captured this:

> It is the irony of Mother India that whereas other religions spend their money in establishing hospitals and schools for the use of the people belonging to our religion, Hinduism enjoins its followers to waste crores on smoke, in memory of the 'heroic' deed of one of its Trinities. And the protagonists of this religion have no shame in cringing the Government for bits of charity. …. The cross-word puzzler wanted the name of a religion which deprived its people of health, wealth and intellect and yet was loved by them. We suggest Hinduism. (Cited in Geetha and Rajadurai, n.d., p. 288)

Two dimensions of Periyar's critique can therefore be discerned. First, caste society creates incentives to emulate the consumption practices of elites, leading to a drain of the wealth of poor, lower-caste households. Second, such drain feeds into the pockets of the priestly class, a class that contributes little towards productive economic activity. As a corollary, it also drains the national economy of resources that can be invested productively in domains such as education, health, and modern industries. The appropriation of such wealth by the priestly class led Periyar to identify the 'stone capitalist' as an axis of economic power.

The 'Stone Capitalist' as Rentier

Temples have historically been repositories of wealth and power. Wealth accumulation by temples, religious mutts, and temple authorities was therefore a subject of Periyar's persistent ideological attention. He used the example of the income accruing to the Tirupati temple to illustrate how money flowing into temples in the form of donations was a drain on the nation's wealth (*Kudi Arasu*, vol. 1, pp. 121–123). Lower-caste people also incurred expenses to propitiate gods to address setbacks in their economic or bodily well-being. Siphoning off poor people's incomes through this route was compelled by a web of beliefs backed by Brahminical authority that had no place in a modern egalitarian society. As in the case of donations to the Tirupati temple, such income could have been spent more productively. This phenomenon indexes an important axis of economic exploitation in caste society. A rentier class of caste elites with no disposition for productive labour or investment in the larger economy appropriates the wealth generated by productive castes. According to Periyar, this needed to be addressed before the exploitation of the modern working class by the capitalist is taken up because this is not only more widespread, but importantly does not translate into any productive redeployment of the surplus.

In a speech in Bombay on 12 February 1950, on the differences between the communist movement in the West and the SRM (Anaimuthu, 1974, vol. 1, p. 640), Periyar contended that Christianity as the dominant religion in the West had ensured social equality. It was therefore possible for the communist movement to discuss economic equality. In India, on the other hand, the hegemony of Vedic Hindu norms did not allow for political mobilization that prioritized economic equality. Economic equality would not last if the norms that enforced caste divisions and hierarchies are rendered redundant through social reform. In Gramscian terms, building up a 'commonsense' against such norms and their religious sanction had to precede any struggle for economic justice. 'The communists should realise that before the abolition of the rich capitalist, the priestly Brahmin capitalist, the "stone" capitalist [temples] and the mutt capitalist [religious heads] must be abolished …' (Anaimuthu, 1974, vol. 1, p. 640). For this task, building an ethic based on rationality and self-respect had to take precedence. Here, we see how Periyar integrated his earlier Congress nationalist vision of wealth drain with his critique of the nationalist movement that failed to interrogate the basis of wealth appropriation by the priestly rentier class. A related aspect that he highlighted was the set of norms in caste society that generated perverse economic incentives and negated the development of a productive ethos.

Caste and Productivist Ethos

Appropriation by a non-productive class importantly generated a negative feedback loop that affected the macro-economy. It undermined incentives to invest in improving the efficiency of various productive tasks, and hence, reproduced a low productive economy (Anaimuthu, 1974, vol. 3, pp. 1637–1639). The caste-based division of labour did not generate incentives for innovation and improvements in productivity as the productive castes had little possibility of appropriating the higher returns thus generated. Posing the question why India continued to be a poor country despite abundant natural resources, Periyar identified three primary reasons (Anaimuthu, 1974, vol. 3, pp. 1640–1641): to begin with, such resources were not shared among the bulk of the population because the caste system denied lower castes any right to accumulate. The varnashrama dharma slotted members of each caste into particular occupations and hence acted as the primary barrier to economic democracy that is critical to a productive economy. Second, Manu dharma dictated that the Shudra had no perennial right over property and the Brahmin could usurp the Shudra's property whenever he chose to. As a result, 90 per cent of the citizens had little incentive to accumulate.

Third, citing the case of the agricultural sector, Periyar next pointed to the stagnation of technology for 2,000 years given that the same primitive tools continued to be deployed (Anaimuthu, 1974, vol. 3, p. 1737). Economic freedom was denied to a large majority in India by virtue of their birth. It was the priests, those who held government offices, lawyers, traders, capitalists, zamindars, and *mirasdar*s who owned wealth and importantly had economic rights. The others constituting the majority were denied any such right because of their birth and were forced to labour just to survive. The denial of economic rights on account of the social undermined the prospects for economic mobility among the latter and, importantly, aspirations for such mobility. For example, the son of a Brahmin selling idlis could become a judge in the high court, but such a trajectory was impossible for a scavenger's son. One of the tasks of the Dravidar Kazhagam (DK) was to therefore modernize all sectors of the economy and abolish private property. Highlighting the productivity differences between Indian agriculture and that in the West, Periyar made a case for modernizing agriculture, which in turn required that modern education too be democratized.

British rule had weakened the hold of these scriptural sanctions and opened a few economic spaces that allowed some Shudras to become wealthy. But those demanding self-rule such as Gandhi only wished to perpetuate the regressive system when they called for people to pursue their traditional occupations. Unless those who sought political sovereignty or economic independence engaged with this social injustice, their agendas would only serve the interests of the social elites (Aaimuthu 1974, vol. 3, p. 1640). Periyar's critique of *khadi* and self-reliance emanated from this position.

On *Khadi* Self-reliance

By the 1930s, Periyar had developed a critique of the economic logic underlying the 'swadeshi' movement and support for *khadi* (Aaimuthu 1974, vol. 3, p. 1654). The typical argument for self-reliance was the possibility of creating jobs for more workers and hence improvement in overall living standards of people in the country. But workers would gain very little in the process, Periyar pointed out. Neither backed by employment security nor given a decent share of the returns from production, justifying self-reliance would serve only the interests of the economic elites. The poor were likely to be better off buying cheaper imported goods. Those who campaigned for *khadi* production ignored the fact that mill-made clothing was cheaper and hence more affordable.

There were other reasons Periyar cited as to why the demand for a sustainable *khadi* eco-system as a politico-economic goal of self-reliance was untenable. To begin with, the call for diffusion of *khadi* production did not consider the market conditions under which inputs were available as well as competition in the output market. It could not be sustained without government support as it was neither productive nor cheap. The economic logic of small-scale home-based production went against the trends in the global market where collective large-scale manufacture and mechanization dominated. To Periyar therefore, this valorization of the *khadi* eco-system was a call to return to older forms of manufacturing which were less productive and hence would leave workers with little time for leisure. Importantly, this system of production would prevent labourers from coming together, reflecting on their common conditions, and organizing themselves. It would therefore only serve the interests of the rentier classes who could live off the labour of such small producers.

Periyar also read a demand for a return to the traditional caste-based social division of labour in the demand for *khadi*. He therefore pilloried Gandhi's glorification of people labouring with their hands. 'Why should people work so much to earn a living?', he asked, especially when the priest, the zamindar, the king, the trader, and the official led comfortable lives with no sweat (Anaimuthu 1974, vol. 3, p. 1660). He also pointed to the culture of poverty that *khadi* reproduced. The weavers were expected to labour on their looms through the day, but given the low productivity, they were unlikely to earn anything more than what was required for bare sustenance. As Periyar noted, this production arrangement was not only inspired by a celebration of India's caste tradition but would also serve to reproduce it. He thus built a strong case for reconstituting the economy on modern lines to ensure both social and economic justice, as modern production would allow for the possibility of undermining pre-existing social hierarchies as well as improve worker incomes.

Rather than the colonial government, Periyar therefore held that it was the nationalist agenda of self-reliance that thwarted the prospects of building communism or socialism in the country. Modern machinery was not the scourge of labour as was made out by Gandhi and his supporters, rather it was the caste system. Further, the premise that each household should be able to produce all that it required subverted the evolutionary logic of human development rooted in more sophisticated forms of cooperation and social organization of labour. Discouragement of *khadi* might lead to unemployment and hence poverty in the short run. But Periyar provocatively argued that it may be in the best interests of workers (and the country) to launch a struggle against the rich and survive in jail rather than be pacified by labouring in *khadi* production. His recognition of the lifelong labouring of the lower castes as they were 'born to labour' led him to a distinctive conception of the labour question.

The Labour Question in Caste Society

Periyar, along with one of his close associates from the SRM, translated (from English) and published *The Communist Manifesto* in the movement's Tamil weekly *Kudi Arasu*. This was the first translation of the manifesto in Tamil. It was accompanied by several articles on Lenin, socialism, and progressive changes in the USSR. The Erode Programme that Periyar drafted in 1932 along with the communist leader Singaravelar made demands for nationalization of land and key sectors such as banks, the railways, and other modes of transport (Geetha and Rajadurai, 2008, p. 511). Periyar addressed several meetings advocating the socialist cause, was arrested for supporting strikes, formed workers' unions, and defended their rights in several forums. Simultaneously, he launched a critique of both the communist movement and segments of the nationalist movement that espoused socialism, particularly on their formulation of the labour question in the context of India.

In the early years of labour mobilization, the left and nationalist movements primarily organized wage workers in modern sectors such as textiles, the railways, and tramways. Periyar had a more expansive understanding of who a labourer was in a country like India. Through several pieces published in *Kudi Arasu* (vol. 1, pp. 80–82; vol. 23, pp. 205–207, for example), he questioned the dominant narrative of these movements that privileged the wage worker labouring for a capitalist at the expense of the self-employed labourer. This invisibilized the numerically more dominant self-employed workers or 'born workers' and importantly the processes that rendered them labourers by birth. Those who were working on modern machines could not be the only ones to stake claim to the status of workers. On the contrary, all those who had to labour to survive in this world such as the cartman, the *dhobi*, the sweeper, the scavenger, the potter, and the weaver were all workers as dictated by Manu dharma. To Periyar, the dominance of the former category implied a legitimacy of the struggles that they pursued vis-à-vis the employer or capitalist for higher wages, and the use of strikes as a bargaining tool.

Periyar further argued that such struggles for higher wages were not always helpful. His reasoning was as follows: he drew a parallel between these struggles and those of the working classes in the metropole. The latter, according to him, were keen to get a better share of the spoils from the colonial exploitation of labour, rather than identifying themselves with the hardships that workers in the colonies faced. When wage workers demanded more wages, the capitalist often conceded to the workers' demand because they could pass on the increase in wages to consumers by hiking the prices of their products. In other words, the demand by workers did not lead to a reduction in the profit of the capitalist but rather ate into the real incomes of the mass of consumers who were largely self-employed workers. These workers were therefore forced to spend more out of their pockets for the commodities produced in sectors where such labour bargaining succeeded. To support his contention, he cited the example of the strike by tramway and railway workers in the Madras Presidency. The demand for higher wages only led to an increase in ticket fares at the cost of the welfare of poor consumers, leaving the profits of the owners intact. Similarly, when mill owners conceded to mill workers' demands for higher wages, they could again pass on the higher wages in the form of higher prices to the consumer. But the mill worker would be spending more on train fares while the railway worker would be paying more for his clothing. As a result, Periyar argued, actions such as strikes neither contributed to industrial production nor to overall economic well-being.

Here, it is insightful to recognize the parallels with Lenin's (1902) critique of the economism of the trade union movement when it was not embedded in social-democratic struggles, and the pitfalls of the presence of a labour aristocracy in developing a revolutionary worker consciousness. Writing as he did in the first half of the twentieth century, we need to bear in mind that he was critiquing the politics of labour emanating from mobilizing workers primarily in the small modern capitalist segment. To Periyar, this prevented the foregrounding of substantive issues faced by the large mass of self-employed 'born' workers. The persistence of the self-employed as a significant category of India's workforce well into the twenty-first century attests to the salience of his concern.

Similarly, Periyar did not believe that inciting workers to strike and damage machines helped their well-being in the long term. Any damage to the machines would not harm the owners as they could always tax the people to buy new ones. His critique of the mode of negotiation by labour unions also alluded to the market power wielded by modern enterprises which were often monopolies or oligopolies and hence could pass on price hikes to consumers. Workers, on the other hand, would suffer when factories were closed. And so would the overall economy and the lay person. He therefore urged workers to chart strategies based on local conditions and not merely imitate what workers did in other parts of the world. To say that we should do what Marx or Lenin said was meaningless as they did not live in a world where workers were condemned to labour by the virtue of their birth and caste status. He held that the contradiction and animosity between the worker and the capitalist could be addressed by making workers equal partners in the production process, thus sharing the returns from it. While this position overlapped with the cooperativism advocated by Gandhi, Periyar's critique should be read in conjunction with his critique of appropriation by an unproductive priestly class that was highlighted earlier.

The DK was a union for labourers, he asserted (Anaimuthu, 1974, vol. 1, p. 614). Unlike the mainstream workers' unions that merely sought to get better conditions or incomes for the worker, the DK sought to destroy the basis on which the social division of labour and its attendant hierarchies operated. The DK was a movement not just for workers who got an opportunity to be workers, but also those who were condemned to a world of labour by virtue of their birth, by the Shastras, and by the gods, Periyar said. This was the labour question that the Dravidian movement sought to address.

> Our worker is concerned about his wages but not concerned at all to know why we have been slaves and of lower caste status for 2,000–3,000 years, or why the Brahmin has a high caste status and can eat without having to labour for 2,000–3,000 years? And when we say that we want to study, they say that we are not eligible or do not have the capability to study. Should we not worry about this? How can a society be without the capability or eligibility for 100 years? ... Higher education is exclusively for them. Because of that, modern jobs and higher end jobs are exclusively for the Brahmins. Who is thinking about these things, except us? ... (Anaimuthu, 1974, vol. 3, p. 1741)

He proceeded to ask when a worker's son would go on to study enough to get a modern job? This passage reveals the emphasis that the Dravidian movement placed on addressing the structural barriers to inter-generational mobility, by problematizing the reproductive domain and the ideological basis that perpetuated them. None of the other parties or movements took any steps to educate workers about how religion prevented them from thinking about the larger issues that they ought to be fighting for, Periyar contended. They were content to intensify the conflict between the worker and industrialist, but did not want workers to question or rally against the Brahmin or the state. It was the state that enacted the laws that upheld the right of the capitalist to appropriate the wealth generated by workers. This reading of the labour question is close to Lenin's call to workers' movements to politically expose the autocracy in all aspects of oppression (1902, p. 53).

Periyar posed a further question: Why was it that Brahmins who did not uphold or support the demand for equality of experience or equality of rights, supported economic equality when they joined the communist party? His answer ran as follows: the communists demanded only an equal share in property or wealth. While this was important, a struggle for experiential equality in Indian society had to precede this. Else, when Brahmins called for economic redistribution but failed to address the question of caste, it would only serve their interests. As long as lower-caste labourers were denied experiential equality, the hegemonic control wielded by caste elites would certainly ensure that the redistributed property would flow back to the Brahmins as the lower castes would continue to venerate them and feel beholden to them for their overall well-being. He contrasted the destinies of non-Brahmin elites like Annamalai Chettiar and R. K. Shanmukam Chetty (the first finance minister of post-independence India) who had accumulated a fortune with that of the poor Brahmin. Periyar contended that in caste society, economic wealth did not change one's status. As a result, the degree of freedom and rights enjoyed by the non-Brahmin wealthy could not match that of the poor Brahmin. Further, on account of the rights he enjoyed by virtue of being a Brahmin, he could also make sure that his children would get into the Indian Civil Service (ICS) and become a collector or a judge, or become the head of a mutt. Periyar's anti-Brahminical position was therefore rooted in opposition to a hierarchy that denied the entire society a common experience (*sama anubhavam*). This experiential injustice had to be addressed before the narrative of socialism could gain ground in caste society.

Another aspect of labour that Periyar highlighted was the differential valorization of manual and non-manual labour. 'Sitting under a fan in a comfortable room, working at a desk … fetches a *gumastha* 100 rupees, but a worker who forges metal in a furnace with a hammer is paid merely 30–50 rupees? (Anaimuthu, vol. 3, p. 1741). While this logic stemmed from the casteist denigration of manual labour, it also had implications for the inter-generational mobility of lower-caste households undertaking manual occupations. Because of relatively lower incomes, they were less likely to get their children into higher education or afford better healthcare. Periyar went on to point out how difficult it was for children from a worker's household to study up to the postgraduate level and become eligible for a government job when the worker was paid just enough to subsist. He therefore made a case for equalization of wages for different kinds of work. Wages should help workers lead a life with basic comforts and not merely suffice for food; he also demanded that the state build colleges for workers' children, opening long-term pathways for economic mobility and freedom from caste-encoded occupations.

The Dravidar Vivasaya Thozhilalar Sangam (DVTS) initiated by the SRM did mobilize lower-caste agricultural labour in the Thanjavur delta to demand better terms of work. There were trade unions that the SRM backed in the textile mill sector as well. However, the difference between the left movement and the DK was the latter's emphasis on addressing the basis of the social division of labour that imprisoned lower castes in low-status manual occupations.

Caste Consciousness and Labour Solidarity

The caste system also denied the possibility of labourers coming together to forge a collective consciousness that could undermine the power of the rentier castes. As Ambedkar famously argued in his 'Annihilation of Caste', the caste system was not merely a division of labour, but a division of labourers. Though workers across diverse occupations were exploited by a common set of actors, their caste consciousness undermined any incentive to collectively resist. Brahmanical hegemony therefore operated along two axes simultaneously: one, by sanctifying status hierarchy and two, by generating differential access to the means of production and livelihood. If Shudras were deemed to serve the caste elites, no exploitation could be resisted as appropriation of Shudra labour had legitimate sanction. To the Shudra, labouring was their duty that would be rewarded in their next birth. Further, the division of labourers implied that labourers from other castes were not seen as part of the common collective of exploited labourers. In other words, the caste system did not sustain the formation of a collective class consciousness.

The latter dimension is best exemplified by what happened during the Buckingham and Carnatic Mills strike in Madras in 1921 when the management used caste divisions within the workers to break the strike (Venkatachalapathy and Sivasubramanian, 1990; Rajadurai and Geetha, 2009). This was followed by clashes between caste Hindu and Muslim workers on the one side and Dalit workers on the other. This inability of the orthodox left to take cognizance of the existing caste divisions within the working class and how they deterred the forging of solidarities was at the heart of Periyar's reading of the labour question. Caste consciousness therefore needed to be addressed ahead of the class question. To Periyar, the inability of the left movement or its leaders to recognize this was a consequence of the privileged caste positions of most left leaders. Writing in 1928 in *Kudi Arasu* (vol. 6, pp. 62–63), Periyar said that the labour movement in the Madras Presidency was unlikely to take off. To paraphrase, none of the leaders of the movement such as Annie Besant, S. Srinivasa Iyengar, B. Shiva Rao, S. Satyamurti, or P. Varadarajulu Naidu were workers or had experienced the living conditions of workers. Under such circumstances, it was important to ask why such elites were interested in guiding and mobilizing workers. Periyar read this as yet another means adopted by caste elites to preserve their privileges.

Periyar also identified the economic illogic of caste pride whereby lower castes staked claim to a higher social status based on a perceived past where they had once held a high status (Anaimuthu, 1974, vol. 3, pp. 1748–1750). Such claims for status mobility once again reduced incentives to forge horizontal solidarities across labouring caste groups. Responding to demands made by lower castes classified as Shudras to be brought under Kshatriya status, Periyar pointed out that however high a labouring social group may be in the ascribed caste status, they should continue to have another social group above them. Rather than trying to abolish the basis of such differences, some caste groups were seeking higher status. 'If the stone mason and the weaver is seeking the status of a Brahmin, another worker is seeking to become a "rishi".' Such aspirations conceded higher standing to the Brahmin or the 'rishi' and therefore only perpetuated the caste system as well as their occupational status and did not help in reforming the mode of organizing social production. To democratize the social division of labour across castes, two things had to happen simultaneously. Just as workers' children had to be able to access modern education to escape from their lifeworld of manual labour, the Brahmin had to be encouraged to undertake tasks that were otherwise carried out by low-caste workers. When they undertook such low status work, the status of the work itself would change. For example, when the Devadasi women were performing the traditional dance *sadir*, it was deemed low status. But when the Brahmins appropriated it and named it 'Bharatanatyam', the status of the dance transformed and it became a classical art form (Anaimuthu, 1974, vol. 3, p. 1750).

The Educated as Oppressor

An important insight of Periyar was his recognition of the economic power that emanated from monopoly over education, modern education in particular, and hence, employment in the colonial administration. The jobs in the colonial bureaucracy were not only high-paying but also allowed those occupying higher echelons to shape laws and policies. Periyar was particularly aware of the power wielded by lawyers and judges under such conditions. The colonial legal regime generated the need for a set of legal experts to mediate between the letter of the law and the lay person, including the landed. The landed classes, given their Shudra status, were denied education and hence an understanding of modern law. The imposition of the colonial property regime led to a series of disputes and litigations that demanded the mediation of the lawyer. Periyar saw the landed lower castes as a class of people who were at the mercy of mediating lawyers. This reading inverted the classical distinction and hierarchy between the propertied and the labouring classes. In orthodox class terms, a lawyer is a worker while his landlord client is propertied and hence more powerful. In India however, the latter's ignorance of laws and inability to defend themselves in courts on account of a lack of education forced them to pay educated lawyers heavily to defend their property.

This power relation was illustrated through a fictional conversation between an uneducated but landed client from a middle caste (he is addressed as a Gounder) and a lawyer, with the latter appropriating a large sum of money for helping the client deal with land disputes.[4] Status hierarchies could thus serve to transfer economic resources to caste elites. Just as caste power inscribed in ritualistic hierarchies involved transfer of wealth to the priestly Brahmin, the same continued in the modern domain as the case of the lawyer suggests. The new articulations of Brahminical power proved to be critical to Periyar's conceptualization of caste power in colonial India. As the narrative suggests, the non-Brahmin protagonist was not at the bottom of the class–caste hierarchy. Nor was he poor and had access to land. Despite that, it was the Brahmin who wielded power over him on account of his monopoly over knowledge of modern law. The narrative thus highlights a transition of caste power from the traditional sphere into the modern colonial domain. While Periyar recognized the re-articulation of Brahmin power by virtue of access to modern education, he was also cognizant of the role of temples and religion and the priestly class in continuing to impoverish the worker. The monopoly over education by caste elites therefore needed to be addressed. 'The selfishness of the educated class and the misguided blind belief resulting from the ignorance of uneducated people keep us away from the search after truth and justice' (Anaimuthu 1974, vol. 1, p. viii). This in turn called for democratization of education and rational thought.

Landed Power

Though his primary emphasis was on Brahminical power and monopoly over modern administration through access to modern education and social networks, Periyar was also cognizant of the power wielded by other 'non-productive' castes or classes like the moneylender, the trader, and the zamindar. The series of articles he authored on socialism on various occasions made this abundantly clear (Veeramani, 2019). He highlighted the importance of land redistribution and the need for abolition of the zamindari system. Addressing the non-Zamindari conference in Salem in 1933, he said that there was a strong case for organizing similar conferences on various non-exploiting or non-elite sections like a 'non-moneylenders' conference, non-capitalists' conference, non-industrialists' conference, non-house-owners' conference, non-upper-castes' conference, and so on' (Anaimuthu, vol. 3, pp. 1682–1685).

Periyar has however been criticized by ideologues of the left for not sufficiently reproving landed power and at times being sympathetic to landlords. This allegation found backing particularly in the purported non-response of Periyar to the massacre of Dalit agricultural workers by landlords in Kilvenmani in the Cauvery delta in 1968. However, as Thirumavelan (2018) and Manoharan (2020) observe, he was neither silent on nor indifferent to the incident. Along with Thiruneelakandan (2017), they point to the strong mobilization of agricultural workers by the DVKS against both Brahmin and non-Brahmin landlords apart from Periyar's vocal support on several occasions for land reforms as well as better wages for agricultural workers. Periyar also demanded that administrative posts in villages (which were held hereditarily by upper castes) such as that of the accountant be given to Dalits.

However, this did not stop him from aligning with the non-Brahmin landed or business elites to articulate a political frontier when addressing Brahminism in the social sphere became his primary political project. We therefore see a complex articulation of economic power where the axes of differentiation tend to be fluid. This ability to simultaneously address multiple sources and spatial scales of power even as he prioritized them in terms of political action was critical to his approach. His support for zamindari abolition was also accompanied by an argument in favour of the landed vis-à-vis the educated urban elite.

Town and Country

In a piece provocatively titled, 'Villages Should be Abolished', Periyar (2007 [1944]) articulated a vision of social justice that was completely in opposition to that of Gandhi. It resonated in many ways the arguments made by Ambedkar about the oppression prevalent in villages (Rodrigues, 2002). Addressing a group of trainee village officials in Erode in 1944, Periyar claimed that the village as a spatial entity occupied the same status as that of the 'panchama' under the varnashrama dharma (2007 [1944], p. 6). Just as the Shudra and the Panchama were expected to attain salvation by labouring for the upper castes, the only role of those in the villages was to serve those residing in urban spaces. The number of towns in India too was much fewer than the lakhs of villages, mirroring the numerical split between the upper and lower castes, with the top three varnas accounting for just a small share of the total population.

Raising the question, 'What is a village?' he answered that a village was a place that had no school, no hospital, no theatre, no park, no court, no police, no road, no lights, no quality drinking water, no progressive values, and had the means only to earn enough to keep away hunger and not enough to lead a good life. But it was the produce of the villages that fed the townsfolk as well as the government coffers and sustained the deities, the temples, and all the rituals. To illustrate, he called upon the audience to think about how the landed even from a well-irrigated region led their lives in contrast to the opulent lifestyle of traders and moneylenders like the Nattukottai Chettiars and the Marwadis who lived in dry, desert-like regions (2007 [1944], p. 5). Here, he pitted the landlord (mirasdar) and the cultivating peasant together against the moneylender, the trader, and the official.

A key source of such disparity and exploitative relations was the lack of education among the rural classes. It was the lack of awareness of these exploitative relations and the varna-imposed belief that it was their lot to toil in poverty that perpetuated such relations. The urban trader was able to appropriate the bulk of the profits from the sale of the farmer's produce precisely because of the lack of awareness of market prices and the resultant inability to bargain. The spatial divide, to Periyar, also translated into an educational and hence economic divide over time. He contended that while the children of a sweeper in a city would be able to access modern education, the children of even those with 100 or 200 acres of land in a village had less access and had to spend substantially to go and study in the city (2007 [1944], p. 8).

He listed a set of reasons as to why the city had to be the destination for villagers (Periyar, 2010 [1936], pp. 21–22).

1. The cruelties of caste restrictions are not present. The city is also free of the barriers to exercising one's individual freedom and rights that exist in a village.

2. There are provisions for education and healthcare.

3. There are facilities and support to undertake entrepreneurial activities and for industrial development.

4. There are means and facilities for intellectual development as well as for leisure.

5. Wages are commensurate to the amount of labour spent.

6. There are more resources that help one progress to the extent of one's intellectual capabilities.

7. Anyone can compete in any domain.

The city was therefore not only a place where the traditional caste-based division of labour was undermined by modern production regimes and modern education, but also a place where people learnt the ethos of equality and treating fellow human beings with respect.

Periyar also proceeded to map the set of new processes that drove the appropriation of the lands of labouring farmers by urban elites such as lawyers, the judiciary, high-ranking officials, and capitalists (2010 [1936], pp. 20–21). Having been dispossessed of their lands, they became tenant farmers or worked on small parcels of land that were insufficient for sustenance. This forced them into debts that were not repayable given their meagre incomes, leading to further dispossession. This happened to even the big landlords because of the narrow-mindedness brought about by village life. They often entered into conflicts with one another on account of such attitudes which landed them in the hands of urban lawyers and officials who siphoned off their wealth. Pointing out that there was hardly any village where such conflicts were absent, he said that the liberal and broad-minded views that life in the city could provide were completely lacking in a village. Lawyers and officials thrived only through such narrow-mindedness among the rural land-owning classes. The case of the landless agricultural labourer in the village was even worse, working as he did for meagre food and not even enough to light a lamp in his house in the evening. The lives of those who could move out of the village to work in nearby villages or towns were only marginally better. To state that such lifestyle should be upheld, he said, amounted to treachery and deception.

In order to progress therefore, lower-caste workers had to move to the city and imbibe the values of modern civilization. He narrated what was likely to happen when the Adi Dravida workers who had migrated to work in plantations in places like Colombo, Penang, and Singapore returned to their native villages. They would have some savings, but importantly, they would not be willing any longer to slog for the landlords through the day for measly food. They would not want to return to such uncivilized lives. On seeing them, their kin and the members of their community would also aspire to move away from such a life. This discontent was likely only when they were exposed to the possibilities of life in the urban. Another recurring theme in his writing, therefore, was the emphasis on modern education and knowledge of English to diffuse a worldview that acknowledged the importance of equality and scientific reason. To him, such ideas disseminated through modern education alone had enabled people to raise their voices against Brahminical authority and the validity of its basis.

Apart from advocating rural to urban mobility, Periyar called for reconstruction of agricultural production on industrial lines using modern technology, as stated earlier. He envisioned a role for cooperatives to avoid middlemen as well as to collectively use inputs. He also envisaged the setting up of urban amenities for a cluster of villages: not only schools, hospitals, and recreational services, but also small-scale industries established on the basis of modern technologies so that the division of labour between the town and village could be destroyed. Given the nature of modern progress, he said that there was no place for the village in the future. Big cities would proliferate while villages would disappear.

Indian Big Business and Geographies of Economic Domination

Periyar, along with the DMK, has been accused of being a separatist as he called for the creation of Dravida Nadu. Though it was given up in 1965, the demand has been re-articulated as one for greater federal autonomy. There were a few factors that drove this demand. To begin with, it was in opposition to the nationalists' articulation of an independent India that would uphold the privileges of the caste elites and an 'Indian tradition' that sanctified and legitimized caste hierarchies. It was increasingly becoming clear that such a nationalist imagination would be hard to contend with given the dominance of upper castes in articulating this vision and their hold over the tools of propaganda. Such conditions made the political struggle for a secular and genuinely democratic republic that would destroy the basis of caste at a pan-Indian scale extremely difficult. Further, the articulation of India as a nation was rooted in conjuring up a historical past that was bound by common traditions. This 'national' homogeneity was articulated through the idea of a Hindu–Hindi–India that had little space for the vernacular or for an alternative democratic vision of modern India. The need for a common language to unite the country too saw a demand by the nationalist movement for the Sanskrit-based Hindi. Periyar and the Dravidian movement saw this as an attempt to erase the Dravidian–Tamil identity that invoked a future rooted in the modern and the secular.

Another significant factor was the dominance of the Brahmin–Baniya nexus that allowed for the imagination of a pan-Indian market that Baniya elites with their country-wide networks sought to exploit. Periyar's vision of the economic therefore had a spatial expression in the form of resistance to the power wielded by the Brahmin–Baniya nexus. In India, big business was (and continues to be) monopolized by members from a few social groups with strong roots in trading such as the Baniyas and Marwaris. By virtue of their long history of trading, they had not only managed to establish trans-regional networks and institutions to strengthen their economic power but had also worked with the British government and the Indian nationalist movement to advance the economic space in which they could operate in colonial India. To secure the terrain of social justice, Periyar therefore proposed an alternative nation as a place holder for an alternative community that he labelled Dravida Nadu. This was not, as many believe, a territorial identity but an alternative republican political space juxtaposed against the Indian national identity that to him was a place holder for a nation that upheld caste hierarchies and the credibility of the religious texts that dictated such hierarchies (Pandian, 1993). Addressing a public gathering in 1951 (cited in Rajadurai, 2012, p. 590), he outlined the kind of society that would flourish in Dravida Nadu: 'In this country, you cannot see any Brahmins. Similarly, you also cannot see *panchamar*s, *parayar*s, *chakkiliyar*s, or any other caste members. You cannot even hear these names. "We are all humans, humans" would be the call that would be heard everywhere. This is our first political goal.'

Analytical Summary

Periyar engaged with the priorities put forward by other political parties. To the nationalists, it was political power that was paramount, while for those on the left, it was the economic drain of wealth that was of primary importance. He questioned both, using arguments that resonated with those of Ambedkar. Political power was meaningless without reconstitution of the social. When citizens of a future nation refused to see each other as equals, political power would have little meaning for those at the lower end of the hierarchy. The same would hold good for those privileging economic drain. One needed to ask, whose wealth was being drained to locate the hidden elite bias in this contention. Against these two positions, he privileged the need to address the ideological validation of social hierarchies that undermined both political and economic justice.

It is worth bringing his position into conversation with Karl Polanyi's thesis on the 'Great Transformation' (1944) brought about by capitalist development. Polanyi argued that for the first time in history, the economic domain had been disembedded from the social. Tracing the evolution of the economic domain in capitalist society in the eighteenth and nineteenth centuries, he established how political interventions during this period disembedded the market from social institutions. This was an inversion of past human history where economic transactions had always been embedded in and guided by social norms. Reading the emergent colonial modern in Indian society, Periyar clearly recognized that such disembedding of the economic had not happened, as a consequence of the caste elites seeking to preserve a social order that perpetuated their power. Any demand for economic justice in such a context therefore had to recognize how economic behaviour and inequality were shaped by and embedded in social institutions. He further drew attention to the shifts brought about by the colonial administration that enabled new forms of articulation of traditional social power in the modern economic sphere. In doing so, he made visible the power wielded by those with access to modern education and jobs in the bureaucracy and how that interlocked with premodern sources of power rooted in monopoly over education and property. As a corollary, he viewed democratization of education and access to such jobs along with the destruction of the ideological basis of caste society as critical to ensuring social as well as economic justice. His insights also therefore speak to neo-Polanyian calls to re-embed the economy in social institutions in order to mitigate the costs of unbridled capitalist expansion. Periyar's call to recognize the power inherent in non-modern social institutions resonates with the problematization of the 'social' by scholars like Nancy Fraser (2013).

In *Capital and Ideology*, Piketty (2020) demonstrates how ideology naturalizes inequality across all societies and is the basis for all 'inequality regimes'. Using a comparative perspective on the relationship between economic inequalities and ideologies that justify status-based inequalities, Piketty identifies the inequality regime 'as a set of discourses and institutional arrangements intended to justify and structure the economic, social, and political inequalities of a given society' (2020, p. 2). He identifies a trifunctional structuring of premodern societies that was dominated by a priestly (religious) elite and further comprised of a warrior and landowning nobility, and a working class, with the former two classes constituting the elites. In India, Piketty, points out, the explicit ordering of status and class by the *Manusmriti* (seen by orthodox Hindu elites as the code book that ought to govern Hindu society), is quarternary, with a trading or mercantile class added to the trifunctional stratification. The *Manusmriti* locates the primary authority in the Brahmin as kings and the warrior classes too are expected to abide by the counsel of the Brahmins. Despite considerable fluidity of power relations, especially across caste groups in practice, the power of the Brahmin elite was consolidated vis-à-vis the warrior classes in the immediate pre-colonial period. This power was further rigidified with the colonial administration's efforts to govern the numerous social groups by fixing categories based on censuses.

Piketty contends that caste ideology therefore played a critical role in sustaining economic inequality in India. It produced a commonsense that legitimized social and economic inequality. The overlaps with Periyar's insights are not hard to see. Periyar saw caste norms as constituting the basis for justifying the inequality regime being perpetuated in India. His ideas hold particular allure at the current conjuncture when mobilization based on Hindu nationalist ideology holds sway in the country. The mainstream left movements that emphasize mobilization based on economic classes have been less successful in resisting the politics of Hindu majoritarianism that invokes a pan-Indian unity based on a common civilizational ethos stemming from Vedic Hindu norms. This inability arises from a failure to effectively engage with a politics based on the social rather than the economic. On the other hand, movements inspired by a vision of caste-based social justice such as the Dravidian movement have been able to not only resist the incursions of such majoritarian politics but also offer a repertoire of tools that can be potent in this regard. However, even in the case of caste-based movements, mobilization of lower castes based on an imagined glorious past (of their castes) has proved to be problematic. Aspirations for improved social status within the varna fold can easily dovetail into efforts to incorporate lower castes into the imagination of a Hindu nation. Periyar's arguments on the illogic of such demands for improved status thus continue to offer lessons for mobilizations around questions of social and economic justice. His insights on the operation of power in Indian society remain relevant in twenty-first-century India.

Notes

1. *Kudi Arasu*, 9 August 1925 (*Kudi Arasu*, vol., 1, pp. 159–160).
2. *Kudi Arasu*, 9 August 1925 (*Kudi Arasu*, vol. 1, pp. 159–160).
3. On several occasions, Periyar had criticized the division of spaces in public eating places such as restaurants and canteens into spaces exclusively meant for Brahmins and those for the rest.
4. *Kudi Arasu*, 16 August 1925 (*Kudi Arasu*, vol. 1, pp. 165–167).

References

Ambedkar, B. R. 1936. 'Annihilation of Caste'. Speech prepared for the annual conference of the Jat-Pat-Todak Mandal of Lahore but not delivered.

Anaimuthu, V. 1974. *Periyar Ee. Ve. Ra. Chinthanaigal* (Thoughts of Periyar E. V. R.), 3 vols. Tiruchirapalli: Thinker's Forum.

Fraser, N. 2013. 'A Triple Movement? Parsing the Politics of Crisis After Polanyi'. *New Left Review* 81: 119–132.

Ganeshwar. 2022. 'Periyar's Spatial Thought'. *CASTE: A Global Journal on Social Exclusion* 3(1): 89–106.

Geetha, V., and S. V. Rajadurai. 2008. *Towards a Non-Brahmin Millennium: From Iyothee Thass to Periyar*, 2nd edn. Kolkata: Samya.

———. eds. n.d. *Revolt*: A Radical Weekly in Colonial Madras. Chennai: Periyar Dravidar Kazhagam.

Kudi Arasu. n.d. *Kudi Arasu: Periyarin Ezhuthum Pechum* (Kudi Arasu: Periyar's Writings and Speeches), vols. 1–26. Chennai: Periyar Dravidar Kazhagam.

Manoharan, Karthick Ram. 2020. 'In the Path of Ambedkar: Periyar and the Dalit Question'. *South Asian History and Culture* 11(2): 136–149. DOI: 10.1080/19472498.2020.1755127.

Pandian, M. S. S. 1993. '"Denationalising" the Past: "Nation"' in E V Ramasamy's Political Discourse'. *Economic and Political Weekly* 28(42): 2282–2287.

Periyar. 2007 [1944]. *Graamangal Ozhiya Vendum*. Chennai: Periyar Dravidar Kazhagam.

———. 2010 [1936]. *Graama Vaazhkai Purattu*. Chennai: Periyar Dravidar Kazhagam.

Piketty, T. 2020. *Capital and Ideology*. Cambridge, MA: Harvard University Press.

Polanyi, K. 2001 [1944]. *The Great Transformation*. Boston: Beacon Press.

Rajadurai, S. V. 2012. *Periyar: August 15*, 3rd edn. Coimbatore: Vidiyal Pathippagam.

Rajadurai, S. V. and V. Geetha. 2009. *Periyar: Suyamariyadhai Samadharmam*, expanded edn. Coimbatore: Vidiyal Pathippagam.

Rodrigues, V. (ed.) (2002). *The Essential writings of B.R. Ambedkar*. New Delhi and Oxford: Oxford University Press.

Thirumavelan, P. 2018. *Aathikka Saathikalukku Mattume Avar Periyara?* (Is He, Periyar, Only for the Dominant Castes?). Chennai: Nattrinai.

Thiruneelakandan, A. 2017. *Niitaamankalam caatiyak kotumaiyum tiraavita iyakkamum* (Needamangalam: Caste Oppression and the Dravidian Movement). Nagercoil: Kalachuvadu Publications.

Veeramani, P. (ed.). 2019. *Thanthai Periyarin Podhuvudamai Chinthanaigal* (Periyar's Thoughts on Socialism), vols. 1–3. Chennai: Periyar Suyamariyadhai Prachaara Niruvanam.

Venkatachalapathy, A. R., and A. Sivasubramanian. 1990. *Binny Alai Velainirutham 1921* (The Binny Mills' Strike 1921). Madras: Ponni.

13

Liberation Notes, Dignity, and Periyar

A Radical Cultural Psychology Perspective

Ramaswami Mahalingam

In the Korean drama *My Liberation Notes* (Netflix, 2022), written by Park Hay-Young, three office workers sit in the human resources (HR) manager's room. They have been asked to meet with the HR manager to address a specific issue related to the company's HR policy. As part of a neoliberal workplace well-being initiative, the company encourages employees to join a club to explore their hobbies and other interests. According to its institutional logic, if employees are allowed to pursue their personal interests at the workplace, it will make them 'happy' and creative, eventually leading to greater productivity. The HR manager regularly emails employees about various clubs, such as photography, hiking, and pottery to encourage them to choose a club.

Three colleagues from different departments receive regular club invitations via email, but none of them find the clubs interesting enough to join. To them, the exercise seems absurd, especially given their challenges, such as the high cost of living, normalized overwork, and dignity violations in the workplace. The HR manager's attempts to persuade them to join a club seem meaningless and futile in the face of their existential crisis. They are tired of the monotony of their lives, which limits their hope and possibilities. Consequently, they frequently reject club suggestions. Eventually, the HR manager asks them to meet her in the office and they provide vague answers, but as they leave, they realize they can create their own club to avoid the pressure of joining one. They name it the 'Liberation Club', whose objective is to journal their existential struggles to overcome personal and social reifications. When the HR manager discovers what they are doing, she attends one of their meetings and is impressed by the authentic expressions of liberation notes in their journal entries. She joins the club herself.

I consider Periyar a radical cultural psychologist who inspired people to write their own liberation notes, helping them overcome personal and socially reified self-horizons. I argue that Periyar was a *radical cultural psychologist* who made people recognize the need to restore personal and social dignity (Mahalingam, 2019) by providing tools to infuse a new meaning in life. As a courageous, compassionate, and mindful leader, Periyar helped people to expand the horizons of their possible selves and social connections by transcending social and personal reifications (that is, prescribed restrictions) circumscribed by identities such as caste, class, gender, and religion.

The discussion in the chapter proceeds in four sections. In the first section, I delineate the radical cultural psychological framework after an overview of existing cultural psychological research, followed in the next section by four examples of ordinary people whose lives were touched and transformed. In the third section, I make a case using my mindful mindset framework that Periyar was a courageous and compassionate leader. In the last section, I set out the implications of Periyar's radical cultural psychological framework for personal, intersubjective, and processual dignity (Mahalingam, 2019).

Radical Cultural Psychology

Let me first briefly review the various strands of research in cultural psychology before outlining a framework for radical cultural psychology. Cross-cultural psychologists examine the role of culture in shaping cognition, perception, and emotion, which has contributed to a growing body of empirical research documenting the differences between East Asian and American cultures (Markus and Kitayama, 2010; Nisbett et al., 2001). Such cross-cultural psychological approaches focus on cultural differences in self-construals. The interdependent self (that is, the self as embedded in a social context) is the dominant mode in Eastern cultures. By contrast, the independent self (that is, the self as abstract and context-free) is viewed as the dominant mode in Western cultures. Some cultural psychologists focus on the integral role of cultural practices in shaping meaning-making, learning, and moral reasoning (Shweder and Sullivan, 1993). In contrast, I argue that power differences within a cultural context shape psychological processes (Mahalingam, 2007a).

Emerging scholarship on intersectionality has underscored the need to examine how various intersections of identities (for example, race, class, gender, age, caste, and ethnicity) shape how we make sense of our lives (Cole, 2009; Crenshaw, 1989). We embody multiple identities with differing degrees of privileges and marginalities. Privilege awareness is an essential element of intersectional approaches to studying culture. Mahalingam and Rabelo (2013) have proposed three approaches to using an intersectional framework for cultural psychological research. Intersectional approaches can focus on how embodying intersecting identities shapes our attitudes, behaviours, and emotions. Intersectional approaches can further consider how intersecting cultural–ecological contexts shape psychological processes in a community. Intersectionality is also conceptualized as an awareness that our identities are fluid, situational, and associated with varying levels of privileges and marginalities.

According to Mahalingam (2007b, p. 43), 'intersectionality is a triangulation of a subject vis-à-vis his or her social location and social positioning along race, class, gender, and caste. This process is dynamic, multidimensional, and historically contingent.'

Postcolonial psychologists have argued that colonialism is a form of oppression where colonial discourses assign people to new categories, creating communities disrupted by space, with shared cultural histories (Bhatia, 2018; Okazaki, David, and Abelmann, 2008). For Bhatia (2018), decolonizing cultural and psychological approaches that essentialize cultures is critical for several reasons. Dominant approaches to cultural psychology do not pay sufficient attention to intracultural variations shaped by gender and social class due to increasing global cultural contacts. Bhatia calls for decolonizing psychological research by carefully interrogating essentialist representations of culture (East versus West) and the motivation to cast cultures in stark contrasts (for example, collectivist versus individualist societies). Bhatia (2018) also calls for a de-essentialist approach to studying culture where culture is viewed not in monolithic or essentialist terms but, instead, as a contested space for belonging. Caste location and gender and class hierarchies shape one's capacity to fully participate in culture production and consumption. Mahalingam, Jagannathan, and Selvaraj (2019) argue that even in the neoliberal economy, caste location plays a critical role in reproducing inequalities and caste hierarchies.

The neoliberal colonial context also creates newer forms of social capital often entrenched in caste hierarchies, perpetuating inequalities and reproducing such hierarchies (Mahalingam, Jagannathan, and Selvaraj, 2019; Mahalingam and Selvaraj, 2022). For example, Mahalingam, Jagannathan, and Selvaraj (2019) observe that Dalits continue to work as manual scavengers in exploitative working conditions that undermine their safety and dignity, with technology failing to make any change. They further point out that we need to decolonize Indian minds from the shackles of their taken-for-granted cultural assumptions about caste. Only by decasticizing essentialist notions of caste can we build an egalitarian society where we recognize people not on account of birth-based assumptions of caste but of shared values (such as liberty, equality, and fraternity). More than a century ago, Periyar started a movement that questioned birth-based assumptions about caste and gender, foregrounding human dignity to decasticize Indian minds of fossilized notions of culture, language, religion, and identity. I argue that Periyar was a radical cultural psychologist who worked tirelessly throughout his life, directly speaking to communities to liberate them from reified notions of self and others.

Periyar's Radical Cultural Psychology

Several scholars have studied Periyar's political acumen and social justice framework (for example, Geetha and Rajadurai, 1998; Irschick, 1969; Manoharan, 2020, 2022; Pandian, 2007; Venkatachalapathy, 2019). Some have examined how his Dravidian movement contributed to shaping politics in Tamil Nadu (for example, Pandian, 2007). In contrast, others have studied the economic impact of social justice with a focus on Dravidian government policies, documenting the effect of the Dravidian model on social and economic development (Kalaiyarasan and Vijayabaskar, 2021). While there has been considerable research on the cultural, historical, and political significance of Periyar's work, there is a lack of research on Periyar from a cultural psychological perspective. Considering his direct engagement with people through public meetings and his writings, we can identify the contours of his radical cultural psychological framework. His radical cultural psychology unsettles our taken-for-granted assumptions about culture, identity, language, and nation, thus liberating us to reimagine our possible selves with courage, compassion, and a commitment to preserving the dignity of self and others.

Thiong'o (1983) called for the need to decolonize the mind, which internalized the hegemonic colonial assumptions that invalidate the unique epistemic positions of African writers, language, and literature, making them invisible. If Thiong'o deconstructed race, Periyar deconstructed caste and gender to decolonize the mind and challenge the intracultural hegemony that reified possible selves and the freedom to preserve one's dignity. Although several cultural psychologists recognize the need to decolonize cultural psychology, they primarily focus on the impact of the external colonization of the mind. By contrast, as a radical cultural psychologist, Periyar challenged the internal colonization of minds by hegemonic cultural beliefs and practices about gender and caste.

Periyar dedicated his life to decolonizing the mind from the clutches of casteism and patriarchy and blind devotion to religion, nation, language, and culture. He questioned privileging practices in the name of culture, religion, or national identity if they reify one's capacity to freely pursue life goals to build an egalitarian society.

Reification, or the process of treating an abstraction or concept as though it were a real object or material thing, can be personal, social, or ecological. *Personal reification* refers to our tendency to fossilize our perceptions of who we are, which restricts our formerly expansive, fluid, creative, and playful notion of self. For example, we hesitate to explore our potential because we have constructed a restricted sense of who we are based on the prescriptive norms of a society like India, where caste plays a critical role in defining our social position.

Social reification is the hardened sense of social realities nurtured by essentialist thinking about caste, gender, social class, sexuality, and religion. Social reification ossifies our perceptions of life around us, curtailing our capacity to be open, curious, and trusting—the essential ingredients for social connections. A reified representation of 'others' structures how we interact, judge, and connect with them. Social reification closes our minds and limits our ability to recognize the humanity in others and trust them. It depletes our capacity to develop a meaningful, nuanced, and contextual understanding of and connection with our fellow human beings, perpetuating inequalities. It also becomes a barrier to building a diverse, equal, and inclusive society.

Ecological reification refers to our restricted, fixed, and essentialist view of nature, which legitimizes the exploitation of natural resources.

Periyar challenged people to overcome their personal and social reification. He questioned cultural traditions, especially Brahminical and *varna*-based prescriptions of caste and gender. For Periyar, any exclusionary cultural practices and superstitions degraded the humanity of historically marginalized caste groups and women. According to Manoharan (2022), Periyar's *political atheism* used rationality to appropriate the moral sensibilities and capacity to question the hegemony of culture, religion, language, and patriarchy. Periyar's radical cultural psychological perspective directly appealed to the common sense of ordinary people, helping them find ways to transcend their personal and social reification by providing them the interpretive, rational, and rhetorical tools to re-examine their assumptions about caste, gender, religion, culture, and nationalism. Foregrounding dignity as an ethical yardstick, Periyar provided a tapestry of analytical and innovative tools to let people create their own liberation notes, empowering them to overcome their alienation. In the following section, I provide four examples of ordinary people whose lives were transformed by Periyar.

Four Liberation Notes

My choice of these four narratives is dictated by the fact that their subjects came from very different social locations and had varying degrees of personal contact with Periyar. T. P. Rajalakshmi Ammal (TPR) was an iconic actress, a Brahmin, who maintained a lifelong fraternal relationship with Periyar. Ranganathan did not finish high school and worked all his life as an assistant to a cook in a small town. Arangarasan was in the seventh grade when he attended a talk and left home to follow Periyar's ideals. Olichengo (Pillai, 2016) was a small farmer who worked for Periyar briefly, leading to a lifelong commitment to his ideals.

Liberation Note 1

TPR was a popular star of the Tamil film industry, whose career started with silent films. She appeared in *Kalidas*, the first Tamil talkie (1931). Born in 1911 to a Brahmin family, she got married at eleven. The marriage did not last because her family could not afford to pay the dowry, and she was sent back to her natal home. TPR decided to become an actress despite her family's opposition. Soon, she married a fellow artist and adopted a baby girl to save it from the possibility of female infanticide. A woman with reformist views and active in fighting for women's causes, TPR admired Periyar's progressive ideas and was inspired by his commitment to empowering women. TPR faced discrimination because of her social class and gender.

Once, Periyar spoke at a public meeting near TPR's home. In his speech, Periyar attacked Brahminism and casteism as the root cause of the oppression of marginalized caste groups and women. He called for abolishing child marriage, dowry, and sati, and emphasized the importance of the remarriage of widows, especially Brahmin widows who were mistreated and shunned by their own families. After this speech, when Periyar was about to leave, he remembered that TPR lived nearby. He liked the coffee in her house. So he asked his driver to drive to her home. TPR received him warmly, and Periyar, as usual, asked for coffee. When Periyar was enjoying his coffee, TPR told him she had listened to his speech that day and said, 'Innaiku soodu konjam kudathan' (Today, it [the critique of Brahminism] was hotter than usual). Periyar smiled and appreciated her comments and coffee.

TPR maintained a cordial relationship with Periyar, and his radical views, especially those about women's empowerment, resonated with her deeply. TPR's daughter, Kamala, recalls her mother and Periyar's regard for each other in the following terms.

> Remembering Periyar on this day: Fond memories of Periyar Ayya are with us. Periyar Ayya greatly loved and respected my mother, Cinema Rani TPR. I still recall the times when Periyar Ayya used to come to my home to visit and spend time with my mother. He addressed my mother as 'thangachi' [younger sister]. He loved the coffee prepared in our house and used to ask for coffee whenever he visited. My mother has sung several songs and performed stage plays honouring Periyar Ayya. Even today, thinking about these fond memories brings immense happiness. May Periyar Ayya's legacy live forever. (Kamala, daughter of 'Cinema Rani' T. P. Rajalakshmi)

TPR's daughter's quote attests to TPR's admiration for Periyar and her commitment to performing songs in deep appreciation of his work. TPR maintained a kinship with Periyar until she died in 1964, reaffirming her dedication to social justice and women's empowerment.

Liberation Note 2

Ranganathan hailed from a low-income family and did not finish his schooling. He worked as an assistant cook during the wedding season and other village festivals. His distant relative, Muniammal, who had been disabled due to polio, finished high school and got married in an arranged marriage. After she gave birth to a baby boy, Muniammal's husband divorced her and got sole custody of their son. Muniammal returned home bearing the stigma of her disability and divorcee status, a significant source of stress and social exclusion in the 1950s.

Ranganathan was independent and led a carefree life, supporting himself through various jobs in the village. He was neither affiliated with any political party nor active in any reform movement. He knew Muniammal from childhood because they had grown up in the same village. Aware that Muniammal was studious, he decided to marry her and help her pursue her studies and become independent. It was a simple wedding ceremony. He encouraged her to continue her studies to get the certification to teach elementary and middle school children (a one-year programme in those days).

Since it was customary at the time to admit only single women, not young mothers, to teacher training programmes, Ranganathan and Muniammal decided not to start a family until she completed her education. Muniammal completed her teacher certification and found a job in a government school in Vettavalam. The couple raised three sons, and Ranganathan maintained a cordial relationship with his wife's son from her previous marriage, who was treated as part of the family. All three of their sons went on to study up to college, and one settled in the United States and is active in social justice initiatives in diasporic communities.

Ranganathan and Muniammal are in their eighties now. Ranganathan's son, who lives in the United States, interviewed his father about his motive for marrying his mother.[1] Ranganathan told him he had attended one of Periyar's meetings, where the latter had talked about women's oppression and the need to educate them. Periyar had also talked about widow remarriage. The speech made a deep impression and inspired his decision to marry Muniammal.

What is impressive about Ranganathan's story is that he had never met Periyar in person or read his books. Periyar spoke in colloquial language, appealing to the common sense of people from various walks of life. Ranganathan was neither an ideologue nor a Periyarist; nevertheless, Periyar's speech was instrumental in his making a life-changing decision. Ranganathan's story illustrates the power of Periyar's persuasion in overcoming personal and social reification by encouraging people to explore new possibilities. Ranganathan wrote his liberation note, dramatically altering his life's course. His son, who is active in socially conscious initiatives, is an attestation to the enduring legacy of Periyar's ideals in diasporic communities in the United States.[2]

Liberation Note 3

Arangarasan grew up in a devout family and was a militant follower of the Samarasa Suddha Sanmarga Sathiya Sangam, a movement started by the nineteenth-century saint-poet Ramalingam (also known as Vallalar) to promote communal harmony and non-violence.[3] Arangarasan lived in Manachanallur, a town near Tiruchirappalli, his family being engaged in agriculture. His father was a strict disciplinarian with little tolerance for youthful transgressions. When Arangarasan was in the seventh grade, he attended one of Periyar's meetings. Periyar's provocative and rational ideas, especially his attack on the theory of karma (that predetermined human destiny), inspired him. Arangarasan felt empowered and questioned traditional beliefs and practices that legitimized the caste hierarchy and the privileged status of Brahmins in society. Through Periyar, unfettered from the constraints of religious practices and beliefs, Arangarasan learned to re-examine his own religious values. Soon after, he destroyed all the pictures of deities in his house as a sign of his growing conviction in Periyar's rationalist ideals and humanism.

Arangarasan's actions earned his father's ire. A devout Saivite, he threw Arangarasan out of the house. Arangarasan left home, went to a wholesale banana dealer, bought a bunch of bananas, and hawked them on the street. Soon, he began to support himself and became a successful businessman, thanks to his entrepreneurial acumen. He also joined Periyar's Dravidar Kazhagam (DK) and held various positions in its local chapter. In 1957, Arangarasan was sentenced to two years of rigorous imprisonment for participating in a protest in response to Periyar's call to burn the Constitution of India. While in prison, he befriended a fellow activist, Ganapathi, from Pettaivathalai in Trichy district. Later, he married Ganapathi's sister. His father boycotted the wedding because the bride was from a different caste. The marriage was a 'self-respect' marriage conducted without any priest or religious ceremony.

Periyar's speech made a strong impression on a teenager and turned him into a lifelong Periyarist committed to anti-caste struggles and women's liberation. A self-taught man, Arangarasan read voraciously and built a library of Dravidian literature for local people. He was active in the field and led many agitations. Arangarasan's life is an example of how influential Periyar was in shaping the minds of young people.

Periyar's influence on Arangarasan continued in the next generation. All his children married into different caste groups. For example, his daughter Arivumathi, a civil engineer, married Gowthaman, a fellow Periyarist, in a 'self-respect' ceremony. Arangarasan hailed from a reasonably affluent family and could have had a good education and led a comfortable life. Periyar's ideals inspired and liberated him from the clutches of traditions and superstitious practices. His newfound appreciation of rationality and science and respect for the dignity of self and others transformed his life and the lives of his children. Arangarasan's liberation note illustrates his active participation in and commitment to creating an egalitarian and inclusive society where people are not judged based on caste or gender.

Liberation Note 4

Olichengo hails from a village in Tiruvarur district, Tamil Nadu. Swarnavel Pillai interviewed him as part of a documentary series on the influence of Periyar on ordinary people (Pillai, 2016). I examined Olichengo's narrative to analyse how and why Periyar inspired him. In the interview, Olichengo talks about his humble beginnings. His father was an agricultural labourer, working under landowners who controlled workers with brute force. The feudal setup did not allow workers to wear their dhotis below their ankles, nor could they put on any footwear. Any transgression or resistance by the worker was met with a severe beating and the forced ingestion of cow dung. Periyar started the Dravidian Farmers' Association (DFA) to improve the working conditions of agricultural workers who were Dalits or belonged to the most backward caste groups (also see Gowthaman, 2018). Olichengo benefitted from the critical empowering work of the DFA.

Olichengo's family worked as labourers on the farms of powerful landlords. After the ninth grade, Olichengo could not continue his schooling as his family could not afford the tuition fees. He had to drop out of school, but he still wanted to complete the training to become a Tamil teacher. He wrote the entrance examination for the course but did not qualify.

Olichengo continued to educate himself and found a job as a reporter for *Malai Mursau*, an evening newspaper. While working as a reporter, Olichengo attended a public meeting addressed by Periyar. Listening to his speech was a turning point in Olichengo's life. He was impressed by many of Periyar's rationalist thoughts, especially his call for annihilating masculinity (*azhiyatum aaanmai*; Ramasamy, 1942). He became a follower of Periyar, worked as a reporter for the latter's newspapers, and wrote regularly in *Viduthalai*.

Periyar had a profound impact on his life. Even in his seventies, Olichengo recalls his interactions with Periyar with awe and admiration and talks about the significance of Periyar's influence on multiple levels of society. He points out the pragmatics of Periyar's ability to get resources from landlords to empower workers further. Whenever there was a dispute or standoff with farm workers, even landowners approached Periyar to mediate and find an acceptable solution for both parties. In one such instance, a landlord from a village in Thanjavur reached out to Periyar to resolve a longstanding conflict. Periyar agreed to mediate on the condition that the landlord make arrangements for a week-long rationalist workshop for thirty participants, including space, food, and other expenses. Olichengo stayed with him the entire week as his personal assistant for the workshop.

Using the resources provided by the landlord, Periyar taught workers about rationalist thinking, particularly anti-casteism, women's empowerment, religious superstitions, and dignity. Olichengo thus had firsthand experience of Periyar's working style. Periyar woke up at 4 a.m. and started taking notes for the workshop. By the time Olichengo was up, Periyar had already written many pages of notes for the day. Periyar was in his late eighties then and would enthusiastically greet Olichengo every morning.

Olichengo was very actively involved in the Dravidian movement. He organized public meetings where Periyar would address a few thousand people. The following day, Olichengo would conduct discussions on the ideas Periyar had proposed. When asked how people reacted to Periyar's speeches, Olichengo said there was heterogeneity in people's response to his ideas. Since Periyar's thoughts were radical and transformative, Olichengo observed that what people retained depended on their *mental sieve*.

Olichengo's life was profoundly transformed by his association with Periyar. Despite being a farmer in his village, he made regular trips to Tiruchirappalli to meet Periyar, who always greeted him with enthusiasm. Periyar's commitment to making his works accessible to ordinary people was evident in his first question to Olichengo: 'What are the books you are reading now?' He was genuinely interested in what Olichengo had learned from these books. Olichengo greatly admired Periyar's curiosity about learning new things from people. After each public meeting, people lined up to meet Periyar, who charged a few rupees to name a baby or sign an autograph—money that was deposited in the party funds. Books would be sold at all his public meetings; and at the end of the meeting, Periyar would always enquire about the sales. On one occasion, when Olichengo said that 400 rupees worth of books had been sold, Periyar was rather pleased. Periyar's impact on Olichengo was profound, transformative, and enduring. Olichengo's marriage was a 'self-respect' marriage. All his children were given Tamil or Buddhist names, and their marriages too were inter-caste and 'self-respect' marriages. Olichengo felt very content with his life and fortunate that he had met and worked with Periyar.

Periyar, Dignity, and Liberation

These four vignettes illustrate the complex and heterogeneous ways Periyar touched people's lives. TPR experienced discrimination and mistreatment in her Brahmin community, propelling her lifelong commitment to social reform and women's empowerment. Periyar's rationalism and dedication to empowering weaker sections of society worked synergistically with her commitment to improving the status of women. Periyar's affection for her was fraternal, and his ideas shaped her liberation notes to challenge Hindu religious prescriptions that restricted women's agency. TPR overcame her personal and social reification by challenging the nexus between caste and patriarchal control of women and the role of Brahminism in subjugating women and non-Brahmins.

Ranganathan's encounter with Periyar was accidental. However, he was moved by Periyar's ideas and decided to marry a woman who was disabled and also a divorcee. Arangarasan left home and charted a new course in life after listening to Periyar's call for a fair and just society, recognizing the dignity of fellow human beings. His active involvement in the DK and lifelong commitment to Periyar's principles are a testament to his courage and dedication. He followed Periyar's ideals in his marriage and was able to pass on his values to all his children. Olichengo, a farmer, was inspired by Periyar's rationalist movement. Like Arangarasan, he was self-taught and worked as a reporter for *Viduthalai*. He followed Periyar's ideals in raising his children and transmitted Periyar's commitment to social justice to the next generation.

Periyar and Mindful Leadership

Periyar's leadership appeal was not confined to any particular social group; it resonated with people from diverse backgrounds. The four cases discussed here illustrate his inspiring leadership qualities, especially the unique aspects of Periyar that shaped the minds of people from different social locations. Drawing from an interdisciplinary perspective, I view Periyar as a mindful leader and argue that his holistic approach to leadership was compassionate, courageous, and contextual.

I define dignity as an *embodied praxis* (Mahalingam, 2019), a constellation of processes by which we embody, recognize, intervene in, preserve, and cherish the very core of what makes us human. When such processes are trampled and systemically violated in the name of religion, tradition, or culture, they trigger and naturalize dehumanization. Finding the moral courage to preserve dignity around us with an audacious commitment to recalibrating our moral compass is challenging. Periyar took on this responsibility because no one was stepping forward. He articulated the motivation behind his work with much humility:

> I, E. V. Ramasamy, am committed to reforming Dravidian society with self-respect and dignity like other societies in the world, which has been my intention for being in public service. Since no one has come forward to take up this task, I have undertaken it irrespective of whether I am qualified for it or not. Since my ideology and plans are based on rationality, and I do not have any other materialist concerns or attachments, I consider myself qualified to undertake this service. (Ramasamy, 2017a)

Periyar used a variety of rhetorical strategies and interpretive frameworks to examine the supernatural elements of folklore, religious myths, the Puranas, and literature. Cognitive psychologists have argued that paradoxes play a significant role in fostering conceptual change (Carey, 1985).

Through his public speeches and writings, Periyar effectively used the paradoxes in cultural narratives to decolonize people's minds. As an iconoclast, he questioned the taken-for-granted assumptions about dominant cultural narratives, providing tools to reinterpret the texts critically. Such reinterpretation brought to light new insights into the ideological underpinnings of the subtexts of these narratives that valorize and naturalize caste and gender hierarchies. Periyar's provocative interpretation of the Ramayana is a case in point (Richman and Geetha, 2007). Specifically, he drew attention to the contradictions and paradoxes in popular narratives with wit and common-sense-layered wisdom. For example, one of the most popular Puranic stories is that of Kuchela, a childhood friend of Lord Krishna. Kuchela had twenty-seven children and was poor. His wife persuaded him to visit Krishna and seek his help. Finally, he became rich due to Krishna's benevolent grace. While talking about the story, Periyar pointed out that since Kuchela had twenty-seven children, the oldest son must be at least twenty-seven years old and a few younger ones in their early twenties. Periyar posed the question of why the grown-up sons were doing nothing for the family. While the number of children is a plot device often used to highlight the poverty of Kuchela, which has been the most common understanding, Periyar used it to highlight the logical flaw in the narrative to push home his argument.

Like his reading of Kuchela's story, Periyar critically examined traditional Hindu Brahminical wedding rituals that gave an exalted status to Brahmin priests. As an alternative, Periyar created a secular Tamil marriage ceremony. The 'self-respect' marriage was conducted without a *thaali*, a priest, or Sanskrit mantras. Speeches from members of the DK often marked the wedding. The 'self-respect' marriage subverted traditional Hindu weddings that reaffirmed the privileged and sanctified status of Brahmins and Sanskrit rituals.

One of Periyar's staunch followers, Kuthoosi Gurusamy, wanted to marry Kunjitham, who belonged to the Isai Vellalar caste. Gurusamy came from the Mudaliar caste, a dominant caste group. His parents disapproved of the marriage and did not attend the wedding. Periyar was so happy for the couple that he decided to step in and organize the wedding. Being a Periyarist, Gurusamy wanted a 'self-respect' marriage without a *thaali*. Periyar told Gurusamy that he should tie the *thaali* because Kunjitham came from a caste group that historically denied women the right to have a *thaali* because young girls from her community were dedicated to temples as *devadasi*s. For Periyar, a 'self-respect' marriage did not include a *thaali* for women from all other caste groups because it was a sign of subjugation of women, signalling to the world that she was a married woman and belonged to her husband. However, for women from the Isai Vellalar caste, tying a *thaali* could be empowering (Sundaravadivelu, 2010). Prodding Gurusamy to tie the *thaali* reveals his contextual, compassionate, and nuanced understanding of the oppression of women at various intersections.

In his obituary for Nagammai, his first wife, Periyar paid a moving tribute to her and wrote of his inability to live up to his own gender standards.

> I strongly advocate for the liberty and freedom of women. However, I cannot say that I have applied even one per cent of that advocacy in the case of my beloved Nagammal. Nagammal was ten times more compliant in abiding with the harshness and cruelty of the dictates of the Puranas and Shastras that speak of the enslavement of women and the domination of men. I am ashamed to say that I accepted and approved this submissiveness of hers. (Ramasamy, 2017b)

The obituary reflects his awareness of his male privileges and acknowledgement of his shortcomings as a husband.

Periyar could stand by an idea, even if it led to uncomfortable and vexing realizations. He showed courage and prescience in speaking about the limitations of caste-based associations in empowering marginalized caste groups. As the keynote speaker at various caste-association conferences, Periyar had the courage to say that reasserting caste pride by claiming to become a Kshatriya would only reinforce, not annihilate, the caste system. This was a recurring theme in all his addresses at such conferences (Subgunarajan, 2018).

Periyar's public speeches were provocative, challenging his audience's unexamined assumptions and beliefs. However, he always concluded with a humble plea: 'Please do not believe whatever I have said. Please use your rational mind to take what is right.' As mentioned, in his interview, Olichengo recalled that the first question Periyar used to ask him was about the books he had been reading and was curious to learn more about them. Periyar was open to learning from anyone, irrespective of age or social standing.

Wonder is a transformative passion because it makes us notice the extraordinary in ordinary things (Mahalingam, 2019). While artists cultivate wonder to gain a new perspective, Periyar, as a social reformer, wondered about the normalization of inequalities and dehumanization of human beings because of their gender, caste, or religion. For example, in the early twentieth century, men openly had several mistresses. Periyar argued that this was unfair to women and that if men could be polygamous, so should women. He averred that women were not childbearing machines and strongly advocated for birth control pills. He encouraged women to follow their dreams through gaining an education and lead independent lives. Periyar wondered why caste- and gender-based discrimination existed and proposed a rational approach to annihilate patriarchy and casteism to preserve the dignity of women and members of marginalized communities.

Periyar was intellectually generous in empowering people to find the courage to pursue their liberation notes. His material generosity for social causes was also legendary. For instance, he donated liberally towards building a hospital wing for children as well as money and land to build a college, both in Tiruchirappalli. When Anna (C. N. Annadurai) was leaving for cancer treatment in America in 1968, Periyar carried 25,000 rupees to the airport to help with his medical expenses, which Anna graciously refused while expressing his gratitude (Samas, 2019). Periyar was also magnanimous in his personal interactions with many people with whom he had severe political disagreements. For instance, he had a cordial relationship with Kundrakudi Adigalar, the leader of a Saiva *mutt*, who believed in the power of spirituality in fostering social change. Periyar always addressed him as Mahasanithanam (the great revered one) just like his followers. Periyar's personal friendship with Rajaji, one of his staunch political rivals, has been well documented. In his obituary for Rajaji, Periyar was generous in his praise. He observed that Rajaji ate and sat with everyone equally, whether in his house or outside, irritating many orthodox Brahmins. When Godse, a Chitpavan Brahmin, assassinated Gandhi, there was a backlash and violence against Brahmins across the country. Periyar, a staunch critic of Brahminism, magnanimously agreed to speak on the All India Radio, pleading with people to stop the violence against Brahmins. His speech prevented imminent violence against Brahmins in Tamil Nadu.

I characterize Periyar as a mindful leader using my mindful mindset and dignity perspective. This framework consists of seven features: (*a*) compassion, (*b*) sympathetic joy, (*c*) negative capability, (*d*) situated intersectional awareness, (*e*) cultural humility, (*f*) wonder, and (*g*) generosity. Periyar's holistic approach to leadership inspired his followers. He deeply cared about the marginalization and sufferings of women, Dalits, and other oppressed caste groups whose lives were constrained by dominant Hindu religious prescriptions and practices. He tirelessly fought against the subjugation of women through superstitious cultural practices. Despite his earlier political differences with Anna and Karunanidhi, Periyar rejoiced at their success as also at the personal development of followers like Olichengo. Privilege awareness was his lifetime mission, and he significantly raised consciousness of gender and caste privilege. With negative capability, he honestly reflected on his shortcomings (for instance, in his tribute to Nagammai) and the pitfalls and limitations of caste-based identitarian politics in eradicating caste. Wonder was his transformative passion for critically engaging with normalization of social hierarchies based on gender, caste, and religion. I argue that these qualities endeared Periyar to people from various social locations.

Periyar, Dignity, and Liberation Notes: Contemporary Challenges

We are living in a hyperconnected and yet hyperpolarized world. Periyar worked tirelessly to decolonize our minds of intracultural hegemonies. In contrast, the postcolonial approaches to decolonizing our minds focus on the hegemony of the West. Periyar's motivation to decolonize our minds was to help us overcome our personal and social reification. In the process, we can expand the realms of our possible selves while preserving our dignity. Periyar's critical focus on intracultural hegemonies remains relevant even today. Shivasundar (2022) observes that in Karnataka, in the name of decolonization, Brahminization is legitimized in the education system, the very danger Periyar warned against in his speeches in caste-association meetings (Subagunarajan, 2018). By foregrounding dignity, we can critically engage with all forms of decolonization, including Brahminization. We need to use Periyar's critical tools of rationality to interrogate with courage any hegemonic knowledge system that limits our freedom and dignity, like the four protagonists of my case studies.

We have to understand dignity as an embodied praxis (Mahalingam, 2019) to intervene to preserve the dignity of ourselves and others. Unfortunately, pride-fuelled caste identity politics often undergirds a darker conception of dignity. For instance, in so-called honour killings (*aanava kolai*), dignity is conceptualized as zero-sum (that is, a belief that the dignity of any marginalized group would be an affront to the dominant person's dignity). Such conceptions become a trope to justify everyday dignity injuries and violence perpetuated by dominant caste groups (for example, the murders of Dalit men for marrying or falling in love with women from other caste groups). A zero-sum misconception of dignity is pervasive in right-wing authoritarian identity movements, such as White supremacy, resulting in perpetuating and valorizing violence and dignity injuries against marginalized communities.

We have to adopt Periyar's conception of dignity as fundamental to recognizing the humanity of our fellow human beings by overcoming our social reification and embracing the radical interdependence advocated by Ambedkar (Mahalingam and Selvaraj, 2022). Often, caste-identity-based organizations valorize their caste identity by claiming an idealized past resulting in a situation where we are bewitched and struck by its beauty instead of using it to open the doors to recognize the dignity of all by deepening our realization of the interdependent nature of our existence with compassion, humility, and generosity. Periyar always maintained a warm personal relationship with his political rivals while challenging their political ideas. We can draw inspiration from him in maintaining compassionate and generous personal relationships without hatred while critically engaging with those whose political beliefs differ from ours.

Periyar's leadership approach was holistic, tempered by a courageous and compassionate commitment to dignity. He embodied this commitment in his everyday practices. In his daily interpersonal interactions, he addressed all, regardless of age and social status, using a respectful form of Tamil. In public meetings, he referred to his wife Nagammai as *thozhar* (comrade). Such symbolic acts endeared him to his followers and signalled his commitment to dignity. Periyar was a natural-born mindful leader. By cultivating a mindful mindset, we can commit ourselves to preserving the dignity of ourselves and others and a dignity culture in our communities.

Periyar's lifetime work offers a set of tools for writing our own liberation notes and leading a life with compassion toward ourself and others.

> Rationality and dignity are essential for humans at the individual and collective level to justify the claim that humans are a highly evolved species. These two qualities are primarily absent from people's lives because of God, religion, lack of education, and socioeconomic conditions.
> (Gowthaman, 2018, p. 667)

I have provided the contours of Periyar's radical cultural psychology that transformed many people. His radical humanism offers a colourful palette for reflection and action to decolonize our minds. Periyar can inspire us to write our liberation notes to free us of rigid, fossilized, and idealized notions of identity, religion, nationalism, and language. Instead, we should commit to leading a life with a vision for personal, intersubjective, and processual dignity.

Notes

1. T. Ranganathan, personal communication, 2018.
2. T. Ranganathan, personal communication, 2018.
3. G. Arivuchelvi, personal communication, 2022.

References

Anaimuthu, V. (ed.) 1974. *Periyar Ee. Ve. Ra. Chinthanaigal* (Thoughts of Periyar E. V. R), 3 vols. Trichy: Thinker's Forum.

Athiyaman, Pazha. 2020. *Vaikam Porattam* (Vaikam Agitation). Nagercoil: Kalachuvadu.

Bhatia, S. 2018. *Decolonizing Psychology: Globalization, Social Justice, and Indian Youth Identities*. New York: Oxford University Press.

Carey, S. 1985. *Conceptual Change in Childhood*. Cambridge, MA: MIT Press.

Cole, E. R. 2009. 'Intersectionality and Research in Psychology'. *American Psychologist* 64(3): 170–180. doi:10.1037/a0014564

Crenshaw, K. 1989. 'Demarginalizing the Intersection of Race and Sex: A Black Feminist Critique of Antidiscrimination Doctrine, Feminist Theory, and Antiracist Politics'. *University of Chicago Legal Forum*: 139–167.

Geetha, V., and S. V. Rajadurai. 1998. *Towards a Non-Brahmin Millennium: From Iyothee Thass to Periyar*. Calcutta: Samya.

Gowthaman, P. (ed.). 2018. *E. V. Ramasami Engindra Naan* (I, E. V. Ramasamy), vol. 2. Chennai: Bharathi Puthagalayam.

Irschick, E. F. 1969. *Politics and Social Conflict in South India: The Non-Brahmin Movement and Tamil Separatism, 1916–1929*. Berkeley: University of California Press.

Kalaiyarasan, A., and M. Vijayabaskar. 2021. *The Dravidian Model: Interpreting the Political Economy of Tamil Nadu*. New York: Cambridge University Press.

Mahalingam, R. 2007a. 'Beliefs About Chastity, Machismo, and Caste Identity: A Cultural Psychology Perspective'. *Sex Roles* 56(3–4): 239–249.

———. 2007b. 'Essentialism, Power and the Representation of Social Categories: An Integrated Perspective'. *Human Development* 50(6): 300–319.

———. 2019. 'Mindful Mindset, Interconnectedness, and Dignity'. *Global Youth* 1: 230–253.

Mahalingam, R., and P. Selvaraj. 2022. 'Ambedkar, Radical Interdependence and Dignity: A Study of Women Mall Janitors in India'. *Journal of Business Ethics* 177(4): 813–828.

Mahalingam, R., S. Jagannathan, and P. Selvaraj. 2019. 'Decasticization, Dignity, and "Dirty Work" at the Intersections of Caste, Memory, and Disaster'. *Business Ethics Quarterly* 29(2): 213–239.

Mahalingam, R., and V. Rabelo. 2013. 'Theoretical, Methodological, and Ethical Challenges to the Study of Immigrants: Perils and Possibilities'. *New Directions for Child and Adolescent Development* 141: 25–41.

Manoharan, K. R. 2020. 'In the Path of Ambedkar: Periyar and the Dalit Question'. *South Asian History and Culture* 11(2): 136–149.

———. 2022. *Periyar: A Study in Political Atheism*. New Delhi: Orient Blackswan.

Markus, H. R. and S. Kitayama. 2010. 'Cultures and Selves: A Cycle of Mutual Constitution'. *Perspectives on Psychological Science* 5(4): 420–430.

Nisbett, R. E., K. Peng, I. Choi, and A. Norenzayan. 2001. 'Culture and Systems of Thought: Holistic Versus Analytic Cognition'. *Psychological Review* 108(2): 291–310.

Okazaki, S., E. J. R. David, and N. Abelmann. 2008. 'Colonialism and Psychology of Culture'. *Social and Personality Psychology Compass* 2(1): 90–106.

Pandian, M. S. S. 2007. *Brahmin and Non-Brahmin: Genealogies of the Tamil Political Present*. Raniket: Permanent Black.

Pillai, S. E. 2016. *Periyon*. https://www.youtube.com/watch?v=CN0psNrSaJo&t=33s. Accessed 8 May 2025.

Ramasamy, E. V. 2007 [1942]. *Penn Yen Adimaiyanal?* (Why Were Women Enslaved?), translated by Meena Kandasamy. Chennai: Periyar Self-Respect Propaganda Institute.

———. 2017a. *Periyar Indrum Endrum* (Periyar Then and Now). Coimbatore: Vidiyal.

———. 2017b. *Naan Sonnal Unakku Yen Kobam Vara Vendum?* (When I Point Out Why Do You Get Upset?), edited by P. Gowthaman. Chennai: New Century Book House.

Richman, P., and V. Geetha. 2007. 'A View From the South: Ramasami's Public Critique of Religion'. In *The Crisis of Secularism in India*, edited by A. D. Needham and R. Sunder Rajan, pp. 66–88. Durham: Duke University Press.

Samas. 2019. *Maaperum Tamil Kanavu* (The Great Tamil Dream). Chennai: Tamil Thisai.

Shivasundar. 2022. 'Decolonisation or Brahminisation: What's the Thrust behind Karnataka's NEP Position Papers?' *The Wire*, 14 July. https://thewire.in/politics/decolonisation-brahminisationkarnataka-nep-position-papers. Accessed 8 May 2025.

Shweder, R. A. and M. A. Sullivan. 1993. 'Cultural Psychology: Who Needs It?' *Annual Review of Psychology* 44(1): 497–523.

Subagunarajan, V. M. S. (ed.). 2018. *Namakku En Intha Izhinilai?* (Why Is Our Life So Degraded?). Collection of Periyar's Keynote Addresses in Caste Association Conferences. Chennai: Kayal Kavin.

Sundaravadivelu, N. T. 2010. *Ninaivalaigal* (Waves of Memory). Chennai: Tamil Kudiarau Publishers.

Thiong'o, N. W. 1983. *Decolonizing the Mind: The Politics of Language in African Literature.* Oxford: James Currey.

Venkatachalapathy, A. R. 2019. 'Periyar E. V. Ramasamy.' In *The Oxford Research Encyclopedia of Asian History*, edited by David Ludden. New York: Oxford University Press. 10.1093/acrefore/9780190277727.013.340.

For Further Reading

Aloysius, G. 2019. *Periyar and Modernity*. New Delhi: Critical Quest.
Anandhi, S. 1991. 'Women's Question in the Dravidian Movement c. 1925–1948'. *Social Scientist* 19(5–6): 24–41.
Arni, Abhimanyu. 2024. 'Taking Periyarism Seriously: The Dravidian Identity as a Universality'. *Global Intellectual History* (August): 1–22. DOI: 10.1080/23801883.2024.2386600.
Arooran, K. Nambi. 1980. *Tamil Renaissance and Dravidian Nationalism, 1905–1944*. Madurai: Koodal.
Barnett, Marguerite Ross. 1976. *The Politics of Cultural Nationalism in South India*. Princeton: Princeton University Press.
Bate, Bernard. 2009. *Tamil Oratory and the Dravidian Aesthetic*. New York: Columbia University Press.
Chatterjee, Debi. 2022. 'Periyar E.V. Ramasamy'. In *Revisiting Modern Indian Thought: Themes and Perspectives*, edited by Suratha Kumar Malik and Ankit Tomar, pp. 96–109. Oxon and New York: Routledge.
Diehl, Anita. 1978. *Periyar E. V. Ramaswami: A Study of the Influence of a Personality in Contemporary South India*. New Delhi: B. I. Publications.
Eswaran, Swarnavel. 2017. 'Periyar as a Biopic: Star Persona, Historical Events, and Politics'. *Biography* 40(1): 93–115.
Ganeshwar. 2022. 'Periyar's Spatial Thought: Region as Non-Brahmin Discursive Space'. *CASTE: A Global Journal on Social Exclusion* 3(1): 89–106. DOI: https://doi.org/10.26812/caste.v3i1.358
Geetha, V. 1998. 'Periyar, Women and an Ethic of Citizenship'. *Economic and Political Weekly* 33(17): WS9–WS15.
Geetha, V. and S. V. Rajadurai. 2008. *Towards a Non-Brahmin Millennium: From Iyothee Thass to Periyar*, 2nd edn. Kolkata: Samya.
Hardgrave, Robert L. 1965. 'The DMK and the Politics of Tamil Nationalism'. *Pacific Affairs* 37(4): 396–411.
———. 1965. *The Dravidian Movement*. Bombay: Popular Prakashan.

Hodges, Sarah. 2005. 'Revolutionary Family Life and the Self Respect Movement in Tamil South India, 1926–49'. *Contributions to Indian Sociology* 39(2): 251–277.

Irschick, Eugene F. 1969. *Politics and Social Conflict in South India: The Non-Brahmin Movement and Tamil Separatism, 1916–1929.* Bombay: Oxford University Press.

Krishnan, Rajan Kurai, and Ravindran Sriramachandran (eds.). 2018. *Seminar* 708 (special Issue on Dravidianism). https://www.india-seminar.com/2018/708.htm. Accessed 1 January 2024.

Manoharan, Karthick Ram. 2016. '"Anti-Casteist Casteism?" A Fanonist Critique of Ramasamy's Discourse on Caste'. *Interventions: International Journal of Postcolonial Studies* 19(1): 73–90.

———. 2020. 'An Ethic Beyond Anti-Colonialism: A Periyarist Engagement with Fanonism'. In *Rethinking Social Justice*, edited by S. Anandhi, Karthick Ram Manoharan, M. Vijayabaskar, and A. Kalaiyarasan, pp. 159–178. Hyderabad: Orient BlackSwan.

———. 2020. 'Freedom from God: Periyar and Religion'. *Religions* 11(1). DOI: https://doi.org/10.3390/rel11010010

———. 2020. 'In the Path of Ambedkar: Periyar and the Dalit Question'. *South Asian History and Culture* 11(2): 136–149.

———. 2022. *Periyar: A Study in Political Atheism.* Hyderabad: Orient BlackSwan.

———. 2022. 'Sudras and the Nation: Periyarist Explorations'. *Economic and Political Weekly* 57(44–45). https://www.epw.in/engage/article/sudras-and-nation-periyarist-explorations. Accessed 1 January 2024.

Pandian, M. S. S. 1993. '"Denationalising" the Past: "Nation" in E. V. Ramasamy's Political Discourse'. *Economic and Political Weekly* 28(42): 2282–2287.

———. 2007. *Brahmin and Non-Brahmin: Genealogies of the Tamil Political Present.* Ranikhet: Permanent Black.

———. 2009. 'Nation Impossible'. *Economic and Political Weekly* 44(10): 65–69.

Ram, Mohan. 1974. 'Ramaswami Naicker and the Dravidian Movement'. *Economic and Political Weekly* 9(6–8): 217, 219, 221–224.

Richman, Paula. 1991. 'E. V. Ramasami's Reading of the Ramayana'. In *Many Ramayanas: The Diversity of a Narrative Tradition in South Asia*, edited by Paula Richman, pp. 175–195. Berkeley and Los Angeles: University of California Press.

———. 1995. 'Epic and State: Contesting Interpretations of the Ramayana'. *Public Culture* 7(3): 631–654.

Saraswathi, S. 1994. *Towards Self Respect: Periyar on a New World.* Madras: Institute of South Indian Studies.

Sivathamby, Karthigesu. 2006. *Understanding Dravidian Movement: Problems and Perspectives*, 2nd ed. Chennai: New Century Book House.

Subramanian, Narendra. 1999. *Ethnicity and Populist Mobilization: Political Parties, Citizens and Democracy in South India.* New Delhi: Oxford University Press.

Venkatachalapathy, A. R. 1995. 'Dravidian Movement and Salvites, 1927–1944'. *Economic and Political Weekly* 30(14) (8 April): 761–768.

———. 2017. 'From Erode to Volga: Periyar EVR's Soviet and European Tour, 1932'. In *India and the World in the First Half of the Twentieth Century*, edited by Madhavan K. Palat, pp. 102–133. London and New York: Routledge.

———. 2019. 'Periyar E. V. Ramasamy'. In *Oxford Research Encyclopaedia of Asian History*. https://oxfordre.com/asianhistory/view/10.1093/acrefore/9780190277727.001.0001/acrefore-9780190277727-e-340. Accessed 1 January 2024.

———. 2021. 'Against the Hustings: Periyar, Elections, and Democracy'. In *Crisis of Liberal Deliberation: Facets of Indian Democracy*, edited by Manas Ray, pp. 64–79. Delhi: Primus Books.

Visswanathan, E. Sa. 1983. *The Political Career of E. V. Ramasamy Naicker: A Study in the Politics of Tamil Nadu, 1920–1949*. Madras: Ravi & Vasanth.

About the Contributors

Darinee Alagirisamy is a historian of modern South Asia and the Indian diaspora in Southeast Asia. She is Senior Lecturer and Deputy Head of Department in the South Asian Studies Programme at the National University of Singapore. She earned her PhD in History and MPhil in Modern South Asian Studies from the University of Cambridge. Her research examines state–society interactions in the late colonial and postcolonial periods. She has published her research on the Dravidian movement's transnational circulation and alcohol prohibition in the British empire in the *Modern Asian Studies* and the *Indian Economic and Social History Review*. Her first monograph, 'Sober State: Origins of Alcohol Prohibition in India', is currently in press.

Pazha. Athiyaman is an independent research scholar and Tamil writer based in Chennai. A PhD from the University of Madras in modern Tamil literature, he has been working on the social, cultural, and literary history of colonial Tamil Nadu for nearly forty years. He has written and edited more than fifteen books in Tamil, which include biographies of George Joseph, P. Varadarajulu Naidu, Va. Raa., Thi. Ja. Ranganathan, and Vai. Govindan. He has completed 'a Dravidian trilogy' that includes monographs on P. Varadarajulu Naidu, the Cheranmadevi Gurukulam controversy, and the Vaikom Satyagraha. He is currently engaged in publishing the collected works of Gu. Azhagirisamy. The Government of Tamil Nadu announced in the state legislature that his book on Vaikom will be published in English and in all south Indian languages. He retired from the All India Radio in 2021.

Matthew H. Baxter is Regional Programs Manager for Asia at the Maxwell School of Citizenship and Public Affairs at Syracuse University; Assistant Professor by courtesy appointment in the Political Science Department at Syracuse University; and Associate Researcher in Tamil Studies at the Institut Français de Pondichéry (French Institute of Pondicherry). He earned his PhD from the University of California, Berkeley, in 2013. He previously served on Ashoka University's faculty, held postdoctoral positions at Harvard University's Mahindra Humanities Center and Rutgers University's Center for Cultural Analysis, was a visiting scholar at Cornell University's South Asia Program, and was Associate Editor for South Asia at *Asian Survey*. His scholarship has been generously supported by the Fulbright-Hays Program, the American Institute of Indian Studies, and the Oberlin Shansi Memorial Association. He is interested in questions of comparative political theory with a particular focus on Tamil-speaking south India, non-Brahmin politics, and the worldwide travel of critical imaginaries.

Swarnavel Eswaran is Professor in the Department of English and the School of Journalism at Michigan State University, where he teaches film history, theory, and production. He graduated from the Film and Television Institute of India, Pune, and the University of Iowa. His documentaries include *Nagapattinam: Waves from the Deep* (2018), *Hmong Memories at the Crossroads* (2016), *Migrations of Islam* (2014), and *Unfinished Journey: A City in Transition* (2012). His research focuses on Tamil and Indian cinema's history, aesthetics, politics, contemporary digital cinema, and concomitant changes. His essays have appeared in *Screen* (2017), *Jump Cut* (2022, 2019), *South Asian Popular Culture* (2012) and *Caste: A Global Journal on Social Exclusion* (2022). His books include *Tamil Cinema Reviews: 1931–1960* (2020) and *Madras Studios: Narrative, Genre, and Ideology in Tamil Cinema* (2015). His fiction feature *Kattumaram* (2019) has been screened in over fifty international film festivals, including Frameline, InsideOut, and Kashish.

Sundar Kaali researches and writes on diverse fields in cultural studies, including literature, film, theatre, myth, ritual, and cultural history. He has written and published in both Tamil and English for more than thirty years. He has served as faculty in the American College, Madurai; Madurai Kamraj University; University of Wisconsin; University of Chicago; and the Gandhigram Rural Institute, Gandhigram.

K. R. Vignesh Karthik is a postdoctoral research fellow in Indian and Indonesian politics at the Royal Netherlands Institute of Southeast Asian and Caribbean Studies, Leiden (KITLV), and a research affiliate at King's College London (KCL). He earned his MA and his PhD in Politics and Public Policy from KCL. He has over five years of experience in legislative research and political consulting. He has advised the Indian National Congress on provincial elections and legislative matters (2015–2018) and contributed to the 2019 general election manifesto. He also devised electoral strategies for two parties (the Dravida Munnetra Kazhagam and the All India Trinamool Congress) in the 2021 elections and drafted development blueprints, resulting in the implementation of income support schemes. He co-leads the 'Social Media Networks and (Dis)information' research group, coordinates the 'Confronting Caste' seminar and podcast series at KCL, and is a postdoctoral affiliate at the Center for Information, Technology, and Public Life (CITAP), University of North Carolina at Chapel Hill. He is the author of *The Dravidian Pathway: The Dravida Munnetra Kazhagam (DMK) and the Politics of Transition in South India* (2025).

Ramaswami Mahalingam is a cultural psychologist, award-winning researcher, teacher, mentor, artist, filmmaker (www.mindfuldignity.com), and a Barger Leadership Institute professor at the University of Michigan, Ann Arbor. He has developed a pioneering social justice-focused mindfulness framework, 'mindful mindset', which places a strong emphasis on dignity. His leadership and contributions were recently acknowledged with the Harold R. Johnson Diversity Service Award from the University of Michigan. His research, viewed through an intersectional lens, delves into three key themes: essentialist beliefs about social categories (such as caste, gender, race, social class, and sexuality) and discrimination against socially marginalized community members; the psychological impact of dignity injuries experienced by women engineers and janitors on their well-being; and cultivation of mindful mindset and leadership development.

Karthick Ram Manoharan is Assistant Professor of Social Sciences at the National Law School of India University, Bengaluru. He was previously Marie Sklodowska-Curie Actions Individual Fellow at the University of Wolverhampton, working on the research project 'Freedom from Caste: The Political Thought of Periyar E. V. Ramasamy in a Global Context', funded by the European Union's Horizon 2020 research and innovation programme. He is the author of *Periyar: A Study in Political Atheism* (2022) and *Frantz Fanon: Identity and Resistance* (2019) and the co-editor of *Rethinking Social Justice* (2020). He received his PhD from the University of Essex in 2015. He was Bliss Carnochan International Fellow at Stanford University in October 2023. He will be Smuts Visiting Research Fellow at the University of Cambridge from October 2025.

Vilasini Ramani is a translator, publisher, and an independent filmmaker. She received her MA in English literature from Bengaluru City University. She was awarded the 2024 New India Foundation Translation Fellowship towards translating a book of M. Singaravelar. She was the editor and publisher of *Pragnai* from 2014 to 2020. She has translated four books from English to Tamil and has published articles on cinema and culture. She is interested in the representations of gender and caste in Tamil cinema.

A. Thiruneelakandan is Associate Professor of History at the MDT Hindu College, Tirunelveli. After completing graduate studies at the Madurai Kamaraj University, he received his PhD from the Manonmaniam Sundaranar University, Tirunelveli. His research interests are in the social and political history of Tamil Nadu, with special reference to the Dravidian Movement. He is the author of *Needamangalam: Sathiya Kodumaiyum Dravida Iyakkamum* (Needamangalam: Caste Oppression and the Dravidian Movement, 2017) and the joint translator of *A Shudra's Story* by A. N. Sattanathan.

Antony Arul Valan is an independent scholar, translator and editor based in Chennai. He holds a PhD in English from Ashoka University, Sonipat. He works in the field of critical caste studies, with a focus on language and rhetoric in English and Tamil texts. His writing has appeared in the peer-reviewed journal *J-Caste*, the feminist online archive 'The New Historia', and the edited volume *Keywords for India: A Conceptual Lexicon for the 21st Century* (2020). He graduated with a BTech in Agricultural Engineering from Tamil Nadu Agricultural University, Coimbatore, and was a Young India fellow in 2011–2012. Before pursuing academic research, he was an editor for several years at the academic publishing house Orient BlackSwan.

A. R. Venkatachalapathy is Professor at the Madras Institute of Development Studies, Chennai. He has taught at universities in Tirunelveli, Madras, Singapore, and Chicago. Apart from the V. K. R. V. Rao Prize (History, 2007), he has received the Vilakku Pudumaippithan Award (2018) and Iyal Virudhu (2021), both for lifetime contribution to Tamil. He has won the Sahitya Akademi award (Tamil, 2024). Apart from his scholarly writings in English, he has written or edited over thirty books in Tamil. His publications in English include *Swadeshi Steam: V. O. Chidambaram Pillai and the Battle Against the British Maritime Empire* (2023), *The Brief History of a Very Big Book: The Making of the*

Tamil Encyclopaedia (2022), *Tamil Characters: Personalities, Politics, Culture* (2018), *Who Owns That Song? The Battle for Subramania Bharati's Copyright* (2018), *The Province of the Book: Scholars, Scribes, and Scribblers in Colonial Tamilnadu* (2012), and *In Those Days There Was No Coffee: Writings in Cultural History* (2006). Presently he is working on biographies of Periyar and V. O. Chidambaram Pillai.

M. Vijayabaskar is Professor at the Madras Institute of Development Studies. His research centres on political economy of development with a focus on labour and land markets; technological change; and rural–urban linkages, transformations, and their intersections with policymaking. In addition to publishing in numerous scholarly journals and media outlets, he has co-authored the book *The Dravidian Model: Interpreting the Political Economy of Tamil Nadu*, published by the Press (2021), and co-edited monographs including *Rethinking Social Justice* (2020) and *Participolis: Consent and Contention in Neoliberal Urban India* (2012). He has held visiting faculty positions at École des hautesétudesen sciences sociales (School for Advanced Studies in the Social Sciences), Paris; University of Lausanne, Switzerland; SOAS University of London; and Indian Institute of Technology (IIT), Madras. He is on the editorial advisory board of the *Oxford Development Studies*, the *South Asia Multidisciplinary Academic Journal*, and the *Indian Journal of Labour Economics*.

Index

Adi-Dravida Mahajana Sabha, 39
Adi Dravidars, 36, 38, 46, 48, 81, 150, 229
adult franchise, 36, 39–41
*agraharam*s, 82, 104, 138
All-India Anna Dravida Munnetra Kazhagam (AIADMK), 12, 140, 179
All-India Depressed Classes Association, 43, 44
All-Malaya Central Dravida Kazhagam, 153
Ambedkar, B. R., 35, 39–40, 217
   Annihilation of Caste, 9, 136–137, 225
   conversion to Buddhism, 10, 126
   credentials to represent the Depressed Classes, 41
   critical analysis of the caste system, 80
   difference of opinion with Gandhi, 42
   idea of leaving Hinduism, 136
   and the Poona Pact, 35–50 (*see also* Poona Pact)
   position on annihilation of caste, 116
   views on double voting by Depressed Classes, 37
Anaimuthu, V., 4, 93
Anna, Arignar. *See* Annadurai, C. N.
Annadurai, C. N., 4, 9, 73, 82, 89n6, 138, 198, 244
   differences with Periyar, 94, 96–97
   Ilatchiya Varalaru (1947), 96
   first meeting with Periyar, 93
   personality of, 94
   role in the Self-Respect Movement (SRM), 93
   strategy to tweak Dravidian ideology, 96
Annadurai Resolution, 94
anti-Brahmin violence, Periyar's statements on, 139
anti-caste Dravidian politics, 79–80
anti-casteism, 241
anti-caste spiritual leaders, 126
anti-colonial nationalism, 65, 174, 178
anti-Hindi agitations, 7
   of 1937–1939, 89n1, 93–94, 122
   of 1963–1965, 102
   violence and, 102
Arundhathiar, 38. *See also* Depressed Classes/Castes
Aryanism and Anti-Aryanism
   Aryan racial–cultural superiority, 130
   discourse of Aryan invasion, 130
   Dravidian response to, 132
   Periyar's approach to, 130–132
Arya Samaj, 26, 121
atheism, propagation of
   Periyar on, 1, 5–6, 11–12, 103, 106, 113–116, 118, 120, 126n2, 133, 167, 207, 237
Ayyamuthu, C. A., 21, 22, 23
Ayyappan, 'Sahodaran' K., 23

backward castes, 43, 80, 94, 240
Bahishkrita Hitakarini Sabha, 39

Index

Besant, Annie, 226
Bezbozhnik (anti-religious newspaper), 6
Bhagavad Gita, 184
    Periyar on, 136
Bhaktavatsalam, M., 10, 138
bhakti (devotion), 8, 98, 120, 184, 188, 192–193, 204
Bharathidasan, 199, 207, 210
Bharati, Subramania, 98, 182, 190–191
Bharatiya Janata Party (BJP), 12
black humans, Dravidians as, 62
Black militants 139
Blavatsky, Madame, 131
Bradlaugh, Charles, 133
Brahmanical hegemony, preservation of, 188
Brahmanical political theology, 186
Brahmin–Aryan–Sanskrit, idea of, 130
Brahmin–Baniya rule, 101
    of New Delhi, 9
    scale of economic domination, 218
Brahminical Hinduism, 5, 124. *See also* Vedic Hinduism
    Periyar's exposure of caste injustice in, 126
    politics of, 122
    value-system in, 88*n*1
Brahmin identity, 136, 137
Brahminism, 58
    Periyar's struggle against, 82
Brahmin–non-Brahmin divide, 184
Brahmins, 2
    belief in superiority of, 136
    in creation of the caste system, 134
    exploitation through spirituality, 133
    overrepresentation in jobs, 135
    'reverse casteism' towards, 130
Buckingham and Carnatic Mills strike (1921), 225
Buddhism
    Ambedkar's conversion to, 10, 126
    opposition to Brahmin dominance, 132
    and Poona Pact, 45–50
    Periyar's support for, 121
    revivalism in Madras, 133
    social rationality of, 121

Caldwell, Robert, 8
capitalist development, 231
caste
    and productivist ethos, 220–221
    -and-religion-inspired nationalism, 132
    annihilation of
        Ambedkar's notion of, 116
        Periyar's notion of, 137
    -based associations, 244
    -based discrimination, 35, 81, 150
    -based division of labour, 130, 220, 229
    -based political mobilization, 84
    -based violence, normalization of, 80
    consciousness, 141
    destruction of symbols of caste, idea of, 138
    hierarchies, 83, 126, 129, 220, 236
    identities, 126, 129, 245
    injustice of, 114
    and labour solidarity, 225–226
    society
        economic relations in, 217
        labour question in, 222–225
    and women's question, 170
category-rights, Periyar's definition of, 87
centre–state relations, 88*n*1
chastity, concept of, 172
Chengalpet Self-Respect conference (1929), 171
Cheranmadevi Gurukulam controversy, 3, 17
Annamalai Chettiar, Raja Sir, 224
Chidambaranar, Sami, 116, 185
Christianity, 133, 220
    failure to erase caste distinctions, 121, 126
'Citizen of the World', 64, 69
citizenship, 66, 132, 147–148, 152, 159–160
colonial administration, 86–87, 131, 174, 226, 231
colonial–missionary discourse, 8
Communal Award of 1932. *See* Poona Pact
communal harmony, promotion of, 239
Communist Manifesto, The, 6, 222
Communist Party of India (CPI), 100
communists, 6–7, 11, 95, 98, 100, 220, 224
Constitution of India, 102, 240
    burning of copies of, 138, 240
    criminalizing desecration of, 138

cosmopolitanism, 58, 63–71
cultural–linguistic activism, 161
cultural literacy, 58
cultural psychology, 235–237, 246

Dalit Panthers, 141
Darwin, Charles, 133
de Beauvoir, Simone, 174
decolonization, 148, 156–157, 235–237, 242, 245
degree of freedom, 224
democracy, 39, 90, 100, 220
Depressed Castes/Classes
  freedom and welfare of, 173
  Gandhi on political representation for, 51*n*21
  under leadership of Ambedkar, 35
  mobilization of, 35
    political, 79
  Periyar on, 35
  political unity of, 43
  representation in the legislatures, 48
*devadasi*s, 243
diasporic communities, legacy of Periyar's ideals in, 146–149, 160–161, 239
dictatorship of the proletariat, 63
division of labour, 220–221, 225–226, 229
Dravida Munnetra Kazhagam (DMK), 1, 73, 93, 99, 138
  anti-Hindi agitations, 10, 102
  dethroning of the Indian National Congress (Congress), 93
  relationship with DK, 93, 96, 106
  electoral politics of, 101
  formation of, 82
  identity politics, 99
  and self-respect marriages, 11
  politics of Tamil pride, 10
  response to Periyar's agitations, 102–105
  victory in 1967 election, 93, 105
Dravidan (Tamil daily), 35, 44, 46, 136
Dravida Nadu, 9, 89*n*6, 96, 98
  demand for, 139, 151
Dravidar Kazhagam (DK), 9–11, 82, 93, 99, 137, 169, 198, 221, 240

anti-Brahmin propaganda, 139
creation of, 57–58
goals of, 138
principles and practices of, 106
rivalry with Dravida Munnetra Kazhagam (DMK), 93–106
Dravidar Vivasaya Thozhilalar Sangam (DVTS), 225
Dravidian cinema
  golden era of, 210
  Periyar's views on, 205–209
  women's question and, 209–211
Dravidian family of languages, 88*n*1
Dravidian Farmers' Association (DFA), 240
Dravidian identities, 62, 81, 83, 131
Dravidian ideology
  dominance of, 93
  in Tamil cinema, 199
Dravidian movement, 1, 36, 72, 93, 123, 149, 151, 153, 224, 230, 236. *See also* Dravidar Kazhagam (DK); Dravida Munnetra Kazhagam (DMK); All-India Anna Dravida Munnetra Kazhagam (AIADMK)
  in Malaya, 153
Dravidian Negroes, 142*n*4
Dravidian parties, 7
  politics of, 78
Dravidian politics, 2, 5, 11–13, 79–80
Dravidian Self-Rule, 70, 73
Dravidian–Tamil identity, 78–79, 82, 230
  Periyar's definition of, 88
Dravidian transnationalism, 149
dual citizenship, 159
Du Bois, W. E. B., 142*n*4

economic equality, 220, 224
economic freedom, 221
economic independence, 8, 173, 175–176, 221
economic inequalities, 81, 217, 231
economic justice, 231

education, proportional representation for non-Brahmins in, 7
egalitarianism, 2, 5, 8–9, 13, 61–62, 68, 71, 78, 88, 126, 132, 142, 174, 201, 209, 212, 220, 236–237, 240
electoral politics, 82, 94–96, 198
equality
  politics of, 80
  of rights, 224
Erode Programme (1932), 7, 222

feminist politics, 167–168. *See also* Periyar on women's empowerment
Gandhi, Indira, 177–178
Gandhi–Irwin Pact, 41, 45
Gandhi, M. K., 3, 19, 70, 138, 203
  and Vaikom Satyagraha, 19
  difference of opinion with Ambedkar, 42
  and Poona Pact, 40–50
  model of economic reconstruction, 218
  Non-cooperation Movement, 85
  opposition to separate electorates, 41–45
  participation in Round Table Conference, 42
  and political representation for the Depressed Classes, 51n21
  and varnashrama dharma, 218
  on *khadi* and economic self-reliance, 218
Ganesan, Sivaji, 204–205
Government of India Act
  of 1919, 85
  of 1935, 7, 79, 94
Government of Madras, 6, 30, 96
Gurusamy, Kunjitham, 96, 169
Gurusamy, 'Kuthoosi' S., 96
Guruswami, L. C., 38
Narayana Guru, Sree, 18, 30

hate speech, 139–140
hereditary property, equal right to, 173
Hindi language
  as national language of India, 11
  protests against, 83, 89n1, 93–94, 122
  in schools in Tamil Nadu, 7 (*see also* anti-Hindi agitations)

Hindu Freethought Union, 133
Hinduism, 133
  Brahminical order of, 86
  Periyar's opposition to, 6
  socio-economic and political realities, 80. *See also* caste system
Hindu Mahasabha, 41–43, 46, 49
Hindu Marriage Act of 1955, 179n1
Hindu Marriage (Tamil Nadu Amendment) Act of 1967, 179n1
Hindu Matha Aachara Aabasa Dharsini, 133–134
Hitlerism, 72
Hitler, Adolf, 70, 137
human beings
  concept of, 118
  dehumanization of, 244
human collectives, 115
human dignity, 116, 236

identity politics, pluralism in, 78, 99, 159, 245
ideological purity, 83
Ilatthu Adikal, Karuvur, 121–122
inamaanam (racial dignity), 203
India Councils Act (1909), 36
Indian civilization, racial theory of, 131
Indian National Congress, 3, 35, 79, 218
  all-India committee to eradicate untouchability, 19
  idea of nationalism vis-à-vis caste, 85
  model of self-rule, 87
  Periyar's break from, 17, 149
  policy of non-interference in native states, 19
  'Quit India!' slogan, 138
  vision of wealth drain, 220
  Swarajist phase of, 94
Indian Penal Code (IPC), 45
Indian Statutory (Simon) Commission. *See* Simon Commission (1928)
Indian Union Muslim League (IUML), 101
Indo-Pakistan wars of 1965 and 1971, 9, 121
Inivarum Ulagam (The World to Come, 1944), 9, 13
inter-caste marriages, 175, 177

Islam, 6, 42, 70, 119-121, 126, 152, 172
Iyengar, A. S. Krishnamachari (A.S.K.), 140

jaathi ozhippu (annihilation of caste), 4, 12, 142. *See also* Ambedkar, B. R.
Jayalalithaa, J., 12, 140, 179
Jinnah, M. A., 9
  joint electorates, 45. *See also* Poona Pact
  and reserved seats, 40
  universal adult franchise, 41
Joseph, George, 20–21, 25–26
Justice (English journal), 7
Justice Party, 7–9, 35, 38, 78–79, 83, 85, 93, 171, 177 (*see also* Dravidar Kazhagam [DK])
  renaming of, 94

Kalinin, Mikhail, 6
Kamaraj, K., 10, 89n6, 100, 103, 138
  K-Plan, 102
  pachai Tamilan (trueborn Tamilan), 100
  resignation as chief minister, 102
Kanchipuram 'Separation Conference' (1940), 62
Karunanidhi, M., 4, 11, 98, 100, 102, 198. See also *Parasakthi*
Kerala Congress Anti-Untouchability Committee, 19–20
Kerala Provincial Congress Committee, 19
Kerala Temple Entry Conference, 29
Krishnamachari, T. T., 100, 105, 139
Krishnan, N. S., 199, 204
Kundrakudi Adigalar, 244
Kudi Arasu (weekly), 4–6, 9, 30, 41–45, 48, 58, 97, 116, 121, 149, 169, 200, 202, 222, 226
  publication of Bhagat Singh's *Why I Am an Atheist*, 6
kula kalvi thittam (caste-based education scheme), 10, 100
Kurdistan Workers' Party, 141

labour mobilization, 222
Lakshmi Narasu, P., 5
land distribution, agenda for, 7
League of the Militant Godless, 6
Lenin, Vladimir, 223
liberation of women, 4–5, 142, 168, 178, 243
linguistic reorganization of states, 84
literary merit, notion of, 184
Lohia, Ram Manohar, 6, 138

MacDonald, Ramsay, 45
Madhavan, T. K., 19, 22, 26–27, 29
Madras Adi Dravida Central Sabha, 39
Madras Arundhathi Mahajana Sabha, 38, 39
Madras Legislative Council, 36
Madras Mahajana Sabha, 45
Madras Presidency, 7, 18, 79, 130, 148
  anti-Hindi-imposition protests in, 151
  non-Brahmin elites of, 2
Madras Provincial Committee, 37
Madras Provincial Depressed Classes Federation, 38
Madras Secular Society, 2, 5, 133, 135
Madras State
  Buddhist revivalism in, 133
  renaming as Tamil Nadu, 84
  Tamil-speaking regions of, 84
  as Tamizhagam (Abode of Tamils), 89n6
Madras Times, 133
Malaya
  approaches to Indian politics in, 147
  Dravidian ideology among the Tamils of, 156
  Dravidian movement in, 153
  Periyar's visit to
    addresses to Malayan Tamils, 152–153
    and Tamil consciousness in, 155–160
    first visit, 149–151
    Malayan Tamil engagements with, 150
    second visit, 151–155
    upper-caste resistance to, 150
  plantation economy, 154
  Tamil cultural–linguistic assertion in, 154
  Tamil identity, 153
  Tamil linguistic politics and Malayan nationhood, 161
  use of Tamil language in, 155
  value of the Tamil 'race' to, 158
Maniammai, E. V. R. (Periyar's wife), 9, 169, 177–178

Index

Manu Smriti, 5, 71, 122, 130, 133, 193, 220, 222, 231
   public burning of, 136
Maraimalai Adigal, 5, 122
masculinity, 156, 174, 212, 240
materialism, 117, 127*n*3
Mayo, Katherine, 150
midday meal scheme in schools, 7
Minorites Pact, 43. See also Poona Pact
Mouffe, Chantal, 89*n*16
Ramaswamy Mudaliar, A., 38
Masilamani Mudaliar, M., 133
Muniswamy Pillai, V. I., 38, 44, 50
Muslim League, 9, 72

Nagammai/Nagammal (Periyar's wife), 3, 7, 22, 29, 169, 171, 178, 243, 245–246
Ramasamy Naicker, E. V. (EVR). See Periyar (E. V. Ramasamy)
Manicka Naicker, P. V., 123, 190
Venkatappa Naicker, 2
national-flag-burning agitation, 103–104
national flag, criminalization of desecration of, 138
national identity, 85, 230, 237
nationalization of land, demands for, 222
National Secular Society (England), 5, 133
Arumuga Navalar, 124
Somasundara Nayagar, 5
Venkatachala Nayakkar, Athipakkam, 5, 133–135
Nedunchezhiyan, V. R., 98, 104
Neelambigai Ammaiyar, 8
Negritude movement, 130
Nehru, Jawaharlal, 138, 153
Nehru, Motilal, 19
Periyar Suyamariyathai Prachara Niruvanam, 177
non-Brahmin castes, 8, 35
non-Brahmin constitutional politics, 7
Non-Brahmin Manifesto, The, 7, 78, 85
non-Brahmin movements, 2, 83
non-Brahmin political theory, 58, 61, 63–64, 67, 70
non-Brahmin rights, Periyar fight for, 138

Non-Cooperation Movement, 3, 20, 85, 94, 98
'Non-Oppressor', 82, 84

Olcott, Colonel, 131
oppressed castes
   psychological slavery of the Brahmans, 132
   unity of, 80–83

Pagutharivu (Tamil periodical), 4
Iyothee Thass, 5, 35, 121, 133
Parasakthi (1952), 199, 206
Pasha, Kemal, 121, 126, 151
patriarchal ideology, pervasiveness of, 170, 172
penn viduthalai (liberation of women), 4, 12, 142
Periya Puranam, 103, 122
Periyar (E. V. Ramasamy)
   advocacy for
      Dravida Nadu, 58, 71
      education for women and their economic independence, 8
      reservation for the Depressed Castes, 8
   agitation against Rajaji's education scheme, 103
   agitation of burning the Indian national flag, 103
   ancient Dravidian society, vision of, 132
   anti-Aryanism, Periyar's approach to, 129
   anti-Brahmin speeches, 10, 139, 141–142
   anti-Brahminism, Periyar's approach to, 129
   art and cinema, Periyar's view on, 199–202
   Aryan–Dravidian difference, Periyar's views on, 137
   and Brahmins, 129
   break from the Indian National Congress, 17
   call to burn the Constitution of India, 240
   creation of anti-caste political consciousness, 130
   criticism of Brahmanical religion, 126
   definition of category-rights, 87
   demand for autonomy for south Indian states within India, 9
   differences with Anna, 94, 96–97
   dignity, Periyar's conception of, 80, 245
   Dravidian nationalism, 70
   early life and views on religion, 2–3, 114
   electoral politics, 82, 94–96

friendship with Rajaji, 3
godmen comrades, of Periyar, 121–122
Hindu texts, Periyar's view on, 186–189
idea of 'love', Periyar's views on, 172
on women's empowerment, 8, 12–13, 22, 27, 121, 126, 133, 146, 167–179, 199, 204, 207, 209–210, 212, 237, 241–245
on Independence Day, 9
on Indian big business, 230
Indian materialist traditions, Periyar's belief in, 116–117
influence of Kaivalya Swamiyar on, 5
key goals and ideas of, 4–6
as leader of the Justice Party, 7
leadership of, 242–245
as materialist, 116–119
marriage with
    Maniammai, 9
    Nagammai, 3, 22
meeting with
    C. N. Annadurai, 93
    Mikhail Kalinin, 6
    Ram Manohar Lohia, 138
nationalism, Periyar's idea of, 87
non-Brahmin cosmopolitanism, 58, 70
notion of anti-casteist casteism, 130
and notion of dignity, 80
opposition to
    caste system, 1
    Hinduism, 6
    oppression of women, 1, 8
periodicals published by, 4
Penn Aen Adimaiyaanal? (Why Was the Woman Enslaved?), 8
political atheism of, 237
and Poona Pact, 36–50
propaganda against caste and religion, 10
as radical cultural psychologist, 234, 236–237
rationalism (*pagutharivu*), 5–6, 11–12, 98, 103, 107n20, 120, 132, 134–135, 137, 140, 169, 241
    Periyar's concept of, 124
reflection on Brahminical order of Hinduism, 86

religion as a private affair, Periyar on, 119–120
religious critique, 116
social justice, Periyar's struggle for, 27–29
statues of, 88
struggle against
    Brahminism, 82
    colonial and Brahminical forces, 88
support to the anti-Congress opposition, 100
'Tamil Nadu for Tamils' slogan, 8
title of 'Periyar', 8
town and country, Periyar's views on, 228–229
'uncivil' language used by, 140–142
and Vaikom Satyagraha, 17–31
version of reason, 124–125
visit to
    British Malaya, 147, 149–155
    Europe, 6, 168
    Singapore, 147
    Soviet Union, 6, 168, 218
visualization of category-wise rights, 88
writings on women, 167
Periyar Kalanjiyam, 4, 168, 169
Periyar Self-Respect Propaganda Institution, 4
Phule, Mahatma Jyotirao, 8, 132
Piketty, Thomas, 217
Sundaram Pillai, 'Manonmaniam' P., 5, 123
Purnalingam Pillai, M. S., 5, 123, 194n5
Chidambaram Pillai, V. O., 3, 122, 183
Poona Pact (1932), 8, 35, 36, 45–46, 47, 48

Prakrti Vadam Allatu Materialism (1949), 117
Prevention of Insults to National Honour Bill (1957), 138
Provincial Women's Self-Respect Conference, 46
Puratchi (Tamil weekly), 4, 7

race theory, 74n19, 137, 142n5
racial-caste supremacy, 129, 136, 140
Radhakrishnan, Sarvepalli, 8, 131
Radha, M. R., 204–205
radical cultural psychology, 235–236, 246
Rajagopalachari, C., 3, 10, 20, 23–24, 47, 83, 152, 186, 207
    accession to chief-ministership, 100

Periyar's friendship with, 244
political career of, 100
Rajah, M. C., 37–39, 42–43, 46–47
   Rajah–Moonje agreement, 44
Rajiji. *See* Rajagopalachari, C.
Rajalakshmi, T. P., 237–238
Ramachandran, M. G. (MGR), 11, 205, 208
Ramamirtha Ammal, Moovalur 169
Ramanathan, S., 6, 21, 23, 36, 72
Ramayana, 5, 10, 62, 103, 126, 184
   Periyar's perspective on, 123–124, 200–201, 243
   in Tamil cinema, 212
Reddy, Muthulakshmi, 169
regional identity, 83, 84
Revolt (English weekly), 4, 36, 219
Round Table Conference, 40–41
   First Round Table Conference, 40–41
   Gandhi's participation in, 42
   Second Round Table Conference, 41, 43, 45
Roy, M. N., 6

Sahajanantham, Swami, 38
Saiva reform movement, 5
Saivites, 132
Salem prison massacre (1950), 11
samadharmam (socialism), 6, 193
Samarasa Suddha Sanmarga Sathiya Sangam, 239
samathuvam (equality), 4, 12, 142
Sampath, E. V. K., 98, 102
sanatana dharma, 5, 86
Sandamarutham (Self-Respect journal), 43
Saraswati, Dayanand, 131
Sartre, Jean-Paul, 130
Savarkar, V. D., 47
Scheduled Castes, 1, 7, 72, 90, 130, 136, 142n1. *See also* Depressed Classes
Self-Respect Movement (SRM), 4, 6, 17, 35, 38, 43, 46, 58, 61, 67, 79, 93, 115, 134, 149, 167, 168, 200, 219
   establishment of, 80
   influence on Tamil identity, 156
   campaign against the Hindu epics, 184
   women's wing of, 46

self-respect, politics of, 10, 147–148
   dignity and, 81
   as the engine of anti-caste Dravidian politics, 79–80
   feeling of, 57, 67, 70, 78
   notion of, 88
   Periyar's views on, 167
   social reform in alignment with values of, 150
Self-Respect weddings, 151, 153, 240–241, 243
Self-Rule, 57, 62, 65
separate electorates
   Ambedkar on,
   demand for, 37–38, 40
   Gandhi's opposition to, 41–45
   M. C. Rajah on, 44
   representational strategy of, 41
   Periyar on, 38, 44–45, 46
   Simon Commission and, 37–40
sexual freedom, 8, 167
Shudras, 137, 141, 220
Silappadikaram (Ilango Adigal), 5, 176, 183
Singapore
   Dravidian ideology among the Tamils of, 156
   Periyar's visit to, 148–161
   Periyar's relevance in, 160–161
   Tamil cultural–linguistic assertion in, 148, 154, 160
   Tamil reform organizations in, 148
   use of Tamil language in, 155
Singaravelar, M., 5–6, 222
Singh, Bhagat, 6
Singh, Lalai, 12
Sino-India War (1962), 9
Sivagnanam, Ma. Po., 182–183
socialism (*samadharmam*), 217
social justice, 1, 11, 81–82, 140
   caste-based, 232
   Periyar's struggle for, 27–29
   politics of, 80
Social Justice Day, 1
Soundarapandian, W. P. A., 85
South Indian Liberal Federation. *See* Justice Party
Sree Narayana Dharma Paripalana Yogam (SNDP), 18

Srinivasan, Rettamalai, 38, 41, 43, 50
Srinivas, M. N., 80
Stalin, M. K., 1, 12
state power, concept of, 139
suyamariyadhai, 6, 79, 80. *See* Self-Respect Movement
Swamigal, Sivacharya (Gnaniyar Swamigal), 4, 121
Swamiyar, Kaivalya, 5, 121, 122, 134, 135
swaraj, 29, 57, 136

Tamil Arasu Kazhagam (Association for Tamil Autonomy), 182
Tamil Brahmins 140
Tamil cinema, 198
  Dravidian ideology in, 199
Tamil consciousness, 80, 155–161
Tamil cultural imagination, 184
Tamil cultural–linguistic activism, 158, 160
Tamil diaspora, 147, 152, 155, 158
Tamil enlightenment, idea of, 124
Tamil identity, 155
  linguistic–literary imaginings of, 149
  Malayan Tamil identity, 158, 160
  Self-Respect Movement's influence on imagining of, 156
Tamil *inam*, 62, 158–159
Tamil language, 84, 159, 201
  education, 159
  romanticization of, 172
Tamil Nadu Backward Classes (Sattanathan) Commission (1969), 87
Tamil Nadu Congress Committee (TNCC), 3, 20
Tamil nationalism, 8, 171
Tamil Nesan, 150
tamilpparru, 148
Tamil Saivite, 8, 103, 124, 130
temple entry movements, 126
  Travancore Temple Entry Proclamation (1936), 18, 28
Thanthai Periyar Dravidar Kazhagam, 5, 12
Thathuvavivesini (Tamil journal), 133
Thinker, The (English journal), 133

Thirukkural, 5, 189–193, 194n4, 5. *See also Thiruvalluvar*
Thirumular (Tamil Saivite poet), 103
Thiruneelakandar, 98
Thiruvalluvar, 172, 191. See also *Thirukkural*
Tilak, Bal Gangadhar, 8
Union of Soviet Socialist Republics (USSR), 6–7, 176, 218–219, 222
universal adult franchise, 36, 40–41. *See also* separate electorates; Poona Pact
Unmai (Tamil monthly), 4
untouchability, 20, 98, 168
  issue of, 48
  Periyar's campaign against, 24
Untouchability Eradication Day, 62
'untouchable' communities, 2
  freedom from low-caste tag, 121 (*see also* Depressed Classes/Castes)
upper castes, 18–20, 35, 37, 40, 47, 49, 67, 80, 131, 135, 150, 227–228, 230

Vaikom Satyagraha, 3, 17–30, 121, 171
  challenges to, 26–27
  Mahatma's approval for, 19
  outcome of Periyar's leadership of, 29–30
  Periyar's role in, 17, 20–23, 29–30
  proceedings against Periyar, 23–26
  struggle for social justice, 27–29
  as temple entry movement, 18–20
Vallalar Ramalinga Adigal, 5, 116, 124, 132
varnashrama dharma, 42, 71, 86, 136, 218, 220, 228
Veeramani, K., 96, 140
Viduthalai (daily), 4, 97, 101, 204, 240
Vivekananda, Swami, 18
Voltaire, 133
voting rights, 79
  for women, 121
V. V. S. Aiyar, 3

Western materialism, influence on Periyar, 117
widow remarriage, 151, 171, 175, 238–239
women enslaved, Periyar's views on, 171–174

women's emancipation, Periyar's ideas on, 171, 199
women's freedom, centrality of, 174–177
women's liberation, principles of, 169, 178
women's rights and liberation, 178
Woolf, Virginia, 172
World Buddhist Conference (Rangoon), 152

For EU product safety concerns, contact us at Calle de José Abascal, 56–1°,
28003 Madrid, Spain or eugpsr@cambridge.org.

www.ingramcontent.com/pod-product-compliance
Lightning Source LLC
LaVergne TN
LVHW080305260326
834688LV00039B/1144